The **Simonsens** of **St Kilda**

ROGER NEILL is an expert on the innovators, artists, writers and musicians of the late nineteenth and early twentieth centuries. He was founding director of the Centre for Creativity at City University London. He helped Sam Wanamaker to re-build Shakespeare's Globe in London and was founder of the contemporary music orchestra Sinfonia 21 and chairman of Endymion Ensemble. He curated the exhibition *Legends: The Art of Walter Barnett* for the National Portrait Gallery in Canberra. His most recent book is *Divas: Mathilde Marchesi and her Pupils* and he was co-producer of the 4CD set, *From Melba to Sutherland: Australian Singers on Record*. He started his working life as a rock musician.

For Dora and Isobel

In memory of Adrienne Simpson

Per Diem Projects
King's Sutton, OX17 3RG

First Published 2023

A catalogue record of this book is available from the National Library of Australia.

Designed by Avril Makula
Edited by Fiona Sim
Set in 11/15 Minion Pro

ISBN 978-1-3999-4219-5

Front cover image: Frances Saville by Arthur von Ferraris (Australian Performing Arts Collection, Arts Centre, Melbourne)

www.perdiemprojects.com

The Simonsens of St Kilda

A Family of Singers

Roger Neill

PER DIEM PROJECTS

Ô grandes leçons du passé!
Grand enseignement de l'histoire!
Ici le drame s'est glissé …
Éclair sombre dans la nuit noire!

O great lessons from the past!
Great teaching from history!
Here the drama is slippery …
A muted flash of light in the black night!

La Grande-Duchesse de Gérolstein,
Henri Meilhac and Ludovic Halévy / Jacques Offenbach

Contents

Preface

In 2006 I did a series of talks in Australia entitled 'Melba vs Alda'. In each talk I played recordings by the two great divas, Nellie Melba and Frances Alda, and at the end I ran a straw poll: 'From what you have heard, which of them do you prefer?' Extraordinarily, given Melba's pre-eminence as The Australian Immortal, Alda won resoundingly in every venue, including at the Athenaeum Theatre in Melba's hometown, Lilydale, which was filled with Melba faithful (including Melba's granddaughter, Lady Vestey, in the front row). I'm not sure who was more shocked by the result – me or the audience.

Frances Alda was part of an astonishing musical family. The founding parents of the dynasty were French soprano Fanny Simonsen and her Danish husband, violinist-conductor Martin Simonsen, who together toured the world performing, before settling at St Kilda, Melbourne, in the 1870s.

There they raised ten children, no less than six of them becoming professional singers. And there they formed a pioneering opera company (including several of their young offspring), which toured Australia and New Zealand over the following decades. A speciality of the Simonsens was to entertain gold rush mining communities – in California, in Victoria and New South Wales, and in New Zealand.

One of their daughters, Frances Saville, having established a successful career in Australia, then studied with Mathilde Marchesi in Paris, going on to be an international prima donna, who crowned her career by becoming a leading member of Gustav Mahler's famous company in Vienna.

Saville's niece Frances Alda, granddaughter of Fanny and Martin Simonsen, followed her aunt as a pupil of Marchesi in Paris, making her European debut with the Opéra-Comique in that city before becoming a diva at the Metropolitan Opera in New York over twenty-one seasons. There she established a celebrated partnership with the finest tenors of the era, including Caruso and Gigli, and with the legendary conductor Arturo Toscanini. Alda became a major star of the gramophone, then of the burgeoning new medium of radio in the USA. In her memoirs she wrote of her childhood home in Melbourne:

> Certainly a great deal of the secret of Frances Alda was to be found in the impulsive, fiery-tempered, ardent little girl playing prima donna in the lath and burlap theatre in the garden at St Kilda.

Not all the Simonsens' children were so successful: one, soprano Martina, decided that domesticity was preferable to a life of constant touring, while another, tenor Jules, went off to ply his trade in San Francisco, but, turning to robbery to make ends meet, was sent to Folsom Prison for twelve years, accompanied by much shock-horror reporting.

In total, between Fanny Simonsen, her children and grandchildren, I have been able to identify twelve who became professional singers, some a great deal more successful than others. Of these, ten were women, two men. And another three were professional violinists, including father of the dynasty, Martin Simonsen.

Although there have been other families of singers, none have been so extensive, nor so long-lasting, nor to have travelled the world so comprehensively as the Simonsens of St Kilda, performing as they did across five continents for almost a hundred years.

Roger Neill
King's Sutton

Acknowledgments

Anyone planning to write about the Simonsens is indebted to the late Adrienne Simpson. She worked and published on various aspects of the family at regular intervals between 1990 and 1999. Before she died, she was researching a full biography of Frances Alda, but sadly was not able to complete the task. At some point in time, we realised that we were working in parallel and I took the decision to step back. In 2018 I was lucky enough to be able to study all of Adrienne's materials, published and unpublished, at the Alexander Turnbull Library in Wellington, New Zealand. This book is dedicated to her memory.

Special mention, as always, of Tony Locantro's contributions in terms of his wide knowledge of musical matters and his pre-editing skills.

My grateful thanks go to a wide range of colleagues and friends whose expertise I have been able to tap, including Stephen Allday, Donald Baillie, Chris Ball, John Dagfinn Bergsagel, Alan Bilgora, Tim Bonyhady, Margot Costanzo, Nathan B Davis, Richard Copeman, Anne Doggett, Charlotte Dorneich, Thomas Dorneich, Frank Heckscher, Stanley Henig, Susan Imgrund, Michael Letchford, Michael Magnusson, Rosie Marson, David Mason, Stephen Rothman, Roger Swearingen, Frank Van Straten and Alice Wilson.

Experts at various academic institutions have been unstinting in offering assistance and advice, including Jessica Bram and Eleni

Papavasileiou (Jewish Museum of Australia), Michael Brown and Llewelyn Jones (National Library of New Zealand, Wellington), Mark Everist (University of Southampton), Claudia Funder and Margaret Marshall (Arts Centre, Melbourne), Liz Kelly (St Kilda Historical Society), Thorkil Mølle (Royal Danish Academy of Music), Kerry Murphy (University of Melbourne), James Nye (University of Chicago Library).

Special thanks go to Nathan B Davis and Larry Lustig for allowing me to include their discographies of Frances Saville and Frances Alda respectively. Also to super-skilled editor Fiona Sim and brilliant designer Avril Makula.

Members of my own family – Sophie Wilson, Kate Neill, Dora Neill and the singing Isobel Slattery – have, as usual, put up with a good deal of speculative chat about singers from long ago.

Illustration credits

Following page: Über dem Altonaerthor *by Friedrich Rosenberg, 1796,*

view from the Hamburg city gate towards Altona

Chapter 1
Martin and Fanny

1

The year 1857, during which Martin Simonsen married Françoise de Haes in Paris, was not especially portentous for music. Hans von Bülow married Liszt's daughter Cosima in Berlin; Richard Wagner, later to be Cosima's second husband, moved into the Zürich house of Otto and Mathilde von Wesendonck, starting an intimate relationship with Mathilde; the first version of Giuseppe Verdi's *Simon Boccanegra* had its poorly received première at the Teatro La Fenice in Venice; 'Jingle Bells' was first published in America. In Paris, seven now forgotten operettas of Jacques Offenbach had their premières at the Théâtre des Bouffes-Parisiens; Gustave Flaubert published *Madame Bovary*, and Louis Pasteur's application to be elected to the Académie des sciences was turned down. In Australia, British prima donna Anna Bishop sang the lead roles in Bellini's *Norma* and *La sonnambula* (and much else besides) at the Princess Theatre in Melbourne;[1] and the colony of

Victoria, having been established in 1851, was into its seventh year of gold rushes.

Martin Simonsen has usually been presented in Australia and New Zealand as German-Jewish, born in Hamburg on 30 January 1830. Three years later, Johannes Brahms was born in Hamburg.[2] However, the family, to which Martin and his wife Fanny often returned from their early travels, lived not in Germany or for that matter in Hamburg, but at Altona, now a western suburb of Hamburg, but at that time a separate city, part of the Danish Duchies of Schleswig and Holstein.[3] Martin would have grown up from early childhood being at the least bilingual. We do not know who his early teachers were, but he was clearly something of a child prodigy as a violinist. When he and Fanny first arrived in Australia in 1865, he proudly presented himself as 'Solo Violinist to His Majesty the King of Denmark'.[4] This was a common form of publicity for ambitious musicians in the nineteenth century.[5]

Situated on the north bank of the River Elbe, Altona had a Jewish community which had been founded in the early seventeenth century, receiving its charter in 1641 from the Danish king, Christian IV. First to arrive there were Ashkenazy Jews from Germany and Eastern Europe, to be joined later by Sephardic Jews, initially from Portugal. Over time it became an important centre of learning – theological, legal, philosophical and musical. In 1815 many more Jews moved from Hamburg to Altona after the emancipation that had been instigated by Napoleon in 1810 was annulled by the Prussians, and restrictions were imposed on the number of Jews allowed to live in Hamburg. Altona's economy was further enhanced by the Danish crown in the form of special commercial privileges. It was only after the Second Schleswig War of 1864 between Denmark and Prussia-Austria that the duchies of Schleswig and Holstein were ceded to Prussia.[6]

The parentage of Martin Simonsen has always puzzled researchers, so many of the relevant archives having been destroyed by a combination of the Holocaust and Allied bombing during the Second World War.

However, very recently the following sentence appeared online on Ahnforschung.net (AncestryResearch.net):

> Simonsen, Martin, born Hamburg 30.01.1830 (German-
> Israelite Community). Son of Salomon David Simonsen of
> Altona, barber, and his wife Leonore née Heckscher of Altona.[7]

This all seems highly credible. Up until the nineteenth century, barbers were not only hairdressers, they were also surgeons, routinely conducting surgical operations (using their razors among other equipment). And many were Jews. It is not known whether Martin Simonsen's father was also an amateur musician.

That Martin's mother was a Heckscher is particularly fascinating. The Heckschers had first arrived at Altona in the seventeenth century, and by the middle of the following century, members of the family were in prominent positions in the city and in the Jewish community. At

Martin Simonsen

Altona

the same time, Heckschers started to migrate, first to other parts of Denmark, where the taxation systems were more lenient towards Jews. Later, Heckshers from Altona migrated to the rest of Scandinavia, to North and South America, and to Australia and South Africa.[8] As with Martin's father, Salomon David Simonsen, it is not known if Leonore Simonsen was a singer or musician.[9] However, she made sufficient of an impact on the Simonsen family that Martin and Fanny's first child was named Leonore, as was their granddaughter Leonore, daughter of Louis Simonsen. Both were to become professional singers.[10]

Salomon David Simonsen and Leonore Heckscher, both born in Altona, were married at Hamburg on 6 June 1826. They had three children (maybe more): Zerline (born 22 May 1827), Siegmund (born 19 August 1831) and Martin (born 30 January 1830).[11]

While it has always been difficult to verify Martin's claim to have had a formal role at the Danish court as 'Solo Violinist' to the King, the

Christian VIII, by Wilhelm Marstrand

fact that he was born and brought up to be Danish as well as German makes it more likely. The Danish king at that time was Christian VIII, who reigned from 1839 until his death in 1848. Christian was a highly educated man, who offered practical support to scientists, artists and musicians. Prominent among the musicians that the king supported was the composer-pianist-pedagogue Carl Heinrich Reinecke, who was born in 1824 also in Altona, six years before Martin Simonsen. The court and the city had an established musical culture and, responding to this, Georg Philipp Telemann composed festive works there between 1741 and 1764, one of these describing Altona as 'the Athens of the Danes'.[12]

As a child, Reinecke studied in Altona primarily with his father, JPR Reinecke. On his first tour of Sweden and Denmark in 1843, Reinecke came to the attention of the King and was given financial support to continue his musical education under Mendelssohn at the Conservatorium in Leipzig. In 1846 he was appointed court pianist to the King in Copenhagen, a role he held until 1848, and it seems likely that the teenage Martin Simonsen was there at the court too, for some or all of that time.[13]

The year 1848 saw the start of the First Schleswig War, as Prussian dissidents endeavoured to take control of Schleswig-Holstein from the Danes, and Reinecke was forced to leave Copenhagen. It seems likely that Martin also left the city, beginning a life of travel and performance.[14] By the time he arrived in Australia in 1865, he could boast of having performed for a range of other crowned heads in Europe in addition to King Christian, including the Emperor of Austria, the Kings of Prussia, Hanover and Saxony, and the King of Sweden.[15]

By the 1850s, having toured extensively in Europe, Martin moved his focus to the United States, living initially in the new state capital of California, Sacramento. The city's metropolitan area now has some 2.5 million inhabitants, but in 1850 its growing population was still only 6800. Nevertheless, the whole area was in the grip of gold rush fever, many of the rapid influx of population being so-called 'forty-niners', accompanied by all the usual growth of gold miners' 'support services': banks, stores, gambling dens, saloons, brothels and so on. By June of 1850, twenty years old, Martin had established himself at the Humboldt Saloon in Sacramento, where the following 'ridiculous and yet laughable scene' occurred:

> A quite respectably dressed individual entered the Humboldt
> Saloon while young Simonsen, the violinist, was playing one
> of his best pieces. The man stood listening and gazing for a
> few moments, apparently riveted to the spot, though evidently
> under the influence of liquor. Presently he pulled off his hat,
> and handing it up to the performer, insisted upon his taking
> it as a reward. Simonsen very good humouredly took the hat,
> and proceeded to play another tune, which he had no sooner
> finished, than his auditor pulled off his coat, and compelled
> him to accept that also.

The comedy progressed with Martin playing pieces and the drunk taking off and giving him articles of clothing. Finally, Martin, tired of the joke, handed back to the man all his apparel.[16] A month later he played two concerts at the nearby town of Marysville, George Pettinos his accompanist.[17] In Sacramento, his performances took place in crowded, noisy saloons, and in September it was announced that Martin and Pettinos

> ... are to open, during the week, a new saloon nearly
> opposite the Empire ... Pettinos on the piano and Simonsen
> on the violin furnish a rare combination of musical talent
> which can seldom be met with, even on the other side of the
> mountains.[18]

Martin was to become a regular at the El Dorado Saloon, 'crowded with enraptured audiences during the entire evening'.[19]

The following year he started to move his centre of activity from Sacramento to San Francisco, appearing in a packed programme at the Jenny Lind Theatre in May 1852. He gradually built up his work in the city, performing with a diverse range of 'artists'. At the Metropolitan in January 1855 he followed 'the gorgeous melodramatic, operatic and ballet spectacle of the *Ice Witch* (or *Frozen Hand*);[20] by May he had gained a booking to perform solos on alternate Sundays at the orchestra of the Turn-Verein Hall's concerts in Bush Street;[21] in November he started at Musical Hall what was to become a partnership with the Italian prima donna, Drusilla Garbato.[22] According to the advertisements for the series of concerts, she had been a principal soprano at La Scala in Milan. The Philharmonic Concert Society Orchestra was conducted both by Garbato's husband and by Simonsen. Perhaps it was the performing relationship with this singer that showed to Martin how successful a soprano and violin combination could be in concert.

But soon Martin was to turn for the first time to Asia. In 1856 he played in Singapore, Calcutta, Madras, Bombay and Colombo, including performances at the private residences of the various governmental leaders. He arrived in Singapore from San Francisco towards the end of February, and gave two concerts there at the Theatre Royal, followed by two more at the Assembly Rooms. The *Free Press* was highly apologetic that such a distinguished musician should attract such a 'scanty' audience.

He left for Calcutta on 25 March,[23] where he played for the recently installed Governor-General of India, Lord Canning (son of British Prime Minister George Canning), who wrote for Martin: 'Mr Simonsen performed twice on the violin at Government House before the Governor-General and Lady Canning, who much admired the skill and beauty of his execution.' In similar vein, in Madras, the Governor, Lord Harris wrote: 'I have had the pleasure of hearing Mr Simonsen perform on the violin on four occasions, and have no hesitation in expressing my complete satisfaction at his performance, and my great admiration of the skill and taste which he displayed on each occasion.'

In Bombay, it was the private secretary (Richard Peele) to the Governor (Lord Elphinstone) who wrote the commendation, and in Colombo, the Governor, Sir Henry Ward.[24] Simonsen left India just a few months before the Indian Rebellion of 1857–58 (then known as the Indian Mutiny and put down by Lord Canning), and travelled to Shanghai (at that time organised into three concessions – British, French and American), where he played for the Minister Plenipotentiary, Lord Elgin (son of the purchaser from the Turks of the Elgin Marbles), and then to Hong Kong (performing for the Governor, Sir John Bowring). At each city, the fact that he was able to gain entrée to and commendation from the various governors doubtless enabled him to sell more tickets for his public concerts.

2

Without the 1400-word feature article in *Table Talk* of 1 November 1889, we would know little of Fanny Simonsen's life before her arrival in Australia with husband Martin in August 1865. What is clear is that the newlyweds toured around the world, performing wherever they went. The article tells us that Martin Simonsen married Françoise de Haes in March 1857.[25] He was twenty-seven, she twenty-two. When and where they first met is not currently known, but it seems likely that he had swiftly returned to Europe for the wedding, which probably took place in Paris.

Françoise de Haes was the child of Belgian parents, said in the Australian press to have been aristocratic. Certainly, the de Haes family was and is a well-established family in the Netherlands and Belgium, the males usually referred to as Jonkheer or Écuyer, roughly the equivalent of baronet in Britain. She was born in Paris on 10 February 1835 and was brought up and educated in Brussels. In later life, she spoke of the many languages she had acquired, partly from her education and partly from her extensive travel – French, English, German and Italian, with 'a smattering' of Spanish and Portuguese. Curiously, there was no mention of Flemish. In the article, she spoke of studying singing at the Conservatoire in Paris from the age of sixteen, where she said her singing teachers were 'Duprez, Garcia, Bordogni, Madame Damorcau Ciuti [sic]'. Alfred Guidant taught her the piano and 'lyric declamation was perfected under Duprez'.[26] This is a glittering array of pedagogues.

The French tenor Gilbert Duprez was born in 1806, studied at the Conservatoire in Paris and made his debut in 1825 as Almaviva in Rossini's *Il barbiere di Siviglia*. His great breakthrough came at Lucca in 1831, when, in the Italian première of *Guillaume Tell*, he sang for the first time in an opera house a high C with full chest voice, without resorting to falsetto (as others had done up to that point). This changed not only Duprez's career, but also the future course of tenor singing and composition. From 1851, aged forty-five, Duprez turned his career to teaching, a course which he had first embarked on in 1842 at the Conservatoire. Françoise does not make clear whether Duprez was first or last among her teachers, so Duprez will have taught her sometime during the period 1852 to 1856.

The second teacher mentioned by Françoise was baritone Manuel Garcia, son of Spanish tenor Manuel Garcia, for whom Rossini had written the role of Almaviva. While Manuel Garcia II had a short performing career, his real vocation was as a teacher, which he did for some seventy years. Most celebrated among his pupils was the soprano Jenny Lind, but he also taught Mathilde Marchesi, who in turn taught a stream of young Australasian women, among them Nellie Melba, plus the daughter of Françoise and Martin Simonsen, Frances Saville, and their granddaughter Frances Alda.

The oldest of the singing teachers named by Françoise was Italian tenor Marco Bordogni, who was born in 1789 and whose career was primarily based in Paris, becoming a teacher at the Conservatoire as early as 1823. He published a singing method which influenced singers over future generations. Françoise must have studied with him in the latter years of his life – he died in 1856. The last of the pedagogues mentioned by Françoise was (more correctly) Laure Cinti-Damoreau, who was herself a pupil of Bordogni and of Angelica Catalani. She made her debut in 1816 in Martin y Soler's popular *Una cosa rara*. The heart of her performing career was in the operas of Rossini, with whom she studied. In fact, all of Françoise's teachers were devoted to Rossini, so it is no surprise that she herself had all the bel canto skills associated with his music, skills that she passed on to her children (and granddaughter). Cinti-Damoreau was another of her teachers who published an influential bel canto method.

Central to her presentation of herself in advertising when she and Martin arrived in Australia was that she had been 'Prima Donna from the Opéra-Comique, Paris'. The works that she claimed to have performed in at that house are *The Crown Diamonds* (*Les diamants de la couronne*) by Daniel Auber, *L'étoile du nord* by Giacomo Meyerbeer, *Galathée* by Victor Massé, *Le toréador* by Adolphe Adam and *Les dragons de Villars* by Aimé Maillart. These were all comic pieces, first performed between 1841 and 1854 at that house – excepting *Les dragons de Villars*, which was first given at the Théâtre-Lyrique in 1856, having been turned down by the Opéra-Comique.[27] Françoise de Haes does not appear among the named roles in any of the premières – so presumably she sang in later performances (or was covering a principal, or was in the chorus).[28] Of these five works, it was only *Les dragons de Villars* that was later to be toured regularly by the Simonsens' company in Australasia (as *The Hermit's Bell*, with Françoise/Fanny in the lead role).

It was also reported that Françoise performed at Lyon, Marseille, Bordeaux and Brussels.[29] Although there is no mention of a previous marriage in newspaper reports, the Simonsens' opera company that toured New Zealand in 1880–81 included a young soprano, Eugénie Dehaes, who was said to be the daughter of Fanny Simonsen.[30] She disappeared from the company mid-tour, not to surface again.

Opéra-Comique, Salle Favart 2, Paris

In her memoirs, granddaughter Frances Alda writes of her grand-mother as 'of the nobility ... She ran away from home, her church, her titles to marry the impecunious violinist ... [an] exquisite little aristocrat to her fingertips.'[31] It seems clear that, although Martin Simonsen retained close links with his family home at Altona, Fanny severed relations with her family in Paris and Brussels.

Was the fracture caused by the family rather than by Fanny? This does seem likely. After all, as an aristocrat (albeit a minor one), she might be said to be marrying beneath her. And she was marrying not only a jobbing musician, but, having been brought up a Catholic, a Jewish one. French aristocracy had a long heritage of anti-Semitism, vividly captured in the anti-Dreyfusard rants of the Duc and Duchesse de Guermantes and others in Proust's *À la recherche du temps perdu*, and it seems likely that Belgian aristocracy shared those prejudices.[32] When reconnecting with the previous generation, it was always to Martin's family at Altona that the Simonsens would return.

At the same time, middle- and upper-class women in the 1850s (and until the First World War) were not expected to work for a living, still less to spend their lives touring the world. Rather, they were expected to remain at home, either single or married. Exceptions to this rule were actors and singers, but there persisted the connection in many minds between acting and prostitution (or its more dignified cousin, the courtesan). Perhaps opera and concert singing had a somewhat higher status than acting, but nevertheless ...

It is not widely known that throughout the seventeenth and eighteenth centuries, travelling star sopranos had generally been male castrati rather than female singers, women only gradually taking to the road as the castration of boys steadily became socially unacceptable and then illegal.[33]

3

Following their marriage in 1857, Françoise de Haes – becoming Fanny Simonsen – and Martin Simonsen immediately started touring together. These were lengthy affairs in, for the young couple, unknown territories and cultures, requiring reserves of courage, stamina and resilience to deal with all the obstacles and hardships involved, not least simply in travelling from place to place. They started with Martin's return to Asia, where they performed over a two-year period in India, China, Japan, Batavia (now Jakarta), Manila, the Cape of Good Hope (South Africa), Mauritius and Réunion. Martin was reported as performing at Mauritius in May 1857, although there was no mention of Fanny.[34]

In 1859 they returned to Europe, presumably staying with Martin's family at Altona, and then setting off the following year for a second, long tour together, this time to South America. As granddaughter Frances Alda was to note in her memoirs nearly seventy years later:

They went in sailing vessels to South America. They crossed
the mountains in mule carts heaped with scenery, costume
trunks, and musical instruments. They gave *The Barber of
Seville* and *Don Giovanni* and *Robert the Devil* to audiences of
Spanish grandees and mestizos and unkempt Indian herdsmen
in tattered serapes. Grandmother … had a baby in each one of
half a dozen cities.[35]

According to Fanny, in South America they performed in Uruguay
(Montevideo), Argentina (Buenos Aires, Rosario, Santa Fe and
Concepción del Uruguay), Brazil (Paysandu/Belém in Pará, Porto
Alegre, Rio de Janeiro), Dutch Guiana/Surinam (Pernambuco Batavia),
British Guiana/Guyana (Georgetown) and Jamaica (Kingston). Judging
by the 'Souvenir de Caracas et Puerto Rico, Op 16' by Martin Simonsen,
they had performed in both those places too.[36]

Teatro Solís, Montevideo

In Montevideo they were clearly established as a duo – she now billed as Françoise de Simonsen – beginning at the recently-opened Teatro Solís on 10 November 1859. Their pianist was Arthur Loreau, who had trained at the Conservatoire in Paris. Françoise opened with Leonora's Cavatina 'Tacea la notte' from *Il trovatore*, followed by Frederick Crouch's ballad 'Kathleen Mavourneen' and Variations from Auber's *Les diamants de la couronne*, a role which she had previously sung at the Opéra-Comique. Martin played two of his own compositions – a Fantasia 'Ricordo de Bellini' and 'Introduction and Variations after *La fille du régiment*', then Ernst's 'Andante spianato' and Paganini's 'Carnival of Venice'. Two days later they gave a second concert, this time with orchestra: Martin opened with his own 'Life on the Ocean', followed by his 'Fantasia after *Ernani*' and the Ernst and Paganini pieces he played previously with piano; Françoise opened with Schubert's 'Serenade' ('Ständchen') arranged for soprano, violin and orchestra, which she followed with Pierre Rode's air with variations, 'Al dolce canto'. Their third and final concert at Montevideo, again accompanied by Loreau, was on 19 November, with a similar mix of repertoire.[37]

Already it was apparent that their musical tastes coincided, fundamentally based on the bel canto repertoire, both vocal and instrumental, with its agile runs, leaps and elaborate ornamentation. In their future performing careers, neither of them embraced the 'new music' of Wagner and Brahms. It was at Montevideo on 24 November 1859 (just five days after their last concert) that their first child, Leonore, was born, establishing a pattern that Françoise/Fanny was to follow for future births – of travelling and performing to the last possible moment.

By September 1860 they were performing in Buenos Aires, although how many venues they had appeared at in the meantime, or whether they had stayed for a while in Montevideo after the birth, is not so easy to discern. Argentina in the 1860s was still a comparative backwater economically, the great expansion of its GDP not occurring until the 1880s. In her book on the Teatro Solís, Susana Salgado outlines the typical itinerary of touring musicians in South and Central America:

> It was very unusual for a company to be engaged only for
> Montevideo ... Most of the time they would start out in
> Buenos Aires and, after the conclusion of the season there,
> would go on tour. There was no regular pattern for these
> tours, but the most frequent second stop would be either
> Rosario (often followed by Córdoba) in Argentina ... After
> Montevideo, they might return to Argentina, or go directly to
> Brazil, primarily Rio de Janeiro followed by São Paolo. On rare
> occasions, they might also go to Santiago, but that presented
> a problem, as it necessitated either crossing the Andes, or
> rounding South America.[38]

Without the benefit of Salgado's handy summary and without any prior experience of the continent, the Simonsens achieved an extraordinarily comprehensive schedule. They arrived in the West Indies at the end of this tour, performing at Kingston, Jamaica, where their second child, Martina, was born in 1862.

4

By this stage, Fanny and Martin, together with their two very young daughters, must have been in acute need of rest and recuperation, and they made the long journey to Martin's family home at Altona, their second return since marriage. There they stayed for a short while, leaving Leonore (three) and Martina (one) to be looked after by grandmother Leonore, before embarking on their next expedition together, this time (1863) to Caraçao in the Dutch Antilles, followed by the northern part of South America – Puerto Cabello on the north coast of Venezuela and Santa Marta in Colombia – then returning to California. Although it was some eight years since he had been there, Martin was well remembered in San Francisco as an outstanding virtuoso, possibly the finest violinist to have performed to the west of the Rockies. And now he had a performing partner – his wife Fanny.

Although California was not directly involved in the fighting, in 1863 the American Civil War was at its peak, the population of the state evenly split as to which side they supported, together with a substantial movement in favour of secession. Many men joined militia companies in support of either the Confederates or the Unionists. It must have been a worrying time for Martin and Fanny. They arrived (without children, who were still in Altona) on the steamer *Golden Age* from Panama at the beginning of March 1863.[39] Their arrival was warmly greeted in the local press, and in early March they were already advertising their concerts:

> MARTIN SIMONSEN, the celebrated and world-renowned
> violinist, begs leave to announce to the citizens of San
> Francisco that he will give his FIRST CONCERT … AT
> PLATT'S NEW MUSIC HALL on Saturday Evening March 7th
> … assisted by Mme FANNY SIMONSEN.

At the concert Fanny sang a Romance from Rossini's *William Tell*, the ballad 'Kathleen Mavourneen', Schubert's 'Ständchen' (presumably with Martin) and the Grand Cavatina from Bellini's *I puritani*, while Martin played two of his own compositions – his 'Souvenir de Bellini' and 'Remembrances of Germany' – plus two regulars from his virtuoso dazzlers, the Ernst 'Andante spianato' and the Paganini 'Carnival of Venice'.[40] Platt's on Montgomery Street was to become a regular venue for the Simonsens.

Although Martin and Fanny sang and played excerpts from many of the popular operas of the day in San Francisco, the city was by that time well used to the production of whole operas. Since the start of the Gold Rush in 1851, the most popular works were by Bellini, Donizetti and Rossini, then Verdi. The only German on the scene was by Weber, the only French by Auber and Meyerbeer. The major 'British' (actually Irish) works were by Balfe and Wallace, *The Bohemian Girl* and *Maritana*.[41] In short, the repertoire was very similar to that which prevailed in the late 1860s in Australia. This is not so surprising when one considers that the leading opera company in San Francisco in 1860 was WS Lyster's, which went on to become the leader in the field in Australia from 1861.

On St Patrick's Day 1863 (17 March), the Simonsens gave 'a grand olio'[42] between the acts of Harrigan's *Our Irish Cousin* at Maguire's Opera House,[43] and in April they gave concerts at Sacramento and Marysville, where Martin had previously performed extensively in 1850, although on this occasion in Sacramento the venue was a Congregational church rather than a rowdy saloon.[44] It was reported that Fanny had given birth to a son on 21 September 1863 in San Francisco.[45] This was their first son, Louis Martin Simonsen, who would return with his family as an adult to live in Northern California.[46]

By July 1864 Fanny Simonsen was back, singing in a vaudeville show with the San Francisco Minstrels at the Eureka Minstrel Hall in Montgomery Street, repeating the performance at the Metropolitan Theater in Sacramento.[47] The third daughter (fourth child) of the Simonsens, named Fanny Martina, was born in San Francisco on 6 January 1865.[48] In due course, she was to become their most successful singing offspring – as prima donna soprano Frances Saville.

However, by late January the Simonsens had decided after two years in California that it was time to move on. They gave a 'Grand Farewell Concert' at Platt's Music Hall on 26 January 1865, apparently intending to travel to Japan, China and Australia.[49] They do not appear to have got either to Japan, or to Australia, but they were certainly in Hong Kong in April, 'creating a decided sensation'.[50] Later that year they returned (for the third time since their marriage) to Martin's family home at Altona, this time together with baby Fanny Martina and her elder brother Louis

Martin. At Altona, they were reunited with Leonore and Martina after some two years apart. The city of Altona had recently been transferred from being part of the Danish Grand Duchies of Schleswig and Holstein to be part of Prussia.

Between their marriage in March 1857 and their arrival in Australia in August 1865, they had travelled and performed constantly in Asia and North, Central and South America. So, after a brief rest in Altona, next stop … Adelaide and the goldfields of Victoria.

Notes

1   Anna Bishop first arrived in Sydney on 3 December 1855 together with celebrity harpist Nicholas Bochsa; she had left her husband, composer Sir Henry Bishop and children for Bochsa in 1839. Bochsa was a bigamist, and had previously been convicted in Paris of forgery and fraud; Bochsa died 6 January 1856 in Sydney

2   Johannes Brahms was born in Hamburg on 7 May 1833; his father, Johannes Jakob Brahms, was church organist in Altona and taught the four-year-old Johannes the violin; in 1845, Brahms started to study piano with Eduard Marxsen in Altona

3   *Argus* (Melbourne), 14 May 1869, 4

4   *Argus*, 14 August 1865, 8. Enquiries with current leading Danish musicologists have thus far been unable to substantiate this claim; it is possible that Martin Simonsen played in the court orchestra, which had been originally founded in the reign of Christian I (1448–81) and is now the Royal Danish Orchestra

5   For example, in Arthur Schnitzler's novella *The Spring Sonata*, one of the characters is presented as 'Emil Lindbach, Violinist to the Court of Bavaria'

6   Altona did not become administratively a part of Hamburg until 1939

7   https://forum.ahnenforschung.net/showthread.php?t=19870&page=3

8   Information from Frank Heckscher of Yateley, England

9   It may be relevant that one branch of the Heckscher family came from Altona to set up a piano manufacturing/supplies business at Camden Town, London, in 1883; the firm Heckscher & Company still exists, run by Martin Heckscher

10 A charming poem by the Dane, Jens Baggesen (1764–1826), 'To Mrs Leonore Heckscher', addresses the dedicatee as '… adorable Flower Angel'; that Leonore may or may not be an ancestor of our Leonore

11 Hamburg Births Records (online); in June 1920 an Eleanora Simonsen, mezzo-soprano, said to be a 'grandniece' of Martin Simonsen, performed in concert with Danish pianist Haagen Holenberg in Sydney – perhaps a granddaughter of Siegmund Simonsen – who then disappears from view; *Sydney Morning Herald*, 5 June 1920, 8

12 Telemann: *Ode to King Frederick V of Denmark for the Christianeum in Altona*, 1764
13 Klaus Hellwig, 'Carl Heinrich Reinecke: Piano Concertos 1–4', CPO/Westdeutscher Rundfunk Köln, Georgsmarienhütte, 1994; Reinecke was to return to Leipzig in 1860 as director of the Gewandhaus Orchestra and professor at the Conservatorium, where he was to remain for thirty-five years. Among his pupils in Leipzig were Grieg, Stanford, Sinding, Janáček, Albéniz, Bruch, Ethel Smyth and Australasians Ernest Hutcheson and Alfred Hill; both Grieg and Smyth were unimpressed by Reinecke as a teacher of composition
14 In the First Schleswig War, the Danes prevailed; it was not until after the Second Schleswig War that control passed to Prussia (in 1864)
15 *Argus*, 16 August 1865, 8
16 *Sacramento Transcript*, 3 July 1850
17 *Sacramento Transcript*, 15 July 1850
18 *Sacramento Transcript*, 24 September 1850
19 *Sacramento Transcript*, 24 July 1851
20 *Daily Alta California*, 22 January 1855, 2
21 *Daily Alta California*, 20 May 1855
22 *Daily Alta California*, 2 November 1855
23 *Straits Times* (Singapore), 26 February 1856, 4; *Free Press* (Singapore), 6 March 1856, 2 and 13 March 1856, 2; *Straits Times*, 1 April 1856, 4
24 *Bombay Times*, 6 September 1856, 569; *Argus*, 16 August 1865, 8
25 Adrienne Simpson, 'The greatest ornaments of their profession', 7
26 *Table Talk* (Melbourne), 1 November 1889, 5
27 At the time that Françoise de Haes was said to be singing with the Opéra-Comique, the director of the theatre was Émile Perrin, who was concurrently running the Théâtre-Lyrique
28 And she does not appear in Soubies and Malherbe's survey of performances at the Opéra-Comique 1840–60
29 *Argus*, 14 July 1867, 5
30 *New Zealand Herald* (Auckland), 11 November 1880, 6
31 Frances Alda, *Men, Women and Tenors*, 24
32 Proust was the son of a Jewish mother and Catholic father
33 Among the earliest prima donna women to travel were Francesca Cuzzoni and Faustina Bordoni in the 1730s–50s, but they were exceptional, and the travelling international prima donna did not come about widely until the generation of Giuditta Pasta and Maria Malibran in the 1820s and 1830s, and then Adelina Patti and many others from the 1860s to the end of the century; see Henry Pleasants, *The Great Singers*, 1967, and John Rosselli, *Singers of Italian Opera*, 1992
34 *Empire* (Sydney), quoting the *Port Louis Commercial Gazette* of 6 March, 6 May 1857, 2
35 Frances Alda, *Men, Women and Tenors*, 24; it seems unlikely that they performed whole operas – their performances were more likely mixtures of excerpts
36 The piece was dedicated to Mrs Peregrine Poole of Kingston, Jamaica; Peregrine Poole worked in the Customs Department at Kingston – his wife was previously Harriet Moffat; this work and several others by Martin Simonsen may be found at the National Library of Australia in Canberra
37 Susana Salgado, *The Teatro Solís*, 213–14
38 Salgado, 8–9; resonance of Werner Herzog's 1982 film, *Fitzcarraldo*
39 *Daily Alta California*, 1 March 1863, 1
40 *Daily Alta California*, 6 March 1863; Martin Simonsen's compositions, all for violin and piano or orchestra, are typically called 'Souvenir de …', 'Variations sur …', 'Fantaisie sur …', and are clearly influenced by the important violinist-composers – Italian, Germanic and Scandinavian – of the previous generation (Paganini, Ernst, Ole Bull, JF Frøhlich and Niels Gade)

41 From 1853, the first resident opera company in San Francisco was run by a French couple, Louis Théophile Planel and his soprano wife, Hortense. They were followed by Anna Bishop's company in 1854, then by Eugenio and Giovanna Bianchi in 1858

42 Olio: it is not clear from the context whether this is a general usage, as in a miscellaneous collection, or a vaudeville/burlesque usage, as in a short dance or song as an encore or entr'acte; Kern and Hammerstein's *Show Boat* has an 'Olio Dance'

43 *Daily Alta California*, 17 March 1863; impresario Thomas Maguire had opened his redeveloped 'New Opera House' in Washington Street in November 1856

44 *Marysville Daily Appeal*, 27 March 1863; *Sacramento Daily Union*, 3 April 1863

45 *Sacramento Daily Union*, 26 September 1863

46 While the Simonsens eventually had ten children, when interviewed for *Table Talk* in Melbourne in 1889, Fanny specifically mentioned that she had had eleven children – five daughters and six sons; *Table Talk*, 1 November 1889, 5

47 *Daily Alta California*, 3 July 1864; *Sacramento Daily Union*, 25 July 1864

48 *Sacramento Daily Union*, 10 January 1865

49 *Daily Alta California*, 17 and 23 January 1865; *San Francisco Chronicle*, 19 January 1865, 2

50 *Marysville Daily Appeal*, 4 June 1865

Chapter 2
Touring in Australasia

1

What was it that attracted the Simonsens to Australia in 1865? Was it the prolonged rush following the discovery of gold in 1851, and the consequent need for entertainment, that encouraged them to try their luck there? Certainly by this stage they had plenty of experience of performing for the diggers in California. Perhaps living through the Civil War years in America made them apprehensive that the situation might remain unstable there. The greatest excitement in Australia that year seems to have been generated by the shooting dead of various bushrangers in New South Wales and Victoria.

Together with two small children, Martin and Fanny Simonsen first arrived in Australia on 6 August 1865, at Adelaide's dock at Glenelg by the P&O mail steamship *Northam* from Galle in Ceylon.[1] But which children? By this stage of their lives, they already had three daughters

– Leonore (born in Montevideo, now six), Martina (born in Jamaica, three) and Fanny Martina (born San Francisco, seven months), plus one son, Louis Martin (also born San Francisco, two). Two of them – the the oldest, Leonore and Martina – were probably the ones left behind with Martin's family at Altona. After their long voyage, they finally disembarked at Port Melbourne six days after reaching Adelaide.

What were their intentions? To travel and perform continuously, from town to town, city to city, country to country, as they had done up to that point? Or to consider Australia as a potential new home base for their steadily growing family? Or to do both of those things?

Australia in the mid-nineteenth century was going through a period of rapid growth and change. Between 1850 and 1870 the population quadrupled, with the city of Melbourne growing from fewer than 25 000 in 1851 to little short of half a million by 1891; the discovery of gold in Victoria and New South Wales in the 1850s meant that the economy had moved on from being overwhelmingly pastoral, based on sheep; increasingly (and successfully) wheat and vines were cultivated; and in Melbourne, manufacturing, particularly of foodstuffs, was developing quickly.[2]

By 14 August both Simonsen parents were advertising in Melbourne as having arrived by the overland mail, Martin as 'Solo Violinist to His Majesty the King of Denmark' and Fanny as 'Prima Donna from the Opéra-Comique in Paris'[3] – both claims which would be reiterated frequently in publicity over subsequent years – and giving notice that they would be performing vocal and instrumental concerts 'as soon as their arrangements are complete'.

These arrangements seem to have taken no time at all, as just two days later an advertisement in The Argus announced 'for seven nights only' Grand Vocal and Instrumental Concerts to be given by Fanny and Martin, together with a hastily recruited company.[4] By now, additional to the King of Denmark, Martin was also giving notice that he had

Left: Fanny and Martin Simonsen

23

played for the Emperor of Austria, and the Kings of Prussia, Hanover, Saxony and Sweden, plus the Governor-General of India, Lord Canning, and several other British aristocrats in various diplomatic roles around the world, together with gushing tributes from several of them.

The Simonsens' first performance in Australia took place at St George's Hall in Melbourne just five days after arriving in the city – on Saturday 19 August 1865. 'The new artists were very warmly received', wrote *The Argus*, 'and before the concert closed they had established themselves in high favour'.[5] The reviewers from both *The Age* and *The Argus* praised Fanny's performance extravagantly – Martin too, but more briefly. They performed for seven nights. Already Fanny and Martin had assembled a small concert party, including soprano Geraldine Warden, contralto Maggie Liddle, Frank Howson and brother John, pianist Cesare Cutolo and a string quartet led by Edward King.[6] The audience for this debut was 'not large', the performers having yet to build a following.

Scarcely a week later, the Simonsens' little company was for several nights at the Mechanics' Institute at the port city of Geelong – gateway to the goldfields – the audience 'scanty', but 'the event a great success if considered from an artistic point of view.'[7] By early September, they had moved on to Adelaide, arriving by ship from Melbourne on 4 September, their two young daughters still in tow.[8] They opened at White's Assembly Rooms on Monday 11th. This time it was Martin who garnered the most praise, the *South Australian Advertiser* comparing his playing admiringly with the Austro-Hungarian Miska Hauser,[9] who had been the first internationally known virtuoso fiddler to tour Australia in the 1850s. After a week of nightly concerts at White's, the Simonsen company moved on to tour smaller towns and cities in South Australia, generally to smallish but appreciative audiences. One stop, at the Oddfellows' Hall at Gawler, was notable for the meagreness of numbers, a fact recalled vividly by Fanny in a scathing speech she made from the platform, when they made a return visit six years later.

White's Room as Star Theatre, Adelaide

By the end of September, the company was back at White's Room in Adelaide, the numbers by now picking up, 'their entertainment one of the most elegant and refined ever offered to an Adelaide audience,'[10] and two weeks later they had returned for a second season to St George's Hall in Melbourne, the venue gratifyingly crowded.

Next, they went to Tasmania, opening at the Town Hall in Launceston. The economy of the colony was at that time dependent on farming and shipbuilding, and it was not many years since it had been decided that they would no longer accept convicts from Britain. The Simonsen company was now reduced to soprano-pianist Geraldine Warden and contralto Margaret Liddle, presumably in order to slim down their costs. 'The audience made up in some measure for their limited number by the enthusiasm of their applause,' reported the *Cornwall Chronicle*.[11] They gave concerts in a series of small towns on their way to Hobart, where they opened at the Mechanics' Institute on

6 November, 'an evening [which] throughout gave exquisite delight, and deservedly elicited the most marked approbation.'[12]

Following their short season at Hobart, the Simonsens, together with Leonore and Martina and accompanying artists, sailed to Sydney on 14 November, opening at the School of Arts in Pitt Street on the 20th, the first of many concerts they would present there. This was followed by the Exchange Hall on the 23rd, the audience, as usual, 'not so numerous', but their reception 'very enthusiastic',[13] and the next day they performed at the Masonic Hall in York Street – Martin, it emerged, was a mason.[14] In Sydney, the Simonsen company was joined by pianist John Hill, who was later to become piano accompanist (and third husband) to touring prima donna Ilma di Murska.

January 1866 found the Simonsens in gold rush Bathurst (200 kilometres to the west of Sydney), where they encountered their first organised opposition. It appears that for some reason the good folk of the city objected to the Simonsens performing in their theatre. The consequence was that the company was forced to relocate its two final performances to a 'Monster Hall'.[15] By the end of the month, they were back in Sydney, this time for a brief season at the Prince of Wales Opera House in Castlereagh Street. This must have been quite a significant risk – the theatre having a capacity of 2500 – and the *Sydney Morning Herald* reported an audience 'very inadequate to their merits'.[16]

On 6 February, together with Fanny, 'Brother Martin Simonsen' gave a 'Grand Complimentary Farewell Benefit' at the Masonic Hall in York Street, the event sponsored by the leaders of Sydney's masonic lodges.[17] Taking their leave of Sydney, the company toured some of the smaller pastoral cities of southern New South Wales – Goulburn, Queanbeyan and Wagga Wagga. It was in the last that they encountered their next opposition. There was an escalating series of disasters, all reported by the *Wagga Wagga Express*:

> The concert which was to have been given by the [Simonsen]
> company at the Court House on Saturday night last did not

take place in consequence of the non-arrival of the vocalists themselves. Monday evening's concert also collapsed owing to the general absence of the townspeople on holiday excursions. Tuesday night two meetings were held and attendance at the concert was extremely scant ... The impersonations of male character by Mdme Simonsen were, however, scarcely to the taste of a Wagga Wagga audience ...

In 1866, the 250 km road across the mountains between Queanbeyan and Wagga Wagga was rough and barely ready, the transportation horse- or bullock-drawn; although rail travel in Australia started in 1831, by 1865 the network was still very limited. Fanny Simonsen was in no mood to bow down to the tastes of an outback town. The report continued:

Mdme Simonsen advanced to the front of the stage and complained of the treatment she had received at the hands of the Wagga Wagga ladies. One lady, she said, had characterised her acting as disgusting, another had declared her singing to be only squeaking. In reply to these accusations she begged to state that the pieces that had given such offence to the Wagga Wagga ladies had been acted before Lady Young [wife of the serving governor of New South Wales] and the first families in Sydney, and had never been thought disgusting there. As to the singing being only squeaking ... she could well afford to put up with the adverse verdicts of people who evidently did not know what good music was ...[18]

Ouch! During the course of her rant, Fanny 'was repeatedly interrupted with loud bursts of cheering, and finally retired from the stage amidst a hurricane of applause.' This was not to be the last time that Fanny was to round on her audience from the stage. And, being a good story, it was repeated in the press from coast to coast in Australia and as far as New

Zealand, and must only have served significantly to raise the profile of the Simonsens. In her recent essay, 'Operatic performances two hundred miles in the Australian bush', Nicole Anae points out not only that it would have been the first occasion on which a woman had been seen in men's clothes on stage in Wagga Wagga, 'violating prevailing social mores', but also that it may have been the first concert of its kind (with opera excerpts) in that city.[19]

On their overland trip back south to Melbourne, the Simonsen troupe performed to excited audiences at the gold rush town of Beechworth, and then opened at the Princess Theatre in Melbourne on 15 May – another barn, this time seating some 1650 – where they gave five concerts. In spite of the Wagga Wagga publicity, or perhaps because of it, *The Age* reported that 'it is rather surprising that so small a number of persons should have visited the Princess's last night, considering the real musical treat that was offered to the public.'[20]

Princess Theatre, Melbourne

While transportation by railway train was becoming gradually more possible in the late 1860s in New South Wales and Victoria,[21] many of the constant travels of the Simonsens and their troupe would have been horse-drawn on rough roads. In the dozens of concerts they had performed since their arrival in Australia, certain pieces stood out as crowd-pleasers. For Fanny these included: 'Casta diva' from Bellini's *Norma*, the Cavatina from Meyerbeer's *Robert le diable* and the Romanza from Rossini's *Guillaume Tell*, plus Arditi's 'Il bacio', the Irish ballad 'Kathleen Mavourneen' and the Scottish song 'Comin' thro the rye'. For Martin they were: Paganini's 'Carnival of Venice', together with several composed by Martin himself – 'Remembrance of Germany', 'Souvenir de Bellini' (variously described as by Artôt and by Simonsen), 'Variations on *The Daughter of the Regiment*' and the dazzling 'The Echo'.

Clearly, while Martin and Fanny had worked hard to establish themselves in Australia over the past eleven months, travelling constantly and performing almost nightly, they had found it hard to build a sustainable audience. Fanny's operatic credentials as a prima donna at the Opéra-Comique in Paris could be asserted, but where was the evidence? A new strategy was conceived – necessitating a switch to the operatic stage.

2

The first 'proper' operas to be mounted in Australia were presented in 1833 in Sydney by a Jewish merchant and auctioneer from England, Barnett Levey. Previously, Levey had introduced pioneering concerts and plays in the city, his first opera production being a version of Mozart's *The Marriage of Figaro* (arranged and with interpolations by Sir Henry Bishop). Yet, as early as 1796, the ballad opera *The Poor Soldier* by William Shield (first performed as *The Shamrock* in Dublin in 1777, then at Covent Garden in 1783) was given at Robert Sidaway's convict-built theatre in Sydney on 9 June 1796 – just eight years after the arrival of the First Fleet.[22]

From these small beginnings, opera performances in Sydney gradually became more frequent. From the 1830s, two British-born actor-sopranos – Mrs Taylor and Mrs Chester – vied for supremacy at Hobart and Sydney. Often said to be the first opera composed and performed in Australia was Isaac Nathan's *Don John of Austria*, which was given at the Royal Victoria Theatre in Pitt Street on 3 May 1847. The goldrushes of the 1850s attracted Irish soprano Catherine Hayes, star of La Scala and Covent Garden, to give Donizetti's *Lucia di Lammermoor* and *Don Pasquale* in Sydney and Melbourne.

If there were precursors to the Simonsen family of singers in Australia, they were the Howsons – brothers Frank and John, plus sister Emma and various sons and daughters, who toured in the 1840s and 1850s – and the Carandinis, including five daughters of contralto Marie Carandini (1826–94), who came from Hobart to Sydney from the mid-1840s and toured with Balfe's *The Bohemian Girl* and other works.

However, the first touring opera company to build sustained success in Australia and New Zealand was WS Lyster's, which started at the Theatre Royal in Melbourne in 1861. William Saurin Lyster, was not a musician or singer, but an impresario and manager. Born in Dublin in 1828 to Protestant Irish parents, he had visited Sydney and Melbourne on a round-the-world voyage taken for his health at the age of thirteen. As a young man he fought both in the Cape Frontier War of 1847 in South Africa and in Nicaragua in 1855. Some two years later, he joined his brother Fred Lyster's opera company in New Orleans, and, shortly after, he formed his own company to tour California, the leading artists being two Americans – soprano Lucy Escott and tenor Henry Squires – and he came with them to Australia in 1861. The company played the major cities and toured constantly in both Australia and New Zealand, so by the time that Fanny Simonsen joined them in 1866, they were already firmly established.[23]

William Saurin Lyster

Fanny Simonsen

Donizetti by Chardigny

Fanny Simonsen made her debut as an operatic prima donna in Australia with WS Lyster's Royal Italian and English Opera Company at the Theatre Royal in Melbourne on 25 June, and, starting at the top, she sang the title role in Donizetti's *Lucia di Lammermoor*. 'On Madame Simonsen's coming on the stage, she was cordially but not demonstratively greeted, and went through her opening recitative and aria with evident nervousness,' wrote *The Argus* reporter. Nevertheless:

> Her clear, fresh, bird-like voice appeared to take a portion of
> the audience by surprise, and the applause which this first
> effort elicited soon restored her confidence.[24]

The Age was less circumspect about the new arrival: 'Her first appearance in opera was a complete and undeniable success.' In the third act,

> ... her acting here rose to grandeur. The utter despair with
> which she fell on her knees ... sent a thrill through the
> audience, and when she fell prone to the earth ... a very
> general impression prevailed, so natural was her acting, that
> she had fainted.[25]

Lucia di Lammermoor was the most celebrated and enduring of Donizetti's many operas. It was premièred on 26 September 1835 at the Teatro San Carlo in Naples, and at the heart of its appeal lies a combination of expressive melody coupled with complex coloratura decoration, especially for the singer of the title role. In many ways singing it was to create Fanny Simonsen's high reputation, just as it did for Adelina Patti, Nellie Melba, Luisa Tetrazzini, Maria Callas, Joan Sutherland and many others.

Just three days after her debut as Lucia, Fanny was back, this time as the sleepwalker Amina in Bellini's *La sonnambula*, then on Saturday as Elvira in Auber's *Masaniello*. On the following Monday she was Sélika in Meyerbeer's *L'Africaine*, a role in which she alternated with the established prima donna in the company, Lucy Escott. Tenor Armes Beaumont was Vasco da Gama. Altogether it was an extraordinary eight-day period, one that would never be attempted by a current leading soprano. Fanny first sang the courtesan Violetta in Verdi's *La traviata* at the Theatre Royal on 25 July. *The Age* thought her performance

> … was stamped by all the graceful finish of her Lucia and her
> Sélika. Vocally she achieved in the part her greatest triumph.
> The music is exactly suited to the range of her voice, and
> throughout she rendered it with pure delicacy of expression.[26]

Violetta was a role that would be taken up in later years by two of Fanny's daughters, Martina Simonsen and Frances Saville, and by her granddaughter Frances Alda. Would any of them reach her level of excellence in the role? *Traviata* had been first performed in 1853 at the Teatro la Fenice in Venice.

Three days later, Fanny made her highly praised debut in Meyerbeer's *Les Huguenots* as Marguérite de Valois, with the company's other prima donna Lucy Escott as Valentine.[27] Her performance on 26 August in Meyerbeer's *Le prophète* – Fanny as Bertha, Lucy Escott as Fidès – seems only to have taken place because the planned steamer to Adelaide was postponed. She first sang that role on 30 July. These were Fanny's third and fourth Meyerbeer operas (following *L'étoile du nord* at the Opéra-Comique and *L'Africaine* with Lyster in Melbourne).

Such was her sustained success that season, Fanny was recruited to Lyster's company on a permanent basis in July. How were Louis and Fanny Martina cared for while Fanny and Martin were on tour? By servants in Melbourne? Certainly, by early August 1866 they were travelling by ship to (and later from) Adelaide without the encumbrance of small children.[28] As yet her husband Martin had virtually no role in the company, the conducting being undertaken by the German Julius

Siede. However, Martin was occasionally allowed to play virtuoso violin solos between the acts of the operas.

In Adelaide, Lyster's company opened at the Victoria Theatre, where Fanny opened as Lucia, as previously in Melbourne. Aside from Lucia, in the first week Fanny also sang Amina in *La sonnambula* and the title role in Flotow's *Martha* and the company also gave *Lucrezia Borgia*, *La fille du régiment*, *Il trovatore* and *Faust* – Lucy Escott taking several of the other principal soprano roles.[29] Fanny later added Elvira in Bellini's *I puritani* with 'the utmost brilliancy of execution'.[30] On 14 September came a novelty for the period – a single performance of *The Marriage of Figaro*. Mozart's operas had substantially fallen out of the repertoire by the middle of the nineteenth century. Fanny sang the Countess, 'her singing … deserving of all praise'. This was a role she would have learned with one or other of her teachers in Paris.[31] Perhaps the Adelaide season did something to restore marital parity for the Simonsens, as Martin was there hired by Lyster to conduct all the operas – usually without comment in the press. These performances were quite likely his first assignments as an operatic conductor.

October 1866 found the company back at the Theatre Royal in Melbourne – with Fanny's re-entry as Elvira in *I puritani*. *The Age* commented: 'We have already had occasion to remark how well the music of Bellini was suited to her voice; *I puritani* has given another example.'[32] At the end of the month, Fanny was Princess Isabella in Meyerbeer's *Roberto il diavolo*, which *The Argus* stated was 'by far the most ambitious effort yet attempted on the Melbourne stage'.[33] By this stage, Fanny had established herself as the number one soprano of the Lyster company.

In the mid- and late-nineteenth century, Meyerbeer's operas were very popular in Australasia and around the world – each of them with brilliant and demanding roles for prima donnas. Originally staged in French as *Robert le Diable*, this opera, with its five acts, great spectacle and ballet sequences, effectively established the genre of 'grand opera', a turning point in the history of the artform. First performed at the

Opéra in Paris in 1831, by 1834 it had been staged 300 times at that house and around the world in seventy-seven theatres.

On 12 November, Fanny sang Agathe in Weber's *Der Freischütz*, 'with exquisite finish and with a vocalisation which almost might be pronounced perfect'.[34] A rather extraordinary occurrence happened three nights later. Fanny Simonsen was to take the part of Inez in *L'Africaine* to Lucy Escott's Sélika, but at the last moment Escott's cold got the better of her and she withdrew. The substitute could not be dressed in time, so in the first act Fanny sang both roles. The two leading Melbourne newspapers seem to have been thoroughly bamboozled by this turn of events, *The Age* not appearing to notice that it had happened at all, *The Argus* simply noting that Escott was indisposed, her role taken by Simonsen.[35]

By December, Lyster's company had moved on to the Prince of Wales Opera House in Sydney, with Martin Simonsen as the season's conductor. Again, Fanny opened as Lucia.[36] The whole Sydney season was flagged by Lyster as a 'Farewell', and, following a series of concerts given by the Simonsens in Sydney, their own Simonsen troupe went on to tour some country cities of Victoria, gold-rush Ballarat and Geelong among them. In Ballarat, they opened 'for six nights only' at the Theatre Royal on Saturday 20 April, Fanny Simonsen billed as the main attraction. The *Ballarat Star* reported:

> It is needless for us to attempt to describe this lady's finished
> vocalisation or to claim for her the possession of histrionic
> powers of a high order. These are points long ago conceded to
> her ... [However], it is to be borne in mind that she labored
> under the disadvantage of being without her wonted support
> from band, scenery and appointments ...[37]

Clearly, to the disappointment of the *Star*, the company was performing 'in concert', without an orchestra or sets, accompanied by piano. Martin Simonsen gave his usual 'refined' performances on the violin. It is worth noting that the city of Ballarat had not existed at all until the discovery of gold in 1851. Yet, so speedy was development that by the late 1850s there were already four substantial theatres and three brick-built churches, and soon to join them several halls suitable for concerts. The Theatre Royal, in which the Simonsens were to perform regularly, opened in 1858. Touring international artists who had come to the city to perform included erotic Irish dancer Lola Montez in 1855 and prima donna Anna Bishop in 1856.[38]

Amidst all this performing work, Fanny had given birth to her second son (fifth child), Julius Martin, on 2 April 1867 – at their temporary home in Melbourne, 162 Collins Street East.[39] As tenor 'Jules', Julius was to have a chequered life. Next, Fanny re-joined Lyster's opera company for a short season at the Princess Theatre in Melbourne in May, returning to Ballarat with the Lyster company again at the Theatre Royal in late June, where she opened as Lady Harriet in Flotow's *Martha*, followed by her Lucia, and, among other operas, *La sonnambula*. 'Madame Simonsen was in glorious voice and sang with delightful purity and feeling,' reported the *Ballarat Star*.[40] The Theatre Royal in Ballarat was the first permanent theatre in the city, just eight years after gold was discovered and the township founded.

Next came another gold rush boom town, Bendigo, where Fanny opened as Princess Isabella in *Roberto il diavolo*.[41] She seems to have worked steadily at concerts and operas on a nightly basis, without a hint of 'indisposition' throughout her pregnancy. However, she had a whole clear week at home in Melbourne before the next birth.[42] It was perhaps not so surprising, given that the Simonsens had a short break from work, that Martin was able to do some thinking about the future, and on 13 April, eleven days after the birth of Julius, *Bell's Life in Victoria* reported: 'We are given to understand that Mr Martin Simonsen contemplates the formation of another opera company.'

The newspaper report went on to name the artists that he was thinking of engaging – nearly all of them members of Lyster's company.[43] Had Martin discussed this plan with Lyster, or had the impresario been

Theatre Royal, Ballarat

forced to read about it in the newspapers? Whatever the answer to that question, April 1867 marked a first clean break for both Fanny and Martin with Lyster's company and the Simonsens returned to touring with their own concert troupe.

By the end of August, the Simonsens were back at St George's Hall in Beechworth, a town which had responded so positively to them the previous year,[44] and, following concerts at Albury on the New South Wales/Victoria border, they gave a Farewell Concert on 12 October at the Princess Theatre in Melbourne. Fanny was said by *The Australasian* to be 'shortly going to Calcutta'.[45] In the event, it was not to India that they went, but to Tasmania, where they gave a few performances in Hobart, being rumoured to be bound next for Sydney, Newcastle and San Francisco.[46] This was wrong again, and on 28 November 1867 they sailed, together with their concert party (and their new young son), for the first time to tour New Zealand.[47]

3

The first touring concert party featuring operatic music to visit New Zealand had been the Marie Carandini company in 1863, just four years ahead of the arrival of the Simonsens troupe, closely followed by Lyster's fully staged Royal Italian and English Opera Company, which toured in 1864. They all post-dated the discovery in 1861 of gold in the Otago region of South Island. As earlier in California and Australia, the finding of gold brought a rush of immigrants and Dunedin became the city with the largest population in the whole colony, a city substantially built by immigrant Scots, and subsequently called the 'Edinburgh of the South'.

Publicised in advance as an eight-week tour, the Simonsen troupe was actually to spend the next four and a half months travelling around New Zealand. They opened at the Princess Theatre in Dunedin on 6 December 1867,[48] their party including soprano Rebecca Jones from the Lyster company and pianist Eugène Artôt.[49] The critic from the local press was somewhat circumspect in first making the acquaintance of Fanny as an artist: 'Madame Simonsen has a light soprano voice … She showed that her voice has also a good range and power, and that she can use it well.' Less guardedly, it was reported that 'Herr Simonsen is evidently a very talented violinist.' On the opening night in Dunedin,

> … very heavy rain commenced about seven o'clock, and …
> there was not an instant's cessation until near midnight.
> Consequently, the concert, from first to last, had a loud
> accompaniment from rain-pour on the roof of the theatre.[50]

Presumably the Princess had a resonant corrugated iron roof (a material popular for domestic dwellings in New Zealand to this day). They performed nightly in Dunedin, except on Sundays. Towards the

Princess Theatre, Dunedin (interior)

end of the run, they gave two performances of Bellini's *La sonnambula*, Fanny, as usual taking the lead role. The rest of the cast had been pulled together from whoever was available in the other works being performed at that time at the Princess. Afterwards, Fanny gave one of her impromptu speeches from the stage:

> I am only sorry it has not been in my power to get up pieces
> such as have been played this evening … We got *Sonnambula*
> up in two days …[51]

The 'general agent' for the Simonsens in Dunedin, named as such in advertisements, was one George F Price.[52] Born at Bath in England, Price had emigrated from London in 1865, arriving initially in Melbourne, where he worked as a shop assistant and journalist, then crossing the Tasman to work in the recently discovered goldfields on the west coast of

South Island. There he was both digger and journalist (again). He clearly made a musical impression on the Simonsens, because approximately halfway through their tour, he joined them – as an 'admired tenor and buffo comic vocalist', according to advertisements (written presumably by Price himself).[53]

Leaving Dunedin, the Simonsen company moved steadily northwards up the east coast, to give performances at tiny Waikouaiti, then at Oamaru. They next needed to cross the dangerous (and bridgeless) Waitaki River between Oamaru and Timaru. Five years later, the English novelist Anthony Trollope made the same crossing:

> It was a piercingly cold morning, and we felt aggrieved greatly
> when we found that we had to leave the coach and get into
> a boat. But the dimensions of our own hardships lessened
> themselves to our imagination when we found that two of the
> boatmen descended into the river and pushed the boat for half
> a mile up the stream. During a part of the way three men were
> in the water, and yet the boat hardly seemed to move. For this
> service we were charged 2s [shillings] apiece.[54]

By 30 December, they had arrived at the Town Hall in Christchurch for a three-week season, where the critic of the *Lyttelton Times* compared Fanny Simonsen favourably with Christchurch's previous soprano tourist, Madame Carandini. Of Martin's performances on the violin, 'we are able to speak in terms of unqualified praise'. By this stage, George Price was co-opted as a performer and was allowed to sing an unnamed recitative and air. He was said to have 'a voice of no mean quality', a judgement not widely shared later in the tour.[55]

The company next arrived at the Odd Fellows' Hall in Wellington, capital city since 1865, opening on 22 January 1868, Anniversary Day in New Zealand,[56] where the hall was 'crowded to overflowing ... [and] Madame Simonsen's execution was everything that could be desired.'[57] At their performance a week later, a young couple were observed canoodling in the reserved seats, provoking the wrath (and pomposity) of 'An Onlooker', who wrote to the editor of the *Wellington Independent*:

> I shall not be ungallant enough to comment upon the conduct
> of the lady, and must leave her to her own sense of shame;
> but I will inform the male offender that, were he a gentleman
> … I would remind him of the way in which his companions
> would punish such conduct.[58]

The editor headlined the letter 'Cads at Concerts'. On 1 February, the Simonsens took a side trip to perform at the Masonic Hall at nearby Hutt, and, following a concert in aid of the Fire Brigade back at the Odd Fellows, they gave their last performance of the Wellington season on the 7th in the presence of the recently-appointed Governor of New Zealand, Sir George Bowen and Lady Bowen.[59]

4

From Wellington they went on to Nelson in the South Island, where a local critic observed that

> Madame Simonsen possesses an exceedingly pure and flexible
> soprano voice, and … it is equally true and measured in the
> heaviest passages of opera or the lightest and most plaintive
> notes of a ballad.[60]

The next area where gold was to be discovered was on the west coast of the South Island in 1865–66, precipitating a rush of miners, particularly from Victoria, where the phenomenon was already declining. The Simonsens' manager George Price knew about it at first hand, having worked in the west as both digger and journalist, so the Simonsens headed there next. For Martin and Fanny, this was their third gold rush entertainment of a mining community (following California and Victoria).

It was to be a packed schedule over the following six weeks, with nightly performances in Westport, Charleston, Greymouth and Hokitika – all towns that had virtually not existed before the discovery of gold, but since that time bursting with immigrants and activity. Travelling between them was not at all easy: the Simonsen troupe went from Nelson to Westport by dirt road; from Westport to Charleston they went by Cobb's coach; but the journey to Hokitika from Westport was accomplished by paddle steamer, the *Nelson*, making the dangerous crossing of the sandbar off Hokitika before arriving at the wharf. Between 1865 and 1873 there were no fewer than forty-two shipwrecks at the mouth of the Hokitika River, including the stranding of the *Nelson* on the sandbar in June 1865.[61] Aside from Martin and Fanny

The SS Nelson *at Hokitika by William Marshall Cooper*

(and two of their four young children), the travelling company still included Rebecca Jones, George Price and pianist Eugène Artôt.

They began at the newly opened Assembly Room at Westport on 15 February 1868, followed the next day by their first performance at the Theatre Royal of the Casino de Venice (no less) at Charleston. Gold on the west coast of the South Island turned out to be a somewhat scarce commodity and coal more plentiful.[62] However, the town had mushroomed since the first diggers arrived in 1866, and the *Westport Times* saw the arrival of the Simonsens as clear evidence of the increased maturity of their community:

> The presentation of such a splendid and costly entertainment
> is a marked evidence of the extraordinary rapid progress of
> Charleston within the past twelve months.[63]

After the planned four (increased to six) nightly concerts there, they returned to Westport, then went on to give concerts at Kilgour's Union Theatre at Greymouth, then the Prince of Wales Opera House at Hokitika (which was already said to have seventy-seven pubs). This 'Opera House' had opened in March 1866 with the Lenton Troupe of clowns, gymnasts and trapeze artists – well suited to an audience of diggers – and the only professional 'opera' singer to have appeared there before the Simonsens was the London-born prima donna, Julia Mathews, famous in opéra-bouffe.[64]

So the Simonsens' company was very much a pioneer in these gold rush towns of New Zealand. At Hokitika they gave twelve concerts, and in the later performances there they included the whole of the Fifth Act of Meyerbeer's *L'Africaine* (in English).[65] At the time, the town was in the middle of Fenian demonstrations in support of the 'Manchester Martyrs'.[66] From Hokitika, the party returned to perform again at Greymouth (including the third act of Weber's *Der Freischütz*), before returning by the *Nelson* from Westport to Nelson to complete their time with the New Zealand gold rush.[67]

Finally, they went back to Wellington. This return was timed to coincide with the planned visit of Queen Victoria's second surviving son, the twenty-three-year-old Alfred, Duke of Edinburgh, following his tour of Australia. However, the visit was cancelled because of an earlier assassination attempt on the Royal Duke in Sydney. After surviving a shot from point-blank range by an Irishman on 12 March 1868, the prince returned home to Britain without visiting New Zealand and leaving behind an outbreak of anti-Irish hysteria throughout Australia and New Zealand. The Simonsens gave the last concert of that first New Zealand tour at the Odd Fellows' Hall on 6 April, the performance concluding with a specially re-worded second verse of the national anthem:

> God save our widowed Queen
> God bless our own lov'd Queen
> Give her great joy
> On her young Alfred pour
> Blessings for evermore
> Preserve her and soon restore
> Her noble boy![68]

It was said in the press that the company were to leave for Europe the following day, but if that was the plan, they seem to have gone by the *Rakaia* first to Panama,[69] from where they sailed on to San Francisco – and from there travelling on eventually to Altona, where they were reunited with their older daughters.[70] The implication of the press reports was that they might be in Europe and North America for a lengthy period, perhaps for several years. At Altona, where they stayed with Martin's family, they had another son, their third (and sixth child), Herman Martin, born on 2 March 1869.[71] Just five months later, they were back in Australia and performing in Melbourne, this time leaving four of their six children behind at Altona.[72]

5

For the Simonsens, musical life back in Australia re-started rather slowly. Were they beginning to address the question as to whether Australia would make a good home base for their growing family? On 5 August 1869 they performed before a small but appreciative audience at the Academy of Music (previously Princess Theatre) in Melbourne.[73] However, on that same day they were required to be witnesses at the trial of the captain of the ship they had arrived on, who had been accused of being constantly drunk during the voyage, a situation confirmed by both Martin and Fanny. She told the court that during the passage it was the exception for the captain to be sober.[74] In the following weeks they performed in the suburbs of Melbourne and the country towns of Victoria, their troupe now including German mezzo-soprano Rebecca Nordt, tenor Arthur Moule and pianist Harcourt Lee.[75]

By January 1870, their tour had extended into country New South Wales, and on the 18th they returned to Wagga Wagga, where they had received criticism previously. This time, the concert went well, 'the greatest musical treat', reported the *Wagga Wagga Advertiser*. However, during the performance:

> A large patch [of the ceiling] of several feet in diameter
> suddenly gave way and fell with a crash upon the startled
> musicians, half smothering them with dust, and giving
> Madame Simonsen a severe blow on the head.[76]

She sustained two cuts and some severe bruising, but, being the trouper she was, Fanny was back on stage ten minutes later to 'loud and long continued expressions of enthusiastic applause'. After singing 'Comin' thro the rye' with 'so much sweetness', the audience demanded an encore, but Fanny was not amused and 'administered a short but well-deserved rebuke'.[77]

6

Clearly the Simonsens could not sustain a successful career with endless concerts in outback towns, and in February 1870 Fanny was signed up again by impresario WS Lyster for his newly re-formed opera company.

While the Simonsens had been in New Zealand, Lyster and his company had provided constant amusement for the touring Alfred, Duke of Edinburgh, who went six times to see them perform.[78] The problem for Lyster was that his company was gradually going bankrupt and, after that season ended, the company broke up. On top of this, both William and his brother Fred had to defend themselves as Irishmen (albeit Protestants) in the furore of anti-Irishness that followed the shooting of the Duke.

It was clear that Lyster, following a financially disastrous season in San Francisco, needed a new company with new funding. That funding he found in the person of John W Smith, an Australian impresario, who had made a small fortune out of a troupe of Japanese acrobats which had been regularly patronised by Prince Alfred. The money in place, Lyster left Australia for Italy immediately, in search of good new singers. He achieved his goal with the help of the Tasmanian-raised contralto, Lucy Chambers, who was living the opera star life at that time in Milan, and Lyster was able to sign up a series of good Italian singers, plus Lucy Chambers herself.[79]

Adding to this new Italian gang, in Melbourne Lyster was also able to bring in Fanny Simonsen, Armes Beaumont and others from his previous troupe. Together they were now called Lyster and Smith's Royal Italian Opera Company, and they opened successfully at the Theatre Royal in Melbourne on 5 February 1870 with Verdi's *Ernani*.[80] Fanny Simonsen made her *rentrée* with the company five days later in what might be termed her signature role as the Bride of Lammermoor. *The Argus* reported:

> The entrance of Madame Fannie Simonsen was greeted with
> a unanimous and long-continued burst of welcome from all
> parts of the house, accompanied by a shower of bouquets.[81]

Assessing her Mad Scene, *The Argus*'s critic went on: 'In this most trying part, Madame Simonsen rose above the ordinary level of the night's performance.' Her known skills were praised, and 'we were particularly pleased in this instance that she was entirely free from the only fault we could ever find with her, viz, a tendency to shrillness.' Perhaps the major issue for the Simonsens was that Martin Simonsen was not conducting – that role taken, as earlier, by Herr Siede. Was Martin passed over by Lyster because of the untimely revelations of his intention to start his own opera company back in April?

In March Fanny followed Lucia with another part close to her heart – the title role in Bellini's *Norma*. While generally approving Fanny's assumption of the role, *The Argus* was not so pleased with 'embellishments of her own', which she introduced into the last part of 'Casta diva'.[82] This may indicate an early resistance to bel canto decoration, a trend which gathered pace internationally as the century neared its close.

First performed at La Scala, Milan, in 1831, *Norma* was to become Bellini's most popular and enduring opera. The lead role was first taken by Giuditta Pasta, and it was to become one of Fanny Simonsen's signature roles in Australia and New Zealand from 1870. It seems curious that, while three of her talented offspring sang Adalgisa, none followed her as Norma.

Three days later Fanny was back, this time as Arline in Balfe's *The Bohemian Girl* – a great favourite in the years after the composer's death. This was her first assumption of the role and 'Madame Simonsen comes out of her tent a very charming Bohemian girl', wrote *The Argus*.[83] *The Bohemian Girl* had been first performed at the Theatre Royal Drury Lane in 1843, swiftly taking its place as the most popular 'English' opera of the nineteenth century before falling from favour. Over the

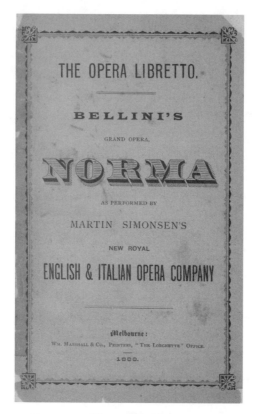

Norma *libretto*

years no less than five Simonsens performed in it, Frances Saville in three different roles.

Next came that other great warhorse of English-language opera of the nineteenth century, Wallace's *Maritana*, Fanny again taking the title role. It had been first performed at Drury Lane in 1845. This too seems to have been a role debut for Fanny. She was a palpable hit:

> In this style of singing, and when abstaining from the use
> of ornaments that are foreign to the composition, Madame
> Simonsen in this country is at the present time unapproachable.[84]

Again, over time five different Simonsens sang in it. In the final production of the season, Fanny was allowed back in an Italian role – as Rosina in Rossini's *Il barbiere di Siviglia*. In it she was surrounded by real Italian singers and the opera's title was given in Italian, a change in Australia:

> Madame Simonsen makes a very nice Rosina, with a strong
> spice of mischief in her composition. She looks the part very
> well ... and she sings Rossini's music correctly – and that is
> saying a great deal in her favour.[85]

The Lyster season at the Theatre Royal in Melbourne of 1870 presented ten operas and had generally moved to performing them in Italian rather than English. In May the company had moved on to the Prince of Wales Theatre in Sydney, where Fanny took the role of Leonora in Verdi's *Il trovatore*, which had been first performed in 1853 at the Teatro Apollo in Rome. The *Australian Town and Country Journal* seized the opportunity to eulogise Fanny's abilities:

> Madame Simonsen is artiste enough to adopt whatever she may
> find good in others ... [Her] voice has improved in strength and
> extended in compass, and she has evidently gained by hearing
> good artists. Her vocalisation is far purer than formerly, and
> her acting gives life and animation to the scene.[86]

In the first week of the Sydney season Fanny also reprised her Maritana and her Lucia ('undoubtedly the best performed opera of the season'), followed by Rosina and Amina.[87] By the end of July 1870, Lyster's company was back in Melbourne, with Fanny ('very warmly received') opening again as Lucia, followed by Marguérite de Valois in *Les Huguenots.*

However, on 9 August came an event important in the growth and development of the city of Melbourne – the opening of the new Town

Hall. The building had taken twenty months to complete and it was regarded as 'by very far the finest municipal building in Australia'. There was to be a gala concert followed by a ball, the central feature of the gala a new cantata, *Euterpe*, commissioned from composer Charles Edward Horsley[88] to words by Australian poet Henry Kendall. 'It may be briefly described as a homage to sound, and an attempt to show how the power of music permeates all phases of life,' wrote *The Age*.[89] The soloists included Fanny Simonsen and Lucy Chambers.

> The solo in A flat, with a subdued accompaniment, was given by Madame Simonsen with a sweetness and tenderness of expression which secured her one of the most hearty rounds of applause.[90]

From late August, Lyster's company took their productions on the road through cities of Victoria outside Melbourne: Ballarat, Geelong and Bendigo. Fanny sang several of her usual roles, and by mid-October they were engaged in a 'Farewell Season' at the Prince of Wales Theatre in Sydney.[91] An important new role for Fanny in the Sydney season was Mathilde in Rossini's last opera, *Guillaume Tell* (performed in English as *William Tell*).

Lyster's contracts with his star Italian singers were ending, and the Sydney season was followed closely by Farewell performances in Melbourne. Among Fanny's Australian-based colleagues in Lyster's company, two tenors stood out as regular 'partners' for her on stage – Henry Squires and Armes Beaumont.

Squires was born in Vermont USA in 1825, and, following a performing career in America and Italy, he was hired by WS Lyster in San Francisco in 1859 and came with that company to Australia in 1861. He was admired for his sweetness of tone and security of intonation, singing over forty roles with the company. Beaumont was born in Norfolk, England, in 1840, and arrived at Melbourne aged seven. He joined Lyster's company in 1863, praised for his richness of voice and fine acting. In 1867 he went shooting with Lyster and was accidentally shot in the eyes with pellets, blinding him in one eye and severely damaging the sight in the other. Nevertheless, he continued his performing career, which encompassed over eighty operatic roles.

Pregnant with another child, Fanny gave birth to a fourth son (seventh child), Albert Martin, at the Simonsen's home in Melbourne (Gertrude Street, Fitzroy) on 26 January 1871.[92] The season at the Princess Theatre ended on 4 February, and Lyster came before the curtain to speak candidly about his situation, that his company, having been together for fifty-two weeks:

> So far as Melbourne was concerned … he and his partner
> had reaped a profit. (Cheers.) But every place was not
> Melbourne, and he regretted to say that in Sydney the season
> had proved an awful failure. Indeed, so bad was it that at
> times he had almost bethought himself of the insolvent
> court.[93]

Lyster went on to announce that, following the closure of his 'Italian' company, he would be launching a less expensive 'English' company, which would open with Offenbach's *The Grand Duchess of Gerolstein*. Now virtually vanished from the repertoire, this operetta had enjoyed immense international success following its première at the Théâtre des Variétés in Paris in April 1867. It had its première in Australia at the Princess Theatre in Melbourne on 27 February 1871 with Fanny Simonsen in the title role.[94]

The libretto for *The Grand Duchess* was by Offenbach's regular team – Henri Meilhac and Ludovic Halévy – and was filled with military and political satire from the reign of Napoleon III. This all seemed to translate with great success to the stages of Vienna, Budapest, Berlin, New York and Covent Garden, London (where Australian-raised soprano Julia Mathews took the lead), before arriving in Australia.[95]

While it has substantially maintained its place in Paris to this day, elsewhere it has gradually given way to other operettas by Offenbach. From the beginning, it was clear that this was an ideal role for Fanny – one that would become a cornerstone of her career in the Simonsens' own opera company. Over the course of the following decades, various Simonsens would sing in seven different operettas by Offenbach.

In Lyster's English season in Melbourne, Fanny followed *The Grand Duchess* with the title role in Balfe's 1858 opera, *Satanella*, its first outing in Australia. While Fanny's performance was regarded as a 'great treat', it was not destined to threaten *The Bohemian Girl* in the public's affections.[96] The same might be said concerning her next role with the company – in the title role of Wallace's *Lurline*, which had been premièred at Covent Garden in 1860.[97]

Thus far in Australia, Fanny had rarely ventured into oratorio, but in April 1871 she took on Haydn's *Creation* at the Princess with the Melbourne Philharmonic Society. *The Argus* concluded that 'the style of singing necessary to do justice to this class of composition is one which, it would appear, has not hitherto been cultivated by Madame Simonsen.'[98] Of course, it may simply be that Melbourne critics were not ready for Fanny's lightness of bel canto delivery, being more used to mid-Victorian religiosity in oratorio singing.

7

Lyster's 'English' season completed, the Simonsens formed again their own concert party for a 'Farewell' tour of Victoria and South Australia starting in May 1871. Farewell maybe, but what next? This was by no means clear. Their repertoire mixed items from earlier Simonsen concert tours together with more-recently performed arias from Lyster's operas. At the same time they tried out some new whole works, none of them to be taken forward beyond that tour, including two operettas by Offenbach – *Breaking the Spell* and *The Rose of Auvergne* – and (in October at Wagga Wagga) a 'musical charade' by Comyn Vaughan, curiously entitled *£. S. D.*[99] Unusually, Martin was often accompanied at the piano by Fanny. The company performed at many towns and cities, concluding with twelve evening concerts back at White's Assembly Rooms in Adelaide.

At Gawler in South Australia, Fanny remembered the meagre size of the audience when they had visited the town six years before. The numbers were just as negligible in July 1871 and Fanny harangued them for it.[100] By this stage, Fanny was becoming quite famous for responding vigorously, either from the stage, or in print, to real or imagined slights – '*cacoethes loquendi et scribendi*'[101] as the correspondent for the *Weekly Times* in Melbourne put it.[102]

On 28 November the company gave what *The Age* reported as 'positively the last appearance of Madame Simonsen in Melbourne' at St George's Hall.[103] Of course it was not, and on I January 1872 (and subsequently) the Simonsens performed at the Town Hall in a crowded concert put on by the Early Closing Association – Martin playing a violin Fantasia on 'Annie Laurie' and Fanny singing 'In Convent Cell' from Balfe's *Rose of Castile*. As a prank, someone shouted 'fire' during Martin's Fantasia, causing uproar. 'Mr Simonsen never moved, while Madame Simonsen, who was accompanying him upon the piano, coolly remained in her seat,' while calm was restored.[104] However, this was by no means goodbye. The Simonsens had an important final addendum before leaving again for Europe.

8

Martin Simonsen had divulged in April 1867 – five years earlier – that the intention of the Simonsens was to start their own fully-fledged opera company, and this is what they accomplished in Sydney in January

1872. They had a star singer in Fanny, and now they had a very popular operetta to perform – *The Grand Duchess of Gerolstein*.[105]

The new Simonsen's Royal English Opera Company (only the first of many name variants to come) opened at the Victoria Theatre in Sydney on 29 January with a full cast and orchestra, together with new sets by esteemed Danish scene-painter Alexander Habbe. Fanny was the Grand Duchess; Martin led the orchestra, but did not conduct (this role being taken at this stage by John Hill); Prince Paul was sung by none other than their agent and tenor from New Zealand, George Price – by now re-named George Darrell (who also doubled as stage manager).[106]

The Grand Duchess was an immediate hit with both critics and the public in Sydney. Of the première, the *Sydney Morning Herald* said: 'Judging from what we saw of it last evening, it is certain to be attractive here … [and] Madame Simonsen's reappearance on the Sydney boards called forth rounds of cheers, which she justified by the manner in which she sang and acted as the Grand Duchess.'[107] And reviewing the production a week later, the *Australian Town and Country Journal* concluded:

> One thing is very certain – the prevailing spirit and guiding genius of the opera from beginning to end is Madame Simonsen.[108]

The run in Sydney played to packed houses and ended with a Farewell Benefit for Fanny on 17 February, at which Balfe's *Rose of Castile* followed by Offenbach's *Rose of Auvergne* were performed.[109] Never missing an opportunity, next the Simonsens took *The Grand Duchess*, the *Rose of Castile* and *Martha* on a sell-out tour around New South Wales – to Newcastle, Maitland and Goulburn.

Somehow, between touring, Martin Simonsen also taught a small number of violin pupils in Melbourne, among whom the most successful was the teenage Johann Kruse, who became a star pupil of

Joseph Joachim in Berlin in 1875 before making a brilliant career in Europe as a soloist, with Joachim's and his own string quartet and as an orchestral leader.[110]

9

On 13 April 1872, the Simonsens together with two small children (Julius and Louis) left Sydney on the *Wonga Wonga*, bound for Auckland,[111] from where they planned to continue their journey through Honolulu, on to San Francisco, and thence to Europe and the Simonsen family home at Altona. Somehow the whole journey from Sydney to Altona lasted not weeks, but many months, with performances given at every opportunity *en route*.

After seven years of continuous touring in Australia and New Zealand, it was to be the best part of four years before they were to return, giving plenty of opportunity for the production of further offspring.

Notes

1   *Argus* (Melbourne), 12 August 1865, 5; *Sydney Mail*, 12 August 1865, 9; *Argus*, 25 August 1865, 1; Adrienne Simpson believed that the Simonsens arrived in Australia without small daughters, but this was not so
2   Gordon Greenwood, *Australia: A Social and Political History*, 448–51; Geoffrey Blainey, *A History of Victoria*, 64
3   *Argus* (Melbourne), 14 August 1865, 8
4   *Argus*, 16 August 1865, 8
5   *Argus*, 21 August 1865, 5
6   Warden and Liddle were to be retained by the Simonsens in future Australasian touring

7   *Geelong Advertiser*, 31 August 1865, 2
8   *South Australian Advertiser*, 5 September 1865, 2
9   *South Australian Advertiser*, 12 September 1865, 2
10   *Adelaide Observer*, 30 September 1865, 2
11   *Cornwall Chronicle* (Launceston), 1 November 1865, 4
12   *Mercury* (Hobart), 7 November 1865, 2
13   *Sydney Morning Herald*, 24 November 1865, 4
14   *Sydney Morning Herald*, 24 November 1865, 8
15   *Bell's Life* (Sydney), 20 January 1866, 3
16   *Sydney Morning Herald*, 26 January 1866, 4
17   *Sydney Morning Herald*, 31 January 1866, 2
18   *Wagga Wagga Express*, 7 April 1866, 2
19   Nicole Anae, 'Operatic performances two hundred miles in the Australian bush', *Rural Society*, October 2010
20   *Age* (Melbourne), 17 May 1866, 5
21   In 1864 Australia's first long-distance railway had opened – from Melbourne to Bendigo and on to Echuca on the Murray River
22   See 'Sydney's Early Opera Performances' by Eric Irvin, *OPERA*, September 1969, 764–72
23   Harold Love, *The Golden Age of Australian Opera: WS Lyster and his Companies 1861–1880*, 20–45
24   *Argus*, 26 June 1866, 5
25   *Age,* 26 June 1866, 5
26   *Age,* 26 July 1866, 5
27   *Argus*, 30 July 1866, 4
28   *South Australian Advertiser*, 6 August 1866, 2
29   *South Australian Register*, 30 July 1866, 1
30   *Adelaide Express*, 27 August 1866, 3
31   *Adelaide Express*, 15 September 1866, 2
32   *Age*, 3 October 1866, 5
33   *Argus*, 30 October 1866, 5
34   Argus, 13 November 1866, 4; this review contrasted sharply with the poor reports printed following the Lyster performance of that opera by a B-list cast (without Fanny) in Adelaide just a few weeks earlier
35   *Age* and *Argus*, 16 October 1866, both 4; in his Lyster biography, Harold Love says that this took place on 13 September, but the operas given by Lyster's company that night were *Il trovatore* and *La sonnambula*, Fanny starring in the latter
36   *Sydney Morning Herald*, 7 December 1866, 4
37   *Ballarat Star*, 22 April 1867, 3
38   Anne Doggett, doctoral thesis, 2006
39   *Argus*, 3 April 1867, 4; now between the Town Hall and the Scots Church (both built later in the century)
40   *Ballarat Star*, 16 July 1867, 3
41   *Bendigo Advertiser*, 6 August 1867, 2
42   *Argus*, 26 March 1867, 4
43   *Bell's Life in Victoria*, 13 April 1867, 2
44   *Ovens and Murray Advertiser* (Beechworth), 31 August 1867, 2; the outlaw Ned Kelly was imprisoned in Beechworth for six months in 1870–71
45   *Australasian* (Melbourne), 19 October 1867, 17
46   *Tasmanian Times*, 2 November 1867, 4
47   *Argus*, 29 November 1867, 4
48   *Otago Daily Times*, 28 November 1867, 1
49   Was Artôt a relation of the singing teacher in Paris Desirée Artôt?

50   *Otago Daily Times*, 7 December 1867, 4

51   *Otago Daily Times*, 18 December 1867, 4

52   Price later renamed himself George Darrell, becoming one of the founding fathers of professional theatre in Australia; in his career he wrote fifty-five plays

53   Adrienne Simpson, 'Footlights and Fenians: The Adventures of a Touring Concert Party in Gold Rush New Zealand', 182–83

54   Anthony Trollope, *New Zealand*, 1874

55   *Lyttelton Times*, 31 December 1867, 2

56   Anniversary Day in Wellington celebrates the arrival of the first British settlers on 22 January 1840

57   *Wellington Independent*, 25 January 1878, 5

58   *Wellington Independent*, 30 January 1868, 4

59   *Wellington Independent*, 6 February 1868, 5

60   *Colonist* (Nelson), 11 February 1868, 2

61   *Westport Times*, 17 February 1868; the treacherous crossing of the Hokitika sandbar in 1865–66 is vividly described in Rose Tremain's 2003 gold rush novel, *The Colour*

62   *Westport Times*, 20 February 1868, 3; currently, the combined population of Westport and Charleston is less than 5000

63   *Westport Times*, 19 February 1868, 2

64   *West Coast Times*, 27 March 1866, 3; *West Coast Times*, 8 September 1866, 3; Mathews had been taken to Australia as a twelve-year-old, appearing at Sydney, Melbourne and in the goldfields

65   *West Coast Times*, 16 March 1868, 3

66   Three men, members of the Irish Republican Brotherhood, who were executed by hanging outside Salford Gaol on 22 November 1867 for the murder in Manchester of a policeman

67   *Grey River Argus*, 13 February 1868; *Westport Times*, 15 February and 26 March 1868; Simpson, 'Footlights and Fenians', 190–93

68   *Wellington Independent*, 7 April 1868, 5

69   *Evening Post* (Wellington), 8 April 1868, 2

70   *Australian* (Melbourne), 17 October 1868, 18

71   *Argus*, 14 May 1869, 4

72   It appears that Leonore (9), Martina (6), Fanny Martina (3) and Herman (1) remained with their grandmother in Altona, while Julius (1) and Louis (less than one) travelled to Melbourne with their parents

73   *Argus*, 6 August 1869, 5

74   *Argus*, 6 August 1869, 5

75   *Australasian* (Melbourne), 11 September 1869, 16

76   *Wagga Wagga Advertiser*, 19 January 1870, 2

77   *Ovens and Murray Advertiser*, 25 January 1870, 2

78   Love, *The Golden Age of Australian Opera*, 158–61; His Royal Highness also visited the 'legitimate' theatre several times; plus recitations; a troupe of Japanese jugglers, acrobats and contortionists; various balls; horse-racing; a cock fight and a pantomime; while finding time to pay regular calls at Sarah Fraser's house of ill-repute at Stephen Street, Melbourne

79   Love, 189–92

80   *Argus*, 4 February 1870, 4

81   *Argus*, 11 February 1870, 5

82   132 *Argus*, 11 March 1870, 5

83   *Argus*, 14 March 1870, 5

84   *Argus*, 28 March 1870, 6

85   *Argus*, 8 April 1870, 6

86   *Australian Town and Country Journal* (Sydney), 7 May 1870, 21

87 *Australian Town and Country Journal*, 4 June 1870, 21
88 Born in London in 1822, CE Horsley became a pupil of Moscheles and Mendelssohn in Leipzig, immigrating to Australia in 1861; he was to move on to live and work in New York in 1871
89 *Age*, 10 August 1870, 3
90 *Argus*, 10 August 1870, 5
91 *Empire* (Sydney), 15 October 1870, 2
92 *Argus*, 28 January 1871, 4
93 *Age*, 6 February 1871, 3
94 *Argus*, 27 February 1871, 6
95 Kurt Gänzl and Andrew Lamb, *Gänzl's Book of the Musical Theatre*, 300–05
96 *Age*, 29 March 1871, 3
97 *Leader* (Melbourne), 15 April 1871, 18
98 *Argus*, 8 April 1871, 6
99 *South Australian Advertiser*, 10 June 1871, 1; *Express and Telegraph* (Adelaide), 11 July 1871, 1; *Wagga Wagga Advertiser*, 14 October 1871, 3
100 *Bunyip* (Gawler), 15 July 1871, 3
101 An uncontrollable urge to speak and write
102 *Weekly Times* (Melbourne), 2 September 1871, 9
103 *Age*, 29 November 1871, 2
104 *Age*, 2 January 1872, 3
105 *Sydney Mail*, 13 January 1872, 50
106 *Sydney Mail*, 27 January 1872, 109
107 *Sydney Morning Herald*, 30 January 1872, 5
108 *Australian Town and Country Journal* (Sydney), 10 February 1872, 9
109 *Sydney Morning Herald*, 19 February 1872, 7
110 *Geelong Advertiser*, 23 October 1873, 2; Joachim was the leading solo violinist of his generation, famous for his performances of Beethoven, and giving the first performance of the Brahms concerto
111 *Empire* (Sydney), 15 April 1872, 2

Chapter 3
Settling at St Kilda

1

After all those years of Australasian touring, performing night after night, their various children living in two different hemispheres, Fanny and Martin Simonsen's family were finally together with all their children in one place in the middle of 1873 – at Martin's family home in Altona. The Australian press suggested that there were 'domestic affairs' that created the need for their urgent departure from Melbourne,[1] and a later report homed in on 'unhappiness [that was] likely to lead to the divorce court'.[2] It appears that Fanny had put her foot down, insisting that they take time off from their daily grind in order to bring their still-growing family together.

Nevertheless, unable to pass up an opportunity to publicise and to earn, the journey back to Altona with two small boys was to be interrupted at several stopping places on the route. First, at Auckland for a month of performing at the Prince of Wales Theatre from late April 1872 through to mid-June, including fully staged productions of Gounod's *Faust*, of Verdi's *Il trovatore*, and the professional première in New Zealand of *The Grand Duchess of Gerolstein*.[3] These performances of full operas were interspersed with innumerable concert performances. Fanny was thought to be in top form as a singer, and 'she also showed herself to be an admirable actress of comedy of the very highest kind'.[4]

From Auckland they moved on to Thames, the gold rush city of the Coromandel Peninsula, where they gave several concerts at the Academy of Music,[5] before returning to Auckland intending to leave immediately for Honolulu. However, the Californian Mail steamship was postponed, so they stayed and gave performances for another month, this time at the City Hall.[6] There they teamed up successfully with the 'celebrated American Minstrel and Star Comique Company'. Eventually, they departed New Zealand for Hawaii aboard the *Nebraska* on 13 June.[7]

Unable to resist the temptation, on the tedious twenty-day voyage to Honolulu with 'a very great variety of character amongst the passengers – doctors, squatters, merchants, ex-legislators bolting with other men's wives, etc' – the Simonsens favoured all with an on-board concert,[8] and when they arrived at Honolulu (on 3 July) they and their concert party gave several further concerts at the Royal Hawaiian Theatre[9] for another month, leaving for San Francisco early in August.[10]

They arrived in California early in September and performed 'in conjunction with Maguire's California Minstrels' at the New Alhambra. The Minstrels were a blackface group of white singers and musicians performing 'negro' song and dance. Not to be hurried, Martin and Fanny stayed in San Francisco for several weeks, discovering how their musical skills might be appreciated in the context of a vaudeville show.[11] During the season, Fanny appeared as Arline in a burlesque version of *The Bohemian Girl* and in *The Grand Duchess of Gerolstein*. Popular in the nineteenth century, burlesques were parodies of well-known operas, plays or ballets, played for comic effect. By early November, Fanny was singing in an 'immense programme' (including Adelina Patti's violinist brother Carlo) at Pike's Opera House in Cincinnati. The concert was followed by the title role in *Martha*, *Il trovatore* and *The Bohemian Girl*.[12] Fanny then joined Leonard Grover's German Opera Company, which was formed in St Louis in November 1872 – 'an operatic infliction ... no other man could have woven such a patch work together', said the *Chicago Tribune* – and travelled to several cities, including Boston and Chicago.[13] Sadly,

> Mr Leonard Grover's opera company went to pieces in St Louis
> last week. It is said that some of the artists were compelled to
> walk to Cincinnati after his failure.

In June of 1873, the Simonsens finally arrived in Altona, which since 1864 had become part of Prussia, no longer a dependency of Denmark. This was to be their fifth and final visit after marriage. Their whole family reunited, they had, 'to all appearances, severed their connection with the musical profession', reported *The Australasian*.[14] During their time at Altona, two more children were born to Fanny and Martin, their eighth and ninth, Florence Martina (born 1874) and William Martin (born 1875). Both were to become singers.

In two feature articles in 1891 and 1894 on the emerging prima donna Frances Saville, it is clear that the Simonsens' third daughter, Fanny Martina (as she was originally named), had been taken from Melbourne to live in Altona with her grandmother at around six months old. There she had learned 'pianoforte, painting and singing'.[15] It seems that she was a good painter in her early years and there were various intimations that she might have chosen that path as a career before she started to focus on singing. She was to spend the following years in Altona, her first language German, before returning to Melbourne just after her eleventh birthday.

2

The Simonsens only re-surfaced from Altona in Australia in early 1876, some three and a half years after leaving. The Australian press rejoiced that the Simonsens were returning to Melbourne 'by the *Norfolk*, which left London October last'.[16] A letter from Martin to the Victorian press made clear that they now intended to settle in Melbourne, together with all their children, 'and pursue their professional career'.[17] Martin added that he was bringing with him 'a number of new operas, of which he [possessed] the copyright, and which [had] never been performed in Melbourne'.[18]

The Simonsen family (parents and nine children) arrived at Port Melbourne together with Martin's niece from Altona, Jenny Goldstein, and two servants on 8 January 1876 – two days after Fanny Martina's eleventh birthday.[19] They settled into Royal Terrace, Nicholson Street, Fitzroy,[20] and immediately advertised for performers for their English Opera Company.[21] Clearly, they were planning to be out on the road in Australia again – and soon. However, Fitzroy was but a brief stepping stone on the way to the place that was to be their home for the long term – and on 20 January, they announced that they had moved to Cambo, Carlisle Street, St Kilda.[22] On the corner of Barkly Street at the western end of Carlisle Street, near what is now the National Theatre, Cambo had been built in the late 1860s. It was well equipped to serve the needs of the Simonsens' rapidly growing family, with seven bedrooms, drawing room, dining room and breakfast room.[23]

In the 1870s and 1880s St Kilda was an upwardly mobile seaside suburb with many fine stone mansions. For Melburnians, St Kilda was already something of a fashionable seaside resort, a place of escape from the 'dusty streets' of central Melbourne,[24] carried there by horse-trams and (later) cable-trams. There were hotels, dance halls, sea baths and parks – it was a centre for leisure and entertainment, and it also had a growing immigrant Jewish population. As granddaughter Frances

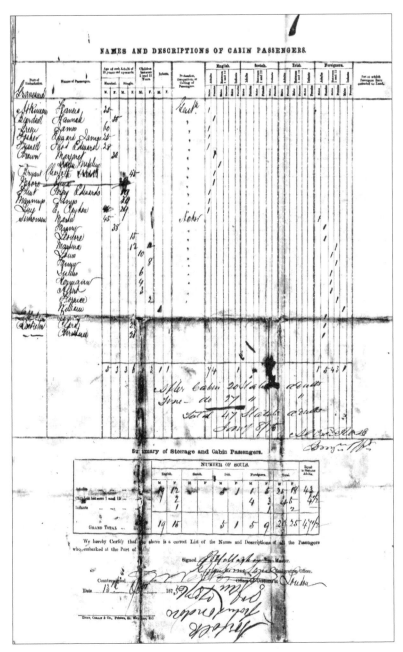

Simonsen family's arrival in Melbourne, 8 January 1876

Alda was to write in her memoirs some sixty years after the Simonsens settled there:

> Grandfather bought a house in St Kilda, a suburb of
> Melbourne, then, in the late sixties [sic], a raw, gangling town.
> But he had faith in the country's future, and in its appetite for
> Italian opera.[25]

The Simonsens advertised their reappearance at the Town Hall on Saturday 29 January 1876, the major fly in the ointment being that the international diva Ilma di Murska was performing in Melbourne at the same time.[26] However, the *Weekly Times* rejoiced in the prospect of seeing and hearing Fanny Simonsen again:

> She does not appear to have encountered many of the storms
> and perils of life, for she looks younger than ever. There is
> perhaps a trifle of added *embonpoint*, but there is also a fresh
> healthy look in the face that speaks volumes in favour of a long
> sea voyage as a recuperative agent.[27]

The report went on to say that because the major theatres in Melbourne were fully occupied, the Simonsens were planning to take their company first to New Zealand. The new company started rehearsals two days before the first Town Hall concert.[28] The re-appearance of the Simonsens at the Town Hall, fully four years after their last performance in Melbourne, 'was welcomed … with a great display of very hearty good feeling towards both', reported *The Argus*, which continued:

> From the first note that she sang it was found that while
> her voice retains all the ringing brilliancy which is known
> to characterise it, there is still an increase of fullness and
> sweetness in tone in … the lower register.[29]

The fact that Ilma di Murska was making her very highly publicised way through Australia at the time that Fanny Simonsen made her re-entrance might well have caused problems for the Simonsens. Di Murska, the 'Hungarian Nightingale', was an extraordinary character as well as an outstanding singer – one of the earliest of Mathilde Marchesi's pupils to become an international star – and the Australian press and public lapped her up. What's more, she sang almost the same repertoire as Fanny Simonsen and was about to tour New Zealand – a progress which would be over precisely the same period as the Simonsens. Nevertheless, preparations by Fanny and Martin for that tour were going ahead apace, and by the first week of February they had 'got together a company of principals and chorus-singers and [had] put popular works into active rehearsal'.[30]

One important consequence of Ilma di Murska's performances in Melbourne was that she was seen and heard by the eleven-year-old Fanny Martina Simonsen, third daughter of Fanny and Martin, who, hearing that di Murska's teacher was the celebrated Mathilde Marchesi, decided 'then and there, that Madame Marchesi should be my teacher'. Fanny Martina would in due course study with Marchesi in Paris and become Frances Saville, prima donna soprano in Gustav Mahler's superb company at the Court Opera in Vienna.

Before leaving for New Zealand, perhaps to try the company out, the Simonsens gave a handful of well-received performances of *The Grand Duchess*, *Maritana* and *The Bohemian Girl* at the Prince of Wales Opera House in Melbourne. On 29 February 1876 the new company sailed on the *Arawata* for Bluff in the far south of South Island, then on to Port Chalmers, Dunedin.[31] Their tour of New Zealand was to occupy the following nine months and was to see Leonore, the oldest of their daughters, married.

3

It is inconceivable that a modern-day prima donna would contemplate the frequency of performances given by Fanny Simonsen in New Zealand in 1876. Over a period of 270 days, she sang in around 200 opera and concert performances – always in a demanding lead role.[32] If one takes away Sundays (as non-performance days in New Zealand at that time), that leaves some thirty spare days, many of which were in reality occupied with travel by ship, by rail, or by stagecoach between cities. So far as one can tell, apart from Sundays, there would have been virtually zero rest days. What is more, although very occasionally she was reported as being somewhat hoarse, she was never 'indisposed' and always seems to have recovered fully by the following day. What a testament this is both to Fanny and to her teachers, implying a rock-solid technique, coupled with vocal cords of steel, allied to an indomitable will.

This was in effect the Simonsens' third season in New Zealand – their first as a fully equipped opera company – and Simonsen's Royal English Opera Company[33] opened at the Queen's Theatre in Dunedin on 11 March 1876 with their proven crowd-pleaser, *The Grand Duchess of Gerolstein*. Previewing their debut, the *Otago Daily Times* summarised the company: they were fifty-seven people in total, of which ten were principals, ten ballet, eleven orchestra, plus 'ballet master, stage manager, scenic artist, property man, stage machinist and costumier'. Aside from Fanny Simonsen, the other principals included the eighteen-year-old German–South Australian mezzo Minna Fischer (anglicised to Mina Fisher in the local press), who, after several years of touring in Australasia, was later to become a distinguished singing teacher in London; the contralto Nellie Lambert, who had toured New Zealand previously with GB Allen's company in 1874–75; the Lisbon-born British tenor Carmini Morley, who had previously come to Australia with prima donna Anna Bishop in 1875; and the experienced

Australian baritone Albert Richardson.[34] It was the largest opera company yet to tour the country.

It may seem surprising to today's readers that the company included so many dancers, but audiences in the 1870s still expected operas to contain substantial ballet components, and in mixed programmes whole ballets could be performed before, during or after the main event.

In *The Grand Duchess*, Fanny was greeted warmly by the audience and by the local press as '… a first class artiste … [with] much artistic feeling and considerable dramatic powers'[35] – as indeed was the whole company. Across a four-week season, Dunedin saw ten out of the sixteen operas brought by the Simonsens to New Zealand. They followed *The Grand Duchess* (2 performances) with *Lucia di Lammermoor* (3); *Maritana* (3); *Martha* (2); *Il trovatore* (2); *Lucrezia Borgia* (2); then the first of their works new to New Zealand, Charles Lecocq's *La fille de Madame Angot* (7); *The Bohemian Girl* (1); *La sonnambula* (1); a second work new to the country, Aimé Maillart's *Les dragons de Villars*, presented as *The Hermit's Bell* (2); and finally a charity concert on 10 April. The new works were to be presented frequently throughout their tour – the Lecocq no less than thirty-six times (more than any other opera) and the Maillart twenty-three times (second most frequent).[36]

First performed at the Théâtre des Fantaisies-Parisiennes in 1872, Lecocq's *La fille de Madame Angot* enjoyed immense popularity internationally in the 1870s and 80s, but has only retained its place in the repertoire in France.[37] This was its first outing in New Zealand, and in Dunedin on 27 March 1876 Fanny took the lead role of Clairette, and the Queen's Theatre was 'crowded in every part'. The *Otago Daily Times* pointed out how rare it was for a company to be outstandingly good in both grand opera and operetta, and, while generally praising the production, felt that some of the performers lacked the true '*vis comica*', substituting for it 'elaborate buffoonery'. Nevertheless, 'Madame Simonsen filled the part of Clairette Angot, and did so with much spirit.'[38]

Poster for La fille de Madame Angot

Maillart's *The Hermit's Bell* (also new to New Zealand) was premièred on 7 April, the theatre again having 'attracted a large and fashionable audience'. *Les dragons de Villars* (now almost totally forgotten) was twenty years old by the time that the Simonsens introduced it, having been first performed at the Théâtre Lyrique in Paris on 19 September 1856. An early opéra-comique, it held its place in the repertoire in France and elsewhere even after the arrival

of Offenbach and Lecocq. 'The performance was a decided success –
and met with a most favourable reception,' concluded the *Otago Daily
Times*, although the paper doubted whether 'the music … is calculated
for lasting success'. Rose Moineau was a role 'eminently suited to
Madame Simonsen'.[39]

The Dunedin season concluded with a concert given by the whole
company for the Jewish Philanthropic Society. Fanny Simonsen sang
an aria from Offenbach's *Les bavards*, followed by 'Comin' thro the
rye', then the 'Inflammatus' from Rossini's *Stabat Mater* and 'Kathleen
Mavourneen', while 'masterly' Martin Simonsen played several of his
party pieces.[40]

On 11 April 1876 the Simonsen company sailed on to Christchurch's
port at Lyttelton, having attracted positive notices and done good
business in Dunedin. The fact that they were able to make this
journey by ship was a substantial step forward from their journey to
Christchurch nine years earlier, facilitated by the founding in 1875 of
the Union Steam Ship Company in Dunedin. The company operated all
around New Zealand, enabling theatrical troupes to move from city to
city much more easily.

At Christchurch they performed twelve of their sixteen operas,
adding two to those already given in Dunedin – Bellini's *Norma* (which
was already a part of Fanny's repertoire) and Offenbach's *La Périchole*.
Adapted from a play by Prosper Mérimée and premièred at the Théâtre
des Variétés in Paris in 1868, the opéra-bouffe *La Périchole* tells the story
of two impoverished street singers in Peru and a lecherous viceroy, who
wishes to make one of them, La Périchole, his mistress. It was this that
caused a press fracas in Christchurch. Houses were well attended and
appreciative, the critics impressed – especially with Fanny Simonsen.
However, it was following the introduction of *La Périchole*, last in the
run, that trouble broke out.

At that time, Christchurch had four newspapers, two of which –
the *Lyttelton Times* and *The Star* – were delighted with the new work,
praising the performance and performers, while the other two – *The*

Press and *The Globe* – condemned it as thoroughly immoral. *The Press* particularly disliked the 'drunken scene at the close of the first act', which it thought 'so degrading to the art in which true opera stands so high',[41] while *The Globe* went further, describing the work as 'a miserable *burletta* … a wretched abortion, which … would be hissed off the stage' even in the East End music halls of London. 'With the exception of an aria in the first act, tolerably well rendered by Madame Simonsen, there was not a single pleasing solo in the whole performance.'[42]

There were two more performances of *La Périchole* there, attendances severely damaged by the assaults of the two newspapers. Not one to take unjust criticism lying down, on the second night, in response to cheers, Fanny Simonsen marched in front of the curtain brandishing the two offending newspapers. She launched into a diatribe:

> I am pretty well endowed with a great deal of patience,
> but there is a limit to all things. And therefore, when I am
> attacked in the manner I have been, I have a tongue to defend
> myself against those who attack me without any reason.
> (Applause.)

Fanny went on to defend the duty of an artist to 'sing any song of the author's as long as it is in accordance with the character, and as long as the artiste can do it pretty well. (Loud applause.)' She laid out for the audience the great popularity of *La Périchole* in Paris and London and then turned on the writer of one (or both) of the offending articles:

> I happen to know who wrote this. The a-a-a-gentleman who
> wrote this was in Dunedin while we were there and, being
> very noisy for a couple of nights in the stalls, he was refused
> admission. He declared at the time that he would make it hot
> for the Simonsens when they came to Christchurch, and he is
> trying to do so now. I am very sorry for him; it is a very poor
> revenge. (Hear, hear, and applause.)

Finally, she advised the proprietors of the papers 'to look twice before they put such a disgusting little thing as that in it', and retired 'amid loud applause'.[43] *The Globe* hit back immediately, and while the faithful were reassured by Fanny's words, others of a more delicate moral constitution stayed away. The writer of the offending articles revealed himself the following day as one John J Utting, 'recently sub-editor *Otago Guardian*, at present on the staff of the *Press*, Christchurch'.[44]

In five weeks in Christchurch, the Simonsens had given thirty-two opera performances, plus a concert, to enthusiastic, generally plentiful audiences. And now it was time to sail on to Wellington. They arrived on the *Otago* on 23 May, staying for five and a half weeks at the Theatre Royal, during which time they gave fourteen different operas, two of them additional to those performed previously in Christchurch and Dunedin – Gounod's *Faust* and Auber's opéra-comique *Le part du Diable* (rendered in English as *Carlo Broschi*). *Faust* proved to be

> a brilliant and well-deserved success [with] a capital house
> and the audience, from first to last, were enthusiastic in their
> recognition of the remarkable excellence of the performance
> … How splendidly Madame Simonsen sang and acted as
> Margaret.[45]

Faust was given four performances in Wellington, followed by two more in Auckland, then single performances as the company moved south in South Island to conclude their tour. It seems ironic that Fanny should have had to wait so long to make her debut in this, her favourite role – so beloved by her that she asked to be buried with the score. However, when the Simonsens first started with Lyster's company in 1866, Lucy Escott 'owned' the role. Fanny will have taught it to her offspring, and Leonore Simonsen and Frances Saville, and granddaughter Frances Alda, all embraced it (though not, apparently, Martina).

Now substantially neglected, the Auber had been premièred at the Opéra-Comique in Paris fully thirty-five years before (in January 1843). It centred on an incident in the life of a 'minstrel', Carlo Broschi, who was in reality the great castrato Farinelli. In its introduction to New Zealand on 28 June 1876, Fanny played Broschi, which was for her another trousers role. Declaring it a 'masterly work', the *Post* was puzzled as to why 'it should never have been performed outside the native land of its gifted composer'. Fanny's performance was judged to be 'a brilliant success throughout'.[46]

As early as 1 June the *Evening Post* declared that the Simonsens were having 'a most prosperous season',[47] a situation which persisted throughout the tour. From Wellington, the company sailed north on 5 July to Napier on the east coast of the North Island, where they gave a successful three-week season including fifteen operas, the novelty being a second work by Auber – his grand opera *La muette de Portici*. It was performed there as *Masaniello* by the Simonsens. It had been given by the Simonsens with Lyster's company in Australia ten years before.[48]

While the company was performing in Napier, there was a burglary at the Simonsens' home at St Kilda. Money was stolen from 'Mark [sic] Simonsen' – six gold sovereigns – by one Theophilus Howell, who was 'boots' (the lowest-ranking male servant in the household). The house was being looked after by Jenny Goldstein, Martin Simonsen's niece from Altona.[49] Exactly where the nine Simonsen children (aged from two to seventeen) were at this point is not clear. Some will have been looked after by Jenny at St Kilda, while others had been on tour with their parents in New Zealand. Two years later, Jenny (a soprano herself) married Henry Susman, a businessman and violinist of Hobart, moving to live with him in Tasmania, where they enjoyed a rich musical life together, including singing with young Tasmanian prima donna Amy Sherwin.[50]

From Napier the Simonsen company sailed around the south of the North Island to Nelson on the north coast of South Island for four nights, then on to the west coast city of New Plymouth. Sadly, 'this talented company received but a very cold welcome ... from the Nelson public, and we fear the miserable attendance both then and at the [recent] Di Murska concerts will go far towards keeping away from us all the real artistes, and that Nelson will be abandoned to jugglers and mountebanks.'[51]

The arrival at New Plymouth was a more hazardous operation than they had encountered previously. There was no harbour, so, after a rough crossing, people and goods had to be brought ashore by surf boat – no small undertaking for such a large group of performers together with all their paraphernalia – props, scenery, costumes and so on. Perhaps not surprisingly, they were the first opera company to visit and perform there.[52]

Safely landed, they opened on 8 August with Flotow's *Martha*.[53] Still wintertime in New Zealand, the weather had been fine in New Plymouth until the day of the company's first performance, when the heavens opened, 'debarring many from attending'. Nevertheless, there was 'a large and fashionable audience in the hall, the ladies appearing in full dress costume', and the performance 'met with a most enthusiastic reception ... [Fanny Simonsen's] singing far surpasses anything that has ever been heard in New Plymouth'.[54] They gave five operas in five nights, special transportation being laid on to bring in settlers from outlying areas, and the whole visit was sufficiently successful for the Simonsens' companies to make return visits in 1881 and 1889.

From the small city of New Plymouth, the company proceeded to Auckland, already the North Island's largest city, where they gave a season of four and a half weeks, for the first time on the tour including all sixteen of the operas in their repertoire. The remaining work not previously performed on the tour was Mozart's *The Marriage of Figaro*. Fanny had sung in this opera as the stately Countess with Lyster's company ten years before, but now in Auckland she was a vivacious Susanna.

The Simonsen company opened their season with the inaugural performance at a state-of-the-art new venue in Auckland, the Theatre Royal. The event was accompanied by appropriate pomp and ceremony, starting with the (British) National Anthem, followed by a recitation by Fanny Simonsen of an extended ode written for the occasion by Auckland journalist John Blackman, which opened:

> Friends, hail and welcome! Triumph and delight
> At your fair presence fill our hearts tonight –
> Within this noble building …

It carried on for a further hundred or so lines in similar mode, but was 'rather long for such an occasion', sighed the *New Zealand Herald*'s reviewer. The performance that evening, 14 August 1876, was of Donizetti's *Lucia di Lammermoor*, the title role of which was a great calling card for Fanny Simonsen. The *Herald* observed:

> The Lucia of Madame Simonsen is a great deal more than a
> successful artistic impersonation. It is an admirable portrayal
> of passionate fervour … It abounds in magnificent effects …
> [and] in the execution of the difficult passages she acquits
> herself without the slightest apparent effort.[55]

It was near the end of the run that *The Marriage of Figaro* was introduced for a single performance. By the middle of the nineteenth century, Mozart's operas, while retaining their high reputation, had mostly fallen out of the repertoire,[56] so it was at the time very much a rarity, not only in New Zealand. Nevertheless, the *Herald* greeted it as a long-lost friend:

> This opera, which is almost incomparable as a harmonised
> composition, has never failed to draw large houses wherever
> a taste for high classic music is genuine.[57]

Minna Fischer was the admired Countess, Nellie Lambert was Cherubino, Albert Richardson the Count, John Barrington was Figaro and Fanny Simonsen, as already noted, Susanna. '[Madame Simonsen] invested the part of Susanna with a sprightliness and variety which caused it to be very attractive,' said the *Auckland Star*.[58]

As in previous cities, in the early part of the Auckland season, the Simonsens performed to crowded houses. In her work on the tour, Adrienne Simpson concluded that Auckland 'turned into a financial disaster as performance after performance was played to a half-full auditorium'. The consequence, she suggested, was that 'in an effort to cut costs, the Simonsens were forced to pay off some of their artists … and reduce the number of operas in their repertoire.'[59] However, Simpson's conclusions are not generally supported by contemporary press coverage.

Certainly, the première of *Maritana* on 18 August had a poor house, caused, according to the *Daily Southern Cross* by miserable weather.[60] However, re-examination of the newspaper reports suggests that this dip was a one-off, and the reviews for the subsequent operas reported plentiful audiences. So, on 7 September, towards the end of the season:

> The production of [*Faust*] last night filled the house in every
> part; indeed the stalls and pit were crowded to excess, the
> passage and entrance doors being so thronged that ingress or
> egress was scarcely practicable.[61]

Indeed, the final production of the Auckland season, *Norma*, was said to have been 'nearly full, despite very bad weather.[62] The downsizing of the Simonsen company may indicate, quite simply, greater commercial insight on the part of Fanny and Martin than Adrienne Simpson allows. What is clear is that, having left Auckland, and starting on a series of short return trips over the final weeks of their tour to cities already visited by the company, there would be likely to be smaller audiences. And this is exactly what happened.

The gradual move south of the Simonsen company, each city given just a handful of performances, started at Thames (at the southern end of the Coromandel Peninsula, previously visited in 1872), then progressed after a very brief return to Auckland, through Nelson, Christchurch and Dunedin, before finally arriving in Invercargill in the far south. They had not performed at that city before, so at the Theatre Royal, they gave eight different operas in nine days (Sunday being a day of rest), starting with *Martha* on 7 November and finishing with *La sonnambula* on 15th. As a parting gift, at that last performance, they also featured an act from *The Grand Duchess of Gerolstein*.

During their second short season in Christchurch, there was a major and joyful occasion for the Simonsens. Their eldest daughter, Leonore, was married to Mr David Davis. She was sixteen and a budding mezzo-soprano. He was twenty-four, a talented amateur musician who frequently played in the orchestras of touring opera companies, and fifth child (of an eventual sixteen) of a prominent wine and spirits merchant in Christchurch, Hyam Davis. On 27 October 1876 they were married at the synagogue in the city.[63] It became a media topic – the Simonsen family by now being celebrities in both Australia and New Zealand and the Davis family being established prominently in various businesses in New Zealand, there was extensive and detailed press coverage of the event throughout both countries. One report started:

> The scene was of an imposing character. Six large wax candles were burning in silver candlesticks on each side of the ark and on the reading desk; the Rabbi wore a *Talish*, or prayer scarf, of white silk ...[64]

... and so on. As the young bride and groom left the synagogue, the orchestra of the Simonsen company played Mendelssohn's 'Wedding March'. This was not a marriage that was to last. It seems that her husband wanted Leonore to give up her operatic aspirations. However, the marriage did have significant consequences – the births, first in 1877 of a son Albert (Alby), and then on 31 May 1879 in Christchurch of a daughter, Fanny Jane Davis, who would in time become a major star at the Metropolitan Opera in New York – as Frances Alda. By 1877, at the age of forty-one, Fanny Simonsen was already a grandmother.

Leaving Leonore behind in Christchurch, on 16 November 1876 the whole Simonsen company sailed from Bluff to Melbourne on the *Alhambra* after nine solid months of performing and travelling in New Zealand and was dispersed.[65]

4

After around ten days of rest and recuperation at their home in St Kilda, the Simonsens were already advertising for singers, musicians and dancers for their next tour – due to start 'on or about 15 December' – and recruiting 'artists of acknowledged ability' as principals.[66]

Unable to find a suitable unoccupied venue in Melbourne, the newly convened company went touring in the western part of Victoria, apparently starting in the gold rush port of Warrnambool (on the south-west coast) during Christmas week,[67] and going then to pastoral Hamilton, Mount Gambier (across the border into South Australia), Portland, Camperdown, Geelong, Ballarat, Castlemaine and Bendigo.

At each town they performed for several evenings, giving operas from their New Zealand tour repertoire, often starting with *Maritana*. The only work new to the Simonsen company was Balfe's *Satanella*, a role which Fanny had previously created in Australia with Lyster's company in 1871. Premièred in 1858 at Covent Garden, *Satanella* is now regarded as a typical mid-nineteenth century mixture of sensationalism and pious sentimentality, but at Ballarat in February 1876, it was 'charming', with

> Madame Simonsen in her brilliant series of transformations
> being as many visions of beauty, and her singing as superb as
> her appearances.[68]

Theatre Royal, Hobart

After another short break at home in Melbourne, the Simonsens' opera company sailed to Tasmania, opening on 16 March at the Theatre Royal in Hobart, as usual with *Maritana*. *The Mercury* was surprised that the Simonsens had 'attempted the rather dangerous experiment of performing on the day of their arrival from a sea voyage', and added that 'the effects of the voyage, and possibly *mal de mer*, were to some extent noticeable in the singing, and even Mdlle Simonsen was hardly up to what we expect to … hear from her.'[69] They followed *Maritana* with *The Grand Duchess*, which was well received, but had a rather sparse audience for its opening.[70]

However, following a performance of *Lucrezia Borgia* a few days later, Martin Simonsen was taken seriously to task by *The Mercury*'s critic, who, following his strictures regarding the poor singing at *Maritana*, weighed in with:

> Mr Simonsen must be singularly blind to the capabilities of
> his company if he imagines that it contains among its members
> the elements necessary to give even a fair representation of the
> opera of *Lucrezia Borgia*.

Praising Fanny, his barbs were aimed partly at the male singers, but principally at the works given, and, not holding back, Martin was advised:

> He has among his repertoire such operas as *Carlo Broschi*,
> *La fille de Madame Angot*, *Giroflé-Girofla*, *The Hermit's Bell*,
> *The Grand Duchess of Gerolstein*, *La Périchole* and *Martha*;
> let him produce and reproduce these, and he will find his
> audiences increase, and the losses of his operatic campaign
> may yet be retrieved.[71]

Although doubtless bruised by the attack, perhaps Martin felt there was some justice in it, for it is noticeable that, after returning from New Zealand, he programmed fewer and fewer operas requiring serious *bel canto* skills. And, given the pride in straight-talking which existed then as now on both sides of the Tasman, it seems remarkable that this was the first considered negative feedback experienced by the Simonsens over the twelve years since they first arrived in Melbourne.

The novelty in the Hobart season was the aforementioned *Giroflé-Girofla*, an opéra-bouffe by Charles Lecocq, which had been premièred very successfully at the Théâtre des Fantaisies Parisiennes in Brussels in March 1874, and was first produced in Australia in May 1875 by Lyster's company (without Fanny Simonsen) in Melbourne. *The Tribune* reported the house in Hobart to be 'a bumper ... filled to overflowing', so *The Mercury*'s man must have felt vindicated in his moral strictures. 'We were glad to note the good taste of Madame Simonsen in passing over several passages in which *double entendre* was perhaps too evident.'[72]

The Simonsen company moved on from Hobart to Launceston in the first week of April, playing to 'overflowing houses, hundreds being turned away nightly at the doors',[73] returning to 'half-empty benches' and a grumpy critic in Hobart just a week later,[74] and finishing their Tasmanian season with a second visit to Launceston.

This last leg caused agitation in the press: it appears that, during a performance, Martin Simonsen was approached by a total stranger – a 'commercial traveller' – who told Martin as a bet that he would go on stage and sing. Ill-advisedly, Martin took the bet and the man went on and sang 'When other lips' in 'anything but a florid style'. There was much laughter, but unfortunately things went downhill from there, with various drunks making a nuisance of themselves and being removed.[75]

The Simonsen company sailed for Melbourne on the *Mangana*, arriving on 3 May 1877, where finally they had found a venue where they might give a season of opera.

5

With the major theatres in Melbourne suitable for opera still occupied, the Simonsens had taken a concert hall, St George's, a decision constantly criticised in the press as the season progressed, the hall being deemed inappropriate. This was the hall in which the Simonsens had made their Australian debut on 18 August 1865, so they knew its characteristics well. They delivered the usual repertoire during the season there, intending to add the first performance in Australia of Nicolai's *The Merry Wives of Windsor*. Others, new to Melbourne, but performed elsewhere previously by the Simonsen company included *The Hermit's Bell* and *Carlo Broschi*.[76] Two young principals in the company had been with them throughout the New Zealand tour and the subsequent travels through western Victoria and Tasmania – Minna Fischer and Charles Florence – both of them constantly praised in the press for their growth and development as artists. The season at St George's opened on 5 June 1877 with Balfe's *Satanella*, Fanny Simonsen lauded as usual:

> Her delineation of the creature whom love converts from demon to angel was marked by careful acting, while her singing of the part was a very great treat.[77]

This had become a time of increased competition in Australia between rival opera companies. In 1876 Samuel Lazar had brought together in Melbourne a company whose principals had been recruited in Italy; WS Lyster's company continued to tour, including in 1877 the first performance of an opera by Wagner in Australia, *Lohengrin*; American actor-soprano Emilie Melville and company was successfully touring Offenbach's *La belle Hélène*; and English actor-director-theatre-manager Emily Soldene had brought her opéra-bouffe company from London to Australia, *La fille de Madame Angot* at the centre of her repertoire.[78] It was for this reason that the opera theatres in Melbourne were unavailable to the Simonsens.

The late arrival of Richard Wagner's operas to Australia and New Zealand was mostly the consequence of the preferences of visiting and resident musicians and singers. Both Lyster and the Simonsens must have been aware of Wagner's growing, dominant reputation from the 1840s to the 1870s, yet until 1877 there had been no performances in either country of *The Flying Dutchman*, *Tannhäuser*, *The Mastersingers*, *Tristan und Isolde* and the *Ring* cycle. Indeed, the *Ring* was not to be performed in Australia until 1913, brought by Thomas Quinlan's company.

In the event, the promised *Merry Wives of Windsor* was not introduced at St George's Hall. Perhaps it was not sufficiently rehearsed, or perhaps Martin Simonsen thought it too risky. Following the Melbourne season, the company went touring country towns again, starting with two municipalities straddling the New South Wales/Victoria border in the Riverina region – the wool town of Deniliquin and the river port of Echuca[79] – followed by Bendigo and Geelong, and on to Adelaide.

It was at the Royal Princess Theatre in Bendigo on 18 July 1877 that the company opened with Nicolai's *The Merry Wives of Windsor* – its première in Australia. The opera – Otto Nicolai's last and most enduring – had originally been presented in March 1849 at the Court Opera in Berlin. The *Bendigo Advertiser* was enthralled by the new work, which 'abounds with lively melodies … very delightful and pleasing to the ear'. Minna Fischer was Anne Page and Fanny Simonsen Mrs Ford. All were praised.[80] The following month in Adelaide, the *South Australian Register* reckoned the opera an improvement even on 'the pages of the great English poet'.[81]

Late in the Adelaide season came another Australian première – Johann Strauss's *Die Fledermaus* – given on 30 August 1877 at White's Assembly Rooms 'before a small but thoroughly appreciative audience'. Premièred in April 1874 at the Theater an der Wien in Vienna, it was the greatest theatrical success of the composer's career and was to become the embodiment of Viennese operetta, regularly performed all over the world. Having praised Fanny Simonsen for her 'usual artistic skill' as Rosalinda, the *South Australian Register* was cautious in its welcome for the work itself:

> The music struck us as being of unequal merit. Sometimes it
> appears to be noisy, without grandeur or any other speciality
> to recommend it, but at other times it is elegant, melodious,
> and almost fascinating.

Home-town girl Minna Fischer 'appeared as Adele and gained the first encore of the evening by her really artistic vocalisation of ['Mein Herr Marquis'] her soubrette song, in which she passes herself off before Eisenstein as Olga'.[82]

The following day the company gave its farewell performance in Adelaide, sailing back home to Melbourne on 4 September 1877. Very unusually, Martin Simonsen was unable to participate in the farewell concert, 'being very unwell',[83] and the following day it was reported that the Simonsen company's forthcoming season in Ballarat had been cancelled as Fanny Simonsen was also ill.[84] Was this cholera? In 1877, there were thousands of cesspits under Adelaide and raw sewage flowed constantly into the Torrens River; epidemics were rife. Presumably this was the cause of the Simonsens' illnesses.

Able to take a few weeks at home to recover, Fanny and Martin next took to the fray on 1 October with Lecocq's *Giroflé-Girofla* in Sydney at the Queen's Theatre.[85] In Sydney, they competed head-on with Emily Soldene's company at the Theatre Royal, so audiences were significantly reduced. They sailed back home to Melbourne on 30 October.[86]

The year 1877 drew quietly to a close for the Simonsens, apart, that is, from having to deal with the fact that their young son Louis was arrested for stealing fruit, a charge that was later withdrawn.[87] And Fanny sang the soprano solos in Handel's *Messiah* with the Philharmonic Society at the Melbourne Town Hall on Christmas Eve.[88]

6

The Simonsens' professional activities in 1878 were concentrated in the first half of the year, opening at the Prince of Wales Opera House in Bourke Street with *Die Fledermaus* – new to Melbourne – on 5 February. At that time, the theatre was managed by WS Lyster, and the company assembled for the season brought together the best elements of both the Simonsen and Lyster troupes, including Fanny Simonsen from the Simonsens' and tenor Armes Beaumont from Lyster's. A newcomer to Australia was the French soprano Camille Dubois, who sang Adele. Martin Simonsen conducted throughout the season, which ended on 29 June with a performance of Balfe's *The Rose of Castile*.[89]

The Merry Wives of Windsor was introduced to Melbourne audiences late in the run, *The Argus* reporting that 'Madame Simonsen, as Mrs Ford, took the audience completely by storm.'[90] The season at the Prince of Wales was interrupted by Emily Soldene's company's production of Offenbach's *Geneviève de Brabant*. Perhaps not so surprisingly given the continuous stretch of performances, *The Argus*'s critic noted 'signs of fatigue' in one of Fanny's performances.[91] Five days later, she was soloist again for the Philharmonic Society at the Town Hall in Mendelssohn's *Elijah*, by now apparently restored to good form.[92]

On 25 May, perhaps worried about her singing voice, Fanny took the plunge in a completely different direction – as a straight theatre actress – taking the role of Lady Teazle in a scene from Sheridan's *The School for Scandal* at the Theatre Royal in Melbourne, in which she was widely admired.[93] However, it was not to lead anywhere for her. From time to time Fanny stepped in to take over from indisposed colleagues on the opera stage, and in June it was announced that the forthcoming season at the Prince of Wales Opera House would be her last.[94] In that season, Fanny sang an admired Agathe in Weber's *Der Freischütz*.[95]

Was Fanny having vocal problems requiring a prolonged rest period? Was she bored with all the travelling? Or with performing itself? Did she want to spend more time with her still growing family? From the middle of 1878 Fanny Simonsen cut back dramatically on her performing commitments. She sang in various benefits for other artists, but by May Martin Simonsen was conducting operas for Lyster's company with other prima donnas in the lead roles, among them the young Tasmanian Amy Sherwin.[96]

At the same time, Lyster's health was continuously declining, and, after a career dedicated to developing the popularity of opera in Australia and New Zealand, he was to die in November 1880. His death left a substantial gap, one that was to be filled in large measure by the extended family of Simonsens.

7

Clearly, if Fanny was reluctant for whatever reason to perform, Martin had to step up and create a situation in which they could earn money. So in April 1879 he sailed away to America, and from there he planned to go on to Europe in order to recruit a new opera company. According to reports, the prime target was a German tenor, an acquaintance of Martin, Theodor Wachtel.[97] Martin had first met Wachtel in Hamburg in 1869; a dramatic and bel canto tenor, Wachtel sang mostly in German and Austrian houses from the early 1850s, and at Covent Garden from 1862 to 1870.

The recruitment of Herr Wachtel did not come about. Instead, Martin returned from California with something completely different – a fully equipped troupe of American vaudeville performers, including singers, dancers and trapeze artists.[98] They opened on 9 August as 'Simonsen's Froliques' at the Guild Hall in Sydney, and were an immediate hit with the public,[99] so much so that they played to packed houses for two and a half months before moving on to a season at St George's Hall, Melbourne, followed in 1880 by Adelaide, Geelong, Ballarat, Bendigo, Hobart, and Launceston, before moving on to tour New Zealand in April 1880. In Adelaide, Fanny joined the show, and 'met with a most cordial and flattering reception from a crowded and well-pleased auditory', and Martin himself displayed 'wonderful skill in bowing and fingering and in sympathetic effects'.[100] However, the *Adelaide Observer* noted that

> … it would be folly to pretend that Madame Simonsen's
> voice is what it was of yore, but time has dealt very leniently
> with it, and it still possesses the extensive range, a great
> deal of sweetness, and much of the expression and delicate
> modulation which characterised it in the past.[101]

Fanny was forty-five years old. Clearly, all those performances, night after night, year after year, had taken their toll. Had her illness in 1877 in Adelaide had a greater effect than expected? Was her decline the result of hormone shifts during early-stage menopause? In fact, Fanny gave birth to the Simonsens' tenth and last child at St Kilda on 10 December 1878, a son named again after his father, this time plain Martin.

While the Froliques was running elsewhere, Fanny and Martin organised the debuts of their two oldest daughters, Leonore (19) and Martina (17). These took place over one week, not in one of the Australian capital cities, but away from the big city press – at Ballarat.

They opened on Boxing Day 1879 at the Mechanics' Institute: Leonore played a piano solo and sang 'Let me dream again' by Sullivan; Martina sang an aria from *La sonnambula*; Leonore and Martina together sang 'The Hunter's Life' by Knucken; Fanny, Martina and John Barrington sang the laughing trio from Balfe's *The Rose of Castile*; Fanny sang a duet from *Maritana* with Pietro Paladini; Martin played his 'Fantasia on English and Irish Airs' and his 'Variations on Themes from *The Daughter of the Regiment*' (presumably accompanied by Fanny); and after the interval Fanny, Paladini and Barrington performed the second act of *Lucrezia Borgia*. Leonore was judged to have 'a very pretty mezzo-soprano voice, which, well cultivated, she uses most gracefully', while Martina had 'a very sweet [soprano] voice of good range, and she has well studied how to use it effectively'.[102] How far might they go as professional singers?

Having introduced Leonore and Martina in Ballarat, Fanny next presented them on 10 July 1880 in their first performance in Melbourne – in the prime concert venue of the city, the Town Hall. Both girls were evidently nervous, and it was unfortunate that Leonore was suffering from a cold. In consequence, it was Martina who received most of the plaudits, *The Age* noting:

> Miss Martina Simonsen's vocal gifts are of a very high order.
> She possesses a light soprano voice, wonderfully flexible, and

Melbourne debut of Leonore and Martina Simonsen

very extensive in range, which has evidently had the best training from a good artist.[103]

Martina's singing of Benedict's 'Variations on the *Carnival de Venise*' was compared favourably with that of the highly esteemed Ilma di Murska, a great compliment. Mother, father and daughters next went to the Mechanics' Institute in Geelong, then on to the Royal Princess Theatre in Bendigo, received with enthusiasm in both cities.

For Fanny Simonsen, the next major challenge was to sing at the opening of Melbourne's massive new Royal Exhibition Building – a venue intended to seat an audience of 8000 – on 1 October 1880. Amid great pomp and ceremony, it was Fanny who led off the first verse of 'God save the Queen', followed in the second verse by a chorus of 900. Next came a suitably grandiloquent cantata, specially created for the occasion by French composer Léon Caron, with Fanny leading a quartet of soloists. *Freeman's Journal* decided that the cantata was 'wearisome from its abnormal length'.[104]

However, in the weeks leading up to the opening of the Royal Exhibition Building, there was another event of great importance to Leonore and the Simonsen family. Quite soon after the sixteen-year-old was married to David Davis in Christchurch, it became clear that Mr Davis expected Leonore to give up on her career aspirations as a singer and settle down as a wife and mother. Their two children, Alby and Fanny Jane, were both born in Christchurch, but the reality was that Leonore had no such intention.

The situation came to a head in September 1880 in a very messy (and public) court case, heard before the divorce court in Melbourne. Leonore alleged that Davis had committed adultery and that he had been cruel to her, 'cruelty of an unpleasant character'; all allegations that he denied. At the heart of the case, Leonore's doctors stated that she had been infected by a 'contagious disease' caught from her husband, presumably an unspecified STD. Davis said that the whole case was a put-up job, and that it all had come about simply because Martin Simonsen wanted his daughter back singing with him and his

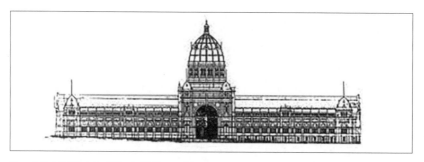

Royal Exhibition Building, Melbourne

company. On 22 September the judges unanimously granted Leonore her divorce.[105]

That settled, Martin and Fanny Simonsen, together with their three oldest daughters, set about bringing together a new opera company which would tour Tasmania, then New Zealand again through 1881.

Notes

1   *Australian Town and Country Journal* (Sydney), 20 April 1872, 9
2   *Hamilton Spectator*, 1 May 1872, 4
3   *The Grand Duchess* had been previously presented in Dunedin in 1869 in a bowdlerised version with a motley cast led by Anna Forde, chiefly renowned as a principal boy in pantomime
4   *Auckland Star*, 27 April 1872, 3; *Daily Southern Cross*, 2 May 1872, 1; *New Zealand Herald* (Auckland), 14 May 1872, 2
5   *Thames Guardian and Mining Record*, 21 May 1872, 1
6   *Daily Southern Cross*, 24 May 1872
7   *Auckland Star*, 14 June 1872
8   *Otago Witness*, 10 August 1872
9   *Hawaiian Gazette*, 3 July 1872, 3
10 *Australasian* (Melbourne), 28 September 1872, 19
11 *Evening Star* (Dunedin), 6 December 1872, 3
12 *Cincinnati Enquirer*, 2 November 1872, 5
13 *Chicago Tribune*, 10 November 1872, 7; *Boston Globe*, 2 December 1872, 2; *Quad-City Times* (Davenport, Iowa), 2 December 1872, 19
14 *Australasian*, 28 June 1873, 19
15 *Table Talk* (Melbourne), 2 January 1891, 4; *Sketch* (London), 11 July 1894, 22
16 *Ballarat Star*, 15 November 1875, 2
17 *Avoca Mail* (Victoria), 16 November 1875, 2
18 *Argus* (Melbourne), 17 December 1875, 4
19 *Bendigo Advertiser*, 11 January 1876, 2; *Age* (Melbourne), 10 January 1876, 2; disembarking from the *Norfolk* at Port Melbourne 8 January 1876: Martin (45), Fanny (38), Leonore (15), Martina (12), Louis (10), Fanny (8), Julius (6), Herman (4), Albert (3), Florence (2), William (1), plus Martin's niece Jenny Goldstein; the children's ages were doubtless guessed by Martin as he filled in the form; several were slightly inaccurate
20 Royal Terrace survives at the corner of Nicholson Street and Gertrude Street (their previous home) in Fitzroy
21 *Argus*, 14 January 1876, 8
22 *Argus*, 20 January 1876, 8

23   Cambo was cleared (and presumably sold) after Fanny Simonsen's death in 1896; *Prahran Chronicle*, 24 October 1896, 2; the house was demolished in 1940, replaced by a block of twelve apartments and shops; *Herald*, 27 March 1940, 10

24   '… dusty streets': from 'Romance' by WJ Turner, who left Melbourne for Europe in 1907

25   Frances Alda, *Men, Women and Tenors*, 24

26   *Argus*, 21 January 1876, 8

27   *Weekly Times* (Melbourne), 22 January 1876, 13

28   *Argus*, 29 January 1876, 12

29   *Argus*, 31 January 1876, 6

30   *Australasian*, 5 February 1876, 19

31   *Argus*, 1 March 1876, 4

32   The full repertoire for the Simonsen opera company in New Zealand in 1876 was: *The Grand Duchess of Gerolstein* (11 performances), *Lucia di Lammermoor* (9), *Maritana* (16), *Martha* (14), *Il trovatore* (9), *Lucrezia Borgia* (11), *La fille de Madame Angot* (36), *The Bohemian Girl* (8), *La sonnambula* (8), *The Hermit's Bell* (23), *La Périchole* (9), *Faust* (10), *Norma* (12), *Carlo Broschi* (7), *Masaniello (La muette de Portici)* (5), *The Marriage of Figaro* (1)

33   They opened their New Zealand tour in February 1876 as Simonsen's Royal English Opera Company; by May they had become Simonsen's Royal English, Italian and Opera-Bouffe Company; in July they were Simonsen's Royal English and Italian Opera Company; and finally, in September they reverted to their initial name

34   *Otago Daily Times* (Dunedin), 11 March 1876, 2

35   *Otago Daily Times*, 13 March 1876, 2

36   Statistics from Adrienne Simpson, *The Greatest Ornaments to their Profession*

37   Gänzl and Lamb, *Gänzl's Book of the Musical Theatre*, 335–36; an opéra-comique, it was premièred at the Théâtre des Fantaisies-Parisiennes in Brussels on 4 December 1872

38   *Otago Daily Times*, 28 March 1876, 2

39   *Otago Daily Times*, 8 April 1876, 2

40   *Otago Witness*, 15 April 1876, 3

41   *Press* (Christchurch), 16 May 1876, 2

42   *Globe* (Christchurch), 16 May 1876, 2

43   *Lyttelton Times* (Christchurch), 17 May 1876, 2

44   *Lyttelton Times*, 18 May 1876, 2

45   *Evening Post* (Wellington), 9 June 1876, 2

46   *Evening Post*, 29 June 1876, 2

47   *Evening Post*, 1 June 1876, 2

48   Set in Naples in 1647, *La muette de Portici* had been premièred at the Opéra in Paris in February 1828, nearly half a century earlier; its first performance in New Zealand was on 13 February 1865, given by Lyster's company in Dunedin, with Henry Squires and Lucy Escott; it was first performed in Australia in September 1838 in Sydney

49   *Leader* (Melbourne), 5 August 1876, 22

50   *Argus*, 23 May 1878, 1; *Mercury* (Hobart), 2 August 1879, 2

51   *Nelson Evening Mail*, 2 August 1876, 2

52   Port Taranaki was established in 1875, but the breakwater not begun until 1881

53   *Martha* was first performed in New Zealand by Lyster's company on 8 September 1864 at Dunedin with Lucy Escott in the title role

54   *Taranaki Herald* (New Plymouth), 9 August 1876, 2

55   *New Zealand Herald* (Auckland), 15 August 1876, 2

56   At Covent Garden through the 1850s *The Marriage of Figaro* was not performed at all; its first performance in New Zealand had been on 19 September 1864, given at the Royal Princess Theatre in Dunedin by Lyster's company with Lucy Escott as the Countess

57   *New Zealand Herald*, 14 September 1876, 2

58   *Auckland Star*, 14 September 1876, 2

59   Adrienne Simpson, *The Greatest Ornaments to their Profession*, 15

60   *Daily Southern Cross* (Auckland), 19 August 1876, 2

61   *New Zealand Herald*, 8 September 1876, 3

62   *New Zealand Herald*, 16 September 1876, 5

63   *Press* (Christchurch), 20 October 1876, 2

64   *New Zealand Herald*, 28 October 1876, 3

65   *Southland Times* (Invercargill), 17 November 1876, 2

66   *Argus*, 30 November 1876, 8

67   *Argus*, 12 December 1876, 5

68   *Ballarat Star*, 6 February 1877, 2

69   *Mercury* (Hobart), 17 March 1877, 2

70   *Tribune* (Hobart), 19 March 1877, 2

71   *Mercury*, 24 March 1877, 2

72   *Tribune*, 4 April 1877, 2

73   *Age*, 9 April 1877, 3

74   *Mercury*, 13 April 1877, 2

75   *Mercury*, 3 May 1877, 2

76   *Weekly Times* (Melbourne), 26 May 1877, 13

77   *Age*, 6 June 1877, 3

78   Soldene settled for a while in Sydney in 1892

79   *Australian Town and Country Journal* (Sydney), 7 July 1877, 7; Riverina Herald (Echuca), 10 July 1877, 2

80   *Bendigo Advertiser*, 19 July 1877, 2

81   *South Australian Register*, 27 August 1877, 6

82   *South Australian Register*, 31 August 1877, 5

83   *Evening Journal (Adelaide)*, 3 September 1877, 3

84   *Age*, 4 September 1877, 2

85   *Sydney Morning Herald*, 1 October 1877, 2

86   *Sydney Mail*, 3 November 1877, 558

87   *Telegraph, St Kilda, Prahran and South Yarra Guardian*, 15 December 1877, 3

88   *Age*, 27 December 1877, 3

89   *Age*, 6 February 1878, 3; Argus, 29 June 1878, 8

90   *Argus*, 28 March 1878, 4

91   *Argus*, 15 April 1878, 4

92   *Argus*, 20 April 1878, 8

93   *Argus*, 27 May 1878, 6

94   *Leader* (Melbourne), 22 June 1878, 18

95   *Age*, 24 June 1878, 3; *Der Freischütz* had been first performed in Australia in Sydney as early as 1838

96   *Age*, 25 May 1878, 4

97   *Ballarat Courier*, 21 April 1879, 2

98   *Argus*, 30 July 1879, 6

99   *Sydney Morning Herald*, 11 August 1879, 6

100 *Express and Telegraph* (Adelaide), 10 February 1880, 3

101 *Adelaide Express*, 14 February 1880, 22

102 *Ballarat Courier*, 27 December 1879, 4

103 *Age*, 12 July 1880

104 *Argus*, 2 October 1880, 4; *Freeman's Journal* (Sydney), 2 October 1880; the architect of the Royal Exhibition Building was Joseph Reed and the builder was Melba's father, David Mitchell; nearly twenty years later, Fanny Simonsen's granddaughter Francie Adler (later Frances Alda) performed in other works by Caron – two pantomime-vaudevilles

105 *Leader* (Melbourne), 18 September 1880, 20; *Argus*, 20 September 1880, 3; *Hamilton Spectator*, 23 September 1880, 2

Chapter 4
Leonore, Martina and the young Frances

1

With the debut of their two eldest daughters, Leonore and Martina, at Ballarat on Boxing Day 1879, the Simonsens' company had become a family business. Now, in November 1880, two singing daughters became three with the incorporation of the fifteen-year-old Fanny Martina, who joined the company under the name Frances Simonsen. Moreover, it might well be argued that there were not three, but four daughters, if we include soprano Eugénie Dehaes, who was to take small roles on tour and was said to be Fanny Simonsen's daughter from Paris.[1] Did Fanny really have a previous marriage and daughter? To a M Dehaes? Or was Dehaes her maiden family name? Thus far, it has not been possible to untangle this issue. When she declared in 1889 that she had had not ten but eleven children, were people not surprised and puzzled?[2]

Five or more performing family members in an opera company is extremely rare, but not unknown. The most famous example from an earlier generation was the Garcia family in the first half of the nineteenth century, who travelled to perform in New York in 1825.[3] There they befriended Mozart's librettist Lorenzo Da Ponte, who had fled to America to escape his creditors. The Garcia family was: tenor Manuel Garcia I (born 1775), for whom Rossini wrote the part of Count Almaviva in his *Il barbiere di Siviglia*; soprano second wife Maria-Joaquina Sitges (born 1780); and their three children: baritone Manuel Garcia II (born 1805), who became the leading teacher of his generation (among his pupils Fanny Simonsen), Maria (born 1808), who became the most famous singer in the world as Maria Malibran and died young, and Pauline (born 1821), who achieved success as Pauline Viardot. However, in reality the five Garcias never performed together – Pauline was just four years old when they arrived in New York, and her sister Maria died in 1836, the year before Pauline made her debut – whereas those five Simonsens did tour and perform together – extensively.

Frances Simonsen followed her older sisters, making her professional debut on 20 November 1880 at the Theatre Royal in Hobart in Gilbert and Sullivan's *HMS Pinafore*.[4] She was fifteen. *Pinafore* had previously been performed in May 1879 at the School of Arts in Sydney by an American burlesque troupe, the Kelly and Leon Minstrels, a pirate production. JC Williamson had just acquired the rights to all Gilbert and Sullivan operettas and was at that time sailing towards Sydney to claim those rights. The Simonsen production was done with Williamson's permission and advertised as such, and, following Tasmania, the company performed it extensively in New Zealand.

HMS Pinafore was followed in Hobart two days later by Wallace's *Maritana*. In both works the young newcomer Frances was given small roles – Hebe in *Pinafore*, she was 'to be congratulated', and the Marchioness in *Maritana*. Between arriving to live at St Kilda aged eleven and her first public performance just four years later, Frances said that she attended 'a fine Academy for girls' in St Kilda, also acknowledging the musical environment of her parents' home in Carlisle Street. Moreover, 'I positively lived outdoors. I accompanied my brothers on fishing and hunting expeditions … joined in their games of cricket and football … could swim like a fish and ride bare-back.'[5] Were there difficulties arising from her lack of English, starting school as a German-speaker in Australia at eleven? She did not say.

As previously, when the Simonsens were going to make a tour of New Zealand (1880–81), they prepared the way with a newly-formed company closer to home – this time with performances at Echuca, then Bendigo, where eighteen-year-old soprano Martina made her full opera debut on 26 October 1880 at the Royal Princess Theatre in the lead role of Bellini's *La sonnambula*, Amina. The *Bendigo Advertiser* said of Martina:

> This young lady has earned her laurels as a concert singer, and we believe her appearance last evening was the first she has made in opera. This being so, much allowance has to be made for lack of experience … A natural awkwardness was apparent, but this will soon vanish … [and] was overlooked by many last evening when absorbed in the clear bell-like resonance of Miss Simonsen's soprano voice, and her chaste vocalisation.[6]

First performed in 1831 at the Teatro Carcano in Milan, the lead soprano role in *La sonnambula*, Amina – with its story of an innocent young bride whose happiness is nearly wrecked by a jealous rival, coupled with its mix of limpid musical lines and challenging coloratura – was often sung by the most promising young bel canto singers. The creator of the role, Giuditta Pasta was already thirty-two at the première, while the great Maria Malibran was twenty-three when she first sang the role. At Bendigo in 1880, Martina Simonsen was just eighteen.

Among Martina's other legendary predecessors in the role were Jenny Lind and Adelina Patti (her breakthrough).

Her mezzo-soprano sister Leonore's debut[7] in opera came three weeks later, on 16 November at the Theatre Royal in Hobart, as Maffio Orsini in Donizetti's *Lucrezia Borgia*. Her mother Fanny was in the title role. *The Mercury* reported:

> Evidently well taught, Miss Simonsen adds to the advantages
> of careful training a picturesque appearance … and a voice
> clear as a bell and powerful in tone – as ringing in the upper
> register as it is full and sonorous in the lower one.[8]

The Simonsens were ready to take on New Zealand again.

2

Simonsen's Royal English and Italian Opera Company arrived at Bluff from Hobart on 29 November 1880.[9] Overall, they numbered thirty-five, twenty-two fewer than the troupe which had arrived in 1876. This time their orchestra was fewer in number – the intention was to pick up good local players as they went along – and there were no dancers, so the weekly wage bill would have been commensurately lower.

The tour took much the same shape as before – they started in the far south at Invercargill, then Dunedin, Christchurch, Wellington, Napier, Auckland, New Plymouth and Nelson – but after New Plymouth, they stopped for six evenings at Wanganui. This time, they were in New Zealand for seven and a half months, giving 184 performances in 223 days – in other words at much the same intensive rate as in 1876. However, they had worked out that it was legally possible to perform on Sundays if they restricted themselves to 'Sacred Concerts'. They brought and performed seventeen operas, one more than in 1876.

Five of their 1876 operas were dropped,[10] and in their place came two by Verdi (*Un ballo in maschera* and *La traviata*), plus *La dame blanche, Der Freischütz, Satanella* and *HMS Pinafore*.[11] It was the last of those which gave the Simonsens the major hit of the tour, and they gave twenty-eight performances of it – far more than any other work. However, it seems that the only one of the new works in the Simonsens' repertoire which had not been heard before in New Zealand was Boieldieu's *La dame blanche* (rendered in English as *The White Lady of Avenel*). Based on two novels by Sir Walter Scott, it had been premièred in December 1825 at the Opéra-Comique in Paris, becoming so popular there that it passed its thousandth performance in 1862.

Following her vocal difficulties of the previous year, in the 1880– 81 tour there was a major easing of the load for Fanny Simonsen. In New Zealand in 1876 she had taken the lead in every one of their 199 performances. On this tour, she was able to share that burden with her two eldest daughters, soprano Martina and mezzo-soprano Leonore. However, the response to fifty-year-old Fanny throughout the tour was just as positive as it had been previously – there seemed to be no suggestion of declining vocal abilities.

They opened on 29 November at Sloan's Theatre at Invercargill with Flotow's *Martha* – most popular then as now for the one melody not composed by Flotow, 'The Last Rose of Summer'. Fanny Simonsen took the lead, 'her acting and singing from first to last were such as to elicit from every part of the house no expression of opinion but that of high admiration.'[12] Fanny took the lead again the following evening in *Lucrezia Borgia*, introducing for the first time to a New Zealand audience her daughter Leonore in the role of Maffio Orsini. Leonore 'played the part … with much vivacity and sang the music of it with sweetness and power'.[13] Also making her debut (in an unnamed role) was the 'other' daughter, Eugénie Dehaes.

On the third evening at Invercargill, Martina Simonsen took the lead as Amina in *La sonnambula* – her mother not on stage. The *Southland Times* was impressed:

> We may at once say that long before even the first act was
> over the young lady had established her right, in the opinion
> of all judges present, to the highest praise which has been
> bestowed on her, and that before the curtain fell she had
> secured a prominent position in the first rank of favourites of
> the local 'musical world'.

The 'compass, quality and volume of her voice [and] the command she has over it' were all exceptional, continued the *Times*.[14] The third daughter, Fanny Martina (now professionally named Frances Simonsen), also took to the stage in New Zealand for the first time that evening in the minor role of Dame Teresa (usually played by a much older singer).[15] In time Fanny Martina was to become the international prima donna Frances Saville, second only to Nellie Melba among Australian-raised sopranos of that generation.

3

Amina in *La sonnambula* was for Martina a role to be repeated in all the subsequent New Zealand cities. In Dunedin, the *Otago Daily Times* was enchanted:

> It would be difficult to imagine a part more suited to her
> appearance and voice ... and the unanimous recall which
> she received at the close of the performance stamped her first
> appearance a brilliant success ... She delivered the florid passages
> of the opera with great apparent ease, and, indeed, more than
> once introduced a series of runs not to be found in the score.[16]

In Christchurch, the *Lyttelton Times* declared that 'it is no exaggeration to say that her success in the part was most unqualified,'[17]

Martina Simonsen as Nanine in Camille *by Falk (H Walter Barnett)*

and the *Evening Post* in Wellington reported that 'she at once proved herself the possessor of a very sweet and powerful soprano voice of extensive compass,' adding that 'her shake [trill] is very promising and her scales are generally excellent.'[18] The *New Zealand Herald* in Auckland concluded: 'Miss Martina Simonsen possesses all the qualities from which the highest lyric eminence can be reached.'[19] This was altogether a remarkable start for a young prima donna.

Martina's other operas in 1880–81 in New Zealand (each sung on multiple occasions) were a mix of soprano and mezzo roles: Adalgisa in *Norma* (to her mother's Norma), Arline in *The Bohemian Girl*, Jenny in *La dame blanche*, Josephine in *HMS Pinafore*, Georgette in *The Hermit's Bell*, Violetta in *La traviata*, Oscar in *Un ballo in maschera*, Aennchen in *Der Freischütz*, and the leads in *Satanella* and *Lucia di Lammermoor* (taking over from her mother). Each was received with handsome plaudits. From the great volume of positive notices received by Martina, this brief one of her Lucia, from the *Wanganui Herald* might stand to represent the response throughout New Zealand:

> The fair debutante produced an effect in which astonishment
> was mingled with delight. To say that she has been well
> trained is only to say that Madame Simonsen was her
> instructor.[20]

Although Martina's sister Leonore Simonsen was equally gratefully received in New Zealand, her mezzo roles were often overshadowed by the soprano ones of Martina. In terms of impact, Leonore's first role there, as Maffio Orsini in *Lucrezia Borgia*, could not compare with Martina's Amina. Nevertheless, she was consistently acclaimed. Her other roles in the tour were: Clotilde in *Norma*, Lazarillo in *Maritana*, Buttercup in *HMS Pinafore*, Ulrica in *Un ballo in maschera*, Azucena in *Il trovatore*, Siebel in *Faust*, Agathe in *Der Freischütz*, Georgette in *The Hermit's Bell*, Agnes in *La dame blanche*, Lilia in *Satanella* and Wanda in *The Grand Duchess*. Of Leonore's Siebel, the *Evening Post* in Wellington wrote:

> For her performance throughout we have nothing but the
> highest praise to give. She looked, acted, and sang charmingly
> throughout, her 'Flower Song' winning a vociferous and
> irresistible encore. She is incomparably the best Siebel yet
> seen here.[21]

The youngest of the daughters, Frances Simonsen, who had had her sixteenth birthday in January, was, not surprisingly, given more minor roles – ones which gave her a chance to get used to being on stage, and to become confident with all the business of a touring opera company – including Marthe in *Faust*, Annina in *La traviata*, Margaret in *La dame blanche*, First Bridesmaid in *Der Freischütz* and Hebe in *HMS Pinafore*. Was there any hint in all this of the star prima donna to come, above the achievements of her two older sisters, eventually becoming a key member of Mahler's company at the Court Opera in Vienna? Not judging by the brief notices she received on that tour, which ranged between the patronising and the grudging.

Fanny's remaining daughter on tour in New Zealand, Eugénie Dehaes was similarly given a range of small roles and seems to have left the company after Wanganui, presumably returning to Europe.

4

Off-stage in New Zealand, little of great note seems to have occurred: Martin Simonsen's Germanic speech to the throng in Dunedin was mocked in a long (and unfunny) letter to *The Globe*;[22] a cricket match, watched by a thousand spectators, was played between a Simonsen company team and an Auckland XI, both in fancy dress;[23] in June, Mr RW Carey was reported as having purchased from Australian impresario JC Williamson the sole New Zealand rights to Gilbert and Sullivan's *The Pirates of Penzance*, a situation which so enraged Martin Simonsen that he blacked Carey's and another man's eyes;[24] and just one day after the ship left New Zealand for Hobart carrying the Simonsen company, there was a breach of promise case brought by one 'M Simonsen' against a Mr Joseph Soloman in Dunedin. The plaintiff was awarded £125 in damages.[25] Was this M Simonsen by any chance Martina?

However, one welcome outcome of the 1880–81 tour by Simonsen's Royal English and Italian Opera Company was that 'Mr Simonsen is so well satisfied … on the conclusion of the New Zealand campaign, which has been pecuniarily successful much beyond his expectations.'[26]

The company returned to Tasmania in July 1881, where they simply picked up where they had left off eight months before. At the Theatre Royal in Hobart, the company gave *Un ballo in maschera*, followed by *The Hermit's Bell*, *Der Freischütz*, *Lucia di Lammermoor* with Martina Simonsen as Lucia, plus lead roles in *Maritana*, *La traviata*, *Norma*, *The Grand Duchess* and *The Bohemian Girl*.

On 18 July 1881, sixteen-year-old Frances Simonsen was married in Hobart to the current agent for the Simonsen company, John Saville Smith.[27] Frances had been advertised to appear that evening as Alisa in *Lucia di Lammermoor*, but did not do so, being otherwise occupied.[28] The two must have known each other at least from the beginning of the New Zealand tour eight months previously, as Smith administrated that tour for the Simonsens, together with the subsequent season in Tasmania. According to Adrienne Simpson, the marriage was a complete surprise and led to a brief rupture with her family, and Simpson speculates that it took place hurriedly as Frances was pregnant. The marriage was not to last, but there were two long-term consequences. First, she gave birth to a son, Frank, on 6 April 1882,[29] so it seems that the conception more or less coincided with the marriage. And second, Frances Simonsen took her husband's middle name, eventually becoming the international prima donna Frances Saville.[30]

It must have been with some relief that, after a further fortnight in Launceston, on 13 August the rest of the family sailed home to Melbourne.

5

There followed a period of relative calm for the Simonsens, and Fanny advertised in Melbourne for singing pupils.[31] In late October 1881, Fanny Simonsen, together with her two eldest daughters, performed in two concerts at the Town Hall in Melbourne. These were advertised as 'Farewell Appearances', the two young ladies said to be departing shortly for Europe, via India, with their father.[32] In the event, it appears that the journey did not reach as far as Europe, their activities as a small concert party being confined to India, where they appeared as the 'Simonsen Vocal and Instrumental Operatic and English, Irish and Scotch Ballad Company' at the Banqueting Hall in Madras (organised for them by the Governor), Calcutta, Lahore and elsewhere.[33] 'During 1881 did the whole of India, concert tour', wrote Martina in her brief notebook, written much later. Father and daughters arrived back in Melbourne on 29 March 1882.[34] Perhaps, given subsequent events, the tour of India was not a positive experience for Martina.

By early May, Martin was said by the *Lorgnette* to be 'on the war-path' again, organising a new company to tour 'the Australian colonies and New Zealand'.[35] Previous New Zealand tours had each been preceded by a brief try-out season around Victoria or Tasmania, but this time the forthcoming twelve-month Australasian tour was split evenly, Australia having the first six months.

They opened at the renovated Gaiety Theatre in Castlereagh Street, Sydney, on 20 May 1882, with *Satanella* – Martina Simonsen in the title role and the young mother Frances, by now billed as Frances Saville, as Lelia. It was six weeks since she had given birth. Not realising that both Martina and Frances had in their early years been brought up German-speaking in Altona by their grandmother, in a generally positive review, the *Sydney Morning Herald* reviewer took exception to their German rolled 'r's, delivered from the back of the throat.[36] At the Gaiety, the Simonsens presented nine operas,

Gaiety Theatre, Sydney

most of them to be taken on to New Zealand in late October. The Sydney season was followed by the Exhibition Theatre at Geelong, the Theatre Royal at Adelaide and the newly refurbished Theatre Royal in Hobart. In Adelaide, *HMS Pinafore* and von Suppé's *Boccaccio* were added to the nine (the latter new to Australasia). And when they reached New Zealand, in Invercargill the Simonsens added Lecocq's popular *Giroflé-Girofla*.

The workload of prima donna roles was throughout spread quite evenly between Fanny, Martina and Leonore, with Frances gradually taking on more demanding roles. Since Leonore had always been presented as a mezzo, and had sung Siebel in *Faust* with success, it was perhaps surprising that she should take over the role of Marguérite from Fanny, with Frances now taking on Siebel.[37] Was Leonore's voice moving up? Was Frances's moving down? Martina retained Lucia and took both Maritana and Clairette in *La fille de Madame Angot* from Fanny. Of the opera season in Adelaide, 'read [the] German critics', commanded Martina in her notebook, and they were indeed full of admiration for her Lucia, comparing her favourably with both Lucy Escott and Martina's mother Fanny Simonsen.[38]

Audiences for the season in Sydney were not numerous enough and it was reported that Martin Simonsen was a 'heavy loser' and had left 'almost broken-hearted'.[39] Geelong was no better. However, things looked up in Adelaide and Hobart. Would another New Zealand tour put things right for them?

In Adelaide, Martin had a new crowd-pleaser in *Boccaccio*. It had been premièred at the Carltheater in Vienna in February 1879 and had quickly become a favourite both in Austria and internationally. The Simonsens presented its Australian première on 22 September 1882 at the Theatre Royal, with Fanny Simonson as the poet Boccaccio, Leonore Simonsen as Fiametta and Frances Saville as Isabella. However, the situation was more complicated than that. A version, said to be inauthentic, had been introduced twenty days earlier at the Prince of Wales Opera House in Melbourne by the London Comic Opera Company with Kate Chard as Boccaccio. That version included forty dancers. Whatever the truth of the matter, the Simonsens' audiences in 'authentic' Adelaide loved it, the *South Australian Register* appreciating the

> ... rollicking humour, rich and rare costumes ... [the]
> lavish display of the nether limbs clothed in closely fitting

hose of many hues ... and the music of this opera [which]
rises much above the level of that of the ordinary opera-
bouffe.[40]

Throughout the Australian tour and on to New Zealand, Frances
Saville's husband John Saville Smith remained as agent for the Simonsen
company.

6

Simonsen's Royal English and Italian Opera Company opened their
1882–83 tour of New Zealand on 30 October 1882, at Sloan's Theatre
in Invercargill again, with *La fille de Madame Angot*. Pre-publicity
announced that it was a company of forty with Martina and Leonore
Simonsen both listed among the sopranos and Frances Saville among
the contraltos.[41] Simonsen brought with him from Australia just eight
orchestral players and augmented the band with local musicians in
New Zealand. Among these (for *Der Freischütz*) was the twelve-year-
old cornet player Alfred Hill, who would in time become the leading
Australasian composer of his generation.[42] Of *Madame Angot* the
Southland Times reported:

> Miss Leonore Simonsen, who has vastly improved since her
> last appearance in Invercargill, has evidently conceived a great
> liking for the part of Clairette, for she plays it throughout with
> a zest which is a pleasure to witness.[43]

As before, following Invercargill, the company gave seasons in
Dunedin, Christchurch, Wellington, Nelson, Auckland and Napier.
The only venues newly visited by the Simonsens were the Auckland
suburb of Parnell and Boylan's Hall in Gisborne. Among the eleven

operas this time brought to New Zealand, three were introductions – Suppé's *Boccaccio* (new to New Zealand), Lecocq's *Giroflé-Girofla* (previously played in New Zealand by Emily Soldene's company in 1877) and Offenbach's *The Brigands*.[44] Overall the company gave 117 performances in 159 days – the tour interrupted more than on previous occasions by illness and bad weather. Although there had been warning signs in Sydney and Geelong, Fanny and Martin must have been bitterly disappointed by the poor audience numbers, a situation that led to the premature closure of the tour at Napier. Several reasons have been put forward for the downturn – among them depression in the New Zealand economy, increased competition from rival opera companies, and too short an interval since the previous tour by the Simonsens. Another concern was the lack of a sure-fire box office winner.

While *Boccaccio* generally pleased both audiences and critics – and received by far the most performances on the tour, thirty-three in all – it simply did not have the drawing power of *La fille de Madame Angot* in 1876, or of *HMS Pinafore* in 1880–81. The three Simonsens in the *Boccaccio* cast constantly gained highly positive notices – Fanny as the poet, Leonore in the soprano role of Fiametta and Frances Saville as the mezzo Isabella. Being nineteenth-century New Zealand, there was a certain amount of moral handwringing as to whether *Boccaccio* was a suitable entertainment for ladies.[45]

The other operatic introduction to New Zealand, *The Brigands*, fared less well. Its première had been in December 1869 at the Théâtre des Variétés in Paris and it was considered to have gaiety, plus music just as dazzling as Offenbach's previous hits. However, lacking a dominant female lead role, it did not establish itself in the repertoire in the way that others had. 'There is a noticeable dearth of taking airs,' noted *The Press* in Christchurch, adding that Miss Martina as the brigand's daughter lacked the 'requisite verve', and Frances Saville as the page Fragaletto 'was so confidential in the delivery of her music as to render it a matter of doubt as to the manner in which she sang it.'[46]

On this tour, cricket matches were played in most of the cities visited, the opera company team usually being dismissed for miserable totals – forty-two in Nelson and just twenty-seven in Gisborne.[47] Perhaps the poor performances on the cricket field mirrored in some mysterious way the lack of audience numbers. Towards the end of the season at Auckland, Fanny Simonsen fainted onstage at a mixed concert on 2 March 1883, having just sung 'He loves me' from *The Hermit's Bell*. The *New Zealand Herald* described the scene:

> Mrs Simonsen did not seem well when she came on the stage. When she attempted compliance with the encore her head drooped, and she presently fainted, falling rather heavily on the stage. The curtain fell.[48]

Martin Simonsen came forward and told the audience that 'this was the first occurrence of the kind in a long professional career.' Fanny was sufficiently recovered three days later to take the lead again in *Boccaccio*. Nevertheless, it will have shocked Fanny profoundly, and may well have contributed in no small way to the fact that, at the end of the tour at Napier, she announced her intention to retire from the opera stage (and to live out the remainder of her life in Australia).[49]

The 1882–83 tour of New Zealand had had to endure several setbacks – bad weather, illnesses and poor box-office receipts among them – so the Simonsens must have returned home to St Kilda in a somewhat chastened mood.

7

Despite their financial setbacks in New Zealand in 1882–83, the future must have looked bright for the three singing Simonsen daughters. Twenty-three-year-old Leonore and twenty-one-year-old Martina had both received highly positive responses, both from audiences and reviewers, and were by now performing major lead roles, while eighteen-year-old Frances Saville had graduated to middle-ground roles and was gaining experience steadily. Yet the latest Simonsen company had now been dissolved, so the young women each had the go out and find work for themselves for the first time.

It was clear that mother Fanny was moving towards retirement from the stage, dedicating herself to teaching. Settled back home in Carlisle Street, she ventured out from time to time in order to perform at concerts and in church services (both Catholic and Anglican). Her conversion to Judaism on her marriage to Martin never seemed to get in the way of Christian musical witness. So, on 13 May 1883, Whit Sunday, she sang in Haydn's *Imperial Mass* and Rossini's 'O salutaris Hostia' from his *Petite Messe Solonnelle* at High Mass in St Patrick's Cathedral, Melbourne.[50]

A rather greater challenge for Fanny must have been to sing the role of Donna Anna in a production of *Don Giovanni*, put on with very little rehearsal by American baritone/impresario Guglielmo Verdi (his real name was William Green) at the Opera House in Melbourne on 7 September. The press tore into Mr Verdi for his lack of proper preparation, yet Fanny was complimented on her 'artistic and well-studied rendering of the great part'.[51] This was likely to have been Fanny Simonsen's first performance in the role. Her daughter Martina was Zerlina. In that Verdi Opera Company season in 1883 at the Opera House in Melbourne, all three Simonsen women – Fanny, Leonore and Martina – took leading roles.

In November, Fanny was the soprano soloist in a performance with the Philharmonic Society at the Town Hall of Gounod's oratorio *Redemption*,[52] and on 15 September 1884 she sang the role of Marzelline (to Elise Wiedermann's Leonore) in Beethoven's *Fidelio*.[53] Just five days later, on 20 September, Fanny gave her final farewell to opera (while making it clear that she might continue to perform in concerts).

That 'Farewell to the Stage' took place at the Princess Theatre in Melbourne, scene of so many of her earlier triumphs.[54] The occasion attracted a 'numerous and fashionable audience', including the Governor of Victoria and Lady Loch. The performance started with the third act of *Maritana*, her rendition of 'Scenes that are brightest' receiving 'enthusiastic applause' as always, and this was followed by the second act of *Lucrezia Borgia*. The great American actress Genevieve Ward, on tour at that time in Australia, recited the poem 'True Heroism'.[55] Since Martin Simonsen was abroad with daughter Leonore in San Francisco, the concert was conducted by Alberto Zelman. Among the performances that remained for Fanny Simonsen, one was to sing on 8 December 1885 in a performance of Frederick Clay's cantata *Lalla Rookh* at a concert in aid of the Chair of Music Endowment Fund at Melbourne University – the other soprano soloist being a Mrs Armstrong, in due course to become Nellie Melba.[56]

By this stage, Fanny was dedicating herself primarily to her role as a singing teacher. Aside from her own offspring at St Kilda, her pupils included three young women who were later to sing with Simonsens' opera companies – Lillie Crowle, Ada Prull and Flora Graupner. However, Fanny's most successful non-family pupil was the contralto Ada Crossley, who started with her in 1888, and who would go on to study with Mathilde Marchesi in Paris.[57] Crossley had a brilliant career as a concert artist, mainly in Britain. She returned to tour Australia in 1903–04 and 1908–09.

8

Leonore Simonsen had had such consistently positive responses from audiences and critics for her performances in New Zealand, it might have been quite natural for her to expect that her good fortune would continue without a hitch. This was not to be the case.

Quite why, after 'resting' for a while at home in Melbourne, Leonore should decide to try her luck in San Francisco, is something of a mystery. Perhaps her father's experiences there in the 1850s and early 1860s had something to do with it. He had been one of the earliest first-rate violinists to perform there. They left together, father and daughter, along with her two small children, for America in June 1883, while Martina stayed home at St Kilda with her mother. It became clear that California was a tougher nut to crack than they had anticipated, but on 15 August they opened at Dashaway Hall on Post Street.[58] In September they were performing with the impresario Cagli's company, who were just off the boat from Australia, at the California Theater,[59] but 'business was far from being large'.[60] In November Leonore sang with Eugenie Pappenheim's company at the Grand Opera House as Ortrud in Wagner's *Lohengrin*.[61] This last was for a Simonsen a rare excursion with a major Wagner opera – probably a first for a Simonsen. The *Daily Alta California* was enthusiastic:

> Miss Leonore Simonsen is an admirable Ortrud, singing the
> difficult music of her role with force and precision, and looking
> and acting the character to the life.[62]

Exactly when and where Leonore met Herman Adler remains a mystery. However, some six months after arriving in California, she was to marry again. The ceremony was conducted on 3 January 1884 by the prominent Rabbi for the Congregation Sherith Israel in the city, Dr Falk Vidaver. They were married at a leading Jewish association in San Francisco, the Concordia Club on O'Farrell Street.[63]

Leonore appeared in October 1884 with Madame Fabbri's Opera Company at the Mission Street Opera House – in Halévy's *La Juive* and *Les Huguenots* (although in which roles is unclear) and *Norma* (Adalgisa). On 8 November, Leonore received a benefit at Irving Hall in San Francisco and was then in New York, Martin having also gone east,[64] but the last musical sighting of her was in early December in

Dashaway Hall, San Francisco

connection with an aborted *Un ballo in maschera* at the Tivoli Opera House back in San Francisco. According to the *Daily Alta California*: 'A large audience was disappointed last night by the postponement of *Un ballo*, on account of Miss Simonsen's refusal, after two rehearsals, to appear as Amelia.'[65] On 20 December, Martin was sighted in Reno, Nevada, 'one of the best violinists ever seen this side of the Rocky Mountains', apparently on his way back to California.[66]

He arrived in San Francisco on Christmas Day 1884 – just four days before Leonore died at her home on Sutter Street.[67] The symptoms of

Grave of Leonore Simonsen Adler, Colma, San Mateo County, California

peritonitis,[68] the illness that was diagnosed as the cause of her death, would have been very evident, not only to father and daughter, but also to Leonore's husband of a few months, Herman Adler, and to her two young children, Alby (seven) and Fanny Davis (five). Leonore was twenty-five. Fifty-three years later, Fanny Davis, by now prima donna Frances Alda, wrote of her mother's death:

> She had a charming voice and had been trained to sing, light
> roles and in concerts. She was determined to make a career
> for herself and support her children. When she was twenty-
> four, she came to America, to California, bringing us with
> her. I never see it snowing that I don't think of my mother …
> We stand at the window with our noses pressed to the pane,
> watching the white flakes come down over San Francisco. It is

twilight … We are waiting for our mother to come home. The
door behind us opens. We turn eagerly … 'Mama!' … Suddenly
she sways and falls forward … Two days later she is dead.

What had caused the peritonitis? We shall never know. 'Her
young American husband, our stepfather … stares at Alby and me in
bewilderment.'[69] Clearly, Herman Adler was in no position to take care
of his new family, so Grandfather Martin swept them up and took them
back to live with Fanny and himself (plus several singing aunts and
uncles) at St Kilda.

9

Leonore had had a difficult time after returning from New Zealand,
but her sister Martina got off to a flying start – recruited by baritone-
impresario 'Guglielmo Verdi' to be Carmen to his Escamillo at the
Prince of Wales Opera House in Melbourne.[70] It opened on 4 August
1883, *The Argus* reporting:

> Much of the interest … in this performance was due to the
> appearance here for the first time in opera of Miss Martina
> Simonsen, and we are glad to be able to record in that
> young lady's favour a most gratifying success.[71]

The Argus went on to point out that the favourable impression of
her singing was even greater because the role lay too low for her – an
opinion positively reinforced by the singer in an interview fifty-five years
later.[72] The following week, with the same company, Martina was Oscar
in *Un ballo in maschera*, and then the lead in *Lucia di Lammermoor*,
both of which roles she had first sung in Dunedin. Of her Lucia, *The
Argus* critic wrote:

> We think highly of this performance, because in it Miss
> Simonsen is enabled to display the good culture she has received
> as a vocalist, and to justify the high expectations which had
> been formed from the reports which had preceded her.[73]

On 25 August Martina ventured into new territory, taking on the role of Sinais (Pharaoh's Queen) in Rossini's grand opera, *Mosè in Egitto* (Moses in Egypt) with Mr Verdi as the Pharaoh. It was the work's première in Australia (having first been performed in March 1818 at the Teatro San Carlo in Naples). The production was greeted positively at the Opera House, running for ten nights, and Martina was particularly praised for her 'true Rossinian style' (which she will have learned from her mother).[74]

Next came another Australian première, this time of a more recent work – Flotow's *L'ombra* – which had been first performed at the Opéra-Comique in Paris in July 1870. This was mounted, presumably because of the popularity of the composer's *Martha*, at the Victoria Hall in Melbourne by an outfit led by Italian bass Filippo Graziosi, which made its bow on 13 October 1883. 'Miss Simonsen gave a very piquant impersonation of the lively young widow [Vespina] and sang the florid music of the part with ease and skill,' wrote *The Age*.[75] For whatever reasons, *L'ombra* remains virtually unperformed to this day.

March 1884 found Martina Simonsen as prima donna in American light opera singer Emilie Melville's company at the Bijou Theatre in Melbourne – first in the lead role in *Maritana*, then as Amina in *La sonnambula* and thirdly in the title role in *Martha*. All were praised. At the last night of *Martha* (18 April), the audience was informed that when Martina left the theatre she would be going straight to her ship, which would carry her to 'some Mediterranean port, from whence she would go to Milan to study'.[76]

In April 1884 she sailed off with her father to Europe. Why it was decided that this would be a good career move for Martina in not clear. Her performing life in Australasia was going splendidly and all the best judges felt that she was a good actress with a fine voice, superbly trained by Fanny. Nevertheless, the long voyage was to have life-changing consequences for Martina, for also on board was a Melbourne-based businessman, George Schreiber.[77] Did they first meet on board, or had they met previously and their encounter on the ship was pre-arranged? Was Martin Simonsen aware of a growing romance? Arriving at Naples, Martina recorded in her notebook that they were initially quarantined on the nearby island of Nisida. Was there smallpox on board? Was it in the infamous Bourbon prison on the island that they were lodged?

In Milan, Martina's main teacher was retired tenor Felice Pozzo – a 'real farce as my mother had taught me everything', said Martina – but she also had lessons with Fanny Salvini-Donatelli (the original Violetta in *La traviata*), and Giorgio Ronconi (the first Nabucco).[78] Several much later reports suggested that Martina also was taught by Mathilde Marchesi in Paris, the leading pedagogue of her era, who was later to teach her sister Frances Saville and her niece Frances Alda, but there is no supporting evidence for this. In truth, Martina and Martin (and George?) were in Milan for a relatively short time, for by October they were in London seeking an opening at Covent Garden,[79] then on to New York.

Neither London nor New York produced work for Martina, and the next we hear of her is that on 30 April 1886 she was married to George Schreiber at the German Evangelical Church at Sydenham (then part of Kent, now in leafy south-east London).[80] Martin was not there, having returned to Melbourne, excited about the prospect of forming a real Italian opera company to tour Australia and New Zealand, and the bride was given away by William Howard Smith junior, son of a shipping magnate. The happy couple honeymooned in Paris and the South of France.[81]

Marriage spelled the end of a very promising career for Martina. She retired from the stage immediately, to become Mrs George Schreiber of Melbourne, wife and eventually mother of four.[82]

Perhaps it was for one of those children that she hand-wrote a brief overview of her life in a little notebook – four pages, less than 300 words – which abruptly stops with her marriage to George in 1886. Preceding that overview is a single page in her own hand outlining five basic precepts for the evangelical Christian life. From the time of her marriage, Martina shifted allegiance away from the Judaism she had grown up with.[83]

In so many ways, Martina's life following marriage was a complete reversal of the path her mother took: while her mother had abandoned the restrictive precepts of womanhood in an aristocratic Christian French/Belgian family to become a constantly travelling, working woman, married to a Jew and embracing his religion, Martina gave all that up to become a non-working wife and mother in Melbourne and a committed Christian, adopting the faith of her husband. Neither her notebook, nor later press interviews reveal Martina's reasons for giving up her promising singing career in exchange for the life of a housewife-mother in Melbourne. One imagines she would not have been impressed by the proto-feminism of Ibsen's *A Doll's House*, which opened at the Princess Theatre in Melbourne three years later, the theme of the play creating controversy and rowdy scenes.[84]

However, George Schreiber, who part owned and ran an import business, ran into deep problems in 1891. Following a fire at his Little Flinders Street premises and trading losses, George was declared bankrupt.[85] And life became more difficult for George and Martina Schreiber during the First World War. It was a troublesome time generally for German-heritage Australians; not only for those in business like George, but also for academic musicians who had made their homes there. In November 1914 it was reported:

> The authorities today carried out a search at the homes of two
> University Professors, Mr Edward Scharf of 40 Park Street,
> South Yarra, and Herr Walter von Dechend of Woodgrange,
> Hawksburn Road, Hawksburn. The officers were given every

assistance in their task of collecting correspondence for transmission to the Federal Attorney-General, who will go through it and report to the Minister for Defence the result of the investigation.[86]

On 11 December 1915 a further report stated: 'Two German professors of the Melbourne University – Herr E Scharf and Herr von Dechend – have had their services dispensed with.'[87] Owning his own importing business, one might think that George could not have his services dispensed with. However, 'not only did he lose his business, but [daughter Laura] was ostracised by her former school friends.'[88] Presumably Laura's mother Martina suffered similar treatment.

On 30 May 1891, in the year of her husband's bankruptcy, Martina returned in a straight play at the Princess Theatre in Melbourne as the maid Nanine to the great French actress Sarah Bernhardt's Camille. Reviews were good, her performance in Sydney in July described by the *Australian Star* as 'bright and unaffected'. Nine years after her last operatic appearance, 'Mrs Schreiber' returned briefly to the concert platform in 1894-95: a Liedertafel concert at the Town Hall, where she sang 'with the perfect vocalisation which reminded old concertgoers very forcibly of her mother, Madame Simonsen'; then with the Melbourne Zither Club at the Athenaeum Hall.[89]

10

With the death of Leonore Simonsen in December 1884, and the withdrawal from performance of her sister Martina sixteen months later, both in their early twenties, the hopes of Fanny and Martin Simonsen rested on their third daughter, Frances Saville. The main problem with this prospect was that Frances was to have a lengthy period of professional struggle.

Compared with both her sisters, Frances was introduced by her parents very gradually to the operatic stage. At eighteen Martina had made her operatic debut as Amina in *La sonnambula* at Geelong, and at twenty Leonore had made her debut as Maffio Orsini in *Lucrezia Borgia* at Hobart, both in 1880, whereas until 1883, Frances had had to make do with relatively minor roles.

Things started well for Frances after she returned from New Zealand and she was signed up by the Montague-Turner Opera Company, initially in mezzo roles – Azucena in *Il trovatore* and the Gipsy Queen in *The Bohemian Girl* – and her husband, John Saville Smith, was hired by the company as its manager. At the time she joined it, the company was touring northern New South Wales and Queensland, and it was at the Theatre Royal Rockhampton in late June, where Frances first took on the roles of Nancy in Flotow's *Martha* and Philine in Ambroise Thomas's *Mignon* (to Annis Montague's Martha and Mignon).[90] In July the company was performing for a week at Mackay, Frances Saville appearing there in all her roles.[91] Curiously, in the audience was a pregnant young wife, Mrs Armstrong. She and her husband were living close by, Mrs Armstrong under pressure from her husband to give up on her operatic aspirations. She saw the Montague-Turner company performances and wrote to her teacher, Pietro Cecchi, in Melbourne, that she had met and liked Mrs Turner (Annis Montague), the American prima donna and manager of the company.[92] It was this meeting that, in effect, determined Mrs Armstrong's future, for it lit the flame that would lead to the glittering career of Dame Nellie Melba.

In October at Adelaide, Frances had a lucky break – Annis Montague was unwell, so Saville took over the lead role, Arline, in *The Bohemian Girl*, at very short notice.[93] However, this did not immediately result in greater things, and by the next week she was back singing the comprimario role of Nancy, in *Martha*.[94] Still being asked to perform as a mezzo, she was Siebel in *Faust* shortly after,[95] and then Philine in Thomas's *Mignon* once again.[96]

However, 'the crowning success of her present season' in Adelaide, according to the *Express and Telegraph*, came as Maffio Orsini in *Lucrezia Borgia* – one of her sister Leonore's main roles previously in New Zealand. 'We think there is a brilliant future for this gifted young lady.' [97] This was a step up from the notices she had been receiving from the Adelaide press. Maybe Frances did have a bright future – although this was not so apparent in the next chapter of her performing life.

Over the Christmas holiday period, she took the role of Morgana in a pantomime – *The Forty Thieves* at the Bijou Theatre in Melbourne[98] – and by April 1884 she was in Hobart with her husband, who had pulled together an Italian troupe, the Milano Opera di Camera Company, which opened with *Il trovatore*. 'To say that the audiences were greatly disappointed is only a mild way of putting it,' reported *The Age*.[99] In May, Frances was Rip's little daughter Alice in Robert Planquette's *Rip Van Winkle* at the Theatre Royal, Hobart.[100]

Later in the year, Frances was back in Sydney in a new comic opera by Christchurch-raised Luscombe Searelle, *Bobadil*. Based on a story from *The Arabian Nights*, it was premièred at the New Opera House in Sydney on 22 November 1884, with Frances Saville as Lulu, and had a reasonably successful eight-week run in Sydney. Frances's performance was a 'praiseworthy delineation', according to the *Australian Town and Country Journal*.[101] Towards the end of the run, Gracie Plaisted, who had been Princess Zorayda, was ill and Frances took over the lead role at short notice to much approval:

> She has made a decided advance in her profession … She
> sang and acted with skill, taste and judgment, and thoroughly
> secured the favour of her audience.[102]

In August the following year, she appeared in another of Luscombe Searelle's offerings (less successful) at the New Opera House in Sydney – the story of a wandering pirate and the daughter of one of his victims,

Isidora – with Frances as Sabina.[103] Was she destined for a lightweight career in musical comedy?

Fortunately for her, by performing in *Bobadil*, Frances Saville had become a member of the Majeroni and Wilson Comic Opera Company, who opened next at the New Opera House with Lecocq's *La fille de Madame Angot*, Frances as Mlle Lange (a role brilliantly taken by her mother in New Zealand in 1876).[104] Neither Eduardo Majeroni nor WJ Wilson were singers. The former was an actor-manager, nephew-in-law of the great Italian actress Adelaide Ristori, with whom he had originally come to Australia in 1875. The latter was primarily a scene painter for the stage, who also managed various theatres in Australia and New Zealand. Together, as joint managers of the New Opera House, they formed their own comic opera company in 1884, with Frances Saville a founder member. The Sydney season ended with Offenbach's *La belle Hélène* with Gracie Plaisted in the title role ('she has not the physique requisite to look the character,' sighed the *Sydney Mail*), and Frances Saville as 'a dashing Orestes'.[105]

In March 1885 *Bobadil*, *La fille de Madame Angot* and *La belle Hélène* relocated to the Theatre Royal in Adelaide, where they had a successful run, the *South Australian Advertiser* finding Saville's Mlle Lange 'greatly pleasing'.[106] These were followed by *HMS Pinafore*, with Frances as Josephine, a role previously taken by her sister Martina in New Zealand.[107]

In June the Majeroni and Wilson company opened at the Bijou Theatre in Melbourne – *La fille de Madame Angot* their first offering, followed by Offenbach's *The Brigands* with Saville as Fragoletto, a role originally intended for a tenor, which she had previously sung in New Zealand in 1883. She 'vocally carried off the honours of the evening', wrote *The Age* reviewer.[108] At the end of the Melbourne season, Frances took over the title role in *La belle Hélène* for the first time, a role she was to repeat at the Court Opera in Vienna in 1902.[109]

By September, the company was back in Sydney at the New Opera House, this time with *Maritana*, Frances as 'a very pretty Lazarillo',[110] followed, as so often at that time, by *The Bohemian Girl* with Saville 'the most disappointing Queen seen in Sydney for a long time', according to the *Sydney Mail*. 'She was imperfect in her part and appeared out of humour with herself and those associated with her.'[111] Perhaps she was bored.

Those two 'British' operas seem to mark the end of Frances Saville's association with the Majeroni and Wilson company, and by May 1886 she had become a regular performer in Sydney in Henri Kowalski's concerts. Taken altogether, up to this time it could not be said that Frances Saville's career trajectory gave any real hint that she might in time become an international prima donna, second only to Melba among Australians of their generation.

11

With first daughter Leonore dead at twenty-five, second daughter Martina about to retire at twenty-four, third daughter Frances Saville at twenty-one struggling to create her own career, and wife Fanny gradually withdrawing from public view, what was still-energetic father Martin Simonsen to do with his life?

In 1886 at fifty-six years old, he was unlikely to forge a viable career from continuing to play the violin, or with conducting, yet he was still filled with the dynamism that had characterised his life up to this point. In April, a brief paragraph in *The Argus* pointed the way forward for him:

> For some time past there has been a freely expressed opinion
> that the time is ripe in Melbourne for another season of
> grand opera. Mr Martin Simonsen, acting on this view, has
> canvassed the leading residents of Melbourne, with the object
> of securing one hundred subscribers to the fund that will

be necessary for bringing out a new company and several new operas.[112]

By late May, his subscribers duly signed up (and paid up), Martin left Melbourne for Naples and then Milan, planning to return, complete with company, in 'about six months' time'.[113] And, being the man he was, he was back in late November with a complete company of Italian singers.[114] Their Melbourne season opened at the Alexandra Theatre (now Her Majesty's) on 11 December with *Il trovatore*, and his new company was an immediate success.[115]

For the first time being entirely without Simonsen family singers, it is not necessary here to cover the progress in Australia of Simonsen's first Royal Italian Opera Company of 1886–87 in detail, nor of his subsequent Italian company which toured Australia and New Zealand in 1888–89.[116] Suffice it to say that they were widely regarded as first rate and among the operas performed were six that were new to Australia – Donizetti's *Roberto Devereux* and *Belisario*, Bellini's *I Capuleti e i Montecchi*, Ponchielli's *I promessi sposi* and *La Gioconda* and Antonio Carlos Gomes's *Il Guarany* – plus a new Australian work, *I due studenti*, composed by British-born Alfred Plumpton, the libretto by Italian artist-writer, Ugo Catani (both Melbourne residents).

Frances Saville, who was living and performing in Sydney, sang a song at a benefit concert for her father on 25 May 1887 at the Theatre Royal in Sydney.[117] On 30 September the semi-retired Fanny stepped in at short notice to sing Valentine in *Les Huguenots* in Melbourne, the Italian soprano being indisposed. It was a role she had not sung before (her usual part being Marguérite de Valois). In the second Italian company's tour, on 5 November 1887 Fanny was La Cieca in the Australian première of *La Gioconda*, and on 5 February 1889 she sang the title role in *Maritana* at a benefit for Martin.

This *Maritana* does signal the end for Fanny Simonsen's performing career. She had first appeared in her late teens at the Opéra-Comique in Paris in 1854–55 and had continued singing in public through the

Martin Simonsen

following four decades. She first announced her intention to withdraw from the opera stage at Napier in March 1883, aged forty-eight, but continued to emerge from time to time over the following six years, in concert, in church and on the opera stage. The last of her ten children, Martin junior, had been born ten years earlier, when Fanny was forty-three. In those final years of performance, it was clear to critics and presumably to Fanny herself, that her great powers were in decline, and so she took the inevitable final decision, concentrating primarily on teaching. Presumably, as with so many women singers, then as now, the vocal change was the result of shifts in her hormones, arising from the menopause that affected her breath control and resulting in an inability to pitch as accurately as in former times. While her most successful daughter, Frances Saville, had a similar end to her career, her granddaughter Frances Alda was able to continue singing professionally until she was fifty-seven.

Sadly, while Martin's first Italian company was adjudged a success, his second was not, and, coupled with the unqualified financial disaster of a troupe of Spanish dancers also brought in by Martin, in February 1889 Martin Simonsen was declared insolvent in Sydney. His many declared debtors included his wife Fanny.[118] Extraordinarily, when that second Italian company disbanded, the glutton for punishment Martin immediately formed a new company to tour New Zealand, starting at Invercargill in May 1889 and finishing in Dunedin on 30 October. A recurring theme in Adrienne Simpson's pioneering writings was Martin Simonsen's lack of competence in financial management. And it is true that his projects swung wildly between success and failure, but then so did most other musician-impresarios in his line of business, before and since.

Again, there were no Simonsen family singers in the new New Zealand troupe, but it is worth noting that the stage manager on that tour was the Tasmanian-born Tom Pollard (born O'Sullivan), who also took on well-received minor roles in several productions.[119] Pollard was to become the driving force behind the various Pollard child and adult opera companies over succeeding decades.

The future was not looking bright for the Simonsens. The next tranche of singing Simonsen siblings – Jules, Florrie and Willie (plus their promising granddaughter Fanny Davis) – was not yet quite ready to mount the stage. Could young Frances Saville retrieve the situation?

Notes

1   *New Zealand Herald* (Auckland), 11 November 1880, 6
2   *Table Talk*, 1 November 1889, 5
3   The Garcias in New York in 1825 gave the first professional opera performances in the USA
4   *Mercury* (Hobart), 22 November 1880, 3; *HMS Pinafore* had been first performed at the Opera Comique in London in May 1878
5   Quoted from *Broadway Magazine*, May 1899, by Adrienne Simpson in her 'Frances Saville: Australia's Forgotten Prima-Donna', 3
6   *Bendigo Advertiser*, 17 October 1880, 3
7   Leonore was usually presented as Leonora in Australia and New Zealand
8   *Mercury*, 17 November 1880, 2
9   *Evening Star* (Dunedin), 29 November 1880, 3
10 *Carlo Broschi, La Périchole, Masaniello, La fille de Madame Angot* and *The Marriage of Figaro*
11 The full repertoire for the Simonsen's opera company tour of New Zealand in 1880–81 was: *Martha* (6 performances), *Lucrezia Borgia* (8), *La sonnambula* (7), *Il trovatore* (12), *Norma* (12), *The Bohemian Girl* (7), *The White Lady of Avenel (La dame blanche)* (11), *Maritana* (9), *HMS Pinafore* (28), *La traviata* (6), *The Hermit's Bell* (11), *Un ballo in maschera* (11), *Lucia di Lammermoor* (8) *Faust* (11), *Der Freischütz* (14), *Satanella* (6) and *The Grand Duchess of Gerolstein* (7)
12 *Southland Times* (Invercargill), 30 November 1880, 2
13 *Southland Times*, 1 December 1880, 2
14 *Southland Times*, 2 December 1880, 2
15 Adrienne Simpson believed that this performance was both Martina's and Fanny Martina's operatic debut, but these had taken place a few weeks earlier at Bendigo and Hobart respectively
16 *Otago Daily Times* (Dunedin), 17 December 1880, 2
17 *Lyttelton Times* (Christchurch), 18 January 1881, 5
18 *Evening Post* (Wellington), 18 February 1881, 2
19 *New Zealand Herald* (Auckland), 9 April 1881, 5
20 *Wanganui Herald*, 21 May 1881, 2
21 *Evening Post*, 19 February 1881, 2
22 *Globe* (Dunedin), 17 January 1881, 2
23 *New Zealand Times*, 18 April 1881, 2
24 *Auckland Star*, 13 June 1881, 2
25 *Evening Post*, 12 July 1881, 2
26 *Otago Witness* (Dunedin), 18 June 1881, 20
27 *Mercury*, 25 July 1881, 1; on the marriage certificate, Frances gave her age as 'above 21'
28 *Mercury*, 19 July 1881, 3
29 Adrienne Simpson, 'Frances Saville: Australia's Forgotten Prima Donna', 4
30 This was the second of Martin and Fanny Simonsen's daughters to embark on a brief marriage at the age of sixteen
31 *Argus* (Melbourne), 15 October 1881, 16
32 *Argus*, 19 October 1881, 8
33 *Argus*, 16 January 1882, 4; *Sydney Mail*, 28 January 1882, 153; *Australasian* (Melbourne), 4 March 1882, 19
34 *Argus*, 30 March 1882, 7
35 *Lorgnette* (Melbourne), 3 May 1882, 2
36 *Sydney Morning Herald*, 22 May 1882, 6
37 *Daily Telegraph* (Sydney), 10 June 1882, 5

38   *Australische Zeitung*, 22 August 1882, 1
39   *Queenslander* (Brisbane), 5 August 1882, 174
40   *South Australian Register*, 23 September 1882, 6
41   *Southland Times*, 18 October 1882, 2
42   John Mansfield Thomson, *A Distant Music*, 17
43   *Southland Times*, 31 October 1882, 2
44   The full repertoire for the Simonsen opera company's 1882–83 tour of New Zealand
     was: *La fille de Madame Angot* (10 performances), *Der Freischütz* (6), *Boccaccio* (33),
     Maritana (7), *Giroflé-Girofla* (19), *Satanella* (9), *The Hermit's Bell* (7), *The Grand Duchess
     of Gerolstein* (8), *HMS Pinafore* (3), *The Brigands* (8) and *The Bohemian Girl* (2)
45   *Observer* (Auckland), 2 December 1882, 2
46   *Press* (Christchurch), 19 December 1882, 2
47   *Colonist*, 16 February 1883, 3; *Poverty Bay Herald* (Gisborne), 21 March 1883, 2
48   *New Zealand Herald*, 3 March 1883, 5
49   *Evening Star* (Dunedin), 3 April 1883, 2
50   *Australasian* (Melbourne), 19 May 1883, 6; presumably the 'Imperial Mass' was what we
     would now call the 'Missa in Angustiis' (Mass for troubled times) or 'Nelson Mass'
51   *Age*, 8 September 1883, 4
52   *Age*, 28 November 1883, 6
53   *Australasian*, 20 September 1884, 26
54   *Age*, 9 September 1884, 8
55   *Age*, 22 September 1884, 5; the author of that 'True Heroism' is undiscovered
56   *Australasian*, 12 December 1885; Mrs Armstrong/Melba was twenty-four; aside from this
     concert, there is no evidence that Melba and Fanny ever met, although it seems likely that
     the young Nellie Mitchell would have seen Fanny perform, both in opera and concert; in
     June 1891, Fanny wrote a letter from Milan to the Italian magazine *Il Mondo Artistico*,
     protesting that Melba should acknowledge the important role of her teacher Pietro Cecchi
     in her success
57   Beth Mary Williams, 'Lineages of Garcia-Marchesi and Other Traditional Italian Vocal
     Pedagogy in Australia, 1850–1950', Vol 1, 82
58   *Oakland Tribune*, 11 August 1883, 8
59   *San Francisco Chronicle*, 24 September 1883, 3
60   *Lorgnette* (Melbourne), 4 December 1883, 2
61   *Oakland Tribune*, 28 October 1892, 8; *Daily Alta California*, 5 October 1884
62   *Daily Alta California*, 3 September 1883, 8
63   *San Francisco Examiner*, 6 January 1884, 3; a founding member of the Concordia Club
     was blue jeans pioneer Levi Strauss
64   *Evening News* (Sydney), 8 December 1884, 5; *Daily Alta California*, 8 November 1884, 4
65   *Daily Alta California*, 9 December 1884
66   *Reno Gazette-Journal*, 22 December 1884, 3
67   *Age*, 14 February 1885, 9
68   Causes of peritonitis include: abdominal wound or injury, ruptured appendix, stomach
     ulcer, perforated colon, diverticulitis, pancreatitis, liver disease, and infection of the
     gallbladder, intestines or bloodstream
69   Frances Alda, *Men, Women and Tenors*, 23
70   *Leader* (Melbourne), 21 July 1883, 26
71   *Argus*, 6 August 1883, 7
72   *The Star*, 29 September 1934
73   *Argus*, 24 August 1883, 7
74   *Australasian*, 1 September 1883, 18
75   *Age*, 15 October 1883, 5
76   *Argus*, 19 April 1884, 8
77   *Evening Journal* (Adelaide), 21 April 1884, 2

78   *Mercury* (Hobart), 28 August 1884, 2
79   The Covent Garden season in June–July 1885 was mounted by Colonel Mapleson, with Adelina Patti and Sofia Scalchi among the singers
80   The German Evangelical Church (protestant) at Sydenham was built in 1883; Dietrich Bonhoeffer was its pastor 1933–35
81   *Argus*, 4 May 1886, 1; *Table Talk* (Melbourne), 7 May 1886, 16; *Evening Journal* (Adelaide), 12 June 1886, 4
82   George Henry, Elsa Emmy, Paula Olga and Laura
83   Now in the Performing Arts Collection at the Arts Centre Melbourne (2013.011.002)
84   *Argus*, 16 September 1889, 6
85   *Argus*, 27 November 1891, 5; *Age*, 20 July 1892, 6
86   *Kalgoorlie Western Argus*, 17 November 1914
87   *Bairnsdale Advertiser and Tambo and Omeo Chronicle*, 11 December 1915, 2
88   Winsome E Matenson, *A Melbourne Family 1848–1948*, 191–92
89   *Table Talk*, 10 August 1894, 6; *Argus*, 20 April 1895, 12
90   *Morning Bulletin* (Rockhampton), 21, 28 and 30 June 1883, 1
91   *Mackay Mercury* (Queensland), 4 July 1883, 2
92   Quoted in Thorold Waters, *Much Besides Music*, 112–13
93   *Express and Telegraph* (Adelaide), 22 October 1883, 3
94   *South Australian Advertiser*, 31 October 1883, 5
95   *Express and Telegraph*, 16 November 1883, 3
96   *South Australian Weekly*, 17 November 1883, 15
97   *Express and Telegraph*, 23 November 1883, 3
98   *Weekly Times* (Melbourne), 29 December 1883, 9
99   *Age*, 9 May 1884, 7
100 *Mercury*, 28 May 1884, 2
101 *Australian Town and Country Journal* (Sydney), 29 November 1884, 28
102 *Sydney Mail*, 17 January 1885, 130
103 *Daily Telegraph* (Sydney), 24 August 1885, 6; for Searelle, see Jeremy Commons, 'Who was Luscombe Searelle' in Adrienne Simpson (ed), *Opera in New Zealand* , 47–59
104 *Australian Town and Country Journal*, 17 January 1885, 25
105 *Sydney Mail*, 14 February 1885, 346
106 *South Australian Advertiser*, 23 March 1885, 5
107 *Express and Telegraph*, 18 April 1885, 3
108 *Age*, 8 June 1885, 5
109 *Herald*, 30 June 1885, 2
110 *Sydney Mail*, 12 September 1885, 590
111 *Sydney Mail*, 3 October 1885, 743
112 *Argus*, 5 April 1886, 4
113 *Argus*, 29 May 1886, 8
114 *Age*, 29 November 1886, 4
115 *Age*, 13 December 1886, 5
116 Detailed coverage of Simonsen's first Italian company in Australia in 1868–88 may be found in Alison Gyger, *Opera for the Antipodes*, 38–49; and of his second Italian company in 1888–89 in Gyger, 59–70; and of his next company in New Zealand in 1889 in Adrienne Simpson, *The Greatest Ornaments of their Profession*, 105–29
117 *Sydney Morning Herald*, 26 May 1887, 8
118 *Daily Telegraph*, 7 February 1889, 5
119 *Star*, 22 June 1889, 4; *New Zealand Herald*, 26 August 1889, 5

Chapter 5
The Ascent of Saville

1

If Frances Saville was to start the climb towards the top of the tree in the world of opera, there had to be a decisive change in the way she was going about it. Thus far, she had built a fine level of skill and technical ability, the result of years of training with her mother, at the same time accumulating a good deal of practical experience – after all by late in 1885 she had been performing continuously, mostly in opera and operetta but also in musical comedy, for nearly five years professionally, and was approaching her twentieth birthday. Yet there was thus far no real lift-off in her career. She seems to have realised that, if she was to make significant progress, she needed to shift her artistic focus from comic opera to more 'serious' music.

So, initially in Sydney, she joined a concert troupe – the Sydney Artistes Concert Company. Formed in 1866, this was the brainchild of composer-conductor Charles Huenerbein – an ensemble of singers, together with violinist (Rivers Allpress) and Huenerbein as accompanist. In their short season at Grafton on the Clarence River in northern New South Wales in January 1886, his troupe had included another promising soprano – a Mrs Armstrong – who was shortly to leave Australia, becoming first a pupil of Mathilde Marchesi in Paris, then the international prima donna, Nellie Melba.[1] In the previous month, a visitor from Melbourne had come to sing *Messiah* at the Sydney Exhibition Building, conducted by Henri Kowalski. This was that same Mrs Armstrong.

Saville joined Huenerbein's company as the principal soprano early in 1887. The intention was to perform six concerts in suburban Sydney venues, starting at the School of Arts in Burwood. However, audiences were so meagre that the series was soon abandoned.

The change in Saville's fortunes came about – largely unnoticed until now – when Saville met, and performed with and was coached by Henri Kowalski in Sydney. Composer-pianist-conductor Kowalski was born in 1841 in Paris and had first come to Australia in 1880 to

Henri Kowalski
by H Walter Barnett

give piano recitals at the Melbourne International Exhibition, staying on to give concerts in 1881–82. He went back to Europe the following year, returning to Sydney in 1885, where he was to remain for twelve years. He was born at Bordeaux in 1841 to a Polish father (who had fled to Britain in 1830) and a French mother of Irish ancestry, supposedly (like Fanny Simonsen) a minor aristocrat. At the Conservatoire in Paris, he studied piano and composition, and, by the time he arrived in Australia, he was skilled in both disciplines and was also conducting regularly. In Melbourne, then Sydney, Kowalski wrote many works on Australian themes, including *The Belles of Melbourne* and *Nuits Australiennes*.[2]

Saville seems to have first met Kowalski not long after he had arrived in Sydney in 1885, and in October she was performing with him in a Liedertafel concert in honour of Austrian composer-pianist Max Vogrich, who was leaving for America. There was a note of surprise in the press that Frances was involved in this event, as she had previously been 'known in Sydney in opéra-bouffe'. However, in 'Ah, fors' è lui' from *La traviata*, she 'succeeded so well that she was warmly encored'.[3]

Over the following five years, Saville was to perform regularly with Henri Kowalski in concert (and occasionally in opera) in Sydney, with Kowalski coaching her on each occasion. Indeed, he was notorious for the rigour with which he rehearsed. These concerts formed the backbone of her work and indicate a serious desire to improve vocally and to move her performing career into the more 'serious' end of music.

Quite quickly, Frances was able to establish herself as the leading lyric soprano in Sydney. There she was to explore a range of repertoire, mostly with Kowalski (who conducted the Sydney Philharmonic Society orchestra and chorus), far wider than she would have encountered with the various Simonsen opera companies, including Handel's *Acis and Galatea*; Haydn's *The Creation*; Dvorak's *The Spectred Bride*; songs by Schubert, Schumann and Mendelssohn, plus arias, duets and ensembles from a wide range of operas (many but by no means all of them favourites of her mother). And she sang in several compositions by her mentor: the cantata *Welcome* (written for the new Governor of New South Wales, Lord Carrington), 'Valse chantée', his opera *Verçingétorix*,[4] and a valse de concert, 'Perles de rose'.

Aside from re-focusing her repertoire (and through that her reputation), Frances also changed husbands. In August 1887 out went John Saville Smith, and in March 1888 in came Max Rown. Both operated in effect as her business managers, but while Smith and Saville had travelled and worked together through a series of campaigns, with various opera companies, Saville had not been able to bring about the success that she sought. And he was penniless, whereas Rown was a well-to-do businessman. The question was, would he do better for her?

The divorce proceedings with Smith got off to a tangled start. Both wanted the same outcome, but, as so often at that time, it was necessary for evidence to be manufactured. However, His Honour 'severely cross-examined the witness' and clearly did not believe a word of what was said about the adultery of Mr Smith. Nevertheless, the petition was granted the following day on the grounds that the petitioner was unaware of the deception. Custody of their son, Frank, was granted to Frances.[5]

In July 1889, Frances organised a benefit concert in Sydney for the promising young violinist Bessie Doyle, who was planning to study at the conservatorium in Leipzig.[6] Frances roped in several of her friends to come and perform, and organised for the Governor's wife, Lady Carrington, to attend. At the concert, Saville sang her current party-piece, 'Elisabeth's Prayer' from *Tannhäuser*.[7]

2

Having successfully rebuilt her career on more stable artistic foundations, Saville now needed a catalyst that might enable her to move up decisively, and this came, quite serendipitously, through the advice and counsel of a famous British baritone touring in Australia, Charles Santley.[8]

Born at Liverpool in the north-west of England in 1834, Santley became a successful oratorio singer from the 1850s, and a celebrated opera singer from the 1860s, performing with Mapleson's company and at Covent Garden in London before going to Italy, where he met Rossini and retrained.[9] After returning, he sang for several seasons with the Carl Rosa company. In 1889–90 he toured Australia and New Zealand, greeted everywhere as a major star.

Saville's opportunity came when Mrs Palmer (Rosina Carandini), the soprano who had been booked for a performance of Mendelssohn's *Elijah* with Santley on 21 October 1889 at the Exhibition Building in Sydney, was unavailable, and Frances was brought in at short notice. This was treated as an important musical event in the city and Saville, according to the *Daily Telegraph*

> … deepened the favourable impression previously made by singing throughout with greater purity of attack and vocal reserve in the English style, whilst at the same time she lent as before to the Widow music all the tenderness and pathos of her richly laden voice.[10]

Frances was retained to sing at the baritone's later appearances in Sydney. However, it is interesting to note that reports of how impressed Santley was with her singing, encouraging her to seek 'finishing' training in Europe in order to pursue a career there, appeared in the British press fifteen days before she sang with him in *Elijah*. Where had he heard her previously? According to press reports, in Santley's view Saville was superior to Melba.[11]

3

Preparing to follow Santley's advice, Saville spent the next twelve months undertaking a handful of high-profile assignments before sailing to London with her new husband Max Rown. Prominent among these was a series of Farewell Concerts for Sir Charles and Lady Hallé at the Town Hall in Melbourne in August 1890. Just as with the Santley concerts the previous year, the fact that Saville was able to take them on was entirely fortuitous, in this case, due to the indisposition of the booked soprano, Annis Montague. Effectively, after living and performing almost exclusively in Sydney over the past five years, these Hallé concerts represented Frances's return to her 'home' city.

Charles Hallé was born in 1819 at Hagen, Westphalia, in Germany and, after studying piano and associating with Cherubini, Chopin and Liszt in Paris, he abandoned that city after the 1848 revolutionary disturbances, settling in London. He moved to Manchester in 1853, starting what was to become the Hallé Orchestra four years later. In 1888 at age sixty-nine he married his second wife, the celebrated Moravian violinist Wilma Neruda. He was knighted that year and together, he and Lady Hallé toured Australia in 1890. Of course, it will have been a bonus that Saville was fluent in German.

The Hallé farewell concerts in Melbourne were high profile affairs, given the full treatment by the press, and Frances, 'of late years almost a stranger in Melbourne', was welcomed back warmly. Over the series she sang arias from many of the operas which would go on to be important in her future career, including *Tannhäuser, Faust, La sonnambula, Il barbiere di Siviglia, Norma* and *Ernani*. *The Argus* noted that

> Her rendering of 'Elisabeth's Prayer' was imbued with earnestness and pathos, and created a most favourable impression, the fair vocalist being twice recalled.[12]

Saville also sang with the Hallés in Sydney and Adelaide, then taking on two final stage roles before going to Europe. Perhaps surprisingly, given the weightiness of her recent repertoire, she was hired by impresarios Williamson and Garner to sing, first the lead role in *Marjorie*, a comic opera by Walter Slaughter, which opened at the Princess Theatre in Melbourne, on 20 December 1890.[13] It had been premièred in July 1889 at the Prince of Wales Theatre in London by the Carl Rosa Opera Company, and had run there for 193 performances. This was followed in mid-January by a revival of *The Pirates of Penzance*, with Saville as Mabel.[14] The Australasian rights to both works were owned by Williamson.

Her Sydney friends put on a fundraising Farewell Concert for Frances – towards her journey to Europe – on 21 March at the Centennial Hall. Among the performers were several who had appeared many times with her, including soprano Lilian Colbourne Baber and Henri Kowalski. Saville sang 'Sombre forêt' from *Guillaume Tell*, the 'Jewel Song' from *Faust* and several ballads.[15] This was followed by a 'sacred concert' on Good Friday at Her Majesty's Theatre.[16] Summing up the position she had reached, *Table Talk* was clear:

> Miss Frances Saville ... who a year or two ago used to appear
> in comic operas, is the leading concert soprano of Sydney, and
> a much sought-after teacher.[17]

On 20 April 1891, Frances and Max, together with her son Frank, sailed from Sydney to London on the *Parramatta*.[18] Shortly before they left, Madame Buesst informed *Table Talk* that Frances had been a piano pupil of hers for five years. While there is no corroboration for this, it seems likely. One of her sons, Victor, became an international piano soloist, while another, Aylmer, became an opera conductor in Germany and Austria and with the British National Opera Company in London.[19]

4

Even before the ship arrived in London, word had reached the local press concerning the Australian traveller. As the *Pall Mall Gazette* reported early in July:

> Australia sends us from time to time the best of its native productions in many departments of life. Lately there has come to London one of the most noted of its vocalists, in the person of Miss Frances Saville, whose father M Simonsen, is a prominent impresario in Australia … Mdme Simonsen, the mother, is also a singer of considerable merit, and under her and competent instructors Miss Saville was early prepared for the concert and opera stage.

The report went on to mention warmly Saville's performances with Santley and the Hallés, concluding: 'It is to be hoped that Miss Saville will appear professionally in London.'[20] However, Mr and Mrs Rown arrived in a London abuzz with the ascendancy of another Australian soprano, Nellie Melba, who had by this stage triumphed at Covent Garden as Lucia, Gilda, Juliette and Ophélie. And shortly before the arrival of the Rowns, the press had broken the story of Melba's passionate affair with Philippe, Duc d'Orléans, pretender to the French throne.

If public concerts were expected in the short term, Max and Frances were to be disappointed, and the only exposure that Frances seems to have achieved in London by late July was, firstly a 'private recital', where Sir Arthur Sullivan was her accompanist (variously reported as having been with the Royal Family, or with an audience of musicians including conductor Hans Richter), and secondly a 'private matinée' organised by Saville's supporters from Sydney, Lord and Lady Carrington, recently returned from the governorship of New South Wales, for several of the bigwigs at Covent Garden, including Melba's great supporter, Lady de Grey.[21] It is possible that these two events were one and the same.

Mr and Mrs Rown and Frank soon moved on from London to Paris in search of Madame Marchesi. By 1891, Mathilde Marchesi was already seventy-six years old and had been teaching for half a century. Among her pupils to date were a dozen or more international divas, including Ilma di Murska, Etelka Gerster, Emma Nevada, Sigrid Arnoldson, Emma Calvé, Emma Eames and Nellie Melba.

Marchesi was born in Frankfurt in 1821 and her own teachers included Felix Mendelssohn and Otto Nicolai. In 1845 she became a pupil of the younger Manuel Garcia in Paris. She found in Garcia an approach and methodology for teaching singing that stretched back to Nicola Porpora in the early eighteenth century. This method would serve her and her pupils well for the whole of her working life.[22] It is no coincidence that Fanny Simonsen and Mathilde Marchesi were both pupils of Garcia – their teaching methods being similar – a fact remarked on by Australian contralto Ada Crossley, who was a celebrated pupil of both women.

Nellie Melba had been the first Australian to be taught by Marchesi, starting with her in 1886 and, aided by Marchesi, becoming a star at the Théâtre de la Monnaie in Brussels the following year. Frances Saville arrived in Paris with letters of introduction in August 1891, ready to start the new academic year in September. In many ways she was the ideal Marchesi pupil, for although Madame was a very thorough teacher, her best pupils arrived already well trained and with a generally sound technique, so that she could provide the finishing touches and help them to launch their European careers. This was true of both Melba and Saville, with Saville having the great advantage at twenty-six of ten years of practical stage experience behind her.

Extraordinarily, Saville's intention to study with Marchesi had been born when, as an eleven-year-old, she had heard Ilma di Murska in Melbourne and had been told by her father, Martin Simonsen, that di Murska's teacher had been Marchesi.[23] Frances spent the year 1891–92 with Marchesi, essentially polishing a well-formed existing technique and preparing herself for her European debut. At the Marchesi École, she was to perform in at least three of Madame's pupil concerts – two in-house 'auditions' in April 1892 and a soirée at the Salle Érard on 25 June, where, according to her teacher, she 'excelled in the grand air from *Hamlet* and in the trio from *Faust*'.[24]

At those Marchesi events she shared the platform with two Australian contemporaries, Lilian Devlin (who had a promising but brief career) and Nellie Rowe (whose career suffered because of her intense shyness, though she later became a well-known teacher in London), plus a fine American, Suzanne Adams.[25] Although Adams had all the hallmarks of the Marchesi style, uniquely she led an angry insurgency against Madame and her methods. Adams was a young soprano who came to reject Mathilde Marchesi's authoritarian teaching style, and 'asserted her rights in true Yankee spirit', said the *Boston Daily Globe*,[26] by walking out of class and taking some other American girls with her. It does not appear that any of the Australians joined the revolt.

Five years earlier, Marchesi had organised for directors of the Monnaie in Brussels to be at one of her own concerts when Melba was singing, and this had led directly to Melba making her triumphant debut at that house. Similarly, for Saville, having been heard at the École soirée, they 'engaged her on the spot', and Marchesi arranged for Frances to make her own debut at the Monnaie on 7 September 1892 – as Juliette in Gounod's *Roméo et Juliette*. On leaving Marchesi, Frances wrote a note of humble thanks to her, quoted in Mathilde's memoirs:

> My gratitude and love, my darling Madame, have grown with the studies, which have been such a pleasure to me … I could fill all the pages of this album with praises and thanks for your loving kindness and patience, and still would fail to express half of what I feel.[27]

Mathilde Marchesi
by Joseph Uphues

The theatre at Aquarium Gardens, St Petersburg

While Melba's arrival at the Monnaie had brought forth high approval from the critics, the response to Saville's first performance there was more muted. On the plus side, 'she had precious gifts: uncommon purity of tone [and] a supple and often charming voice', while, not so positively, 'artistic sentiment, emotion, are lacking. Her Juliette is cold and timid.'[28] Was she very nervous? It was perhaps surprising that this was a role that Frances should be singing for the first time, given that Gounod's *Faust* had been a great favourite of, and frequently performed by, her mother.

During that season at the Monnaie, Saville sang eighteen times, all Gounod – nine Juliettes and nine Marguérites in *Faust* – followed by a Gala Concert together with star violinist Eugène Ysaÿe at the Conservatoire Royal in Brussels on 7 May 1893.

Overall, she must have impressed, because she was next booked to sing in twenty-five performances at the Aquarium Theatre in St Petersburg (where Marcella Sembrich had previously starred) through the Russian summer,[29] opening there (again) as Juliette and during the season singing Marguérite, Lucia, Gilda, Santuzza in Mascagni's *Cavalleria rusticana* and Elsa in *Lohengrin* – her first verismo and her first Wagner operas.[30] Of her season, *The Standard* wrote: 'From the first she pleased both the critics and the house, and in *Lucia* the *furore* was boundless.'[31] Saville was the third Simonsen to star as Lucia, following her mother Fanny and sister Martina. From St Petersburg, in late August she went on to Moscow, where she sang Lucia, Marguérite and Gilda.

Returned from Russia, Saville made her Berlin debut at the Kroll Theatre on 16 September 1893 as Violetta in *La traviata* – she singing in French, her Alfredo in Italian and the remainder of the cast in German – followed by Lucia.[32] A review of her final performance waxed lyrical:

> The artiste is gifted with a beautiful and highly cultured voice,
> especially strong in the higher parts, but also most sweet and

tender in the piano parts. To all this she unites a fascinating
personality with the most charming expression … It is
therefore not to be wondered that she brought down the house
repeatedly.[33]

All this was exactly the kind of lift-off for her career that she sought,
already having performed in top roles at four of the leading opera cities
in Europe, a far cry from the slow operatic progress she had made over
a decade in Australia and New Zealand.

5

There is no doubt that Frances and husband Max would have wished
that the next step in her journey would come at Covent Garden and, in
pursuit of that objective, she performed at a promenade concert there on
6 October 1893, singing the 'Mad Scene' from *Lucia di Lammermoor*.[34]
Clearly, either the right people were not there, or she did not sing well
enough, for there was no booking. So, she did the next best thing in
Britain, taking a season's contract with the Carl Rosa Opera Company.
By this stage, Nellie Melba was well established at Covent Garden, her
interests closely guarded there by her friend, Lady de Grey, although,
unlike others, there has never been a suggestion in Saville's case that
Melba blocked her path at that house.

Started in 1875 by German-born impresario Carl Rosa, the company
presented operas in English, touring the major provincial cities of
Britain, together with regular London seasons. There were many such
companies in the quarter-century following its establishment, but the
Carl Rosa swiftly became leader of the pack. Rosa himself died in 1889,
but the company survived and even prospered in subsequent years.

Frances Saville made her debut with the Carl Rosa company as
Marguérite in *Faust* at the Theatre Royal in Glasgow on 16 November

1893, making an immediate impact as the 'new' Australian prima donna.[35] 'Her rendering was at once artistic and refined ... Histrionically as well as musically Mdme Saville achieved a brilliant success,' wrote the *Glasgow Evening Post*.[36] The cast included Irish tenor Barton McGuckin as Faust and Tasmanian-born bass Lemprière Pringle as Méphistophélès.

After Glasgow, in the following seven months as the Carl Rosa's new star singer, Saville performed in Edinburgh, Newcastle, Bradford, Liverpool and Manchester, before returning for a second season in Glasgow and Edinburgh and going finally to the Theatre Royal in Birmingham. Over the period, in addition to Marguérite in *Faust*, she sang Leonora in *Il trovatore*, Santuzza in *Cavalleria rusticana*, Juliette in *Roméo et Juliette*, the title role in *Lucia di Lammermoor*, and two Wagnerian roles – Elsa in *Lohengrin* and Elisabeth in *Tannhäuser*.

Among the twelve Simonsen singers covered in this book, only Frances Saville sang extensively in Wagner's operas (solely preceded by Leonore Simonsen as Ortrud in *Lohengrin* in San Francisco in 1884). Although Adrienne Simpson thought that Wagner was 'not ideally suited to a voice of her type', nevertheless Saville gained consistently positive reviews for her singing of Wagner – with the Carl Rosa and later with Covent Garden, at the Met and with Mahler at the Court Opera in Vienna.[37] In fact, Wagner had a clear preference for singers with a strong bel canto technique, as was the case with several of Mathilde Marchesi's pupils, Saville among them.[38]

Working with the Carl Rosa company must have brought back memories (positive and negative) of the constant touring in Australia and New Zealand with her parents' company. Saville's first appearance in Manchester as Elisabeth in *Tannhäuser* came about as a consequence of the 'serious illness' of American soprano Marie Duma (another Marchesi pupil), and was highly praised.[39] Summing up her Elisabeth (and her standing at the end of that Carl Rosa tour), the *Birmingham Daily Post* wrote:

> Gifted with a soprano voice bright and pure in quality and a
> charming stage presence, Madame Saville immediately won
> the favour of the audience … Her movements were marked by
> a girlish grace, and her voice … sounded so sweet and true,
> that her success was beyond question.[40]

Interspersed between Carl Rosa cities, Saville was able to appear regularly in ballad concerts at St James's Hall in London, together with a range of colleagues, including her key supporter in Australia, Sir Charles Santley, and she was able also to gain a leave of absence from the company in order to make her debut at Monte Carlo.

The Opéra de Monte-Carlo was designed by Charles Garnier, architect of the Palais Garnier, home of the Opéra in Paris. It had opened in 1879, seating just 524. In effect, it is part of the Monte Carlo Casino, and from modest beginnings climbed swiftly to become one of the leading houses in Europe. Melba had made her house debut there as Juliette in 1890, but Melba's most famous performing relationship – with Enrico Caruso – started at that house later, in 1902. Saville made her first appearance there on 20 January 1894 in a part which was new to her – Desdemona in Verdi's *Otello* – and she had the great good fortune to sing the role with Verdi's original Otello from 1887, the legendary tenor Francesco Tamagno. Of her Desdemona, the *American Register* wrote:

> Her voice is a most perfectly trained soprano, and it would
> certainly be difficult to find an artist to sing the role of
> Desdemona more effectively or more sweetly, while she acted
> most naturally and gracefully. She is in every sense of the
> expression an artist.[41]

At Monte Carlo she followed *Otello* with Santuzza in *Cavalleria rusticana*, a role she had previously sung at St Petersburg and with the Carl Rosa.[42]

Teatr Wielki, Warsaw

Saville's series of concerts with the Hallés in Melbourne in August 1890 paid off for her with an invitation organised by Sir Charles Hallé to perform in a concert at Buckingham Palace for Queen Victoria on 9 July 1894. Saville sang the duet 'Lontano, lontano' from Boito's *Mefistofele* with French tenor Albert Alvarez, and the aria 'Ernani involami' from Verdi's *Ernani*. Saville was by far the youngest of the soloists at the concert, the others being Emma Albani, Sophia Scalchi, Pol Plançon and Mario Ancona. This was substantially the starriest group Saville had been associated with thus far in her career. Then, in September and October, she sang nineteen guest performances at the Teatr Wielki (the Grand Theatre) in Warsaw, including her first appearance as Ophélie in Ambroise Thomas's *Hamlet*.[43]

6

By the middle of 1894, Frances Saville had toured extensively with the Carl Rosa around Britain, and had built a growing international reputation in Europe with her seasons at St Petersburg, Moscow, Berlin, Monte Carlo and Warsaw. What she needed now was operatic success in Paris, New York and London, all of them cities in which Nellie Melba had already established herself.

First came Paris and the Opéra-Comique, where she was to make her debut as Virginie in Victor Massé's *Paul et Virginie* (with Julien Leprestre and Edmond Clément alternating as Paul). Born in 1822, Massé had studied at the Conservatoire in Paris with Halévy and was winner of the Prix de Rome in 1844. Although expected to have a career in 'serious' music, he is most known now for his opéra-comique *Les noces de Jeannette*. Set in Mauritius in the late eighteenth century, his comic opera *Paul et Virginie* had been a great success at the Opéra-Comique in 1876, but had had to wait eighteen years – until 18 December 1894 – for a revival, partly, according to *Le Ménestrel*, because of the lack of suitable Virginies,[44] a role demanding 'an artist who combines with the perfection of technique the qualities of first-rate acting and a charming presence'. The *Morning Post* reported approval of Saville in Paris:

> Madame Frances Saville ... fulfils the varied requirements
> of her part in a very remarkable degree. She has an admirable
> mezzo-soprano [sic] voice, which has been cultivated to the
> very highest pitch of modern technique. She has all the gifts
> of youth and presence to create a Virginie who would have
> flattered the dreams of Bernardin de St Pierre [the novelist]
> himself. Her success last night was immediate and indeed
> triumphant.[45]

However, despite the acclaim for her Virginie, which she gave twenty-nine times, the only other role that she was given at the Opéra-Comique was a solitary performance of Violetta in *La traviata*. So, in March 1895 she returned to Moscow, making eleven guest appearances, among these Micaëla in *Carmen* – a role new to her.

7

If Paris had not embraced her as fully as she might have wished, maybe New York would do so. Always on the lookout for new talent, Maurice Grau from the Metropolitan Opera saw and heard Frances Saville sing at Monte Carlo. He was one of the threesome of agent-impresarios – Abbey-Schoeffel-Grau – who ran the Met at that time, and they needed someone to replace Nellie Melba for the first half of the 1895–96 season.[46] Grau was noted for hiring only the best and that season had an astonishing array of very expensive talent, including, among the women, Emma Calvé, Lillian Nordica, Sofia Scalchi, Lola Beeth and Melba, and among the men, Mario Ancona, Pol Plançon, Jean and Édouard de Reszke, Australian basso Lemprière Pringle and Victor Maurel, of whom more is to be heard, especially in relation to Frances.

The opening for Saville at the Met was at the first night of the new season. On 18 November 1895 she was Juliette to the legendary tenor Jean de Reszke's Roméo, with Jean's brother Édouard as Frère Laurent and Pol Plançon as Capulet. Two days later, she was Micaëla to the equally legendary Emma Calvé's Carmen, with Victor Maurel as Escamillo. Was this where his relationship with Frances started? Another three days passed and Saville was Violetta in *La traviata* with Giuseppe Russitano as Alfredo and Mario Ancona as Germont, and on 24 November there was the First Grand Sunday Night Concert of the season, shared with Plançon and others, at which Frances sang 'Elisabeth's Prayer' from *Tannhäuser* and Tosti's 'Goodbye'. Altogether, this was a triumphant week in her life, performing as she had for the first time at the Met in a variety of roles with a galaxy of world stars. She was clearly very nervous at the start, gradually gaining in confidence as Juliette, as described by the *New York Herald*:

> Her first florid passage, delivered in fresh crystalline tones, with a certain facility, but with rather uncertain intonation, brought her a storm of applause … At the conclusion of the waltz the audience rose at the prima donna, and she had to repeat it … Her voice captivates the listener instantly, for it is a young voice, a fresh voice, and is a voice that has a certain carrying quality. In the garden scene she showed considerable skill as an actress.[47]

The following week she was Marguérite in *Faust* with Albert Lubert as Faust and Plançon as Méphistophélès, followed by the soprano soloist role in Handel's *Messiah* – a first for that oratorio at the Met. At that time, large-scale performances of *Messiah* with massive choruses and big-voiced soloists were the norm, and the reviewer in the *Tribune* thought Saville's voice 'seemed light for the task'.[48] The final production with Frances at the Met itself (before going on tour) was an opera new to her, *Falstaff*, which had been premièred at La Scala, Milan, in February 1893 with baritone Victor Maurel, Verdi's original Sir John Falstaff. Maurel sang with Saville's Mistress Ford throughout the Met run. Saville then sang on 12 January 1896 at the Eighth Sunday Night Concert, and the *Herald* praised her performances:

> Mme Saville sang with brilliant execution 'Ernani involami' and, on recall, 'I dreamt I dwelt in marble halls' from *The Bohemian Girl*. Both were given in charming manner.[49]

Perhaps the latter brought back memories of her mother in the role. However, it was Victor Maurel who had the 'triumph' at that concert.

Next in January, Frances went on tour with the Met company, firstly to the Brooklyn Academy of Music in *Faust*, then on to Boston, Baltimore, Washington DC, Philadelphia, Buffalo, Detroit, Chicago and St Louis before returning to New York. On tour she sang her previous roles at the Met and, as Micaëla in Buffalo, she was 'the pure and gentle maiden to perfection'.[50] The *Chicago Journal* wrote: 'Mme Frances Saville as the sweet, lovable Violetta in *La Traviata* is worth going far to see … Madame Saville is all we have anticipated.'[51]

Victor Maurel

She sang winsome Mistress Ford to Victor Maurel's libidinous Sir John in six different cities, and, with the aid of hindsight, the close proximity of touring would have given every opportunity for a close relationship between the two of them to flourish. Returned to New York in mid-April, they performed together again, this time in *Don Giovanni* with Maurel the licentious Don lusting after Saville's peasant girl Zerlina. *The Recorder* in New York reported: 'Mme Saville was coquettish and sprightly as Zerlina ... She was in excellent voice and sang capitally ... flowers galore, especially for Saville.'[52]

The Met season ended on 24 April with a Testimonial Performance mounted for two of the three impresarios, Henry Abbey and Maurice Grau. Saville sang Micaëla in Act 3 of *Carmen* (with Calvé), Alice Ford in Act 2 of *Falstaff* (with Maurel) and participated in a starry line-up for the 'Soldiers' Chorus' from *Faust* – the only time that Saville and Melba were on stage together – before the now-returned Melba sang the 'Mad Scene' from *Lucia di Lammermoor*. The following day Victor Maurel and Frances Saville sailed away together on the *Gascogne* to France.

Saville's season with the Metropolitan Opera Company – she sang forty-two times with them between November 1895 and April 1896 – points up an ironic reversal of values between the 1890s and the twenty-first century. In the nineties, prima donnas came in all shapes, sizes and degrees of pulchritude, and Frances's good looks were constantly commented upon, whereas now women have to go on diets to get on to opera house stages, but their looks there are rarely commented upon in reviews. So, while 'Jean de Reszke is fatter than he was last season – he must have gained at least twenty pounds in weight', Frances Saville 'is an exceptionally beautiful woman, who can act as well as sing'.[53] Even in her history of the Met on tour, Quaintance Eaton took this line:

> The comely soprano ... left a lasting impression in several
> cities as Marguérite, Mistress Ford and Micaëla. Her

triumph in *Traviata* was complete, according to Chicago's
critics. One called her 'petite, graceful, with features as
clear-cut as a cameo'.[54]

At some point during Saville's 1897–98 season at the Met, she
made her first recordings in the form of cylinders for Gianni Bettini. A
pioneering audio recorder of leading singers, Bettini was born in Italy
in 1860 and opened a studio near Central Park South in New York in
the 1890s. He persuaded many celebrities to make recordings, including
Mark Twain, President Harrison and a range of singers, including Jean
de Reszke and Nellie Melba (neither of whose cylinders have survived)
and Frances Saville (at least one of whose has, 'Caro nome' from
Rigoletto).

While she was in America, the subject of many celebrity interviews,
Frances did some careful repositioning of her nationality, backing
several horses simultaneously: 'I am only half-French', she told them,
'I am an American really. I was born in California, although I passed
many years of my life in Australia. It was there I learned to love outdoor
sports. I shoot, I swim, I hunt and ride a bicycle.'[55] One consequence
was that American journalists started vigorously to promote Saville as
the next Great American Diva. An article in the *Los Angeles Times*,
headed 'San Francisco girl, a favourite in New York,' went on:

> It is a pleasure to record the great success which [a] San
> Francisco girl has scored. I speak of Frances Saville, the new
> prima donna. She resembles Emma Eames absurdly and … she
> can give both Eames and Melba many points as an actress …
> She is a singer of whom any country might be proud.[56]

News broke publicly about the romantic relationship between
Frances Saville and Victor Maurel in October 1896. They had gone
together to perform in St Petersburg. However, the affair had been
apparent to all at the Met by the end of the New York season, and:

> The husband of Mme Saville, who is a very stout man with a
> very small head, announced at the last performance given at
> the Opera House that he proposed to challenge Maurel as soon
> as he reached Paris …

However, that duel does not seem to have taken place. Perhaps Max Rown thought better of fighting with Maurel, who was 'expert with the sword and boxing gloves, and a good shot as well', according to the *New York Sun*.[57] Although the affair with Maurel fizzled out, Frances's marriage with Max was effectively over, and in mid-October it was reported that she was seeking a divorce from him in Paris.[58] It is perhaps not so surprising that Saville is not mentioned in Maurel's book, *Dix Ans de Carrière*, which was published the following year. In September, singing at St Petersburg, she may have received the shock news that her mother, Fanny Simonsen, had died suddenly in Melbourne at sixty-one.[59]

After St Petersburg in January, Saville returned to sing at the Teatr Wielki in Warsaw, where she was again much admired as Marguérite, Desdemona and Ophélie, then to the Opéra-Comique in Paris for five more performances of *La traviata*, before going on to Nice in the south of France, where she gave opera and concert performances in February–March 1897 ('delicious' and 'accomplished' as Violetta and 'sympathetic' as Marguérite).[60] She enjoyed it so much, she purchased land at Roquebrune, Cap Martin (between Monaco and Menton). There, some years later, she built the Villa Miramar, which was to become a favourite home when she retired.

8

After Paris and New York … Covent Garden in London. It was unfortunate that Frances was always following Melba's star, a strategy

Royal Opera House, Covent Garden

that in due course she would need to abandon in order to find her own place in the pantheon. However, quite fortuitously for Saville, in addition to the Met, Maurice Grau had also taken over the management of Covent Garden following the death of Sir Augustus Harris in 1896.[61]

As previously at the Met, Covent Garden in the summer of 1897 was to be another star-propelled season, with Emma Eames, Zélie de Lussan, Ernestine Schumann-Heink, Frances Saville and the inevitable Melba among the women, and Jean and Édouard de Reszke, Ernest van Dyck, Marcel Journet, Lemprière Pringle and Pol Plançon among the men. In the season Saville was scheduled to sing in seven operas – Juliette in *Roméo et Juliette*, the title role in Massenet's *Manon*, Violetta in *La traviata*, Marguérite de Valois in *Les Huguenots*, Micaëla in *Carmen*, the title role in the première of Baron Frédéric d'Erlanger's *Inez Mendo* (now sunk without trace) and the Woodbird in Wagner's *Siegfried*.

LONDON
MUSICAL COURIER
A WEEKLY JOURNAL DEVOTED TO MUSIC & MUSICAL INDUSTRIES.

Price 3d. (by Post 3½d.) Annual Subscription, 10s. 6d.
„   4d. Foreign and Colonial.   „   „   15s.

VOL. III.] [Registered as a Newspaper] LONDON, JUNE 24, 1897. [Transmission Abroad, at Book Rates.] [NO. 25

Photo. by Lafayette, Dublin.

MME. FRANCES SAVILLE.

She made her debut at Covent Garden on 11 May 1897 as Juliette. Was this a wise move, given that she was sharing the part that season with the two most famous lyric sopranos in the world, Nellie Melba and Emma Eames (both Marchesi pupils, as was Saville)? Nevertheless, *The Globe* was generally impressed:

> Her voice is light in quality, and a little wanting in power, but she is such a finished singer that she understands thoroughly how to make the most of her resources … She was at first excessively nervous, but her singing steadily improved in the course of the opera, and she won a very decided and genuine success. A graceful presence and careful and conscientious acting helped to complete the impression created by her excellent singing, and her whole performance is entitled to high praise.[62]

Saville's Manon followed, and, reviewing a later performance in the run, *The Stage* noted:

> Madame Saville, who looked very well in her pompadour dresses, brings out admirably the beguiling and fascinating traits in the character of Manon, and also acts with considerable fervour and pathos, as occasion requires. She uses her bright voice with ease and flexibility in Massenet's essentially French music.[63]

Of her Violetta the *St James's Gazette* wrote:

> The favourite character found last night a charming representative in Madame Frances Saville, who, besides singing the music [to] perfection, presented what one rarely

Left: Saville as Juliette, Covent Garden 1897

meets with on the operatic stage – a consistent impersonation.
From beginning to end Madame Saville is always in the part.[64]

Saville's singing of the Woodbird in *Siegfried* at Covent Garden,
her first venture into Wagner's *Ring* cycle, came along with some
interpersonal conflict. It seems that she felt strongly that, by this stage
of her career, she should be offered a more important Wagnerian
role, and she told the management accordingly that they should have
a suitable substitute ready. The conductor, Anton Seidl, was outraged
and initially refused to rehearse with Frances.[65] In the event, 'the
clear, silvery tones of Madame Frances Saville are well suited to the
trilling "off" of the communicative Waldvogel', said *The Stage*.[66] It was
altogether a starry cast in *Siegfried*, with Jean de Reszke in the title role,
his brother Édouard as the Wanderer, Susan Strong as Brünnhilde and
David Bispham as Alberich. It appears that Saville withdrew from her
scheduled appearance as the Queen in *Les Huguenots* on 3 June.

During the previous year, her teacher Mathilde Marchesi had
published her memoirs, *Marchesi and Music*, in which she wrote of
Saville:

> She comes of a musical family of Australia … Frances showed
> early in life a taste for music and drawing [and] she was sent
> to pursue her studies in Germany. On her return home,
> her mother, noticing her very fine voice, gave her lessons
> and brought her out in concerts, where she was greatly
> applauded.[67]

Clearly, by the middle of 1897 Frances had made a successful entry
at the Opéra-Comique in Paris, the Metropolitan Opera in New York
and Covent Garden in London, but not with a result that had really set
the world alight. She now needed a new path, one that would be her
own, no longer following in the footsteps of Nellie Melba. But where
would that path take her?

Notes

1   *Clarence and Richmond Examiner*, 2 January 1886, 3
2   Kerry Murphy, 'Henri Kowalski (1841–1916): A French Musician in Colonial Australia', 350
3   *Sydney Mail*, 31 October 1885, 950
4   *Verçingétorix* was first performed in Sydney on 1 April 1881 during Kowalski's earlier trip to Australia; the title character was a Gaul, later to become a French national hero
5   *Sydney Morning Herald*, 25 August 1887, 11; *Evening News* (Sydney), 26 August 1887, 6
6   *Daily Telegraph* (Sydney), 30 July 1889, 3; *Sydney Morning Herald*, 4 January 1890, 6; Bessie Doyle went on to study with Hans Sitt in Leipzig, followed by Ysaÿe in Brussels (1895–97), then with Ševčík in Prague (1904–05)
7   Elisabeth was a role Saville was first to sing with the Carl Rosa company in Manchester in April 1894
8   Knighted in 1907
9   Gounod was so impressed with Santley that in 1864, for a production of Faust in English in London, he wrote for him an additional aria: 'Even bravest hearts may swell' (with words by Henry Chorley) which was a big success. It was later translated into French as 'Avant de quitter ces lieux' and has become a standard part of the opera
10 *Daily Telegraph*, 22 October 1889, 6
11 *Blackburn Standard* (England), 5 October 1889, 2; *Table Talk* (Melbourne), 2 January 1891, 4
12 *Argus* (Melbourne), 1 August 1890, 6
13 *Table Talk*, 26 December 1890, 12
14 *Australasian* (Melbourne), 24 January 1891, 22
15 *Sydney Morning Herald*, 23 March 1891, 9
16 *Sydney Morning Herald*, 28 March 1891, 8
17 *Table Talk*, 8 February 1889, 15
18 *Evening News* (Sydney), 20 April 1891, 4
19 *Table Talk*, 16 January 1891, 14
20 *Pall Mall Gazette* (England), 3 July 1891, 6
21 *Daily Telegraph* (Sydney), 18 July 1891; *Ballarat Star*, 18 July 1891, 4; *Maitland Mercury*, 21 July 1891, 2; *Wagga Wagga Advertiser*, 25 July 1891, 2; *Australian Town and Country Journal*, 1 August 1891, 19
22 Marchesi's life is dealt with in detail in Roger Neill, *Divas: Mathilde Marchesi and her Pupils*, 2016
23 *Broadway Magazine* (New York), May 1899, 506, quoted in Simpson, 'Francis Saville', 4
24 *Mathilde Marchesi, Marchesi and Music*, 281
25 *Le Ménestrel* (Paris), 20 March 1892 and 5 June 1892
26 *Boston Daily Globe*, 27 October 1895, 14
27 Mathilde Marchesi, *Marchesi and Music*, 283
28 *Le Ménestrel*, 8 September 1892, quoted in Simpson, 'Francis Saville', 8
29 *Lorgnette* (Melbourne), 6 April 1893, 2
30 *Evening News*, 7 October 1893, 1
31 Review in Saville files at Museum of Performance + Design, San Francisco (MPDSF), *Standard*, 24 June 1893
32 *Le Ménestrel*, 8 September 1892
33 Review in Saville files at MPDSF, unidentified source and date, 1893
34 *Maitland Mercury* (NSW), 14 November 1893, 7
35 *Morning Post* (London), 17 November 1893, 5
36 *Glasgow Evening Post*, 17 November 1893, 3
37 Adrienne Simpson, 'Frances Saville: Australia's Forgotten Prima-Donna', 9

38 See Neill, *Divas*, 99–100
39 *Manchester Courier*, 17 April 1894, 5
40 *Birmingham Daily Post*, 30 May 1894, 8
41 Review in Saville files at MPDSF, *American Register* (Paris), January 1894
42 TJ Walsh, *Monte Carlo Opera 1879–1909*, 76–77
43 Opened in 1833, the Teatr Wielki was/is one of the largest major opera houses, seating over 2000; singing there was an important part of Saville's career, as it was later for her niece, Frances Alda
44 *Le Ménestrel*, 23 December 1894, 403
45 *Morning Post*, 20 December 1894, 5
46 *Daily Times* (Davenport, Iowa), 12 October 1895, 7; from late September through end December 1895, Melba's Operatic Concert Company gave fifty concerts around the USA and Canada
47 *New York Herald* quoted in *San Francisco Call*, 28 November 1865, 6
48 *New York Tribune*, 23 December 1895
49 *New York Herald*, 13 January 1896
50 *Buffalo Commercial*, 18 March 1896, 8
51 Review in Saville files at MPDSF, *Chicago Journal*, 27 March 1896
52 Review in Saville files at MPDSF, *The Recorder* (New York), 17 April 1896
53 *San Francisco Call*, 1 December 1895, 26; *Sunday Leader* (Pennsylvania), 8 March 1896, 14
54 Quaintance Eaton, *Opera Caravan*, 59
55 *Fort Wayne Journal-Gazette* (Indiana), 12 January 1896, 7
56 *Los Angeles Times*, 1 December 1895, 16
57 *New York Sun*, 14 October 1896, 7
58 *Free Lance* (Melbourne), 17 October 1896, 5
59 The death of Fanny Simonsen is covered in Chapter 7
60 *Le monde élégant* (Nice), 14 March 1897; *Le petit nicois*, 13 March 1897; *La colonie étrangère*, March 1897
61 *Record-Union* (Sacramento), 6 December 1896, 5
62 *Globe*, 12 May 1897, 3
63 *Stage*, 1 July 1897, 12
64 *St James's Gazette*, 5 June 1897, 5
65 *Times* (Philadelphia), 4 July 1897, 9
66 *Stage*, 24 June 1897, 10
67 Marchesi, 282

Chapter 6
Saville and Mahler

1

Having diplomatically converted from Judaism to Roman Catholicism, in May 1897 Gustav Mahler was appointed firstly as Conductor at the Imperial and Royal Court Opera in Vienna, then five months later as Director.

When Mahler came to Vienna in 1897, many radical developments were occurring in the city – social, scientific, political and artistic: the revolutionary Viennese version of art nouveau, the Secession, was launched by Gustav Klimt and others; Sigmund Freud began his self-analysis; Arthur Schnitzler wrote *Reigen* (otherwise known as *La Ronde*), a play scrutinising sexual morals and class ideology; the giant Ferris wheel in the Prater, the Riesenrad, was opened; Mahler's friend Hugo Wolf composed his last three songs before becoming incurably insane – to verses of Michelangelo; the election of anti-Semitic demagogue

Karl Lueger as mayor of Vienna was finally ratified by Emperor Franz Joseph.[1]

This was a city steeped in musical culture – Gluck, Haydn, Mozart, Beethoven, Schubert, Brahms, Liszt and the Strauss family, all had lived there – and the performing arts and artists were central to life in the city. 'The first glance of the average Viennese into his morning paper was not at the events in parliament, or world affairs, but at the repertoire of the theatre,' wrote Stefan Zweig, adding that, on the streets, 'a court actor or an opera singer was recognised by every salesman and every cabdriver'.[2]

That October, thirty-two-years-old Frances Saville also made her debut in the city – as Mimì in Puccini's *La bohème* at the Theater an der Wien. It was the first performance of that opera in Austria.[3] Saville's only previous experience with verismo style had been in Mascagni's *Cavalleria rusticana* in 1893 – at St Petersburg and with the Carl Rosa company in Britain. The Viennese critics were unanimous in their praise of the new soprano. Eduard Hanslick, influential critic of the *Neue Freie Presse*, who was famously dismissive of the new work, wrote:

> An extremely attractive discovery was the singer Madame
> Frances Saville, who played the part of Mimì with a pleasant,
> excellently trained voice, heartfelt sentiment and great talent
> for acting.[4]

Richard Wallaschek of *Die Zeit* agreed:

> Madame Saville is a first-rate artist. Possessing a lovely voice
> of perfect training, pure intonation and without distracting
> vocal affectations, this artist is able to act so nobly and truly
> that her performance affords great artistic pleasure from
> beginning to end.[5]

Frances Saville

Postcard from Puccini to Saville, 1897

Hans Buchstein in the *Deutsches Volksblatt* concurred:

> As singer and actress alike, she is an extraordinary artist, in
> possession of marvellous vocal resources that she employs in
> an admirable way throughout the entire evening.[6]

And Albert Kauders in the *Neues Wiener Journal* was equally excited:

> Among the cast Madame Saville, the singer of Mimì, stands
> out; her singing is artistic, inspired, full of true expression
> and ample enough for dramatic effect ... That she lends a
> bold, starkly veristic stroke to her death scene follows as a
> matter of course.[7]

Having fulfilled her obligations at the Theater an der Wien, Frances's intention was to go again for a further season in Russia.[8] The day she first sang *Bohème*, 5 October 1897, was just three days before Mahler was appointed director of the Court Opera. Frances was contracted to sing Mimì fifteen times and Mahler heard her at one of these and wasted no time in signing her up for the Court Opera, along with her Rodolfo in that production, the Slovenian-born tenor Franz Naval. In fact, according to documents in the Court Opera's archives, even before her debut in *Bohème*, Mahler had been in negotiations with Saville through her agent in the city, Ludwig Grünfeld. Initially she was given three performances at the Court Opera as a guest artist, and, if these were successful, she would be offered a two-year contract.

2

In today's world, the symphonies and song cycles of Gustav Mahler make him a dominant figure in the world of classical music, and it tends to be forgotten that this was not always so. In fact, before the great revival of his music that began in the 1960s (led by Leonard Bernstein, Bernard Haitink and Rafael Kubelik), he was something of a marginal figure, his work kept alive primarily by conductors who had known him personally and worked with him (mainly Bruno Walter, Oskar Fried, Willem Mengelberg and Otto Klemperer). Yet, popular and widespread as his work has now become, most music lovers remain unaware that, in his own lifetime, Mahler was most celebrated not as a composer, but as a conductor, particularly at the Court Opera in Vienna, influencing decisively how opera should be produced, designed, acted, played and sung. His symphonies and songs were mostly composed at weekends and on vacation. In short, he was in his own lifetime a professional opera conductor and a leisure-time composer.

Mahler was born in 1860 into a Jewish family on the borders of Moravia and Bohemia (then part of the Austro-Hungarian empire, now the Czech Republic), where as a child he experienced street music – songs, dances, marches and so on – and learned to play the piano. As a teenager, he studied at the Conservatoire in Vienna, where he won prizes for his piano-playing and wrote his first compositions. He was percussionist in the Conservatoire's student orchestra.

In 1880, he took his first conducting job, in the small opera theatre at Bad Hall south of Linz, where the repertoire was mainly operetta. The following year he conducted his first opera, Verdi's *Il trovatore*, at the Royal Municipal Theatre at Olmütz, where he went on to conduct nine more operas. Next, he became musical director at the opera house at Kassel in Germany, then in 1885 director of the Deutsches Landestheater in Prague. It was there that he first conducted the operas of Mozart and Wagner. The succeeding year he took up a contract at the Neues Stadttheater in Leipzig, where he became involved in a feud with his senior colleague, Arthur Nikisch, and by 1888 he was back in Prague. He was next hired by the Royal Hungarian Opera in Budapest, where he conducted *Das Rheingold* and *Die Walküre* for the first time. At each of these many posts, Mahler fell out with the singers, the musicians, with other conductors or with the management – sometimes with all of them.

In 1890 Mahler visited Italy, where he engaged with the newly emerging verismo movement in the form of Mascagni's *Cavalleria rusticana*. Political machinations in Budapest led to Mahler moving on yet again in 1891, this time to the State Theatre in Hamburg, where he was chief conductor. There for the first time Mahler could give rein to his emerging artistic vision, particularly with Wagner, in his initial season conducting and directing *Tannhäuser*, *Siegfried* and a celebrated production of *Tristan und Isolde*, together with the German première of Tchaikovsky's *Eugene Onegin* with the composer present. In Hamburg he started an intense relationship with his leading prima donna, Anna von Mildenburg. Mahler's dictatorial style again caused wide resentment, but in 1892, he took the Hamburg company to perform at a German opera festival in London (at Covent Garden and the Theatre Royal Drury Lane), which included a pioneering *Ring* cycle there.

Even before his promotion to the directorship of the Court Opera, Mahler had created a stir in Vienna with his conducting in May of *Lohengrin* and *Die Zauberflöte*, and in August he gave Vienna's first complete, uncut *Ring* cycle, which stimulated his friend Hugo Wolf to declare that it was 'the first time that I have heard the *Ring* as I have always dreamed of hearing it'.[9] Smetana's nationalist Czech opera, *Dalibor*, which opened on 4 October, was Mahler's first production since becoming director of the Court Opera – producing as well as conducting. It was a controversial choice, given the rising tide of nationalist feeling within the Austro-Hungarian Empire.

Mahler's innovations over his decade at the Court Opera were comprehensive, both in scale and in detail, adding up to an artistic

Right: Gustav Mahler by Emil Orlik

dem lieben freunde, Dr. Th. PollaK
zur Erinnerung an das Original
Gustav Mahler

revolution: Mahler created a true ensemble company – singers, orchestra, conductors, designers – conducting in total 648 performances himself (of sixty-three different operas), a quarter of which were of Wagner. A distinctive, authentic Viennese style for the performance of Wagner and other composers emerged. (Incidentally, the work he chose to conduct more than any other at the Court Opera was Johann Strauss's *Die Fledermaus* – eighty-nine times.)

Wagner was second only to Beethoven in Mahler's eyes. 'When Wagner has spoken, one can only keep silent,' he remarked. In a poem written in 1886 for the third anniversary of Wagner's death, Mahler wrote: 'The world's decay you stripped away, / Creating a new world of melody.'

Mahler's artistic vision for the Court Opera was clear: each production should become a total unity of music, acting and staging in the Wagnerian sense; each production should be at the level of the finest festival performances at Bayreuth or Salzburg; the claque was banned; latecomers were denied entry; and singers were forbidden 'traditional' embellishments and interpolated high notes.[10] Operas by Wagner and others had often been cut severely in Vienna before Mahler. 'Tradition is slovenliness' was his credo.

Singers who were chosen to become members of the Court Opera ensemble were contracted. There were few visits by external celebrities, one exception to this rule being for Lilli Lehmann, who had sung in Wagner's original Bayreuth *Ring*, and who joined the company each year to give what Mahler described as her 'annual singing lesson'.

Whilst Mahler, like Wagner before him, placed acting ability before singing, nevertheless he did not insist on the vibratoless extremes of Cosima Wagner's Bayreuth. Indeed, the evidence suggests that he encouraged both *vibrato* and *portamento*, though less of the former than in subsequent generations. Mahler's approach to singing was faithfully recorded by his close musician friend, Natalie Bauer-Lechner (who wrote down nearly everything she heard him say):

In singing, everything depends on diction. Interpretation,
even from the musical point of view, ought always to be built
on the words. No matter how beautifully a phrase is sung, if
the singer fails to bring out the full meaning of the words, it
will not produce the desired effect, even though the audience
might not always recognise the cause of its disappointment ...
The ideal song must be based on the words; the sound virtually
makes itself, if you speak the words with their full meaning
and sharply accented... The most important thing in a singer
is his 'r'; if he can get that right, strange as it may seem, he
can't be entirely bad.

Mahler summarised all this as 'building on the sound of the words'. In
order to approach Wagner's ideal orchestral sound, Mahler had the pit
lowered at the Court Opera, as it is at Bayreuth. His musicians had to
learn to play as delicately as in chamber music.

Mahler moved the conductor's podium from where it was
traditionally in Vienna, in the centre of the orchestra, to the front,
facing both the whole orchestra and the stage. The lights were now
dimmed in the auditorium during performance. The rehearsal system
was completely overhauled. And Mahler weeded out older singers
who did not meet his new demands, bringing in new ones who would.
Frances Saville was an early one of these incomers.

3

Saville made her debut at the Court Opera (as a guest artist) on 21
November 1897, as Gounod's Juliette, the role with which she had
made three previous debuts – at the Monnaie in Brussels in 1892, at the
Metropolitan Opera in New York in 1895 and at Covent Garden in 1897.
She sang it again three days later, and on 7 December was Violetta in

Court Opera, Vienna, 1898

La traviata. At this stage Mahler seems to have been well satisfied with her, because on 8 December Frances was made a contracted member of the Court Opera company.

She was to be a principal soprano paid 16,000 florins per annum – this was 4000 florins more than Mahler himself was paid – for a maximum eight performances a month, with additional fees for any extra performances, and she had an entitlement of a month of paid leave at Easter and three months in the summer. During leave periods, she could undertake engagements elsewhere. The contract named seven roles which she was expected to perform: in the event, of these seven (at the Court Opera) she did sing Elsa, Marguérite, Violetta, Manon, Ophélie, Nedda and Mathilde in Rossini's *Guillaume Tell*; but Elisabeth and Desdemona she sang elsewhere, never in Vienna.

Altogether it was a fine deal, with many attractive features from Saville's point of view: this was an opera company and house with the highest reputation; she liked the city and spoke fluent German, the language learned initially as a small child with her grandmother in Altona; although Mahler had a reputation for autocracy, he was clearly the coming man, maybe even a genius; she would be part of a real ensemble company, something she had not fully experienced since leaving Australia; and there would be no touring. All was set fair for her, one would have thought.

But in the last three months of 1897, Saville gave just five performances at the Court Opera – two in *Roméo et Juliette*, two in *La traviata* and one as Nedda in *Der Bajazzo* (the Viennese name for Leoncavallo's *Pagliacci*).[11] And she was in conflict with Mahler. It should be said at the outset that Mahler already had a substantial track record for damaging clashes with his singers. For him it was a way of life, a way of asserting his authority. Nevertheless, in his dealings with Frances Saville, there was certainly an extra dimension, and it may be useful to explore the sources of this.

At that time, the social and cultural differences between Austria and Australia were very great. While Austria remained fundamentally a hierarchical, autocratic society, Australia was already relatively democratic with a flatter distribution of power and far more widespread questioning of authority. Similarly, while Austrian authority rested fundamentally with men, with women expected to be followers, not leaders, Australian women could be far more independent, self-reliant and assertive. In Vienna of the late 1890s, Frances Saville was a strong Australian-raised woman in a world dominated by men. Altogether, Mahler may well have felt threatened by her assertiveness, a situation hard for him to deal with or even to come to terms with.

Then, she was unusual in Mahler's company in having come from an intensely musical background with extensive practical experience. Ever since she was twenty years old, she had made her own decisions – where she sang, what she sang, how she sang. All the other members of the Court Opera company had grown up in the Austro-German ensemble system, whereby singers were on contract and expected to follow instructions.

The first problem that we know of between them emerged during the preparations for Leoncavallo's *La bohème* in February 1898, less than three months after Saville's debut. Performing it was a commitment that Mahler had inherited from his predecessor, Wilhelm Jahn. He had already seen the work, having taken a trip to Venice to attend the world première at the Teatro La Fenice on 6 May, taking the opportunity to see Puccini's *Bohème* at the San Benedetto Theatre the following night. Mahler was in no doubt as to which of the two works was superior, writing to Jahn that in his opinion the Puccini was finer by far. And to the Viennese critic, Richard Heuberger, three weeks later, Mahler wrote:

> Leoncavallo's music and his opera are like their creator, hollow, pretentious bombastic and generally tending towards vulgarity. The orchestration is superficial, noisy, and to me literally repulsive. One bar of Puccini is worth more than the whole of Leoncavallo.[12]

By February 1898, at Mahler's invitation Leoncavallo was in Vienna and attending rehearsals, which is where the problems really started. First, the Marcello, tenor Ernest van Dyck, decided that he did not want to sing the role, invoking a get-out clause in his contract. Leoncavallo was beside himself about this. Then the composer criticised the two principals he had seen rehearsing on 17 February, prompting Mahler to respond that 'Frau Saville and Herr Felix [Mimì and Rodolfo] were in fact uncertain of their roles. You know, however, that neither of them is to sing on the evening of the première.' It is clear from the fact that Saville went to Paris to learn the role with her teacher, Madame Marchesi, that she was taking the whole thing very seriously.[13]

However, learning that she was to be in the second cast, not the first, was a bombshell for Saville – not at all a situation that she had signed up for as a leading soloist. She wrote Mahler a letter (which he received on 20 February) in which she announced that, if she had not attended rehearsal that day, it was because she had decided not to sing her role, having heard that Berta Förster-Lauterer was to sing it at the première. She added that she 'felt entitled to the assumption that I would create the part, that is, sing it at the première'.[14] And the following day, Frances informed the Viennese press that she would not agree to a contract extension at the Court Opera, and would be leaving soon.

Mahler did not relent, yet Saville stayed. But he cannot have been used to such treatment from his singers. In the event, the Leoncavallo *Bohème* was well received, but public interest waned, and it was withdrawn after six performances, all without Saville's participation.[15]

4

By February 1898, Frances had moved her furniture and all the rest of her possessions from her flat in Paris to Vienna. Her son Frank was settled at a boarding school in Paris and her brother Willie was continuing his vocal studies in that city.[16]

At the Court Opera in 1898, Saville sang Violetta in *La traviata* (twice), Nedda in *Bajazzo/Pagliacci* (five times), Marguérite in *Faust* (five times), Ophélie in *Hamlet* (once), Juliette (twice) and a minor role in *Die Fledermaus* (once). A total of sixteen appearances over a twelve-month period was not at all what she would have expected, but clearly the row with Mahler had had negative consequences in terms of the frequency with which she was being deployed.

As a consequence, seeking good paying work elsewhere, Frances took leave-of-absence and returned to Covent Garden, where she opened on 9 June 1898 as Elisabeth in *Tannhäuser*, with her colleague from Vienna, Ernest van Dyck, in the title role.[17] Later in the season, she took for the first time the challenging role of Gutrune in Wagner's *Götterdämmerung*, with Lillian Nordica and Milka Ternina alternating as Brünnhilde, and Andreas Dippel (another colleague from Vienna) and Jean de Reszke alternating as Siegfried. The *Evening Standard* decided that Saville's Gutrune at her first performance in the role (11 June) was 'seductive', but, as usual, most reviews focused on Brünnhilde, Siegfried and Hagen (sung by Jean de Reszke's brother Éduard).[18]

Among the prima donnas at Covent Garden that summer were three other Marchesi pupils – Suzanne Adams, Emma Calvé and Nellie Melba – but Melba appeared rarely before departing in August for Lucca in order to study the role of Mimì with Puccini. Saville's Wagnerian summer in London was interrupted by a benefit at Her Majesty's Theatre (together with most of the Covent Garden company from that season) in aid of retired Hungarian prima donna Louise Liebhardt, who had fallen on hard times.[19]

While Saville was in London that summer, Mahler had an operation for haemorrhoids, convalesced at Vahrn in South Tyrol, where he composed two of his *Wunderhorn Songs* – 'Lied des Verfolgten im Turn' ('Song for the Persecuted Prisoner in the Tower') and 'Wo die schönen Trompeten blasen' ('Where the Fine Trumpets Blow').

In September, an inaccurate and spiteful article ran in the Sydney Roman Catholic periodical, *Freeman's Journal*, the gist of which was to boost the prospects of 'their' girl, soprano Amy Castles, and to denigrate the 'Protestant' Nellie Melba and the 'Jewish' Frances Saville, who

> ... speaks English with a foreign accent ... this dark-eyed
> Jewess [who was] disowning Australia ... Neither her
> father nor her mother had any opinion of Miss Frances.
> A a matter of fact, they looked on her as a stupid block, and
> gave her only very small parts, which she sang and acted
> wretchedly.[20]

The piece was signed 'DB'. Hopefully, Saville, back in Vienna for the new season, never saw it. After performing a few more times in Vienna, gradually building a faithful public following there, Frances negotiated with Mahler another leave-of-absence, this time unpaid by the Court Opera, so that she could return to the Met in New York.

It was to be a season of extraordinary competition among prima donnas at the Met, with no less than five Marchesi pupils among them – Nellie Melba, Emma Eames, Suzanne Adams, Sophie Traubmann and Frances Saville – plus Lilli Lehmann, Johanna Gadski, Lillian Nordica and Marcella Sembrich. Was there ever such an assembly in one place of prima donna talent, before or since? And the men were an equally starry bunch. No wonder the performances of Meyerbeer's *Les Huguenots* were dubbed the 'Nuits de Sept Étoiles'. So unfashionable nowadays, *Les Huguenots* was one of the most successful grand operas of the nineteenth century.

Replacing an indisposed Emma Eames at short notice, Saville opened on 31 December 1898 as Elsa in *Lohengrin* with Ernest van Dyck in the title role – previously she had sung Elsa in 1894 at St Petersburg. Sadly, on that very day, a robber entered Frances's rooms at the Madison Avenue Hotel and stole jewellery valued at $22 000. Suspicions pointed immediately towards her personally assigned waiter at the hotel, Emil Becker, who was seen leaving with two trunks (and a wife), not to be seen again. Frances later successfully sued the hotel for the value of the theft.[21]

At the Met, two weeks after *Lohengrin* came Massenet's *Manon* with Saville in the title role, van Dyck as Des Grieux and Pol Plançon as the Count. Naturally, Frances was directly compared by the critics with yet another Marchesi pupil, American soprano Sybil Sanderson, who had previously sung the role there amidst great expectations (and great disappointment) in January 1895. Saville was adjudged to be far superior to Sanderson, but the *New York Times* (probably the scrupulous WJ Henderson) gave her a mixed review:

> Mme Saville's Manon was a pretty performance and was
> deficient chiefly in its pathos. But her voice is well suited to the
> music and, except for occasional flatness, she sang creditably.
> She had to repeat her gavotte, which she sang very well.[22]

Next came *Don Giovanni* with Saville's old flame Victor Maurel as the Don and Frances as Zerlina, exactly as in the 1895–96 season, and the season concluded for her with three Wagner operas – *Götterdämmerung* (as previously at Covent Garden, Nordica was Brünnhilde, Jean de Reszke was Siegfried and Frances was Gutrune again), *Tannhäuser* (Frances as Elisabeth) and *Lohengrin* (Van Dyck in the title role, Frances as Elsa). Altogether she sang ten times in that season at the Met, the *Lohengrin* on 4 March 1899 being her last performance at that house.

During that season at the Met, Saville made a return trip to Bettini's New York studios to re-make her recording of 'Caro nome' and also to make a cylinder of Brahms's 'Wiegenlied' ('Cradle Song'). By late January, Frances would have become aware that her brother Jules had been arrested for burglary in San Francisco, with her name mentioned in every shock-horror newspaper report. So, it must have been with a sigh of relief that she was able to sail back to Europe three days before sentence was passed.

5

Returned to Vienna, 1899 at the Court Opera was more active for Saville, with performances of *La traviata* (5), *Guillaume Tell* (4), *Rigoletto* (6), *Fledermaus* (1), *Manon* (5), *Lucia di Lammermoor* (2), *Roméo et Juliette* (1), *Pagliacci* (1) and *Götterdämmerung* (Gutrune, 1), plus Thomas's *Mignon* (Philine, 2) and Meyerbeer's *Robert le Diable* (Isabelle, 1). She opened on 24 March in one of the roles she was to sing most frequently at the Court Opera, Violetta in *La traviata*, and on 2 May she was (for the first time) Mathilde in Rossini's *Guillaume Tell*. Saville won good notices for her performances in the Viennese press – the *Neue Zeitschrift für Musik*, though dismissive of the quality of the cast in *Lucia*, pronounced Saville outstanding in the title role.[23]

However, all was still not well in her relationship with Mahler. The director was notorious for his 'infatuations' with the leading ladies in his companies. Was Frances not one of these, or – perhaps more ominously – did she reject him? Was she his choice to be brought into the Court Opera company, or was she to some extent foisted on him by the company's Intendant, Baron August von Plappart, or the theatre administrator, Eduard Wlassik? It was even suggested at one stage that the Prince of Wales (later King Edward VII) had personally recommended her, but there is no evidence for this. Knowing that she had won support from the Viennese public, she felt poorly treated by Mahler, who clearly felt that she had defied his wishes on various occasions. One consequence was that Saville actively sought guest performances elsewhere, and Mahler blamed Plappart for extending her leave (while she was at the Met that winter) without consulting him.[24]

Frances had no outside booking for the summer vacation in 1899. Instead she spent time working on her roles with her long-term friend, pianist and French diction coach Emmie Ellis (formerly of Sydney) at Bad Ems in the Rhineland.[25] That summer, perhaps surprisingly, she also negotiated a renewed contract at the Court Opera with Mahler, who wrote to her 'wanting to give proof of how valuable it is to me to retain you in our institution'.[26] Such was the roller-coaster of her relations with the director.

From the end of June by the shores of the lake at Alt-Aussee in Styria, Mahler revised his Third Symphony, corrected the proofs of *Das Klagende Lied* and drafted a complete sketch for the Wunderhorn song, 'Revelge'. He started to work on his Fourth Symphony in mid-July.[27]

Frances was recruited by American impresario Victor Thrane to tour the United States in the period November to January – at a time when the new 1899–1900 season in Vienna had already started. She negotiated this unpaid exeat directly with Mahler, who approved it as she 'had shown herself, particularly recently, to be a very faithful and accommodating member'.[28] Thrane regularly organised American tours with the most celebrated of musicians and singers, starting in the early 1890s with the stratospheric soprano Ellen Beach Yaw, then importing baritone Victor Maurel, violinist Eugène Ysaÿe, cellist Jean Gerardy, pianists Raoul Pugno, Emil Sauer and Mark Hambourg and many others.

Frances must have felt she was back with the Simonsen company, moving constantly from city to city – Los Angeles, Philadelphia, Baltimore, Indianapolis, Nashville, Pittsburgh, Cleveland and so on – often performing with the local symphony orchestra.[29] While touring in November, she may have heard of the suicide of her father, Martin Simonsen, in Melbourne.

6

Before Saville returned from America, Nellie Melba made a brief stop in Vienna. She was there at the invitation of the Emperor Franz Joseph himself and gave two performances: the first, on 18 January, in concert at the Musikvereinssaal and the second, on 19 January, on stage at the Court Opera.[30]

Both would appear to have been triumphant occasions, each attended by the aged Emperor. At the concert Melba sang the 'Mad Scene' from *Lucia di Lammermoor*, and at the opera house she sang Violetta in the Court Opera's current production of *La traviata* – a role often undertaken there by Saville.[31] Was Melba aware of this? In an interval, Mahler presented Melba with a laurel crown, but later he wrote that the evening had only been 'moderately agreeable', and that 'I'd rather listen to a clarinet!'[32]

Frances was back in Vienna by March 1900, and by the time she had returned to the Court Opera, Mahler had recruited a new principal lyric soprano, Marie Gutheil-Schoder, who rapidly became his first choice in several of the roles previously occupied by Saville. In a long career at the Court Opera, among the many roles sung by Gutheil-Schoder – from the lightest to the heaviest – were Despina in *Così fan tutte*, Pamina in *Die Zauberflöte*, Carmen, Octavian in *Der Rosenkavalier*, Adele in *Die Fledermaus*, Eva in *Die Meistersinger*, Kundry, Salome, Elektra and Mélisande. Mahler thought Gutheil-Schoder a 'musical genius', but Viennese audiences were not at first convinced. The *Deutsches Volksblatt* described her as a 'remarkable actress', but with an 'extremely ordinary voice and by no means outstanding vocal talents'. She made her debut on 19 February as Nedda in *Pagliacci*.[33] If the arrival of Gutheil-Schoder was a negative sign for Saville, she was also afflicted in the months after her return with some sort of peritonitis, the gastric illness that had felled her sister Leonore in 1884.[34] In May she had recovered sufficiently to sing Lucia and Violetta at the Neues Deutsches Theater (now the State Opera) in Prague.[35] Mahler completed his Fourth Symphony in the summer break of 1900.

By this stage, Mahler had built an extraordinary company of singers at the Court Opera, including among the sopranos: Anna von Mildenburg, Lola Beeth, Ellen Brandt-Forster, Elise Elizza, Marie Gutheil-Schoder, Selma Kurz, Margarethe Michalek, Sophie Sedlmair and Frances Saville.

Despite the truncation of her performing life in Vienna in 1900 through absence in America and illness, Saville's total number of appearances that year at the Court Opera, at twenty-eight, was only one less than in the previous year. She sang many of the same roles as in 1899, adding Elsa in *Lohengrin*, plus arguably the most important contribution of her six years at the Court Opera, Fiordiligi in Mozart's *Così fan tutte*.

Now widely regarded as one of Mozart's greatest works, by the time Mahler brought it back into the repertoire, *Così fan tutte* had been

neglected for over a century. The third of Mozart's operas created with librettist Lorenzo da Ponte, it had been premièred at the Burgtheater in Vienna in January 1790. Its theme, a frank exploration of human frailty, shocked nineteenth-century sensibilities and it was denounced as 'stupid', even 'disgusting'. Its only reappearances over that period were with sanitised, 'improved' librettos. It was not performed in London until 1811 and then was not seen again until fully a century later in Sir Thomas Beecham's revival in 1910. At the Met in New York, it was not heard until 1922. In his book of 1913 on Mozart's operas, the distinguished music historian Edward J Dent clearly signalled the work's rehabilitation:

> *Così fan tutte* is the best of all Da Ponte's librettos and the most exquisite work of art among Mozart's operas.[36]

Mahler also rightly perceived it to be a great work in desperate need of a first-rate revival. In fact, *Così fan tutte* had last been produced in a drastically cut version at the Court Opera in 1880, with all Mozart's recitatives removed, replaced by spoken dialogue. Mahler's intention was that *Così* should be the first production in a pioneering 'Mozart cycle', but, probably for financial reasons, this was not achieved until 1905–06. His cast was hand-picked from his Court Opera ensemble, with Frances Saville as Fiordiligi, mezzo Laura Hilgermann as Dorabella, Marie Gutheil-Schoder as Despina, Franz Naval as Ferrando, Leopold Demuth as Guglielmo and Wilhelm Hesch as Don Alfonso. Mahler himself played the keyboard recitatives.

The new production opened on 4 October 1900, and the Viennese critics applauded it musically, but remained generally unconvinced by Da Ponte's libretto. Eduard Hanslick thought the singers were 'made for each other', while still condemning the work itself as 'self-consciously vulgar'. Robert Hirschfeld, no great supporter of Mahler's work, was

Left: Frances Saville by Artur von Ferraris

practically alone in finding the value in the opera and in Mahler's presentation of it:

> In Mahler's interpretation, the strictest artistic conscience
> fashioned the airiest orchestral figurations, the subtlest
> nuances, the exquisite grace of the gestures in sound. ... Thus
> Mahler has not only revealed a work, but allowed us with deep
> emotion to gain an insight into the soul of Mozart.[37]

Did Saville and Mahler do battle over decoration in Fiordiligi's music? It seems likely, given her mother's pedagogical provenance and her own time as a pupil of Mathilde Marchesi, that Saville would have expected more, while Mahler, devoted to the composer's score, less. In early November, 'an occasional contributor' to the *Daily Telegraph* in Sydney visited Vienna and

> ... had the opportunity of hearing Madame Frances Saville
> in many of her most successful roles and was most impressed
> with the wonderful progress she has made in her art and the
> unique position she has achieved in the world of music.

She/he does not say which these roles were, but goes on to mention how strongly the discerning Viennese public appreciated Saville's gifts, and, having undertaken two interviews with her, went on to describe her 'beautiful apartment' in Vienna:

> ... in the Jacquingasse, a fashionable locality overlooking
> fine gardens. Her reception rooms are spacious and filled
> with priceless works of art – gifts, for the most part from the
> great ones of the earth before whom she has sung, while their
> autographed photographs, inscribed with complimentary
> phrases, fill every space on her tables and mantelpieces.
> Conspicuous among these is a portrait of her teacher, the

famous Madame Marchesi … and above all a picture of
Alexandre Dumas, with a letter stating that Madame Saville is
the only Traviata who has carried out his ideal of the unhappy
Lady of the Camellias.[38]

Her stolen jewellery having finally been recovered, Saville was in
London in mid-November in order to identify it. One wonders whether
she compensated the hotel in Manhattan which had paid for it all
following the robbery there?

On 25 November 1900, Frances was for the first time the Queen of
the Night in another of Mozart's greatest operas, *Die Zauberflöte*. This
was not a new production, but a revival of Mahler's earlier one from
1897, and Mahler, never satisfied with his cast, kept making changes.
Saville was said to be just about adequate, but that her staccato lacked
precision. She might perhaps have coped better with this most difficult
role ten or fifteen years earlier, when there were many more bel canto
roles in her (and her family's) repertoire.

This was followed in early December by a State Concert in Vienna
given by the Emperor Franz Joseph in honour of the marriage of Robert,
Duke of Württemberg, to Archduchess Maria Immakulata of Austria
at which Saville sang. This event might have passed without notice if
it were not for a mouse. The story ran in newspapers and magazines
around the world, embellished at each stage with reports of panic and
general mayhem. *Table Talk* in Melbourne revealed that:

> … during her number a mouse appeared on the stage, and so
> scared the popular singer that she broke down and was unable
> to proceed until some time after the intruder was banished
> from the platform … The venerable Emperor, who was present,
> laughed heartily … especially when the wife of a diplomat
> stood upon a chair in the orthodox feminine fashion.[39]

Two weeks later, Saville played down the whole incident:

Saville's apartment in Vienna

> She ... wore on her arm the diamond bangle which the
> Emperor Francis Joseph presented to her as a souvenir of
> the state concert ... Madame Saville ridiculed the story
> disseminated by the English press ... His Majesty remarked:
> 'I hope, madame, you don't think that mice run wild in the
> Palace.'[40]

What Saville sang at the concert was not disclosed.

7

The year 1901 brought, for Frances, the most performances of her career at the Court Opera in Vienna – forty-five in all, of fourteen different roles. Twelve she had sung there in previous years, but there were two that were new to her: the title role in Flotow's *Martha* (which had been sung by both her mother Fanny and her sister Martina in earlier decades and was later to be taken by her niece Frances Alda at the Met in New York) and Offenbach's *Les contes d'Hoffmann* (*Hoffmanns Erzählungen*). The Flotow was put on by Mahler in a new production (premièred on 4 May). It was a great favourite with the Austrian public and had a top-flight cast – Saville as Martha, Hilgermann as Nancy, Naval as Lionel and Hesch as Plunkett. The problem was that, following the recommendation of Richard Strauss, he had allowed it to be conducted by a virtual novice, Gustav Brecher, whom the critics took to task for imprecise ensemble. Altogether in 1901 Mahler scheduled many more performances of German operas at the expense of the Italians and the French – more Mozart and more Wagner, as well as *Martha* and others.

Did the Viennese public consider the German-French composer Jacques Offenbach passed that test? *Les contes d'Hoffmann* had not been performed in Vienna since the disastrous fire at the Ringtheater, which had killed hundreds of people on 7 December 1881. It had first been performed at the Opéra-Comique in Paris on 10 February 1881 and quickly established itself as a popular favourite wherever it was played. At the Paris première, the three loves of Hoffmann – Olympia, Antonia and Giulietta – so different as personalities and in singing technique, were performed by the same singer, Madame Franck-Duvernoy, just as Offenbach intended, but since that time, most productions have fielded three different singers.

What Mahler did at the Court Opera was to follow the composer's intention, having one singer play all three roles, but recognising the stress involved, he had two lead-role casts fully rehearsed, so that they could alternate. This must have seemed to him perfectly logical, but unfortunately, while both singers won the approval of critics, Saville, who led Cast 2, was immediately compared, unfavourably, with the brilliant acting and singing of Marie Gutheil-Schoder, who led Cast 1.[41] *Les contes d'Hoffmann* was the seventh and last (and most challenging) work of Offenbach's to be performed by members of the Simonsen family.

On 15 June 1901, Frances Saville was appointed an Imperial *Kammersängerin* – literally 'Chamber Singer' – by the Emperor. This was a special award, usually recognising both excellence and length of service, particularly given to members of the Court Opera ensemble. She will have been recommended for the honour by one of the aristocrats in the house's hierarchy who supported her.[42]

During the summer break in 1901, Mahler composed four of his settings of poems by Friedrich Rückert, going on to complete the fifth, 'Liebst du um Schönheit', the following summer; also in summer 1901 three of his five *Kindertotenlieder*.

At some point, most likely in 1902, Saville was visited in Vienna by her twenty-two-year-old niece Fanny, daughter of her oldest sister Leonore. Following the death of her mother in San Francisco, Fanny had been brought up by her grandparents at St Kilda, and, having done apprentice-type work in Australia, had come with her brother Alby to Europe to further her career. Her trip to Vienna was made in order to seek advice and counsel from the celebrated diva, Aunt Frances. It soon became clear that Frances was not in the mood – perhaps she thought Fanny was just another dilettante and should be discouraged, so Fanny left with her tail between her legs, only to take her revenge on her aunt in her memoirs, several decades later, by which time she was the distinguished prima donna at the Met, Frances Alda.

In 1902 Saville gave thirty-six performances at the Court Opera, the single opera that was new to her repertoire there being Meyerbeer's *Les Huguenots*. The publicity surrounding the 'Nuits de sept étoiles' with Melba and Co at the Met in 1898 had travelled far and wide, and, given the strength of the Court Opera company at this time, it may well have seemed natural that Mahler should mount his own version. Of course, there was a significant difference between the two cases. While the Met's seven were all international stars, who performed in all the great opera houses of the world, Mahler's magnificent seven were at that time mostly household names only in Vienna and other German-speaking territories.

Les Huguenots opened at the Court Opera on 29 October 1902, the cast as follows: Frances Saville (Queen Marguérite de Valois), Sophie Sedlmair (Valentine), Selma Kurz (Urbain), Leo Slezak (Raoul), Leopold Demuth (Comte de Nevers), Wilhelm Hesch (Marcel), Richard Mayr (Comte de St Bris). Not only were the lead roles occupied by outstanding singers, even the minor parts were sung by excellent performers from the company, including Arthur Preuss and Benedikt Felix. Altogether, they would have conceded no edge in terms of quality to the Met's crew. The new production was a major popular success (although the critics attacked Mahler's choice of this supposedly outdated work).

The great success of *Huguenots* might seem to point towards a new chapter in Frances Saville's performing life at the Court Opera, but this was not to be the case. In fact, she was nearing the end. In December, her colleague in the company, Lola Beeth, announced her retirement from the stage after a long career.[43] Beeth had been born in 1862, two and a half years before Saville, and had first performed at the Court Opera in 1880. She was a great public favourite. If Beeth could retire at thirty-nine, why not Saville the following year at thirty-eight?

The reality was that Mahler had probably edged Beeth out, as he had so many before her, and he was effectively doing the same with Saville. In his company by now, he had two outstanding singers who duplicated many of Saville's roles – Selma Kurz and Marie Gutheil-Schoder – and as relations continued to be cool between the two of them, Mahler's tactic was to offer Saville a new contract, but at a reduced salary. Saville was not amused, and discussions reached a stalemate by January 1903.

She did not accept the new terms and so effectively resigned from the Court Opera.

Her last performance there was in *Hoffmans Erzählungen* (*Les contes d'Hoffman*) on 23 February 1903 to a packed house, filled with friends and admirers. Overall, in six years at the Court Opera in Vienna, Frances Saville had sung twenty-one roles in nineteen operas. This final appearance there was followed four days later by a farewell concert with the Vienna Philharmonic Orchestra at the Musikvereinssaal, where Frances sang the 'Bell Song' from Delibes's *Lakmé* and songs by Schumann and Grieg.[44] Frances chose an unknown young American pianist, Ethel Newcomb (a pupil of Saville's friend, the great piano teacher Theodor Leschetizsky), to play the Schumann concerto at it. In her memoirs, Newcomb wrote a touching portrait of the occasion:

> She was a great singer and a beautiful woman, and the
> Viennese admired her exceedingly ... I remember that I
> wore a very pretty soft white chiffon frock. Madame Saville
> was magnificent in a different kind of dress ... In honour
> of Madame Saville's farewell a brilliant and distinguished
> audience had been assembled ...

And Newcomb told this anecdote, which well sums up Frances's relationship over the years with Mahler:

> Madame Frances Saville was another who suffered from
> Mahler's imperious and unjust temper. At a rehearsal she had
> the temerity to disagree with him over a point of phrasing, and
> before several of the company was requested by him to resign.
> Her host of admirers were incensed at this. When [pianist and
> teacher] Alfred Grünfeld heard of the affair, he started for the
> opera house with a horsewhip in hand to avenge the insult but
> changed his mind on the way.[45]

8

Although Frances had made a firm decision to retire, there were still a number of performances to be given, and, luckily, at some time in 1902, she had been recorded in Vienna (along with many others from the Court Opera) by The Gramophone Company. Ten sides were made using the company's still fairly primitive recording apparatus (although far advanced compared with Bettini's cylinder recordings of Saville in 1895–96 and 1898–99). The new recordings were produced by either Franz Hampe or William Sinkler Darby,[46] and they included arias from four of Saville's Court Opera roles – *Manon*, *Hoffmann*, *Lohengrin* and *Martha*, plus a handful of songs.

After the farewell concert in Vienna, Frances left for Warsaw, where she gave ten performances as Violetta, Manon, Gilda, Marguérite and Juliette; then to the Neues Deutsches Theater again in Prague for the final operatic performances of her career – as Olympia/Giulietta/Antonia in *Hoffmanns Erzählungen* on 7 May; and the last one, as Violetta on 9 May 1903. At this performance, Frances organised that her favourite younger brother, Willie Saville (Simonsen) should be her Alfredo. Her professional career finally ended in Berlin on 23 November 1903, as guest artist with the Berlin Philharmonic under Karl Muck at a fundraising concert for flood victims.

It is not at all clear why Frances Saville should have retired at the relatively young age of thirty-eight. Perhaps she was bored. Perhaps she just wanted to get out while she was still at the top. It seems that, having been careful through the years at the top, she had enough money saved. Or maybe the quality of her voice was affected by the early onset of menopause. Usually the symptoms of menopause in women starts between forty-five and fifty-five, but it is not uncommon for it to begin in the late thirties.

Following her retirement, she chose to remain in Vienna, where she had a fine apartment in a city she loved, with a rich cultural life and a host of admirers around her. She had been financially prudent throughout her career, investing her money with care, mainly in Austrian government stock and in property. Aside from her apartment by the Belvedere Gardens at 45 Jacquingasse in Vienna, Frances also owned a villa at Wartburg in Styria, plus the land she had bought at Cap Martin in the South of France in 1897, land which she could now develop with the building of a summer villa. After retiring, Frances usually spent summer breaks in Styria and winters in the South of France.

With her staff of servants,[47] Frances commuted regularly between her Vienna apartment and her two villas, and in 1908 she took on responsibility for her niece and goddaughter, four-year-old Daisy, brother Willie's elder daughter, who came to live with her, sending her to fine schools and later helping her with her career as a violinist. According to Daisy, Frances had an active social life, entertaining frequently, playing tennis, riding and swimming every day. On 23 November 1911 her son Frank Saville-Smith was killed in a motor accident at Oakland, California, where he had been working.

The First World War had a disastrous effect on Frances Saville's life and lifestyle. At first she was lucky. Having been born in the United States, she was not initially treated as an enemy alien in Vienna, but, when the Americans joined the war in 1917, she was placed under house arrest immediately. Influential friends helped to have this restriction lifted, but she remained under surveillance, having to report to the police regularly. In time, she was able to leave, going to her villa at Cap Martin. The war also had a calamitous effect on her financial circumstances: her Austrian government bonds became worthless and property values plummeted. By June 1928 she was living in a two-bedroom apartment in Paris with just one servant.

On 6 June 1930, having sold her French villa, she arrived back in Australia for the first time since 1891,[48] where she lived in Melbourne with her long-retired older sister Martina (Mrs Schreiber). However, as George Schreiber had been of German parentage, the family had been ill-treated and had lost out, as had Frances, both financially and socially in the war. Disappointed with her life in Melbourne, Frances decided in 1932 that she would be better off living with her niece Daisy, by now a violinist in the San Francisco Symphony, at Mill Valley, California. Martina was sad: 'I'd imagined us peeling the peas together,' she told her friend Winsome Matenson.[49] However, California was just as great a disappointment for Frances.

Frances clearly had had trouble throughout her life maintaining relationships. Perhaps being abandoned by her parents to be brought up by a grandmother in Altona was a primary source for this, together with the fact that she had to learn first-language English in her teen years, which must have distanced her from her peers. Perhaps constant touring from the age of fifteen meant that relationships were constantly transitory. She abandoned two husbands and one lover (that we know of). She brushed off her niece Frances Alda, when Alda went to her for help and support (for which she was unforgiven). Following constant battles, she eventually fell out terminally with Gustav Mahler. She lost close contact with her son, Frank, before his death in 1911 and when she went to live with her domesticated sister Martina in Melbourne after retiring, she became bored and left. Daisy Saville, the niece that she 'adopted', was afraid of her. Towards the end, she appears to have lacked friends at Cap Martin, in Paris and at Mill Valley. Her rather imperious diva manner may have served her well in a fine professional career, but not personally, and not after she retired.

Within months of her arrival back in her birthplace, California, she suffered one major stroke followed by others, and she died at the Twin Pines Sanatorium at Burlingame on 8 November 1935. She was seventy and her death passed virtually unnoticed.[50]

Notes

1   Emperor Franz Joseph was strongly opposed to anti-Semitism
2   Stefan Zweig, *The World of Yesterday*, 14
3   Puccini's *La bohème* was first performed the previous year (1 February 1896) at the Teatro Reggio, Turin, Arturo Toscanini conducting; Saville sang Mimì fully 24 months before Melba first performed the role (which Melba was substantially to 'own' until the late-1920s)
4   Eduard Hanslick, *Neue Freie Presse*, 7 October 1897
5   Richard Wallaschek, *Die Zeit*, 9 October 1897
6   Hans Buchstein, *Deutsches Volksblatt*, 6 October 1897
7   Albert Kauders, *Neues Wiener Journal*, 6 October 1897, 1–2
8   *Daily News* (London), 4 September 1897, 5
9   Quoted in Henri-Louis de La Grange, *Gustav Mahler: Vienna: The Years of Challenge (1897–1904)*, 51
10   Fanny Simonsen and Mathilde Marchesi, Saville's two main teachers, both trained by Manuel Garcia II in bel canto skills, would have disapproved of this; it was to be over half a century before 'traditional embellishments' in Haydn, Mozart, Bellini, Donizetti, Rossini etc were reintroduced as 'authentic' by Nikolaus Harnoncourt, Charles Mackerras and others
11   *Week* (Brisbane), 31 December 1897, 13
12   La Grange, 23
13   *Launceston Examiner*, 1 January 1898, 3
14   Letter from Saville to Mahler in Court Opera archives, dated 21 February 1898, quoted in Simpson, 'Frances Saville', 17
15   This whole episode is described in detail in La Grange, 22–24, 92–95
16   *Table Talk* (Melbourne), 18 February 1898, 6
17   *Evening Journal* (Adelaide), 11 June 1898, 4
18   *Evening Standard* (London), 13 June 1898, 4
19   *Morning Post* (London), 4 July 1898, 6
20   *Freeman's Journal* (Sydney), 3 September 1898, 16
21   *Baltimore Sun*, 2 January 1899, 2; *Evening News* (Sydney), 24 February 1899, 6
22   *New York Times*, 15 January 1899
23   Quoted in La Grange, 190
24   Letter from Mahler to Plappart in Court Opera archives, dated 27 March 1899, quoted in La Grange, 167
25   *Australasian* (Melbourne), 20 January 1900, 51
26   Undated letter from Mahler to Saville at Court Opera archive in response to her proposals of 5 June 1899, quoted in Simpson, 20
27   La Grange, 753–54
28   Memorandum from Mahler to the Intendant of the Court Opera, 2 November 1899, quoted in Simpson, 20
29   *Los Angeles Times*, 18 June 1899, 18; *Times* (Philadelphia), 10 September 1899, 9; *Indianapolis Journal*, 8 October 1899, 6, and others
30   Stefan Zweig says in *The World of Yesterday* that the Emperor 'evidenced a definite antipathy to music' (21), but he clearly kept a close eye on Court Opera matters
31   Agnes Murphy, *Melba*, 158–59
32   Natalie Bauer-Lechner, *Erinnerungen an Gustav Mahler*, quoted in La Grange, 220
33   Described in La Grange, 251
34   *Australasian*, 26 May 1900, 43; *Table Talk*, 7 June 1900
35   *Australasian*, 21 July 1900, 43
36   Edward J Dent, *Mozart's Operas*, 190

37 La Grange, 284–87
38 *Daily Telegraph* (Sydney), 10 November 1900, 6; until September 1899 Saville lived at 43 Strohgasse, during that month moving to 45 Jacquingasse
39 *Table Talk*, 13 December 1900, 26
40 *Australasian*, 22 December 1900, 43
41 La Grange, 388–90
42 *Sydney Morning Herald*, 14 December 1901, 4; *Tatler* (London), 19 February 1902, 326
43 *Pittsburgh Press*, 14 December 1902.
44 *Daily Telegraph* (Sydney), 11 April 1903, 4
45 Ethel Newcomb, *Leschetizky As I Knew Him*, 153–54, 257
46 Email from Tony Locantro to the author, 16 March 2013
47 Chauffeur, gardener, cook and two maids
48 *Weekly Times* (Melbourne), 14 June 1930, 30
49 Letter from Winsome Matenson to Adrienne Simpson, 26 March 1989
50 *Baltimore Sun*, 10 November 1935, 6; *Sydney Morning Herald*, 30 November 1935, 12

Chapter 7
Jules, Florrie and Willie

1

While Frances Saville was building an international performing career for herself, three siblings, younger offspring of Fanny and Martin Simonsen – Julius (born 1867), Florence (born 1875) and William (born 1874) – started theirs. In total, six of their ten children had become professional singers. The eldest of the emerging trio, tenor Julius Martin Simonsen, was born in Melbourne and had a career filled with ups and downs, which ended disastrously. He seems to have made his public debut as a member of the Christy Minstrels at Sale in Gippsland, country Victoria, in February 1885 aged seventeen,[1] and by 1889 (already Jules rather than Julius) he was winning praise for his performance as Ralph Rackstraw in *HMS Pinafore* in a local production at Albury.[2]

By December 1889, Jules was a member of Martin Simonsen's new touring opera company, following its final return from New Zealand.

Jules performed for the first time what would become a signature role for him – Don Caesar de Bazan in Wallace's *Maritana* – at the Exhibition Theatre in Geelong. This made 'a most favourable impression' and was regarded as his professional debut in opera.[3] *Maritana* was followed by Count Rupert in *Satanella*, Thaddeus in *The Bohemian Girl*, Manrico in *Il trovatore*, Marasquin in *Giroflé-Girofla* – 'a light and pleasant though not very powerful voice', according to the *Barrier Miner* at Broken Hill – Lionel in *Martha*, Ange Pitou in *La fille de Madame Angot* and Rackstraw again in *Pinafore*.[4] Then came the layabout Jean Grénicheux in Planquette's *Les cloches de Corneville*, 'a rather thankless part', said the *National Advocate* in Bathurst. It was a popular opéra-comique that had been toured by Martin and Fanny Simonsen's company earlier in the year in New Zealand.

This tour of Victoria and New South Wales was an early peak in Jules Simonsen's career, the notices generally positive, with father Martin taking care of the bills. However, a warning siren was sounded in October 1890 by *Melbourne Punch*, which described the company's *Il trovatore* as 'about as cheering to look at and listen to as keeners at an Irish wake', and Jules's Manrico as 'unmistakably not the Troubadour Verdi had in mind'.[5]

The tour with his father's company over, in November Jules was hired to be part of Nellie Stewart's company[6] at the Opera House in Melbourne – this time as the wigmaker Pomponnet in *La fille de Madame Angot*. 'Mr Simonsen [is] improving both as a vocalist and actor, though he has still his spurs to win,' wrote the *Lorgnette*.[7] For Jules, this production led nowhere and by the middle of 1891, he was settling for a small singing role with the Irish female impersonator John F Sheridan's *Betty O'Brien Esq* in Adelaide,[8] which was followed by Phineas Fletcher in Sheridan's version of *Uncle Tom's Cabin* in Hobart with the same company.[9]

Altogether, Jules's career seemed to have stalled, but it revitalised a little after his marriage in 1892 to the young contralto Maud Leamington – birth name Eva Maud Horwitz – a colleague on the

Sheridan tour. Maud claimed to have studied at the conservatoire in Milan with Albert Leoni and Francesco Lamperti, and that she had later sung at La Scala, at the Opéra in Paris and at Covent Garden, although under what name is undisclosed.[10] She had a long career in Australia as a singer and teacher, but, aside from a few light musical comedies and operettas, it seems surprising, given her asserted track record in three of the world's leading opera houses, that she appeared rarely on opera stages in Australasia.

Jules and Maud, who performed together regularly, had three surviving children – Juliette in 1893, Mona in 1895 and Daphne in 1897.[11] Juliette Simonsen became a singer, a soprano, who made her debut (supporting her mother) as the nine-year-old 'La Petite Julie' with the Fredo vaudeville company at Boorowa in 1902.[12] Her younger sister, contralto Mona Simonsen, first appeared (together with both mother and sister) aged ten at a concert at the Balmain Town Hall in Sydney in 1905.[13] In 1906, the thirteen-year-old Juliette took the title role in a school production of GF Root's *Snow White and the Seven Dwarfs*.[14] Juliette married William Sylva in Sydney, but, according to her grandson Bill Forrest she abandoned her two children, who were brought up by her mother-in-law. Becoming pregnant again, she got septicaemia after a botched abortion and died aged twenty in 1914. Mona had a lengthy career, mainly in principal boy roles in pantomime, according to Bill Forrest.

2

In the early part of 1891 Fanny Simonsen travelled to Italy in order to recruit a whole Italian opera company for Australia – the third such for the Simonsens.[15] She returned that July with no less than twelve principal singers (including Signor and Signora Cuttica, tenor and soprano) and conductor Napoleone Maffezzoli.[16] The company opened at the Alexandra Theatre in Melbourne with *Il trovatore*, followed by *Martha*.[17] There were good reviews, but there seem to have been losses incurred from the start, the singers becoming more and more unhappy, and, after short seasons in Ballarat and Adelaide, the management of the troupe was taken over by George Musgrove and JC Williamson for seasons in Sydney and Melbourne,[18] and the company was joined by Jules Simonsen. Fanny was by no means alone in her plight – indeed, in the early years of the 1890s, after decades of constant growth, the economic bubble had burst in Victoria. Many banks and businesses failed, and individuals like Fanny who had borrowed at high interest rates were financially devastated.[19]

Things looked up for Jules in 1892 when he was hired to sing Arturo to Felicina Cuttica's lead role in *Lucia di Lammermoor* at the Princess Theatre in Melbourne. 'His voice is naturally of a very agreeable quality', said *The Age*, 'and if he would guard against the habit of forcing his high notes his career as a singer ought to be a successful one.'[20] This was muted praise of the sort that he was going to have to get used to. He continued in the Cutticas' company as Gastone in *La traviata*.[21]

By June 1893, Jules was in *Giroflé-Girofla* at the Gaiety Theatre in Sydney with the Dean and Manning company.[22] Around this time Jules started to give concerts with Maud at the Coogee Aquarium,[23] and next he returned to *Maritana* and *The Bohemian Girl* at the Imperial Opera House in Sydney, this time with Marchesi pupil Lilian Colbourne Baber.[24] Following a promenade concert at Sydney Town Hall in February 1894, again with Baber, the *Sydney Mail* declared, perhaps somewhat implausibly, that Jules was 'certainly our best tenor at present'.[25]

At this point, Jules decided to form his own troupe, entitled Simonsen's Comic Opera Company. Was he funded by Martin and/or Fanny? Was this the final straw that led to their total impoverishment? In November 1894, four months after the company opened, Fanny was declared insolvent, her liabilities £2161 and her assets just ten shillings. In court two reasons were given for her financial problems: 'The causes of insolvency are set down as the failure of her opera company at the Alexandra Theatre and having to pay interest on borrowed money.'[26]

Jules's company had opened at Wagga Wagga in July 1894 with *Boccaccio*, tenor Jules in the title role (which had been previously taken by his soprano mother, Fanny). There were signs in Dubbo, if anyone cared to look for them, of major trouble yet to come – Jules being there found guilty of 'fraudulently removing goods' and 'malicious injury to property' which belonged to auctioneer George H Taylor (one pound damages), and of assaulting William Henry Parker (thirty shillings damages).[27]

By September 1894, Jules had joined a starry concert troupe led by French soprano Clementine de Vere Sapio and American contralto Belle Cole, who performed in a Sydney Philharmonic Society Festival at the Town Hall, giving Mendelssohn's *Elijah*, Rossini's *Stabat Mater* and Handel's *Messiah*. Most critical response focused on the leading ladies, while Jules was deemed 'too nervous to create much impression by his singing' in *Elijah*.[28]

In early 1895, Jules and his sister Florrie performed in a series of concerts at Hobart and Launceston associated with the Tasmanian International Exhibition.[29] Jules's touring company re-emerged in November 1895 with *Giroflé-Girofla*,[30] but by July 1896, he was said to be teaching music in Sydney.[31] The next blow came late in 1896, when it was reported that his mother Fanny had died.

Not surprisingly, given her long and distinguished career as the leading prima donna in Australasia, in their obituary notices the newspapers gave full reign to Fanny Simonsen's contribution to the growth of popularity of opera in Australia and New Zealand. Apparently, her death had happened suddenly at her home in St Kilda on 18 September 1896, after taking supper with her youngest son Martin and granddaughter Fanny – later to be prima donna Frances Alda.[32] Fanny was sixty-one. The *Jewish Herald* reported:

> On Friday evening after supper she was suddenly seized
> with a paralytic fit, and though medical aid was promptly
> secured, she breathed her last soon after midnight ... In private
> Madame Simonsen was the most amiable woman one could
> meet with, a good wife, an affectionate mother and charitable
> to a degree. She had a large circle of friends who were sincerely
> attached to her ... *Sic transit gloria mundi.*[33]

In her memoirs, Frances Alda recalled childhood with her grandmother with the greatest affection and respect. While it was generally expected that middle- and upper-class women should stay at home as wives, mothers and homemakers in the second half of the nineteenth century, singers and actors seem to have enjoyed an exception to that general rule. And perhaps this was even more the case in Australia and New Zealand, where shoals of young women singers left home to be trained in Europe and then, if they were successful, to have a life travelling the world and performing. This was certainly the case for the majority of the Simonsen women who embarked on that life.

Of all the Simonsen women who became professional singers, it was only Fanny who had to take the brave step of abandoning her aristocratic roots and her childhood religion, presumably resisting pressure from her family, in order to follow the purpose of her life. Fanny Simonsen had a rare combination of gifts: as an artist, she was highly skilled and fully committed, while, as a woman, she was courageous, loyal and loving.

One final spark of musical life for Jules in Sydney was the première of an Australian opera at the Opera House on 27 February 1897 – August Juncker's *The Romance of Corsica* – 'while charming and pleasant to listen to', said the *Australian Star*, 'the performers made it drag.'[34] Juncker had previously had a major hit song, 'I was Dreaming', published in Sydney in 1894 – it sold 85 000 copies, was interpolated in Lacôme and Caryll's operetta *Ma mie Rosette* in 1898,[35] and was included in Joan Sutherland's LP of 1973, *Songs my mother taught me*. Then on

13 May Jules took the title role in the first performance in Australia of Berlioz's *The Damnation of Faust*. It was a concert performance at Sydney Town Hall, Roberto Hazon conducting.[36]

3

Jules's career seems to have become becalmed in Australia at this time, and he decided to try his luck elsewhere, with Europe stated as the destination. But he had a wife with three young children, and they were apparently not to be included in this new chapter. Had he fallen out of love with her, with them? To support his future plans, a benefit was held for Jules at the Sydney Town Hall on 3 July 1897 with many of Australia's finest singers of the time giving their services, including Mathilde Marchesi pupil Eva Mylott and William Burns-Walker, who was a pupil of Marchesi's daughter Blanche, and was later to teach Joan Sutherland's mother, Muriel Alston.[37] Ominously, Jules's wife, Maud Leamington, was 'indisposed', not appearing at this event due to 'unavoidable circumstances'.[38]

Jules did not leave Australia until early in 1898 and he did not travel to Europe. Instead, he went to San Francisco, where the *Oakland Tribune* announced that he had arrived on the *Mariposa* on 11 February 1898, 'making a short visit to his brother in this city'. His brother was Louis Simonsen, who had been working in Oakland 'for a long time with the Laymance Company', a major real estate developer. Louis, who had been born in San Francisco in 1863, as a young man became a piano tuner and manager of a retail music store in Sydney, before settling in California, where he built a successful career in real estate. The newspaper trumpeted both Jules's supposed high reputation as an operatic tenor in Australia and also that of his sister, 'the celebrated singer Frances Saville'.[39] The next to be heard of him was that he was 'lying ill in San Francisco'.[40]

News report of Jules Simonsen as burglar, 1899

In June 1898, Jules was Manrico again in *Il trovatore*, given by Carl Marten's company in Los Angeles, but the *Los Angeles Herald* found him 'disappointing ... both his voice and acting are unequal to the demands of the part'.[41] In that same season at the Los Angeles Theater, Jules was Nanki-Poo in *The Mikado* and Captain Thompson in *The Privateer or The American Hero*.[42]

In September he joined Marten's company again for a one-week season at the Macdonough Theater in Oakland, opening as Nanki-Poo, in which he 'sang unusually well and received well deserved encores',[43] followed the next day by Robert Planquette's opéra-comique, *The Chimes of Normandy* (originally *Les cloches de Corneville*).[44] He had previously sung in this popular musical comedy at Bathurst in 1890, when he sang the fisher lad, Grenicheux. Perhaps by Oakland he had graduated to the larger tenor role of Henri, Marquis de Corneville.

From that moment, things went rapidly downhill. On 15 January 1899, Jules Simonsen was arrested by the police in San Francisco, having been caught in the act of burgling Mr AR Heyman's downtown residence in Eddy Street. It appears that Mr Heyman came home unexpectedly, surprising the burglar, and managing to detain him. The local newspapers carried shock-horror reports that someone who had sung not only lead roles in *The Bohemian Girl* and Oscar Weil's comic opera *Suzette* at the Tivoli, but also at the Bush Street Synagogue, should have led a double life. Jules told police that his name was James Stewart, doing all he could to frustrate their enquiries. Gradually it emerged for them (and for the press), not only that he was a professional singer, but also that his sister, Frances Saville, was a famous international prima donna, born in San Francisco.[45]

It is likely that a part of Jules's financial travails, driving him to turn to robbery, was that the Marten Opera Company with which he had performed in Los Angeles and Oakland became defunct as the Oakland season closed, 'not able to pay the wages due to the members of the company'.[46] Then, as the days passed, it became clear that this Eddy Street burglary was no isolated incident – and in Jules's trunks at his home there were discovered 'many jewels and pawn tickets'.[47] The *San Francisco Call* ran a hilarious feature article on the matter, together with comical line drawings of Jules looking sad, Jules climbing in through an upper window, sister Frances Saville 'of the Royal Opera', with the witty headline: 'Scaling Juliet's Ladder Taught Him Porch-Climbing – Tenor Simonsen's Very Dramatic Story'.

> In a dress shirt, rumpled and rather the worse for wear,
> a tourist's jacket, an uncomely pair of trousers and a
> startlingly unartistic pair of brogans, Jules Simonsen,
> erstwhile Tivoli favorite and brother to Madame Saville, the
> world renowned grand opera prima donna, reposes in his
> prison cell.[48]

All this was not just San Francisco news – it was widely published both nationally and internationally, running back home in Australia by 20 February, just days after the burglary at which he was apprehended.[49] At his trial, Jules pleaded guilty, but proposed in mitigation that this was his first offence, which it clearly was not, and that his wife and children back home in Sydney depended on him for financial support (which seems unlikely). Judge Dunne was unimpressed and sentenced Jules to twelve years in Folsom Prison at Sacramento.[50]

In the prison register, Jules's occupation is noted not as professional singer, but as 'watchmaker'. Perhaps he thought that this might provoke less negative attention among the inmates. With good behaviour, he would have been released after serving seven and a half years of his twelve-year sentence (to be released in November 1906), but in the event he was paroled two years before that date (in October 1904). A letter to the Governor of California (George C Pardee) was received from Sophia Bradbury of Moore Park in Sydney in September 1903 begging for his sentence to be commuted. Mrs Bradbury was an assistant to the Anglican Archbishop of Sydney and her letter emphasised Jules Simonsen's contribution to music in Australia, his responsibilities

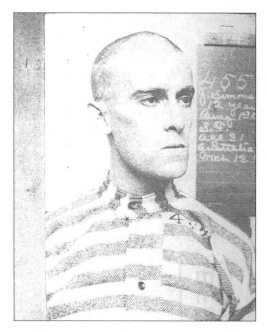

Jules Simonsen at Folsom Prison, Sacramento

towards his wife and young children in Sydney, the fact that it was a
first offence and that he was 'alone in a strange land'.[51]

What happened after his release? Currently little seems to be
known. Where did he go? What did he do? He may be seen again for
a brief moment in June 1908, performing in variety programmes at
the Dreamland Theatre at Chico, north of Sacramento and at Oroville,
where he sang, perhaps with irony, 'In the Valley where my Sallie said
Good-Bye'.[52]

What does seem clear is that his abandoned wife and three children
in Sydney were left to fend for themselves.

4

It is worth pausing at this point to consider what was happening to Jules's younger brother Louis while Jules was being arrested, tried, sentenced and imprisoned. Somehow, although he had been frequently mentioned in the press when Jules first arrived in California, brother Louis managed to avoid all reference to himself in coverage of the case. By this time, Louis was a pillar of the community in Oakland. As a young man, he had been a piano tuner with Steinway in New York and with Neuman in Hamburg,[53] and by 1887, at twenty-four, he was manager of a musical instrument retailer in Sydney.[54] There he must have learned the practical side of running a business, which would be fundamental to his future life in California.

The following year, a daughter, Leonore Simonsen (named in memory of Louis's beloved sister)[55], was born at Ashfield in Sydney,[56] and in 1889 Louis briefly took on the licence of the Surry Hills Hotel in that city and was teaching the banjo before making the move to San Francisco. In California, he joined an established insurance company as a bookkeeper, before moving to a prominent real estate developer, the Laymance Company. He next became postmaster at the newly opened post office at Elmhurst in South Oakland, and then secretary of a hospital board, a senior official of the Mutual Building and Loan Association in San Jose and president of the Californian State Building and Loan League. In short, Louis had built a substantial business career in California and had much to lose by association with a common felon and convict.

Aside from her cousin Frances Alda, Louis's daughter Leonore was to be the most successful of Fanny Simonsen's several singing granddaughters. She was to become a leading mezzo-soprano in vaudeville shows touring America – from 1916 in the New York Hippodrome's *Hip-Hip-Hooray*, its music by Raymond Hubbell.[57] The Hippodrome was the largest theatre in Manhattan, home of spectacular vaudeville shows. It featured in the movie *On the Town* (1949), sung by Betty Garrett and Frank Sinatra: 'My father told me, "Chip, my boy / There'll come a time when you leave home; / If you should ever hit New York, / Be sure to see the Hippodrome".' At the heart of the Hippodrome's spectacular show was John Philip Sousa's famous band and in due course Leonore was to become the regular 'prima donna', the featured soloist with the band.[58] After New York, the show toured and the *Philadelphia Inquirer* was critical of its vastness:

> In its wealth of material, it reminds one of the three-ring
> circus, and the impossibility of seeing everything that is going
> on at the same time ... To say that it is a 'great spectacle' does
> not convey the proper idea of its proportions ...[59]

Leonore Simonsen was 'The Heroine'. By December, Sousa was again fronting his own touring show with Leonore the soloist: 'Miss Simonsen has an excellent soprano [sic] voice of natural tone and wide register,' said the *Berkshire Eagle*.[60] And she regularly sang Raymond Hubbell's most famous and enduring song, 'Poor Butterfly'. She left the band early in 1918, taking on appearances in vaudeville shows around America, and in 1925 was singing on radio.[61] Married, by 1931 she was taking occasional bookings closer to home in Northern California as Leonore Romaine.[62]

5

On 28 November 1899, the father of the dynasty, Martin Simonsen, shot himself in the heart. He died immediately. *The Argus* in Melbourne disclosed the situation the following day:

> Since the death of Madame Simonsen three years ago,
> Mr Simonson had resided with Mr and Mrs Goulding at

588 Elizabeth Street … For some time past he had been very
unsettled, but had never shown any suicidal tendencies.

On his last evening he was visited by his youngest son, Martin,
then twenty-one. They played cards together, Martin senior appearing
cheerful and contented. At two o'clock in the morning, he went to
his room to lie down. About an hour later, there were strange sounds
from the room, and Roberta, the daughter of the Gouldings, went to
investigate, finding Martin on the ground, bleeding. *The Argus* finished
by rounding up his successes and failures, artistic and financial, making
it clear that in the last years there had been more of the failures, and
hinting that it was this that led to his suicide.[63]

What has not been suggested, then or now, was that he may have
been deeply affected by news of the imprisonment of Jules in California,
the most successful of his male children as a musician. At his death,
Martin was sixty-nine years old, having lived in Melbourne for thirty-
four years. In the memoirs of granddaughter Frances Alda, Martin
Simonsen is not recalled with affection:

> Grandfather had never inspired love in his own children or in
> his grandchildren. [Since the death of wife Fanny] he retired
> within himself, bitter and inconsolable … They found his
> body tumbled over on his desk. The bullet that had pierced his
> temples [sic][64] had gone through the photograph of his wife,
> which he held in his left hand.[65]

Shortly before he died, Martin wrote a sad letter to his friend and
solicitor, Henry Westley, which ended:

> I am most miserable and unhappy. I do not think there is
> another man in Victoria who is as much so as I am – lame,
> deaf and getting blind. I know, my old friend, you at least will
> pity me a little.[66]

6

There remain two more Simonsen children who set out on a performing life as singers – Florrie and Willie – in both cases without great success. While Florrie won prizes at the St Kilda Hebrew School as a child,[67] Willie, a year older, went to the State School at St Kilda, also attending Sabbath School for religious instruction, where he too won prizes.[68]

Born at Altona in 1874, Florrie first appeared in public at eighteen on 10 November 1892 in a 'Complimentary Concert' at the Town Hall in Melbourne for leading tenor Armes Beaumont, with whom her mother had sung so often. *The Argus* connected Florrie not particularly to her parents, nor to older sisters Leonore or Martina, but to her other singing sister, Frances Saville, who was 'triumphant in the old world', adding:

> Miss Florrie Simonsen made a very favourable impression
> last night. She has a soprano voice of agreeable quality
> (reminiscent of her mother's), and her method of using it
> shows the results of careful training.[69]

The imposing Town Hall would have been a daunting experience for her if this really was her debut. Florrie followed it in December with another Complimentary Concert at the Town Hall – this time for Nellie Melba's first teacher, contralto Ellen Christian, who was, like Fanny Simonsen, a pupil of Manuel Garcia II. Aside from her solo item, 'Roberto, O tu che adoro' from Meyerbeer's *Roberto il diavolo*, she sang a duet with another of Fanny's pupils, contralto Ada Crossley. *The Australian* noted that

> … she again proved herself to be the possessor of an agreeable
> soprano voice, strongly reminiscent of her mother's, though,

probably owing to nervousness, her intonation was slightly
at fault.[70]

The portents were already not good for Florrie. She sang in
Adelaide in May 1893 – in a 'Popular Concert' at the Town Hall – and
it was there from the *South Australian Register* that she experienced
her first seriously negative criticism: 'Until Miss Simonsen learns
to sing in tune, her performances can by no means be considered a
musical success.'[71]

It was intonation problems that consistently blighted the hoped-
for singing career. Over the coming months, Florrie was booked
several times to sing at the massive Exhibition Building in Melbourne
– including on 7 April 1894 at a Farewell Concert for soprano Lalla
Miranda.[72] In December that year she (a 'prima donna' apparently) sang
at the Mechanics' Institute at Ballarat with her tenor brother Willie.
Willie's first appearance in public was probably a few days earlier at a
Liedertafel 'smoke concert' in Ballarat.[73] While the response to Florrie
was 'irresistible', Willie's recognition was 'cordial'.[74]

As noted previously, Florrie appeared in early 1895 at a series of
concerts together with her older brother, Jules Simonsen, in Hobart and
Launceston, associated with the Tasmanian International Exhibition.[75]

Florrie's performances to date showed no sign of the kind of lift-
off necessary to sustain a career and in May 1895 she became engaged
to Mr Arthur Turrall (variously said to be from Coventry and from
London).[76] As had happened with her older sister Martina, this spelled
the end of her professional aspirations. They were married 'quietly' in
mid-June,[77] and Florrie seems not to have performed thereafter. They
were to have three children – Arthur Edgar in 1896, Florence Clara in
1898 and Winifred Joyce in 1900.

Husband Arthur ran an import business which from around
1900 experienced financial troubles, and Arthur took his own life
with cyanide late in 1903.[78] Florrie remarried two years after the
death of Arthur, to Henry Herbert Lewis, and later became landlady

of the Prince Arthur Hotel in Nott Street, Port Melbourne. She died aged thirty-nine in 1913.[79] If Florrie had assumed that spurning the performing life would lead to settled, contented domesticity like sister Martina, she was to be disappointed.

7

The last of the singing Simonsen children to be brought up at St Kilda before going on to tread the boards was William Martin. He was born at Altona in 1875, the year after Florrie. Little is known of his performing life before leaving for America and then Europe as a young man, but, as mentioned previously, he did sing in two events (one with sister Florrie) in Ballarat in December 1894, and by April 1896 he was Acting-Manager of the Theatre Royal in Sydney where English actor-manager Bland Holt's company was performing *One of the Best: The Drama of Military Life* by Seymour Hicks and George Edwardes.[80] At some point, Willie settled in San Francisco, where, according to the *San Francisco Call*, in 1895 he sang

> ... solo tenor at the Plymouth Congregational Church on
> Post Street, and he will be the tenor soloist in Cowen's secular
> cantata *The Rose Maiden*, which the Harmony Choral Union
> will shortly produce for some local charity.[81]

Shortly after his sister Florrie became engaged to Arthur Turrall, twenty-one-year-old Willie went from California to London, ostensibly to develop his singing career. If this was the plan, it did not seem to get very far. He was spotted there in the audience (along with other Australian singers, including Ada Crossley and Minna Fischer) at the Royal Albert Hall in July 1896 – at a concert where the rising Tasmanian soprano Amy Sherwin was supporting the great diva Adelina Patti.[82] By

September he was in Paris with his sister Francis Saville, 'where it [was] his intention to cultivate his very promising tenor voice'.[83] If this meant engaging a teacher, we do not know who that was, but in June 1897 Willie was said to be on the brink of making his debut on the operatic stage in London, although at what theatre and in which opera was not disclosed.[84] It does not seem to have happened.

The *British Australasian* in London announced that he had adopted the stage name Louis Saville, but later it appears that this should really have been Willie Saville.[85] Neither name seems to have left behind a trail of performances, but he was said to be about to make 'his debut as a tenor at the Opéra-Comique, Paris, during this autumn [1898]'.[86] That performance remains unconfirmed, and in January 1900 *The Australasian* informed readers that 'Mr Willie Simonsen has so far done little to warrant [sister Frances Saville's] enthusiasm over his musical education.'[87] In spite of this scepticism, by the following January the *Evening News* in Sydney was reporting that Willie 'recently made a most successful appearance in opera on the Continent, and will remain in Europe for some time, as he has engagements extending over the next two years'.[88] Details were not available. Two years later, he was said to have appeared in opera 'very successfully in different German towns'.[89]

One of those towns was Munich, where Willie and his wife Anna lived for a while. Anna Margarete Eleonora Auguste Patek had been born at Brno in Moravia on 18 February 1885. She was ten years younger than Willie and was an amateur singer. Presumably they met when he was singing in one or other of those German towns. Their daughters were Frances Margaret Simonsen, who was born at Nuremberg on 9 October 1904, and Edith Marion Altmann (née Simonsen), born at Dresden on 24 June 1906.[90] In their early years, the girls lived with their parents in Munich. There, Anna was said to be an admired hostess and among their guests were the outstanding Wagnerian tenors Heinrich Knote and Ernst Kraus, and the composer Hans Pfitzner.[91]

Around 1905, Willie became separated from his daughters, and perhaps from his wife too, Frances Margaret (Daisy) going on to be

raised by her now retired aunt Frances Saville. Willie was said to have 'served with distinction' in the First World War,[92] but his younger daughter Edith told Adrienne Simpson that in reality he 'served with the American Occupation Army in Germany after World War I'.[93]

A violinist from an early age, Frances Margaret studied at Lausanne in 1919–20 and at the Akademie der Tonkunst in Munich (1920–23). She took the performing name of Daisy Saville and in 1923 was first violin with the Carl Rosa company in England. In 1925 her father Willie was working in business in an office at Wiesbaden, Germany, from where he wrote a long letter to his older daughter, sad about the way his life had turned out:

> Life in an office is very dull and monotonous after having
> lived the life of an artist for years … We artists my dear are
> the happiest, and at the same time, unhappiest mortals in
> the world.[94]

Daisy moved to San Francisco in 1925, joining the San Francisco Symphony Orchestra, whose chief conductor at the time was the German Alfred Hertz, becoming one of the first women to serve in a leading American symphony orchestra. She was to play with that orchestra over nine seasons, while giving occasional recitals (often accompanied by sister Edith) and teaching at her studio in Mill Valley, where she lived.[95]

Aside from Louis, there were three other Simonsen children who managed to evade singing as a profession: Herman Martin, born at Altona in 1869 and who, aged fifteen, did sing a 'Hallelujah' solo 'with very good effect' at the St Kilda Synagogue in October 1884,[96] before running a retail jewellery business in Sydney and Melbourne – he was bankrupted in December 1930;[97] Albert Martin, born in Melbourne on

Left: Willie Saville (Simonsen) and wife Anna Patek in Nuremberg, 1903

9 January 1871, at thirteen he won prizes in arithmetic and French at St Kilda Scotch College,[98] and died aged just forty-four in January 1915[99] – it is not clear how and where he earned a living; and the youngest, Martin junior, born in Melbourne on 10 December 1878, who was a violinist in Germany before returning to Melbourne, where he went into business with brother Herman.

Outcomes for the six children of Fanny and Martin Simonsen who embarked on careers as professional singers ranged from the disastrous to the triumphant: unable to pay his way as a performer, Jules was sent to prison for robbery; difficulty with intonation forced Florrie to abandon ship; lack of bookings in Europe and America saw Willie take a job in an office in Germany; highly promising Martina decided that domesticity was preferable to touring; equally gifted Leonore died from peritonitis; and Frances had a top-flight career as a prima donna in Paris, St Petersburg, London, New York and Vienna.

Could a member of the next generation top them all?

Notes

1   *Gippsland Times* (Victoria), 27 February 1885, 1
2   *Corowa Free Press* (NSW), 20 September 1889, 2; *Table Talk* (Melbourne), 25 October 1889, 16
3   *Lorgnette* (Melbourne), 28 December 1889, 5
4   *Lorgnette*, 4 August 1890, 2
5   *Melbourne Punch*, 16 October 1890, 9
6   Nellie Stewart starred mostly in operetta roles from around 1880 in Australia and England
7   *Lorgnette*, 22 November 1890, 5; *Argus*, 8 December 1890, 6
8   *Evening Journal* (Adelaide), 21 July 1891, 3
9   *Mercury* (Hobart), 18 September 1891, 3
10   *Balmain Observer* (NSW), 26 August 1905, 6
11   Letter from Bill Forrest to Adrienne Simpson, 19 August 1996
12   *Burrowa News* (NSW), 11 April 1902, 2

13   *Balmain Observer*, 26 August 1905, 6
14   *Evening News* (Sydney), 10 August 1906, 4
15   *Melbourne Punch*, 19 March 1891, 13
16   *Evening Journal* (Adelaide), 28 July 1891, 3
17   *Lorgnette*, 3 August 1891, 7; *Weekly Times* (Melbourne), 15 August 1891, 17
18   *Sydney Morning Herald*, 13 February 1892, 2; *Le Ménestrel* (Paris), 13 March 1892, 86;
      Lorgnette, 3 May 1892, 7
19   Geoffrey Blainey, *A History of Victoria*, 147
20   *Age*, 16 May 1892, 5
21   *Australasian* (Melbourne), 28 May 1892, 23
22   *Evening News*, 12 June 1893, 3
23   *Daily Telegraph* (Sydney), 11 November 1893, 4
24   *Evening News*, 22 January 1893, 3
25   *Sydney Mail*, 24 February 1894, 377
26   *Freeman's Journal* (Sydney), 24 November 1894, 19
27   *Dubbo Liberal* (NSW), 22 August 1894, 2
28   *Table Talk* (Melbourne), 13 October 1894, 4
29   *Tasmanian News*, 30 April 1895, 3
30   *Hamilton Spectator* (Victoria), 21 November 1895
31   *Free Lance* (Melbourne), 16 July 1896, 5
32   *Australian Town and Country Journal* (Sydney), 26 September 1896, 14
33   *Jewish Herald* (Melbourne), 21 September 1896, 3
34   *Daily Telegraph*, 27 February 1897, 11
35   Jules's niece Francie Adler was Clochette in that production
36   *Daily Telegraph*, 14 May 1897, 6
37   Many books on Sutherland refer to Burns-Walker as having been a pupil of Mathilde
      Marchesi, but this cannot be so – she only taught women
38   *Evening News*, 5 July 1897, 3
39   *Oakland Tribune*, 12 February 1898, 4
40   *Sydney Mail*, 4 June 1898, 1182
41   *Los Angeles Herald*, 14 June 1898
42   *The Capital* (Los Angeles), 2 July 1898; *The Privateer*
43   *Oakland Tribune*, 7 September 1898, 6
44   *Oakland Tribune*, 10 September 1898, 9
45   *Los Angeles Times*, 18 January 1899, 5
46   *Oakland Tribune*, 13 September 1898, 2
47   *St Louis Post-Dispatch*, 19 January 1899, 2
48   *San Francisco Call*, 19 January 1899, 9; I have found no evidence that Jules Simonsen ever
      sang Roméo
49   *Age*, 20 February 1899, 5
50   *Record-Union* (Sacramento), 12 March 1899, 12
51   California State Archives, Sacramento
52   *Chico Record*, 25 June 1908, 6; in a letter to Adrienne Simpson of 28 February 2001, Jules's
      niece Edith Altmann wrote: 'A brother of him [presumably Louis] helped him to escape
      prison and establish himself in New York'
53   *Narracoorte Herald* (SA), 18 September 1885, 2
54   *Armidale Express* (NSW), 22 February 1887, 8
55   It was Leonore's brother Louis who placed a remembrance notice in the *Sydney Morning
      Herald* marking the second anniversary of her death; ten years old when Louis was
      born, perhaps she had become a surrogate mother for him; *Sydney Morning Herald*,
      29 December 1886, 1
56   *Sydney Morning Herald*, 17 July 1888, 1
57   *Philadelphia Inquirer*, 16 October 1916, 13

58   *St Joseph Gazette* (Missouri), 7 January 1917, 13
59   *Philadelphia Inquirer*, 16 October 1916, 13
60   *Berkshire Eagle* (Massachusetts), 19 December 1916, 4
61   *San Francisco Examiner*, 1 January 1925, 18
62   *Press Democrat* (Santa Rosa, CA), 13 May 1931, 6
63   *Argus*, 29 November 1899, 8
64   Newspaper reports at the time said the heart
65   Alda, *Men, Women and Tenors*, 34
66   *Evening Journal* (Adelaide), 30 November 1899, 3
67   *Jewish Herald* (Melbourne), 5 September 1884, 7
68   *Age*, 4 April 1885, 15; *Jewish Herald*, 4 September 1885, 12
69   *Argus*, 11 November 1892, 6
70   *Age*, 9 December 1892, 6
71   *South Australian Register* (Adelaide), 15 May 1893, 7
72   *Argus*, 9 April 1894, 6
73   *Ballarat Star*, 19 December 1894, 3 & 24 December 1894, 4
74   *Ballarat Star*, 27 December 1894, 4
75   *Mercury*, 18 February 1895, 4; *Tasmanian News*, 30 April 1895, 3
76   *Australian Town and Country Journal*, 25 May 1895, 37
77   *Australian Town and Country Journal*, 22 June 1895, 16
78   *Argus*, 23 November 1903, 6 & 1 December 1895, 7
79   *Age*, 1 September 1913, 6
80   *Era* (London), 16 May 1896, 11
81   *San Francisco Call*, 28 November 1895, 6
82   *Leader* (Melbourne), 1 August 1896, 29
83   *Lorgnette*, 1 September 1896, 2
84   *Daily News* (Perth), 26 June 1897, 4
85   *Mercury*, 28 August 1897, 4; *Table Talk*, 5 August 1898, 2
86   *Telegraph* (Brisbane), 24 August 1898, 6
87   *Australasian* (Melbourne), 20 January 1900, 51
88   *Evening News*, 8 January 1901, 7
89   *Brisbane Courier*, 5 February 1903, 6
90   Letter from Edith Altmann in San Francisco to Adrienne Simpson in Wellington, 21 July 1989
91   Information from Nathan B Davis
92   *Melbourne Punch*, 1 March 1917, 32; *Sunday Times* (Perth), 4 January 1925, 30; Willie probably served in the American army
93   Letter from Edith Altmann to Adrienne Simpson, 12 June 1991
94   Letter from Willie Simonsen to daughter Daisy, 9 September 1925
95   *San Francisco Examiner*, 14 November 1926, 51
96   *Jewish Herald* (Melbourne), 13 September 1882, 15
97   *Argus*, 19 December 1930, 1
98   *Jewish Herald*, 26 December 1884, 9
99   *Argus*, 12 January 1915, 1

Chapter 8
The Arrival of Alda

1

Frances Alda started out in life as neither Frances nor Alda, but as Fanny Jane Davis.[1] She was born on 31 May 1879 in Christchurch, New Zealand, to wine and spirit merchant (and amateur musician) David Davis and his wife Leonore, née Simonsen, and named after her grandmother, Fanny Simonsen. Sixteen-year-old Leonore had met David during the Simonsen opera company's tour of New Zealand in 1876, during which David had played violin in the orchestra. Their wedding took place at the Christchurch Synagogue on 27 September 1876.

At some point in her life, Alda put it about that she had been born on 31 May 1883, shaving four years off her true age, and she did this so consistently that to this day many published sources give the later incorrect birth date. The true birthdate was first established by Adrienne Simpson from Alda's birth certificate.

In her early years, Fanny Jane lived first with her parents in Christchurch, then, after the parents' divorce in September 1880, with one or other of them in Christchurch or Melbourne – Leonore having reverted to her own parents' home at St Kilda – or with her father's relations at Nelson. The divorce had come about because Leonore reasserted after marriage that she still had ambitions on the opera stage, and that being a wife and mother was not enough for her.

Accordingly, together with her sisters Martina and Frances, and her parents Martin and Fanny, Leonore toured Australia and New Zealand from November 1880 to April 1883, performing constantly. Then, in June, Leonore decided to try her luck in California, sailing to San Francisco with her father and her two small children. There she performed a little and married again, this time to an American, Jacob Adler, but shortly afterwards she suffered from peritonitis and died on 27 December 1884, aged twenty-five.

Fanny Jane (by now usually called Francie) and her brother Alby were swept up by their grandfather, Martin Simonsen, and carried back to the Simonsen family home in St Kilda, where Martin and Fanny took care of them through childhood. In her delightful, witty and unreliable memoirs of 1937, *Men, Women and Tenors*, Fanny Jane (by then international prima donna Frances Alda) lovingly described her childhood at Carlisle Street, St Kilda:

> Little Francie Davies [sic] had a temper as fiery as her hair.
> She was stage-struck. She gave herself airs. But in spite of all
> this – or was it because of it? – our croquet lawn was the most
> popular lawn in St Kilda. The theatre which Alby built for me
> out of lath and old burlap under the eucalyptus trees against
> the wall played to capacity.[2]

With Francie and Alby at home were grandfather Martin, who 'disciplined us', and grandmother Fanny, who 'adored and spoiled us both', plus Francie's uncle Martin, who had been born in the same year as his niece. Not mentioned in Alda's memoirs, but also there in the house were aunts Martina (who was in her late twenties, not yet married) and Florence, together with several uncles. Altogether, there must have been an extraordinary cacophony when many of them practised singing, violin or piano at the same time. It appears that all of Fanny and Martin's children, plus grandchildren Alby and Francie, were taught basic musical skills, particularly piano and violin by Martin, and those who showed vocal promise were coached by Fanny.

Francie practised violin and piano five hours a day. 'The piano and the violin have remained my good friends through all the years,' she wrote in her memoirs. The consequence in later life was that 'I can play any piece of music at sight.' Regarding singing, she wrote: 'In my childhood I never had a singing lesson.' Perhaps it was not so necessary for her in that particular house of song.[3]

What her grandmother did teach her was darning and mending, while telling her of the great singers she had heard in Europe before coming to Australia, including Jenny Lind, Adelina Patti and Pauline Viardot, the sister of Fanny's own teacher in Paris, Manuel Garcia. The languages spoken at home were German and French, so it was noted of the girls that they spoke (and sang) English with a European 'accent', particularly rolling their 'r's in an un-Australian manner. But it was not only music and mending that occupied Francie's Australian childhood at St Kilda. She also revelled in the outdoor life:

> I cannot remember a time when I couldn't beat my boy
> playmates at tennis, or swim as far and as fast as they
> could. All through the long Australian summers we ran
> on the beach and were in and out of the water half a dozen
> times a day.[4]

By the time she was eleven, Fanny Jane had won a prize at the St Kilda Hebrew School – for regular attendance[5] – and the following year

The Beach at Port Melbourne from the foreshore, St Kilda by GP Nerli

she went as a boarder to Miss Hatchell Brown's Priory Girl's School in Alma Road, St Kilda, where she won prizes for mathematics.[6] By 1896 she was at the Hawksburn Ladies Training School, where she sang a song at the annual concert,[7] but by this time she was seventeen and the lure of the stage already had her in its grasp. On 18 September 1896 Fanny Simonsen died at age sixty-one. Francie was seventeen, and had loved her grandmother greatly and was devastated:

> A languorous summer evening. Grandmother and I alone in
> the Green Room with the sweetness of the daphne drifting in
> the windows. Grandmother saying she was tired, and going
> into her own room while I sat at the piano playing snatches
> of Mozart and Gounod, composers she loved … An hour or
> so later, Alby, coming home from a party and whistling as he
> turned in at the gate, heard a sound of sobbing in the dark
> garden … I tried to tell him: 'Grandmother is dead'.[8]

Although she claimed never to have had a singing lesson in her childhood, nevertheless she clearly learned much from her beloved grandmother, recalling in her memoirs Fanny's 'directness and fine, practical judgement: "To sing, to be an artist, is not enough. You must also live completely, as a woman".[9]

2

Three of the singing aunts of Francie Adler (as she now called herself) had had the great benefit of cutting their teeth on the operatic stage with Martin and Fanny Simonsen's touring companies. This route into the business was by the late 1890s unavailable to young Francie, and with her grandmother recently deceased, she had to find another way into that world. This was how she addressed the situation:

> I went into Melbourne, rapped on the door of the office of
> Williamson and Musgrove's Light Opera Company, and said to
> the astonished Mr Williamson: 'I can sing as well as any of the
> singers in your company. Why don't you engage me?'[10]

Aged seventeen, she was signed by 'The Firm' (as JC Williamson's company was called) on a twelve-month contract in March 1897[11] and made her debut as Princess Zelica in *Matsa, Queen of Fire* at Her Majesty's Theatre in Sydney on 3 April, replacing one of Fanny Simonsen's former pupils, Flora Graupner.[12] *Matsa* was a spectacular pantomime-vaudeville with music by Léon Caron and George Pack – the sort of production that Williamson and Musgrove were famous for. It had previously opened at the Princess Theatre in Melbourne at Christmas, starring soprano Florence Young (later to be another Australian pupil of Mathilde Marchesi in Paris). From Sydney, the show went on to Adelaide,[13] where Francie left the *Matsa* company and joined the glamorous touring actors Mrs Brown-Potter and Kyrle Bellew (Williamson and Musgrove imports) to perform the songs of Jessica in

Shakespeare's *The Merchant of Venice*, 'after *Matsa* like a full-bodied wine after a glass of lemon kali,' said *Quiz and the Lantern*, adding:

> Her voice, while possessing the freshness of youth, has also the
> charm that comes with careful development ... One regrets
> that she has not more to do.[14]

In fact, on stage the role of Jessica was taken by a young Victorian actress, Lena Brasch (the subject of portraits by Tom Roberts and Walter Barnett), but since she was not a singer, she was surreptitiously replaced in the last act by Francie.[15]

Francie followed *The Merchant of Venice* in Brown-Potter and Bellew's company with a minor role in Victorien Sardou's play *La Tosca*, going from Adelaide to Ballarat and then Bendigo.[16] Cora Brown-Potter was to have an important role in the development of Francie's career, not only when she was a member of Cora's touring company, but also later in London. Always known professionally as Mrs Brown-Potter, she was born in New Orleans in 1857 and had married Mr Brown-Potter in 1877, visiting England in 1886, where, already a celebrated beauty, she was 'befriended' by the Prince of Wales. It was in England that she began her acting career, and then later in New York she started her stage relationship with the English actor Kyrle Bellew, who had first come to Australia around 1869, working as a labourer and goldminer before turning to acting.[17] Accompanied by constant publicity, they toured Australasia together first in 1890, then in 1897, which was when Francie joined their company.

It appears that ten- or eleven-year-old Francie had started idolising Cora on her first tour, buying fan photographs which she posted on the walls around her bedroom in St Kilda. And she had written to her idol at the Princess Theatre in Melbourne, where she sent her flowers, and saw her perform from a gallery seat at a matinée. Francie arranged to visit Cora at her hotel:

Her maid opened the door to the Presence. She was lying on
a chaise longue drawn up before the open window ... Her
glorious shining hair was unbound, like one of Rossetti's
ladies, and framed her camellia-white face ... The short,
plump little girl in the white linen frock like a pillowcase stood
speechless and awed.[18]

Cora asked her to play the piano, which she did – Chopin and
Schubert – and then to sing. She chose a song her grandmother had
sung, Isidore de Lara's 'The Garden of Sleep'. They had tea together, and
Cora invited Francie to come and stay with her one day in England.

Cora Brown-Potter by H Walter Barnett

After performing extensively in Brown-Potter's touring company in 1897, in July Francie re-joined Williamson and Musgrove's company in Sydney, taking small roles in a series of popular operettas – Ivan Caryll's *The Gay Parisienne* (as Ethel), followed by Lacôme and Caryll's *Ma mie Rosette* (as Clochette), Alfred Cellier's *Dorothy* (as Phyllis Tuppett), Robert Planquette's *The Old Guard* (as 'Follow the Drum'), Edmond Audran's *La Poupée* (as Marie) and three Gilbert and Sullivans – *The Yeomen of the Guard* (as Kate) *The Gondoliers* (as Fiametta) and *The Mikado* (where she was 'a pretty and vivacious Peep-Bo').[19] In her memoirs, Francie/Frances gives spicy pen-pictures of some of her older, better-established (but unnamed) colleagues in the company:

> There was a peaked, bleached blonde soprano with sharp
> red elbows and sharp high notes. She held herself haughtily
> aloof from the rest of us. I learned, on the first day of my
> engagement that she had an 'angel', a rich shipping man
> in Sydney.

The ironic fact that Francie herself had an 'angel' at the time, pastoralist Sir Rupert Clarke, does not feature in her anecdote. On the other hand: 'The contralto was buxom and friendly with the manager of every theatre we played on tour, and sympathetic with the stagehands and shifters and carpenters about their neuralgia or their wives or their hangovers.' Most intriguing is 'the comedian [who] had a wife who sang in the chorus, [who was] avidly jealous of her husband': 'Anyway, she would jerk herself out of her last act costume and into her street clothes to get to his dressing-room before he had removed all his make-up to keep him from taking any of the other girls out to supper.'[20]

The most likely candidates for these last two are Mr and Mrs Henry Bracy. Born in Wales, tenor Henry Bracy spent much of his long career with Williamson's companies in Australia. His English wife Clara performed with him for many years before leaving for Broadway and Hollywood, where she appeared in some ninety silent films.

Francie (Frances) Adler

In December 1898, still with 'The Firm', Francie was given the part of the Fairy Queen in the Christmas pantomime at Her Majesty's in Sydney, *Ali Baba and the Forty Thieves* (music by Caron and Pack). The production went on to the Theatre Royal in Adelaide in early April, Francie Adler 'pretty and piquant as Morgiana'.[21] Francie was coming to the end of her contract with Williamson and Musgrove, and in February 1899 she joined vaudevillian Harry Rickards's Tivoli company at the Criterion in Sydney, and later at the Bijou in Melbourne, where she regularly received ovations for her renditions of John Stromberg's 'If All the Stars were Mine' and Stephen Foster's 'Old Folks at Home'.[22]

However, having been encouraged by Cora Brown-Potter to try her luck in Europe, Francie was coming towards the time when this would become her priority. In her career to date, how was she doing? *Punch* in Melbourne thought not well enough:

> When Francie Adler first joined the ranks of Williamson's
> Opera Company, prognostications were made that we might
> someday hear a second Frances Saville. The prophecies so far,
> however, have not proved true.[23]

One last tie with her family home at St Kilda was broken on 29 November 1899, with the suicide of her grandfather, Martin Simonsen. Since the death of his wife Fanny three years before, Martin had 'retired within himself, bitter and inconsolable.'[24] Together with her brother Alby, Francie Adler sailed to London on P&O's largest steam liner, *India*, which left Port Melbourne on 14 August 1900.[25]

3

The siblings could afford to travel to England because their mother, prudent Leonore, before she went to San Francisco, had taken out life insurance for the benefit of her two children, which, following her death, would come to them at eighteen. It amounted to £10 000 – a large sum in 1900 (equivalent to around $AU1 400 000 at today's values). And, for two impecunious young people, 'to us the sum seemed enormous'.

> We were decided on one thing: we would go to England. Alby
> would take a degree [in medicine] at St Andrews University in
> Edinburgh [sic]. I would go to the Gaiety Theatre in London.[26]

In fact, Francie had one other trick up her sleeve. One of her performing colleagues in Harry Rickards's Tivoli company was a German, Ludwig Amann, 'a clever facial artist'[27] – a mimic – who had organised for her a short season in one of Berlin's leading vaudeville venues, the Wintergarden. She opened there on 1 January 1901 at 2000 marks a month.[28] Arriving in London in early November 1900, the insurance money gave Francie enough time to get to grips with the city, to see some shows and to do some auditions:

> We had come to conquer London, and we set about it with vigour.
> We went shopping, a regular orgy, up and down Bond Street ...
> On our first night we went to Covent Garden to hear Melba. She
> was singing *Bohème*. That was the first time I had heard the opera.

Francie was not impressed. 'There was something rigid in Melba. She couldn't lose herself in the little grisette.' Although the role of Mimì was to some extent 'owned' by Melba at that time, it was to become one of Frances Alda's most celebrated depictions. That night, Melba followed *Bohème* with the 'Mad Scene' from *Lucia di Lammermoor*, which she did 'marvellously'.[29] The following evening, in their best clothes, Francie and Alby took a box at the Gaiety and had a champagne supper afterwards.

> Very soon I went to see the manager of the Gaiety. He heard
> me sing, and made some vague, non-committal remarks about
> keeping my name and address, in case he should need a singer
> later on, and bowed me out.

Francie was shattered. This was the dashing of her main ambition in coming to England. What was she to do? Of course! She would go to see her friend Mrs Brown-Potter, who was living in style at Maidenhead in Berkshire. This was Francie's first experience of a weekend party at an English country house, and the beautiful Mrs Brown-Potter was a celebrated hostess. It was a world of rich, privileged guests – of porridge, kedgeree and devilled kidneys for breakfast, of croquet, of eight-course dinners and of choreographed illicit affairs.[30]

There in June 1901 she met Mrs BP's guests, among them the cream of artistic society in London, including two leading painters – James McNeill Whistler and John (not yet Sir John) Lavery – also the conductor of the Opéra-Comique in Paris and Covent Garden, André Messager, and the French basso, Marcel Journet, who would later become a close colleague of Alda at the Théâtre de la Monnaie in Brussels, at Covent Garden and at the Met in New York.[31] Of these, it was Messager who was to be of most immediate value to Francie. The weekend over, Cora asked Francie to stay on so that she could go with Cora's party to Derby Day at Epsom, where:

> … everybody seemed to know everybody else. They all called each other by nicknames, and there were many private jokes, awfully funny apparently to those who understood them, and quite incomprehensible to anyone else.

At the Derby, Mrs Brown-Potter introduced Francie to the new King (Edward VII) as a young singer who might one day rival Melba, and the King asked Francie to sing at a benefit for 'one of the regiments'.[32] Her season at the Wintergarden in Berlin in January 1901 must have gone well, for she was invited back there more than once.[33] In May she was hired to sing in variety again, at the Palace Theatre in London at a salary of £30 a week,[34] and at the end of the year she was Principal Boy, Hero, in the pantomime *Oberine* at the Royal Court Theatre in Liverpool. *The Era* declared that she:

> … possessed much of the dash and confidence so necessary to the proper personation of the 'first boy', and she played the role with unflagging 'go', singing her allotted share of the musical tit-bits with verve and effectiveness.[35]

By May 1902, having also performed in the meantime at St Petersburg, Francie went back for a third time to the Wintergarden in Berlin, where the German audience, Anglophobic during the Boer War in South Africa, 'generally hissed [British performers] off the stage'. However, as an Australian, she was 'not only tolerated, but warmly applauded'.[36] By Christmas 1902, Francie was back in pantomime, this time in a show she had done four years earlier in Australia, *The Forty Thieves*, at the Theatre Royal, Nottingham, where she 'disclosed a bright soprano voice, which she used with taste and discrimination'.[37]

Was this to be the limit of Francie's performing career – singing with 'taste and discrimination' at pantomimes and in vaudeville shows? What should she do?

'Let's go to Paris,' brother Alby suggested. So that is what they did.

4

On the train to Dover and then on the boat-train to Paris, they ran into André Messager. Francie talked with him ceaselessly – they talked about her aunt, Frances Saville in Vienna, whom Messager knew, and about Saville's (and Melba's) teacher in Paris, Madame Marchesi. 'Don't forget, mademoiselle; go to Marchesi. There is no one like her,' pronounced Messager.

They stayed in Paris for a few days (without visiting Marchesi) and then went straight to Vienna, which Francie immediately fell in love with:

> Everywhere you went there was music, *tzigane* orchestras
> playing under the chestnut trees in the gardens, beautiful
> women and, to my eye, even more beautiful officers in
> resplendent uniforms, who were not averse to trying to
> impress an English [sic] Miss ... Aunt Frances had a charming

apartment. She was a person of consequence in Vienna, and a strikingly beautiful woman.

However, 'Aunt Frances was anything but encouraging or cordial to me.' Looking back on the situation, Alda speculated that 'the arrival of an unknown niece with strong operatic aspirations was considerable of a nuisance.'[38] It must be said that Francie's track record up to this point, in operettas, vaudeville shows and pantomime, would have given Saville no possible clue that her niece was serious, or that she had any kind of real future in opera. And Francie would not have known that her aunt was herself drawing towards the close of her illustrious career. Alda saw her aunt once more – in 1912 in Venice. By that time, Saville was cordial with her, but now Alda was herself a highly successful prima donna and not in a mood to forgive.

So, somewhat chastened, Francie and Alby went back to Paris to seek out Madame Marchesi. If she could not persuade her aunt of her serious intent and promise, somehow or other she had to persuade Marchesi. By 1903, when Francie visited the École Marchesi in the rue Jouffroy, Mathilde was already eighty-two years old and had been teaching singing, producing a steady stream of international prima donnas, for nearly fifty years. Admitted to the presence, Francie later shared her memories:

> What a czarina she was! Upright and stiff as a ramrod, with snapping black eyes and stern, tightly compressed mouth. She motioned me to the piano. 'I will hear you sing, mademoiselle. Then I will say what I think of your voice and whether I will accept you as a pupil.'

Wisely, Francie did not offer a bel canto aria, rather she sang a somewhat sentimental ballad which gave her the chance to 'open my throat and pour out all the voice I had' – Francis Allison's 'Song of Thanksgiving'. Francie noticed a twinkle in Marchesi's eye, and, when she had finished (according to Francie), Marchesi rose and called out to her husband: 'Salvatore, viens. J'ai trouvé la nouvelle Melba.'[39] ('Come quickly, Salvatore, I've found the new Melba.')

Whether or not this story is literally true, Francie Adler was in. Undoubtedly, she will have made Marchesi fully aware that her aunt was one of Madame's favourite pupils, and that her grandmother was a pupil of Manuel Garcia, as was Marchesi. And, having taken her as a pupil, Francie noted, Marchesi 'assumed direction of all my activities for the ten months I studied with her'. Disappointed not to be accepted at St Andrews University, her brother Alby went back to Australia, eventually to become a pharmacist at St Kilda. In her memoirs, Alda described her daily life at the École Marchesi:

> Every morning at nine I presented myself in the rue Jouffroy for my lesson. I was expected to stay on to hear all the other pupils in order to learn as much and as quickly as possible … Beside the singing lessons, I was studying French and Italian, and later, when I began to prepare myself in operatic roles, Marchesi arranged for me to study mise-en-scène with the famous tenor, Victor Capoul … Nearly every day I lunched with Marchesi and her aged husband the Marquis de Castrone and their various musical guests.[40]

When Francie had been studying with Marchesi for some months, Mathilde organised engagements for her to sing at the private houses of the great and good in Paris, and it was at these functions that she first used her new performing name – given to her by Marchesi – no longer Francie Adler, now the more distinguished Frances Alda. She also sang in Marchesi's own in-house concerts, one of these in June 1903, when two other Australian students of Marchesi also appeared – Victoria Nicoll and Eva Mylott.[41] In Paris, Frances was able to see several of the greatest performers of that era, including the actresses Sarah Bernhardt and Gabrielle Réjane, pianist Paderewski and the sixty-year-old diva, Adelina Patti.

As with Nellie Melba and her aunt Frances Saville before her, Mathilde also organised Frances Alda's operatic debut, which in this case took place at the Opéra-Comique in Paris on 15 February 1904. Coached on a daily basis by the sixty-one-year-old Massenet, she sang the title role in his *Manon*.[42] This was not the sort of bel canto role that had launched Melba's and Saville's careers at the Monnaie, but rather a more modern, proto-verismo role that Marchesi chose for Frances, one that would point the way for her future career.

'Marchesi altered the entire course of my life,' wrote Alda.[43] In her memoirs *Men, Women and Tenors*, she outlined some key aspects of Marchesi's approach and method:

> To teach the art of singing requires that the teacher shall not only train the voice but be able to teach the singer how to preserve the voice for years and years ... Usually it is fright that makes a singer's throat tighten up. Fright, caused by nerves ... The upper part of the voice was conserved with infinite care to avoid early breakdown ... Most girls over-exercise their voices during the years while the voice is immature ... She advised daily lessons of twenty minutes each, and no more ... Marchesi's exercises were little more than scales, sung very slowly ... After these came a more complicated technical drill to prepare a pupil for *fioritura* work.[44]

5

Introduced by Marchesi, Frances Alda was given a three-year contract by the director of the Opéra-Comique, Albert Carré, and in a box at the theatre on the evening of her debut were Mathilde Marchesi and (says Alda) Marchesi's most famous pupil, Nellie Melba. That performance seems to have gone well enough, but by September, Carré had broken the contract and been sued by Alda for damages.[45]

The real reason for the break with the Comique was most likely because Alda had signed a new contract to sing at the Théâtre de la Monnaie in Brussels. Her view was that things were moving too slowly for her in Paris, and when one evening she was heard as Manon by directors of the Brussels theatre, they signed her up on the spot. Marchesi was not pleased with her, but nevertheless the two of them settled down to learn the roles she was to sing in Brussels.[46]

For a young woman with virtually no experience of singing in opera, Alda would find the Monnaie to be an intensive training ground. Her debut there was on 7 October 1904, twelve years after the first performance of her aunt Frances Saville. As previously at the Comique, she was Manon, with Thomas Salignac as Des Grieux and Alexis Boyer as Lescaut. Of her performance, *Le Guide Musical* wrote:

> With emotion, Frances Alda made her debut in the part of Manon. Very beautiful and with graceful elegance, she gave to the role a delicious manner. Her voice has great range, the high notes of great purity, with a charming trill … Her success was complete, but this is not really surprising as she was coached by Massenet himself.[47]

Her next role in Brussels, its opening on 2 November, was as Marguérite in Faust, with Léon Lafitte as Faust and Cécile Eyreams as Siebel. *Le Guide Musical* wrote that Alda 'achieved a real success as Marguérite, one that fully exploits the beauty, the charm, the purity, the facility of her voice [together with] the art of her interpretation of the role'.[48]

She described one aspect of that occasion in her memoirs: she was told by one of the directors of the Monnaie before the performance that the Belgian King (Leopold II) would be in the royal box. As a joke, Alda suggested that she might wink at him while singing 'There was a king in Thule', which horrified the director. 'Leopold was then a bad old man,' Alda wrote, although whether she had in mind his many mistresses or

Alda as Manon, 1905

his ruthless exploitation of the people of the Congo (or both), she did not make clear.[49]

Among her colleagues 'whose friendship touched me deeply' at the Monnaie was the tenor, Ernest van Dyck (whom Alda thought had had an affair with her aunt Frances Saville). And, while she was at the Monnaie, she fell in love: 'He was a singer, and the only singer I ever did fall in love with. Not a tenor … but a big, magnificent man, six and a half feet tall, with a glorious bass voice.'[50] She did not say who this was, but a strong candidate would have been Marcel Journet.

In the first weeks of 1905 Alda was in rehearsals for a revival of Massenet's *Hérodiade,* which opened on 6 February with Alda as Salomé, Pierre d'Assy as Herod and Charles Dalmorès as John the Baptist. This ran for fourteen performances and was followed on 22 March by Ambroise Thomas's *Hamlet* with Alda as Ophélie and Henri Albers as the prince. In her first season at the Monnaie, 1904–05, Frances sang no less than sixty-one times. The following season opened on 17 August 1905 and Alda made her first appearance on the 20th as Marguérite in *Faust,* followed by *Manon* on the 24th, of which *L'Éventail* wrote:

> [Alda] is perfect with the very intelligent composition and the
> searching study of the character, and the charm and security
> of her voice, which reached without difficulty the high D in
> Act 3. Concerning the Anglo-Saxon accent, there remains
> from last year only a few traces that continual work will soon
> eradicate.[51]

Alda claimed that in all she sang fifty-two Manons and seventy-four Marguérites at the Monnaie.[52] Gounod was grandmother Fanny's favourite composer and *Faust* her favourite opera, and Alda was the fourth Simonsen woman to sing that role.

On 9 September 1905, Alda created the title role ('admirably attractive') in the première of Belgian composer Paul Gilson's *Princesse Rayon de Soleil,* and on 11 October she was Marguérite de Valois in Meyerbeer's *Les Huguenots* with a fine Belgian and French cast. This was a role previously taken by her grandmother Fanny Simonsen in WS Lyster's company in Melbourne thirty-nine years earlier, and by her aunt Frances Saville at Covent Garden in 1897. On 30 October, Alda sang her first Gilda in Verdi's *Rigoletto* with Léon David as the Duke of Mantua and Henri Albers in the title role, and on 16 December she was Ensoleillad ('of beauty and of radiant, splendid voice') in the first performance there of Massenet's *Chérubin,* with Jeanne Maubourg in the title role. The work had been premièred at Monte Carlo in February.

Théâtre de la Monnaie, Brussels

On the 150th anniversary of Mozart's birth, 27 January 1906, the Monnaie revived *Les noces de Figaro* (*Le nozze di Figaro*) with Alda as the Countess. Alda disappointed in this, being 'little adapted to sustained singing', and played the role with 'marked coldness'.[53] Alda regularly returned to Madame Marchesi in Paris for coaching in new roles – so perhaps this was Marchesi's conception of the Countess.

Figaro was followed on 23 February by Berlioz's *La damnation de Faust*, with Alda as Marguérite, Dalmorès as Faust and Albers as Méphistophélès, after which came Gounod's *Roméo et Juliette* on 17 March with Alda as Juliette. During her second season at the Monnaie, 1905–06, Alda sang a total of ninety-four times.

Aside from revivals, new roles for Alda in her third season in Brussels, 1906–07, were: on 9 November, Messager's *Madame Chrysanthème* with Frances in the title role; on 21 April Violetta in *La traviata*; and, in a return to the house with Caruso in 1910, as Mimì in *La bohème*, the performance mixed between French and Italian. Of her Chrysanthème, one Brussels paper wrote, 'Alda's kimonos are as brilliant as her voice,'[54] and of her Violetta, *Le Guide Musical* said 'Frances Alda sang the part ... with much delicate nuance, expressing finesse and truth without looking for dramatic effects.'[55] She was the fourth Simonsen woman to sing Violetta, following grandmother Fanny and aunts Martina Simonsen and Frances Saville.

Between her second and third seasons at the Monnaie, Frances was booked to sing for the first time at Covent Garden in London in May–June 1906.

If Frances Alda's seasons at the Monnaie had built a substantial repertoire for her, giving her extensive practical operatic experience and garnering consistent praise from the critics, her brief season at Covent Garden in the summer of 1906 was not so successful. And Alda's brief stay there achieved by no means the same level of respect that her aunt Saville had achieved nine years earlier.

Her Covent Garden debut as Marguérite in *Faust* on 24 May 1906 seems for the London critics to have stimulated three sources of disappointment. First, her voice was adjudged to be too small for the space. The auditorium at Covent Garden is a good size larger than the one at the Monnaie. Second, Alda was thought to have been nervous. There was at that time a pecking order in the status of opera houses, and Covent Garden was in the top echelon, whereas, beautiful as it is, the Monnaie was in the next tier down. And third, she was called upon unexpectedly in order to fill a gap left by the indisposition of the great Melba. What is more, the programme was not even one whole work, it was a mixture of two acts of *Faust*, followed by a relatively short work, Leoncavallo's *Pagliacci*.[56]

The cast for the *Faust* was fundamentally the group of artists from the Monnaie, including Alda, Altchevsky, Lafitte and Journet, conducted by Messager. They would all have been very used to singing that music in the Monnaie's acoustic. The cast for the *Pagliacci* which followed was of a completely different stripe, with two of the most highly esteemed singers in the world in the lead – Emmy Destinn as Nedda and Enrico Caruso as Canio. Not unnaturally, it was not the *Faust*, but the *Pagliacci* that was given top marks.

Could Alda do better with her next offering? It was to be on 13 June as Gilda in *Rigoletto*, and this time Alda was to perform with a truly world-class team – Caruso as the Duke, Mattia Battistini as the court jester Rigoletto and Marcel Journet as the assassin Sparafucile. This time, it was not so much the inadequate size of the voice or the nervousness, but Alda's 'tremolo' that gave offence. Also, according to *The Times*, 'She does but little in the way of powerful acting to make her hearers forget her vocal shortcomings.'[57] And, most damaging of all, she was compared, unfavourably, in the role with Nellie Melba.[58] Ironically, it was the newspaper dedicated to horseracing, the *Sporting Life*, which most appreciated her talents, liking both the way she looked and the way she sang.[59] The 'tremolo' that the London critics viewed unfavourably would have been more than they were used to – certainly more than from Melba, whose very shallow vibrato was gradually becoming old-fashioned as verismo operas (with broader vibrato) took the place of bel canto works in the repertoire.

One gleam of hope for Frances was that, after her first Gilda at Covent Garden, two people came to her dressing room afterwards to congratulate her – 'a gentle old man and a very exquisite old lady' – this was the composer of popular Italian songs, Paolo Tosti, and the great diva, Adelina Patti. Alda was for a while to go to Tosti for 'my daily singing lesson'.[60] In her memoirs, around this time Frances discloses a close personal relationship with another Italian composer, 'a very attractive man', Franco Alfano, most remembered now for his *Resurrezione* of 1904, and for his later completion of Puccini's last opera, *Turandot*.[61] This affair was to remain active for long enough to become the cause of jealousy on the part of Alda's future husband, Giulio Gatti-Casazza.[62]

Perhaps understandably, Alda's version of events that summer at Covent Garden was rather different from what may be gleaned from London newspaper reviews. She claimed that the director, Harry Higgins, 'was gratifyingly admiring of me as a singer and as a woman'. But, if so, why did she sing so infrequently, and why was she not invited back? Alda implies that there were dark deeds afoot among the elite at Covent Garden that got in her way. She does not directly name either Melba in this context, or Melba's great supporter on the board, Lady de Grey, but they both may be noticed between the lines.[63]

Melba's antipathy to Alda becomes much clearer in what happened next. The conductor of Covent Garden's *Rigoletto* was Cleofonte Campanini, who was recruiting top singers for Oscar Hammerstein's intended new competitor to the Metropolitan Opera in New York, the Manhattan Opera. Campanini told Alda that they had already secured the American performing rights to the new operas of Debussy and Richard Strauss, and of Charpentier's *Louise*, and had signed up a magnificent list of prima donnas, including Luisa Tetrazzini, Mary Garden ... and Melba. Would Alda like to join them?

Yes please, she responded and signed a contract. But sometime later, according to Frances, Melba heard of the arrangements with Alda, and sent Campanini a telegram, which simply read: 'Either Alda or myself.' Not one to fight a losing battle – Melba was the most famous singer in the world – Alda agreed that her contract should be torn up.[64] She might get the chance of revenge later.

However, the opportunity to join the Manhattan Opera was not the only carrot that Campanini dangled in front of Frances. In October 1907 he was to conduct Verdi operas in the famous Verdi festival at the composer's birthplace, Parma, in Northern Italy. Would she sing Gilda in his *Rigoletto* there? With one thing leading to another, Parma was to be a fresh turning point in Alda's career.

7

Alda returned to Brussels from London to complete her commitments to the Monnaie's 1906–07 season, to be followed by two concerts in June at the Bechstein Hall (now the Wigmore) in London, before travelling on to Parma in late September 1907.

On the evening that she arrived at Parma, she heard for the first time Catalani's *Loreley*, a work in which Frances would later become admired. Unfortunately, the artist singing the role of Anna, Alice Zepelli, cracked on a high note in her main aria and the Italian audience immediately 'broke into hisses and jeers'. Alda was horrified. She had never encountered such hostility from an audience. 'I can't sing here tomorrow night', she told Madame Campanini, 'I simply can't face an audience like that.'

But face them she did, and the first night of *Rigoletto* at the Teatro Regio on 2 October, was a great triumph for her. The theatre was 'overflowing with a splendid and elegant public', wrote *La Realtà*. 'There were very many people from outside Parma scattered among the boxes and the stalls.' For Frances, although she did not know it at the time, most significant among the guests was the director of La Scala Milan, Giulio Gatti- Casazza. *La Realtà* continued in grandiloquent prose:

> Whoever has dreamed of an ideal performance of *Rigoletto*,
> which, after the performances which made the opera famous
> … seemed something which would be denied to the pleasure
> of the new generation, can now be comforted in their
> nostalgia. After the vibrant, vigorous, intelligent, bold, but
> happy interpretation of yesterday evening, one has to proclaim
> that … it has been granted to take from the wonderful
> performance of the Verdi opera a range of emotions which
> renders unforgettable the great interpreters and their fine
> labours on stage.

The cast included two of the greatest singers of the age – Alessandro Bonci as the Duke and Mattia Battistini as the hunchback, yet topmost among those eulogised was the newcomer, 'Signorina Alda Frances' [sic], who 'deserves our admiring praise':

> She pleased the audience immensely and she was admired
> and applauded with enthusiasm … She was a precise, elegant,
> agile Gilda and she applied her voice, which is fine, fresh,
> penetrating and very secure, to the difficulties of a role which
> combines both passion and virtuosity. In 'Caro nome' her
> clear, agile singing, her impeccable trills and her nightingale-
> like leaps and turns drew from the audience a prolonged
> ovation.[65]

'I sang with Bonci and with Battistini and I was inspired to my best,' was Alda's own assessment. Madame Marchesi would have been proud of her. And the fact that Gatti-Casazza was there to hear it meant that he asked Frances to come and see him in Milan. Up to that time, she did not know who he was. She asked Battistini about him: 'The ablest director of grand opera in the world,' he responded. 'For eight years he has been directing La Scala … He has brought il bel canto back to Italy – he and Maestro Toscanini, his conductor.'

And who was this Toscanini? 'Marvellous … incredible … an extraordinary genius,' Battistini responded. Frances wrote to Gatti-Casazza that she would be in Milan in two days' time at the Grand Hotel Milan, and he could contact her there.[66]

8

At Alda's first meeting in Milan with Gatti, he told her that they were in the very hotel where Verdi had died – and he showed her the room, which Frances would not enter. They spoke in French, as Gatti did not speak English and Alda did not at that time speak Italian. Gatti was thirty-eight, Alda ten years younger. Both were unmarried, although he had been engaged for a time to the Spanish prima donna Maria Barrientos.

Gatti's father had fought with Garibaldi in the Risorgimento campaigns of the 1860s aimed at unifying Italy and expelling foreign powers, and he had later become director of the Teatro Comunale in Ferrara, where the young Gatti was to experience for the first time all kinds of theatrical entertainments – 'opera, ballet, operetta, comedy, tragedy, marionettes, equestrian circuses …' In the meantime, he prepared himself for a naval career at the Accademia Navale at Leghorn (Livorno), but was not sufficiently motivated by the prospect to pass their exams. So in 1893 Gatti followed his father at the theatre in Ferrara – his first role in opera administration – his greatest (and lifelong) passions being Verdi and Wagner. At Ferrara he befriended the young Puccini, organising (among other contemporary works) early performances of his *Manon Lescaut* and *La bohème*. In 1898 Gatti was invited to take over as general director of La Scala, to be joined there as musical director by the young maestro Arturo Toscanini, who had been conducting at Turin.[67]

After the first meeting of Alda and Gatti at the Grand Hotel Milan, Gatti came back, this time with Toscanini. They were planning to introduce Charpentier's *Louise* at La Scala for the first time. Would she come and sing it? It was October 1907, and the production of *Louise* was scheduled for February, so there was plenty of time to learn the role before coming to Milan for rehearsals. Additionally, Gatti asked her to sing the role of Margherita in Boito's *Mefistofele*, with Feodor Chaliapin in the title role. How could she refuse?

On her return to Paris[68] from Milan, Alda's first action was to enlist Marchesi's help in preparing her for her La Scala debut. A new production in Italy of Charpentier's very popular opera, albeit in Italian, excited Marchesi, and they set to work on it. Alda had seen

Mary Garden several times in the role at the Opéra-Comique – Garden had made her sensational Paris debut as Louise in 1900.[69] Alda quickly realised that she must put Mary Garden's performance out of her mind and create her own interpretation of the character. In the New Year, she went to Milan to start rehearsing with Toscanini. Gatti sat in a corner. 'He leaned his elbow on the arm of his chair and rested his cheek against his hand, eyeing me gravely,' wrote Frances.

> Toscanini sat beside the pianist. He kept his eyes closed as he listened, only lifting a finger now and then to mark the time. I began to sing … The pianist struck a final chord. Its echoes died away in the still room. No one spoke. Then Toscanini leaned across the pianist's shoulder and closed the music book on the rack … 'In what language were you singing?'

Alda was furious. Was this to be the end of their relationship even before it had started? She glared at Toscanini, at the pianist, and at Gatti, and marched out of the rehearsal room, out of the theatre, and back to the Grand Hotel Milan. Significantly, she did not go to the railway station to catch a train home. Several days passed before Gatti finally came to the hotel, apologised, and asked her to come back. She refused. Eventually, Gatti came back with an offer: Toscanini would go through *Louise* with her, note by note, word by word (as Massenet had for her with *Manon*) and that way make sure that her pronunciation of the Italian was perfect. She accepted: 'Of course I did.'

At the ensuing rehearsal, Alda was 'careful of her dignity', and Toscanini 'punctilious'. It was the start of a close personal and artistic relationship that would last for decades. Thinking back on the situation, Frances was full of repentance:

> Now [1937], recalling that childish fit of temper and hurt pride on my part, I think too of the innumerable times later on

that Toscanini taught me the roles I was to sing; his infinite patience and inspiring enthusiasm, and all that I owe him. And I feel like humbling myself before the forbearance of a very great artist.[70]

Of Alda's first performance at La Scala in *Louise* on 6 February 1908, *Il Corriere della Sera* wrote:

> The first place among the singers goes to Frances Alda, who was little known to the public here before she came. She is a most elegant singer, full of subtlety, grace and passion. Her voice is full, clear and very beautiful, and her singing is easy, expressive and always well in tune.[71]

The rest of the Italian press echoed that report, praising her intelligence, elegance, liveliness, passion, beauty, stage presence, nobility and dramatic talent, not to mention the charm, harmoniousness, good intonation and power of her singing. This was a long way from the grudging notices of the London critics during her brief sojourn at Covent Garden nine months earlier. And Alda's triumph at La Scala was even more remarkable, given that this was an Australian singing an opera by a Frenchman in Italian.

Before her La Scala *Mefistofele*, Frances travelled across Europe by train from Milan to Warsaw, in order to fulfil a short season booking at the Teatr Wielki. There she opened on 3 March as Marguérite in *Faust*, following on 19 March with her Manon. Of the two, it was again Manon that reaped the greater plaudits, the *Kurier Warszawski* commenting:

> Finally yesterday we saw *Manon*, beautiful and breath-taking … Miss Alda was a superb representative of Massenet's heroine, but if in her there was more delicacy and refinement than deep sentiment, it is the individual quality of a very

talented artist who, with her voice, brings out the most beautiful feelings.[72]

Returned to La Scala on 11 April, Alda opened as Margherita in *Mefistofele* with Chaliapin. However, in this opera it was the great Russian bass who received the ovation. 'Don't ever go to America, Alda,' he advised her, having not been well received there up to that time. 'It's a terrible place.'

But there, of course, is exactly where she was to go for the greatest part of her performing career.

Notes

1   In her memoirs, Alda says that she was christened Frances Jeanné Davies (22); each part of this name is incorrect
2   Frances Alda, *Men, Women and Tenors*, 25
3   Francie was reported later as having been a pupil of tenor Armes Beaumont, who had sung so often with Fanny Simonsen, but there seems to be little corroborative evidence for this; *Herald*, 5 February 1901, 4; *Leader*, 10 March 1906, 21
4   Alda, 26
5   *Jewish Herald*, 10 October 1890, 7
6   *Australasian* (Melbourne), 26 December 1891, 26
7   *Table Talk* (Melbourne), 25 December 1896, 11
8   Alda, 34
9   Alda, 273
10   Alda, 35
11   *Punch* (Melbourne), 25 March 1897, 5
12   *Evening News* (Sydney), 5 April 1897, 3
13   *Advertiser* (Adelaide), 14 April 1897, 5
14   *Quiz and the Lantern* (Adelaide), 13 May 1897, 12
15   *Quiz and the Lantern*, 20 May 1897, 10
16   *Ballarat Star*, 25 May 1897, 1
17   Among much else, Bellew acted at the Solferino diggings in New South Wales
18   Alda, 31–33
19   *Sunday Times* (Sydney), 4 September 1898, 2
20   Alda, 35
21   *Advertiser* (Adelaide), 3 April 1899, 6

22   *Evening News* (Sydney), 19 February 1900, 3; *Advocate* (Melbourne), 22 February 1900, 21
23   *Punch* (Melbourne), 7 June 1900, 23
24   Alda, 34; the suicide is dealt with more fully in Chapter 6
25   *Australasian*, 18 August 1900, 38
26   Alda, 36
27   *Williamstown Chronicle* (Melbourne) 28 April 1900, 3; Frank Van Straten, *Tivoli*, 18
28   *Critic* (Adelaide), 21 July 1900, 21
29   Alda, 37
30   Juliet Nicolson, *The Perfect Summer*, 79–86
31   Alda, 38–39
32   Alda 39–41; Alda met King Edward VII again two years later at Marienbad, where he
     introduced her to golf; she decided that her arms were too short and her bust too large to
     be any good at it
33   *Evening News* (Sydney), 6 February 1901, 3
34   *Referee* (Sydney), 8 May 1901, 10
35   *Era*, 28 December 1901, 14
36   *Leader* (Melbourne), 15 March 1902, 22; *Queenslander* (Brisbane), 31 May 1902, 1178;
     Advertiser (Adelaide), 2 August 1902, 5
37   *Nottingham Evening Post*, 27 December 1902, 5
38   Alda, 42–43
39   Alda, 44
40   Alda, 45
41   *Sunday Sun* (Sydney), 19 July 1903, 4; contralto Eva Mylott was grandmother of
     Hollywood star Mel Gibson; *Daily Telegraph* (Launceston), 14 November 1903, 7; in
     November, there were further reports of Alda and other Australians performing at
     Marchesi's concerts, including Nicoll, Beatrice Oxley and Rosina Pinhey
42   *Sydney Morning Herald*, 27 February 1904, 9; *Daily Telegraph* (Sydney), 27 February
     1904, 15
43   Alda, 45
44   Alda, 297–99
45   *The Week* (Brisbane), 30 September 1904, 2
46   Alda, 55–56
47   *Guide Musical* (Brussels), 9 October 1904
48   Guide Musical, 6 November 1904
49   Alda, 56
50   Alda, 60
51   *L'Éventail* (Brussels), 26 August 1905
52   Alda, 59
53   The negative reception to Alda's Countess was in marked contrast to the warmth with
     which her grandmother Fanny Simonsen had been greeted in the role at Adelaide in 1866
54   No source available
55   *Guide Musical*, 14 April 1907
56   *Pall Mall Gazette*, 25 May 1906, 3; *Daily News* (London), 25 May 1906, 8; *Times* (London),
     25 May 1906, 5; Era, 2 June 1906, 15
57   *Times*, 14 June 1906, 10
58   *Daily Telegraph* (London), quoted in *Sydney Morning Herald*, 21 July 1906, 4
59   *Sporting Life* (London), 14 June 1906, 4
60   Alda, 48, 66–67
61   Alda, 66
62   Alda, 94
63   Alda, 62–64
64   Alda, 65–66, 72

65   *La Realtà*, 3 October 1907
66   Alda, 70–72
67   Giulio Gatti-Casazza, *Memories of the Opera*, 23–59
68   To the apartment at 55 Avenue Bugeaud, near the Bois de Boulogne
69   Article by Mary Garden in *Theatre*, quoted in Michael TRB Turnbull, *Mary Garden*, 26
70   Alda, 85
71   *Il Corriere della Sera*, February 1908
72   *Kurier Warszawski*, 20 March 1908, 3

Chapter 9
The Met: Gatti, Caruso, Toscanini

1

By January 1908, the New York Metropolitan Opera had started negotiations with Giulio Gatti-Casazza with a view to him becoming general manager. The existing boss of the Met, Heinrich Conried, had been in charge since 1903 and had built up the German repertoire, but was now unwell and had indicated that he planned to retire. Banker and chairman of the board, Otto Kahn, had bought out Conried's shares in the operating company and sent Rawlins Cottenet to Europe to find Conried's successor. Cottenet was a New York socialite related to many of the city's most prominent families – including the Schermerhorns and Astors – but who had personally lost his fortune.[1] He was secretary to the board and in 1903 had negotiated for the young tenor Enrico Caruso to come to the Met.[2]

Initially the board's inclination was to appoint Gustav Mahler, who was soon to conduct German-language operas at the house, making his first appearance in Wagner's *Tristan und Isolde* on 1 January 1908. However, Mahler turned them down, so they turned their attentions to the director-general of La Scala in Milan, Giulio Gatti-Casazza. Their initial concept had been that there might be a dual directorship, with Mahler directing the German repertoire and Gatti the Italian and French, but this did not come about. Instead, Gatti was to be sought as General Director, while the German tenor Andreas Dippel would be appointed Administrative Director.[3]

Early in January, Cottenet was in Milan having meetings with Gatti. By 23 January, Gatti had been formally offered the job,[4] and by

The young Arturo Toscanini

12 February he had accepted and the news had leaked in the American press.[5] By the time Cottenet returned to New York on 6 March, not only had Gatti been signed up, but also Gatti's colleague at La Scala, the outstanding conductor, Arturo Toscanini.[6] And not just Gatti and Toscanini were hired, but also Frances Alda, who always claimed that she was signed first of them.

In August, Cottenet sailed back to Italy in order to finalise plans with Gatti and Toscanini for the forthcoming season at the Met,[7] which opened on 16 November 1908 with Verdi's *Aida*, Emmy Destinn in the title role, her Met debut,[8] Caruso as Radamès, Louise Homer as Amneris and Antonio Scotti as Amonasro, with Arturo Toscanini making his house debut.[9] In his recent biography of Toscanini, Harvey Sachs described the impact made by the conductor at his first rehearsal with the Met orchestra:

> The players had heard stories about Toscanini's memory, but there was general astonishment when he began to rehearse Wagner's gigantic work [*Götterdämmerung*] in detail without consulting the score. And the astonishment grew as the new conductor began to hear and correct errors in the musicians' printed parts … at one point, the orchestra spontaneously broke into applause, bravos and a fanfare.[10]

And gradually Toscanini's 'innovations' took hold at the Met: encores were banned; the musicians who played at the rehearsals should also play at the performances; the conductor, not the singers, would decide how arias would be performed – tempo, dynamics etc; accuracy, drive, brilliance – perfection – was the aim; and, not least, Toscanini demanded complete focus and concentration from both musicians and singers towards his and the composers' artistic goals.

2

Before taking up her new contract as a principal soprano at the Met, Alda had other business to take care of – a season in South America at Buenos Aires and Montevideo.

That company was put together by impresario Camillo Bonetti and left for Buenos Aires in May 1908. Mostly Italians, it also included two fine foreign basses – the Pole Adamo Didur and the Spaniard Andrès De Segurola. Also on board ship was the Russian Chaliapin (with whom Alda had been singing at La Scala), who was going to Buenos Aires to perform separately from the company. While Didur and Alda became friends on the tour, it was 'Seggy' who was to become closest to Frances, 'someone with a grand sense of humour to add zest to the party'.[11] By this stage, Gatti, having fallen in love with Frances, warned her off too much fraternising on board with all those basses, Chaliapin in particular. The conductor of the season, not mentioned in Alda's memoirs, was Leopoldo Mugnone, who had a distinguished career mainly in Europe and South America. He was a close friend of Verdi and had conducted the premières of Mascagni's *Cavalleria rusticana* and Puccini's *Tosca*. On the voyage to Argentina, Alda learned to speak Italian more fluently, and, having arrived, she immediately loved Buenos Aires:

> It was big and vigorous and young and rich and kind ... There
> was a frank lavishness about everything, from the scenery
> and the women's figures to the way men made love ... They
> came to the opera not from any grim determination to prove
> themselves cultured and fashionable, but for enjoyment ...
> How easy they were to sing to![12]

At the Teatro de la Opera, Alda opened on 25 May as Gilda in *Rigoletto*, with Fernando de Luca in the title role, Giuseppe Anselmi as the Duke and De Segurola as Sparafucile – a magnificent cast. They gave six performances. Sadly for Alda, on the same night that she opened in *Rigoletto*, there were also two *Aidas* in Buenos Aires – in the inaugural season of the Teatro Colón and at the Politeama.

Rigoletto was followed on 31 May by *La traviata*, with Alda as Violetta, Rinaldo Grassi as Alfredo and Riccardo Stracciari as Germont (also performed six times). Ambroise Thomas's *Mignon* opened on 30 June with Alda as Philine and Livia Berlendi in the title role. *La prensa* commented:

> The role of Philine requires great vocal agility, more than
> Madame Alda has, but she worked diligently to triumph
> over that.[13]

Over time, Alda would focus increasingly on lyric soprano roles that did not demand extreme vocal gymnastics. The final two productions involving Alda in Buenos Aires were *Roméo et Juliette* with Anselmi as Roméo (five performances), and *Faust* with Grassi in the title role and Didur as Méphistophélès (one performance). In all, Alda sang leading roles twenty-one times in Buenos Aires before the company moved across the River Plate to Montevideo, where they performed at the Teatro Solís.

The Montevideo season opened on 12 August with Anselmi and Alda as Roméo and Juliette. This was followed for Alda (with the same casts as in Buenos Aires) by *La traviata, Mignon, Faust and Rigoletto*.[14] Mugnone conducted during the season the first Uruguayan performances of Wagner's *Die Walküre* and Massenet's *Thaïs*. Frances was very conscious that this was the city where her mother Leonore was born, and where her grandparents Fanny and Martin Simonsen had performed (also at the Teatro Solís) nearly fifty years earlier:

> I drove about Montevideo, through the old Spanish streets,
> telling myself it was this frowning-fronted old house, or there

Alda driving her car

that Grandmother had had her lodgings, and where her baby
Leonore – my mother – had been born.[15]

Frances received letters and telegrams from the ardent Gatti every
day, and, when the company arrived back in Genoa, 'Gatti was on the
pier to receive me.'

3

Before heading for her new life in New York, Frances visited Venice with Gatti, where she vacationed on the Lido with her growing circle of rich and famous friends, before returning to her home in Paris, where she gave concerts in several grand houses, and had a motoring accident in which her arm was broken.[16] She arrived in New York on *La Touraine* on 8 November 1908.

Even before her debut at the Metropolitan Opera, the New York press was abuzz with rumour about her relationship with Gatti. Were they to be married? No, not even engaged, said Gatti.[17] But it was clear to all the New York press that theirs was a very close relationship, and the fact that they sought to hide it only increased speculation and resentment.

Until the 1880s, professional opera in Manhattan had been sung at the Academy of Music on 14th Street. It had fine acoustics, but was lacking in other respects, and there were great expectations of the newly built Metropolitan Opera House on Broadway, these vividly expressed in Edith Wharton's *The Age of Innocence*:

> There was already talk of the erection, in remote metropolitan
> distances 'above the Forties', of a new Opera House which
> should compete in costliness and splendour with those of the
> great European capitals.[18]

However, coming to the Met in 1908, only twenty-five years after the new house had opened, and having sung at several of the most beautiful opera houses in the world, Alda was deeply unimpressed:

> It looked more like a storage warehouse. Dirty brown brick.
> Shabby. Old. Weather-stained posters hanging in tatters in the
> sleety winter wind. The sordid everyday business of Broadway

Metropolitan Opera, New York

– the hawkers, the actors and actresses out of jobs, the hotel
touts, out-of-town sightseers, sandwich men, dope peddlers,
gangsters … The dressing rooms were ill ventilated and
unbelievably dirty.[19]

This building was to remain the home of the Metropolitan Opera
until the move to the Lincoln Center in 1966. Alda's first role at the
Met was as Gilda in *Rigoletto* with an all-star cast – Caruso as the
Duke, Pasquale Amato in the title role, Louise Homer as Maddalena
and Adamo Didur as Sparafucile, with Francesco Spetrino conducting.
And Alda was very clear about its importance:

> My life story begins not in the New Zealand city where I was
> born … but twenty-three years [sic] later, on the rainy night
> of December 7 1908, which was the night I faced my first
> American audience.[20]

For a prima donna starting out on what was to become a distinguished performing career at the Met, eventually encompassing 266 performances of twenty-three different roles, her debut there could not have been more dispiriting. The New York press savaged the debutante's performance in every aspect: the *New York Times* said that her voice was 'of very moderate beauty', verging on 'stridence and shrillness', was also 'frequently false in intonation', and her acting showed 'little that approximated to dramatic talent'; the *Evening World* reported that her singing of 'Caro nome' was 'anything but impressive'; the *Sun* decided that she 'sang so badly', and that 'Miss Alda will not take rank with the memorable Gildas of the Metropolitan'.[21]

Not unnaturally, Alda was devastated. Gilda was a role that she had sung, usually with great success, many times – at the Monnaie in Brussels, at Covent Garden (with Caruso), in Warsaw, Parma, Buenos Aires and Montevideo. Theoretically, it held no terrors for her.

> Was I scared? No one who doesn't know from actual
> experience of what stage fright can do to one could possibly
> know *how* scared … In that I am no different from most
> singers. I remember Caruso telling me that he had never
> sung a single performance [but] that he wasn't nervous and
> miserable and afraid. But stage fright is being afraid that you
> won't do the best that you know you are capable of doing.[22]

She wished that Toscanini had been conducting rather than Spetrino. And there was another negative complication: an anonymous letter to the New York critics, which later appeared in the press, was circulated on the day of her opening, which said that she was not Frances Alda at all, but one of the Barrison Sisters, who were well-known at that time in the music halls of England. Alda denied the story vigorously. She was not a Barrison and she had never appeared in a music hall in England.[23] The problem remained that she had indeed performed – regularly – in both vaudeville and pantomime in Australia, in vaudeville in Germany and in pantomime in England, so it seems likely that some of the mud did stick. Alda's maid brought her the newspapers in bed the morning after. On reading the reviews, she recalled:

> … my heart ached and my throat was sore. I shivered all over.
> I hated America. 'I'll never sing in your old opera house again,'
> I stormed at Gatti when he came to see me. 'I'll take the next
> boat back to Europe…' He shook his beard at me gloomily.
> 'You can't. You are billed to sing *Le Villi* ten days from today.'

Then something happened that lifted her mood. Her maid brought her a hand-delivered basket of roses together with a note from the well-established American prima donna, Lillian Nordica. It read:

> There was never a young singer who appeared at the
> Metropolitan who wasn't criticized on her debut. Melba,
> Sembrich, Farrar, myself … all of us have gone through what
> you are going through today. Have courage. Affectionate
> good wishes.[24]

The note made a big impact on Frances, who made the decision to fight it out and turn opinions of the critics around. Nevertheless, she only sang *Rigoletto* once more at the Met – in January 1909 – after which it was dropped entirely from her repertoire. How much the hostility of the New York critics to Alda was based on her singing, and how much on her closet relationship with Gatti, is difficult to untangle. Indeed, some of it may have been the result of hostility to Gatti's own appointment as general director.

4

The turnaround in Alda's reputation was not to be achieved in a day. *Le Villi* was effectively Puccini's first opera, and 17 December 1908 was its American première (coupled because of its brevity with *Cavalleria rusticana*). It has only three roles – Anna (played by Alda), Roberto (Alessandro Bonci) and Guglielmo Wulf (Pasquale Amati). And this time it was conducted by Toscanini, who had gone over the score with Frances, teaching her the part 'note by note'. However, Frances did not much care for it. It had little to show for her – 'no gaiety, no diablerie, no wistful tenderness … Too, I had a deep-seated contempt for any girl who let her lover walk off and leave her, and then died of it.'[25]

The opera was also not much enjoyed by the New York critics: there was 'a large and tiresome portion of last night [which] was wasted at the Metropolitan Opera House on the production of *Le Villi*', wrote Henry E Krehbiel in the *Tribune*. Noting that the musical content was low, Krehbiel went on: 'There was as little in the music assigned to Miss Alda, though she sang what was set down for her with much greater devotion and effort at sincerity [than Amati].'[26] This was better than the response to her Gilda, but not exactly a ringing endorsement. The problem was compounded by the fact that Krehbiel thought *Cavalleria rusticana* a far superior work, particularly in a production with the universally admired Destinn and Caruso.

Born into a poor family in Naples in 1873, as a child Caruso was encouraged in his singing by his mother, who died when he was fifteen. As a young man, he had engagements in provincial theatres and in 1900 he was hired to sing at La Scala in Milan, making his debut there as Rodolfo in *La bohème* with Toscanini conducting. He made his first recordings for The Gramophone Company at the Grand Hotel in Milan in April 1902 – the first major artist whose performing career was substantially helped by the circulation of his recordings. The following month he performed for the first time at

Covent Garden, as the Duke of Mantua in *Rigoletto*, Nellie Melba his Gilda.

Caruso made his debut at the Metropolitan Opera as the Duke in *Rigoletto* on 23 November 1903, and within months he was making more recordings, this time for Victor. Although he continued to perform around the world, the Met was to become his artistic home for the remainder of his career. The arrival of Gatti-Casazza and Toscanini, together with Alda, at the house in 1908 further cemented his commitment to the Met, and overall, he sang thirty-seven roles there over eighteen seasons, giving 626 performances in all.

Alda, Gatti and Caruso became a close-knit trio in New York, all of them living at the fashionable Hotel Knickerbocker on the corner of Broadway and 42nd Street after Alda and Gatti's marriage in 1910. Alda and Caruso first sang at the Met together in her maligned debut performance, *Rigoletto*, on 7 December 1908. Over succeeding seasons, they performed together there on a regular basis, most frequently in *Manon*, *La bohème*, *Carmen* and *Manon Lescaut*. On 18 March 1917, they were together in a Gala Benefit for Britain and America's Italian allies, singing the quartet from *Rigoletto*. Closer to the end of the war, on 14 April 1918, there was another Italian benefit, and this time they sang the Act 3 Quartet from *La bohème* with Lenora Sparkes and Scotti.

In the following three months of 1909, Alda starred in three more operas at the Met: as Marguérite in *Faust* (with Caruso as Faust and Didur as Méphistophélès); in the title role of *Manon* (with Caruso as Des Grieux, Scotti as Lescaut); and as Nannetta in *Falstaff*. Most of these performances were at the Met itself, but she also sang with the company in Philadelphia, Baltimore and Chicago. Of these, the most positive review was in the *Baltimore Sun*, which said Alda was the best of a rather poor bunch in *Faust*.[27] Caruso was not in attendance that evening. Nevertheless, for many American critics, Marguérite provided too many memories of the finest singers in that role – Christine Nilsson, Marcella Sembrich, Lillian Nordica, Emma Eames and Nellie Melba. The competition in their minds was just too hot. The opening night of *Falstaff* on 16 March 1909 at the Academy of Music in Philadelphia (a new production) was a high-profile occasion with Antonio Scotti as Falstaff and Emmy Destinn as Alice Ford, with Toscanini conducting.

It appears that Alda got her opportunity as Manon in New York and Philadelphia because Geraldine Farrar was not well. The *New York Times* was only just on the warmer side of lukewarm regarding her performance.[28] In time, however, Manon would become one of Alda's most celebrated roles at the Met. Of the *Falstaff*, Henry Krehbiel recalled 'a fascinating Mistress Ford in Miss Saville' in the 1895–96 season. Was he aware that Saville was Alda's aunt? He did not say, and of Alda's Nannetta there was not a word.[29]

Meanwhile, Alda and Gatti continued strenuously to deny that they were either engaged or planning to marry, and in her memoirs Frances later emphasised that she kept turning him down.[30] By May, Gatti and Alda were in Europe – he busily recruiting for the forthcoming 1909–10 season at the Met. On their return, he finally announced that they planned to marry – on a yet unspecified date.[31]

Giulio Gatti-Casazza

5

For Alda, the 1909–10 season started with her first Desdemona in Verdi's *Otello*. It opened on 17 November 1909 with her aunt Frances Saville's old colleague in Vienna, Leo Slezak, making his house debut as the Moor, and Scotti as Iago. While Slezak was naturally the centre of attention for the evening, the *Press* noticed a more interesting Alda:

> In Frances Alda, who was heard to greater advantage as
> Desdemona than in any other part she has sung here, Slezak
> had a most sympathetic partner. There was something
> strangely appealing in the very appearance of this little woman
> … She sang charmingly too, and with admirable attention to
> artistic phrasing and expression. … In *mezza voce* Mme Alda
> attained her best results.[32]

At last – a real breakthrough! It should be noted that the old Met was a far larger house than any she had previously sung in. These had risen step-by-step in her career to date: the Opéra-Comique seated 1250, the Monnaie 1700, the Teatr Wielki in Warsaw 1850, La Scala 2030, Covent Garden 2270 and the Teatro Solís in Montevideo 2500; the Met was a big step up again at 3600. No wonder Alda had found it difficult to adjust. But she now had Toscanini to coach her. A clear indication of Toscanini's commanding style of 'coaching' is given in a description by Frances of an intervention by him during the dress rehearsal for *Otello*:

> *Senti, Aldina* … You will kneel and sing the 'Ave Maria'. Then
> you will get up, without turning your face to the audience.
> There will be not one smile. Not one bow. There will be no
> encores. You will not lift your eyes. You will just get into bed
> like a good pure virgin.[33]

There were to be two more Metropolitan Opera roles for Frances before she and Gatti finally were married – Mimì in *La bohème* and Clairette in Lecocq's *La fille de Madame Angot*. *Bohème* opened on 2 December, not with Caruso, but with his great rival Alessandro Bonci as Rodolfo and Pasquale Amato as Marcello. Mimì was to become Alda's most frequent and one of her most praised roles at the Met – she sang it eighty times.[34] Her first opportunity to sing Mimì at the Met came because the current incumbent, Geraldine Farrar, was again ill. Gatti asked her if she knew the role:

> [He] had no way of knowing, for I had never said a word
> of this to anyone, that of all the operatic roles, the one I
> wanted most of all to sing was Mimì. I had practised it to
> myself. And Toscanini, hearing me one day, had sat down at
> the piano and taught me the role, as long ago he had taught
> me Louise.[35]

Madame Angot was performed (with Edmond Clément and Antonio Pini-Corsi) at the Met's recently built New Theater in Manhattan. The venue was intended as a centre for operetta, but from the start the acoustics were poor. Was Frances aware that Clairette was a much-loved role for her grandmother Fanny Simonsen touring in Australia and New Zealand in 1876 (three years before Frances was born), and also sung by her aunt Martina Simonsen on the 1882–83 New Zealand tour (when Alda was three)? Several of the singers in the Met production used pseudonyms, perhaps not wishing to be associated with too-small roles in mere operettas, but Alda was far too down-to-earth for such subterfuge. The opening on 14 December was not a success. 'The night of the première was one of those times when everything seemed to go wrong,' wrote Alda, amongst which her costume for Act 1 arrived at the theatre only minutes before she went on.[36]

Towards the end of the year, the *Musical Courier* in New York carried a misogynistic story about the levels of influence at the Met of two women: one was the wife of Gatti's administrative director Andreas Dippel, the other Frances Alda:

> The era of the operatic petticoat control is in full swing. Signor Gatti-Casazza is supposed to leave the decisive decisions to Signorina Alda. Herr Dippel is known to incline with seriousness and unaffected respect to the judgment of Frau Dippel whenever a question of a German singer or opera or cast is concerned.[37]

6

On 27 December 1909, her friend Caruso took Frances to the Victor Talking Machine Company's recording studios in Camden, New Jersey, to make a test record. It was he, already one of Victor's best-selling artists, who had recommended her to the company:

> He came to me one day and asked if I would sing with him the 'Miserere' from *Trovatore*. He had tried singing it with several sopranos, but the results did not satisfy him. 'You know what I have often told you,' he said. 'Your voice and mine blend perfectly. I have never found that with any other woman singer.[38]

It was the beginning of a major recording career for her, and this first test, unpublished at the time, remains a glorious performance, testament to Alda's excellence at that time (a view still not widely shared by the New York critics). Particularly remarkable (and surprising) is the richness and security of her chest voice. The two of them returned to the Camden studios ten days later to re-record the 'Miserere', this time with chorus, and it was this second take that was released, becoming Alda's first bestseller. Later in January 1910 Alda made five more recordings for Victor – the 'Willow Song' and the 'Ave Maria' from *Otello*, 'Sul fin d'un soffio' from Act 3 of *Falstaff*, and two songs: 'La serenata' by Tosti and Massenet's 'Oh, si les fleurs avaient des yeux'. She returned to the Victor studios twenty more times before the end of the Great War, making around fifty-eight new recordings, with many more still to come after the war.

The fact that Alda became a bestselling artist for Victor resulted in a five-year contract with the company from 1 March 1911. This specified that forty masters were to be recorded over the period, giving Alda a 10 per cent royalty, plus an advance of $US250 per master. In 1916 the good sales of her records justified an improved contract, which specified that she was also to receive an advance of $US12 000 each year – a large sum at that time. Assessing her early recordings, the experienced and perceptive critic JB Steane wrote in his *The Grand Tradition* (1974):

> She is probably the most consistently satisfying lyric soprano
> on pre-electric records. Her voice took to recording better
> than most. It is vibrant but without the marked vibrato that so
> many of the Italians had, and without their tendency to abrupt
> changes of register. More sensitive and interesting than Farrar,
> fuller in voice and easier above the stave than Bori … less
> given to excessive portamento and steadier than Destinn.[39]

Steane's astute assessment of her early recordings might be extended to contrast Alda's voice with other Marchesi pupils. Most of them have a 'white' sound – the result of more limited vibrato – allied to very accurate intonation. On record, Alda displays a warmth lacking in several of Marchesi's students, and this quality will have been of great value to her both in performance and in selling records. By 1910, following the popularity on record of Caruso, Melba and others in the preceding decade, many homes now had gramophones, so that sales of discs reached unprecedented levels.

Enrico Caruso recording, his own cartoon

Aside from those already mentioned, particular successes among Alda's acoustic recordings up to 1918 include: 'L'ora, o Tirsi' and 'In quelle trine morbide' from Puccini's *Manon Lescaut*, four ensemble recordings from Flotow's *Martha* (with Josephine Jacoby, Caruso and Journet), 'Ah dunque, ei m'amera ... Amor, celeste abrezza' from Catalani's *Loreley* and two arias from *Madama Butterfly*. None of those roles had she yet sung at the Met, and in the case of *Butterfly*, sadly she was never to sing it on stage, performing it only in her radio broadcast of 1929. Jewels among her songs from the period are recordings with the twenty-four-year-old violinist Mischa Elman in 1915.

On 28 February 1910 Frances suffered a ruptured appendix during a performance of *Otello* with the Met at the Academy of Music in Brooklyn. She finished the opera, of course, and was carried off to her hotel, where she was operated on at 3 am, her condition 'critical'.[40] In her memoirs, Alda made particular reference to the rough handling she had received from her Otello, Leo Slezak:

> He had tremendous physical force which he threw into
> his acting. When he came to murder me for my supposed

infidelity, he would shake and strangle me with a realism that probably appealed to the audience more than it did to me.

Alda does not actually say that Slezak was responsible for her appendicitis, but the implication is there.[41] Without forewarning, five weeks later (on 3 April 1910) Gatti and Alda were quietly married at the luxurious Ansonia – their current home – with just a handful of guests, including Mrs Randolph Guggenheimer, Albert Weber and Rawlins Cottenet (who had signed both of them for the Met).[42] Gatti had asked Toscanini to be a witness, but he had refused, not approving of the marriage for either party. Built as a luxury 'hotel of apartments' in 1899–1904, the Ansonia had many celebrity tenants, several of them opera singers – including Alda, Feodor Chaliapin and Geraldine Farrar, and later Lily Pons, Lauritz Melchior and Ezio Pinza – and Toscanini.

Leo Slezak

Gatti and Alda left immediately after their wedding lunch by train for Chicago, where she was to sing Desdemona with the Met company three days later. 'It seems to be the best part for her peculiar talents,' said the *Inter-Ocean*.[43] Nevertheless, Alda still had doubts about the marriage: 'If I hadn't had that ruptured appendix and the operation, and been ill for weeks, would I have married Gatti-Casazza? I've wondered …' And the path of their marriage did not run smooth. Alda wrote:

> I suppose the first months of any marriage are full of bumps
> and sharp corners and steep grades, with innumerable chances
> for skidding and landing in a heap at the side of the road. My
> marriage to Gatti-Casazza was no exception to this rule …
> Gatti was over forty years of age and accustomed to his own
> ways of doing everything. I was seventeen years his junior,[44]
> but most of my life I had seen to it that I had my own way.[45]

Perhaps Gatti expected Alda to be more of a traditional wife, but in her memoirs Frances was very clear that she was a modern woman:

> I'm not the kind of dear little woman who runs away from her
> career the minute the curtain is down, and hurries home to
> cook supper for her husband and darn his socks … I'd rather
> dance all night with three men who were crazy about me than
> sew on buttons for any one of them by daylight.[46]

7

Alda and Gatti left for Europe on the Hamburg-America passenger liner *Kronprinzessin Cecilie* on 26 April 1910. It was carrying more passengers than any transatlantic ship up to that time, many of them celebrities.[47] Their stated intention was to have a honeymoon. Gatti had been pressurising Frances to take his name after marriage, but she declined, happy with the one that Madame Marchesi had given her. Perhaps she was reinforced in this decision by the message that feminist American prima donna Olive Fremstad sent her: 'Remember you married as a woman. Don't give up the position you have attained.'[48]

What she did do, however, was to decide that it would be inappropriate for the director of the Met's wife to continue to sing there. One day she was sitting in a box at a dress rehearsal, when she overheard the chairman of the Met board Otto Kahn talking to Henry Russell, director of the Boston Opera. She heard Kahn say: 'As the director's wife, it is much better that Alda should not sing here next season.' Alda pushed back the velvet curtain between them and responded: 'I suppose it would be all right if I were his mistress instead of his wife. I resign right now.'[49] So in May she announced that decision to the press, while also telling them that she would be singing at the Chicago Opera and the Boston Opera in the autumn.[50]

Instead of the supposed honeymoon, Gatti had organised for his Metropolitan Opera company to perform a season of Italian opera at the Théâtre du Châtelet in Paris in late May and early June. It was the first time that a Met company had ever performed a Paris season. The cream of the Gatti-Toscanini company was there, including Destinn as Aida, the recently discovered Lucrezia Bori in the title role of *Manon Lescaut* and Caruso as Radamès and Canio. American and French opera-lovers in Paris stormed the box office and the season was a great success.[51] Alda sang with Slezak again (now more gentle) in *Otello*, and with Scotti in *Falstaff*, both operas conducted by Toscanini.

The season at the Châtelet over, Gatti took Frances to meet his parents at Ferrara for the first time. Ferrara struck her as a dead city, with 'the smell of malarial marshes and old tombs and cerements[52] of the past'. She immediately liked Gatti's father, a retired senator, 'and he loved me', whereas 'la contessa', Gatti's mother, 'was a dark-browed woman, entirely lacking the wit and the social grace that made her husband so charming'. Sadly, Frances thought that Gatti took after his mother. She wrote:

> I saw enough of the life lived within the walls of the Palazzo to
> make me realise how wide was the gulf between my husband's
> early years and my own. I contrasted those close-shuttered,
> formal rooms, filled with relics of the past, the almost
> medieval attitude that prevailed in the relations of parent
> and child, husband and wife, master and servant ... with the
> sunny, breeze-swept house at St Kilda, filled with children and
> pets, with music and the noise of games.[53]

They returned via Brussels, where Alda, Caruso and Amato gave two special performances of *La bohème* at the Monnaie in September. Following that summer in Europe, Gatti and Alda sailed back to New York – he to run the Met, she for the first time to tour the United States in concert. On that American tour, Frances sang in a multitude of cities, winning positive reviews wherever she went, and fitting in seasons at the opera houses in Chicago, Boston and Philadelphia. At each, she was Desdemona again.[54] Of her concert work, the *St Louis Star and Times* wrote:

> One of the features of the present musical season has been the
> overwhelming success in concert of Mme Frances Alda, who
> ... was hitherto known in America only through her operatic
> achievements. She has proven, however, that on the concert
> platform, her singing is no less delightful.[55]

On 3 March 1911, Alda gave a concert at the Mendelssohn Hall in New York 'that drew a large audience in which were to be seen many singers of prominence on the operatic and concert stage'.[56] Included in her programme was one of the *Fünf Lieder*, 'Laue Sommernacht' ['Warm Summer Night'], composed by Gustav Mahler's wife, Alma. When they were married in 1902, Mahler prevailed upon Alma to give up on her ambitions as a composer in order to look after him and their children. While married to Mahler, Alma had an affair with the architect Walter Gropius, but later, following a crisis in their marriage, they became reconciled and Gustav started to encourage her composing, urging her to publish her *Fünf Lieder*, which she did.

This New York concert was in effect Alma's debut as a composer in America. Mahler himself was at that time principal conductor of the New York Philharmonic, and he endeavoured (to no avail) to persuade Alda to include all five songs in the cycle in her recital. Nevertheless, he took time to rehearse the song with Alda.[57] Alma recalled the rehearsal (at the Waldorf-Astoria) in her memoirs:

> 'Is that right?' he kept asking me from the piano. I was so
> nervous I could scarcely open my mouth. I begged him in a
> low voice not to ask me anymore, as he knew better than I. We
> were very near together in those days.[58]

In the event, the song was encored. 'Thank God', said Gustav, when Alma reported back to him.[59] Already ill, Mahler had conducted his final concert in New York on 21 February, and he died in Vienna on 18 May 1911, just eleven weeks after Alda's concert.

In July of that summer Alda sang in Rome at concerts connected with the International Exposition of Art, and in November she opened the new season at the Montreal Opera. There a performance of *Manon* was disrupted by French-Canadian nationalists, who presumably objected to an 'Anglo-Saxon' taking the title role in a French opera. Even the chorus conspired, deliberately singing out of tune and talking among themselves while Frances sang. She left in disgust.

After nearly two years of self-imposed absence, Frances Alda made her return to the Metropolitan Opera in New York on 21 February 1911 – as Desdemona, of course – together with Slezak, Scotti and Toscanini. By this stage of her long career at the Met, she was to get

Alma Mahler

almost universal approval from the critics and had a strong fan base among the opera-going public. Of her return performance, the *Evening World* said:

> Certain prejudices that prevailed have been dissipated and
> Mme Alda could have no doubt that at least she would be
> heard with respectful attention ... She won deservedly a warm
> welcome from a large, fashionable and appreciative audience.
> Mme Alda's Desdemona was a beautiful impersonation.[60]

Nellie Melba, who had defected to Oscar Hammerstein's Manhattan Opera Company in 1907–08 after singing regularly for the Met between

1893 and 1904, found herself blocked at that house after Hammerstein's company folded in 1910. She sang just twice more at the Met – in November 1910 – by which time Alda was well established. As the director of the Boston Opera, Henry Russell, diplomatically put it:

> It was a curious coincidence that Alda never sang in a
> theatre where Melba had the controlling influence, and vice
> versa. Melba has never sung at the Metropolitan since her
> rival became the wife of the director.

An astute judge of singers, Russell added:

> Alda, though her voice was never as great as Melba's, is
> a better actress and has a finer musical intelligence. Her
> flashing dark eyes and beautiful teeth add to the charm of
> her handsome person.[61]

Even without Melba, the Met had an extraordinary roster of outstanding sopranos during Alda's early years at the house, several of them occupying plum roles that Alda might have sung. Prominent among these were Emmy Destinn, Geraldine Farrar, Olive Fremsted, Johanna Gadski, Alma Gluck, Frieda Hempel, Lillian Nordica, Lucrezia Bori and (briefly) Luisa Tetrazzini. Approaching the end of her distinguished career at the Met was another Marchesi pupil, Emma Eames, who was by no means alone in scorning Alda's early performances. Alda reported in her memoirs Eames's caustic opinion that Frances was 'all right for the chorus'.[62]

Her 1910–11 tour of American cities a distinct success, Alda made a repeat expedition the following year, this time with the rather distinguished French pianist, André Benoist (a pupil of Raoul Pugno and Camille Saint-Saëns), who had already toured the US with Emma Eames, Fritz Kreisler, Ernestine Schumann-Heink, Lillian Nordica, Eugène Ysaÿe, Luisa Tetrazzini and Mischa Elman. *En route*, Alda and

Benoist collected consistently laudatory reviews, but she was not to use him again. It may be that she treated him without due deference, as just another accompanist. However, Benoist's frank memoirs disclose some shrewd observations on the diva from a fellow musician who for a while was up-close with her:

> Madame Alda did not have a large voice, but it was rich and velvety in texture, very expressive, and she never forced its volume beyond its natural limits. She was extremely musical and learned with great ease. She was also an exacting and strict taskmistress as well as completely ruthless in anything that concerned her 'rights' ... The reputation she had gained for high voltage vocabulary was thoroughly justified.[63]

8

One of Gatti's prime strategies in managing the Met was to commit to presenting new operas by Americans, and one of the earliest of these was Walter Damrosch's *Cyrano*, which had its première on 27 February 1913 with Pasquale Amato in the title role and Alda as Roxane. Richard Aldrich in the *New York Times* gave *Cyrano* a somewhat muted welcome, but praised the performances of both Amato and Alda: 'Miss Alda gave an excellent representation of Roxane – one that should be set down as one of her best achievements not only in acting, but as well in singing.'[64] The music of *Cyrano* was not respected by the performers, who thought it old-fashioned:

> 'Where do I go from here?' [Alda] asked Amato. Before he could reply, Hageman, the assistant conductor, who was rehearsing us, spoke up: 'From Gounod to Meyerbeer.'[65]

In subsequent years, singing in productions of new American operas was to become a thread running through Alda's life at the Met. In January 1914 she sang the title role in Victor Herbert's *Madeleine*, and in April 1917 she was both Clara and Vox Tentationis in Adriano Ariani's *St Francis of Assisi*. Sadly, most sank without trace after a handful of performances and required a great deal of work and money to put on.

On 6 December 1913 Alda opened as Giulietta in Offenbach's *Les contes d'Hoffmann* at the Met with Frieda Hempel as Olympia, Lucrezia Bori as Antonia and Carl Jörn in the title role. Alda was replacing Olive Fremstad. There are three contrasted soprano roles in *Hoffmann* – Giulietta, Olympia and Antonia. 'Naturally, it is seldom that one artist can play these three entirely dissimilar roles with distinction,' wrote Alda.[66] Presumably she would have been unaware that her aunt Frances Saville had sung all three at the Court Opera in Vienna conducted by Mahler in 1901.

The year 1913 closed for Alda on 23 December with a now legendary rendition of *La bohème* in Philadelphia. Alda was Mimì, with Caruso as Rodolfo, Scotti as Marcello, Pini-Corsi as Schaunard and her friend Andrès De Segurola as the philosopher Colline – altogether the Met's top team in that work. The performance has become famous because basso De Segurola became hoarse during the performance and, unable to sing Colline's big aria 'Vecchia zimarra', Caruso, back to audience, sang it for him. Nobody seemed to notice the deception, least of all the critic for the *Philadelphia Inquirer*.[67] Afterwards Caruso recorded that aria for Victor, and, later still, Alda made a recording, speaking wittily about the incident.[68]

On 30 March 1914, Alda opened at the Met as Susanna in Wolf-Ferrari's *Il segreto di Susanna*, but it was her return as Massenet's Manon (with Caruso as Des Grieux, Toscanini conducting) the following month which brought most praise. 'Her impersonation was more than satisfactory, for she sang well, acted with convincing sincerity and looked charming,' wrote the *Evening World*.[69]

9

Her self-imposed exile from the Met had persuaded Alda that she could well sustain her performing career with concert tours all over America, and from that time forward they formed a consistent part of her life (and a major part of her considerable income), even after she returned to the Met. Many concerts were given with the young Russian cellist Gutia Casini and the accompanist Frank La Forge (with whom she was also to make many recordings), but she also gave concerts with various celebrity co-stars, including violinists Eugène Ysaÿe, Fritz Kreisler and Jacques Thibaud; cellists Pablo Casals and Beatrice Harrison; tenor Giovanni Martinelli; baritone Giuseppe de Luca; and legendary French actress Sarah Bernhardt. Alda gave an annual recital at Carnegie Hall in New York, usually attended in the audience by colleagues from the Met.

Initially her concerts were focused on German and French song – Schubert, Brahms, Wolf, Strauss, Debussy and Hahn – but gradually she introduced popular and new songs of the day. Local organisers often had a problem obtaining from the diva the intended programme for her forthcoming performance, until her manager of the day pointed out to them that they should take a look at the Epistle to the Hebrews (chapter 13, verse 8): 'Jesus Christ, the same yesterday, and today, and forever'.[70] On tour, Alda was usually attended by her secretary Margaret Evans, 'Boo', who had been a long-time devoted fan.[71] Alda knew her own value. She refused to go on stage on 3 November 1915 at the Coliseum in Des Moines when the local manager offered her $300 instead of the $850 previously agreed.[72]

From time to time, Frances would come across talented new singers whom she would recommend to Gatti. One of these moments occurred in October 1913, when she was performing in San Francisco (the city where her young mother had died). She was persuaded, somewhat reluctantly, to go to a performance at the Tivoli Theatre of *La bohème*.

The Rodolfo that evening was a young Italian tenor, Luca Botta, and Alda was bowled over by his performance.

After auditioning for Gatti, Botta made his debut at the Met as Rodolfo on 21 November 1914 with Lucrezia Bori and Scotti. Botta was a success and made a further ninety-two appearances at the house in the following three years, before dying of cancer in 1917 aged thirty-five. Alda felt that Gatti had over-used the young man too quickly, damaging his voice, a problem that she felt recurred several times with promising singers she had found, including with the young American tenor, Orville Harrold. Alda and Botta appeared together at the Met on fifteen occasions, mostly in *La bohème* and in Borodin's *Prince Igor*.

In July 1913 it was reported that Alda had been booked to sing Eva in Wagner's *Die Meistersinger* at the Boston Opera House in the following season, but this did not come about.[73] What did happen was a single performance by her on 27 April 1916 as Aida with the Met company at the Auditorium in Atlanta (with Martinelli her Radamès). This was in the nature of an experiment: would she be able to cope with the heavier, more dramatic role? Clearly, the outing was not regarded by her as a success, as she never repeated the exercise. The *Atlanta Constitution*, however, was full of praise for her:

> The tragic Aida Mme Alda made an impersonation of real
> vitality and vocal brilliance ... she sang with exquisite tone
> and feeling, her work having both charm and strength.[74]

However, she must have been encouraged to some extent, because in August it was announced that she would sing the title role in Zandonai's *Francesca da Rimini* in the Met's next season. Aside from that single Aida, Francesca was to be the heaviest role she was to undertake. It opened on 22 December 1916 with Martinelli as Paolo and Amato as Giovanni. WJ Henderson in the *Sun*, greeted her efforts guardedly:

Mme Alda bent under the burden. She tried bravely to convey
to the audience the experiences of a 'grande dame' whose
world was overturned by the invasion of something elemental
… ready to throw discretion to the winds. The true Francesca
was far more than this, yet Mme Alda's own inadequate
conception was beyond her histrionic abilities. She sang much
of the music with good effect, but her voice was not equal to
the heavier demands of the score.[75]

At a later performance at the Met, the *Brooklyn Daily Eagle* was
a good deal more impressed: 'Mme Frances Alda … sang the long
arias with sustained power and delicate shading, and her efforts were
warmly appreciated at every curtain.'[76] The production was toured
to Philadelphia and Atlanta. Clearly, Alda was more cautious in her
experimentation with heavier roles than Melba had been in 1896, when
she sang Brünnhilde in Wagner's *Siegfried* at the Met and subsequently
had to take six months off in order to allow her vocal cords to recover
from the experience.

The arrival of the Great War in August 1914 gradually brought
about significant changes to the lives of both Gatti and Alda. In April
1915 Alda took a lease on a large country estate at Great Neck on
Long Island, which was to be her main home for the remainder of her
life. This was the month before the *Lusitania* was sunk by a German
U-boat with the loss of 1198 passengers and crew, among them 128
Americans. It was an event that caused extreme consternation on
both sides of the Atlantic and put a stop to the annual pilgrimages
of Gatti and Alda to Europe. As in Australia, Germans in America
suffered increased hostility – including towards singers, musicians
and composers – among them the great Wagnerian at the Met,
Johanna Gadski. Alda virtually ignores her in *Men, Women and
Tenors* and it has been suggested that Gadski was hounded out of the
country in 1917. In fact, she went to live quietly in New Hampshire. It
was fortunate for Gatti that Italy decided in May 1915 to join the war

on the side of Britain, France and Russia, their main adversary being Austria-Hungary.

Nevertheless, unlike Covent Garden, which closed for the duration, the Met ploughed on without a pause throughout that war, and Alda continued to sing there as well as giving innumerable concerts around America. On 19 November 1914, Alda was Micaëla to Geraldine Farrar's Carmen, Caruso's Don José and Amato's Escamillo, with Toscanini conducting. It was the only opera in which Farrar and Alda appeared together. They were never close. *Carmen* remained very popular with New York audiences, but had for some reason not been performed at the Met for six years.

Alda's next role (new to her) was as Yaroslavna in Borodin's *Prince Igor* on 30 December 1915. Extraordinarily, this was the American première, in the completion by Rimsky-Korsakov and Glazunov, and it was only the third Russian opera to be performed at the Met (the first two being Tchaikovsky's *Queen of Spades* in 1910 and Mussorgsky's *Boris Godunov* in 1913). The cast for *Prince Igor* included Amato, De Segurola and Luca Botta, and it was sung in Italian. Frances found it especially hard to learn and difficult to sing.[77] But it was the success of that production that persuaded Otto Kahn to bring Diaghilev's Ballets Russes with the great Nijinsky to New York after the opera season closed.

In January 1916 Alda was Manon again, but this time (for the first time) in a revival of Puccini's *Manon Lescaut* with Caruso as Des Grieux and de Luca as Lescaut. She had made wonderful recordings of two arias from the opera five years earlier.

10

After seven tumultuous and memorable seasons with the Metropolitan Opera, Toscanini left the company in April 1915, sailing with his wife

Carla back to Italy. There seem to have been several reasons for his sudden departure. The one given in the press was that he was tired and wished to recharge his batteries. Toscanini said that there were artistic differences between himself and Gatti. At the same time, Italy had just joined the war on the side of Britain and France, and as an ardent nationalist he wanted to do what he could to support his country. His wife joined the Red Cross in Italy and Toscanini himself applied to join the army but was turned down because of his poor eyesight. A third, more private reason was that his long-time lover, the beautiful and talented Geraldine Farrar, had issued him with an ultimatum: leave his wife and marry her, or lose her. Throughout his marriage, Toscanini had numberless affairs, but in the end always chose to keep his family intact.

Everyone at the Met realised that the departure of the great conductor would potentially have a very damaging effect on musical standards.[78] In his memoirs the tenor Leo Slezak articulated the debt so many owed to Toscanini:

> During the four years I was privileged to sing under his
> direction, I learned to appreciate a personality in him which,
> for sheer genius, has never been equalled by any man. A
> charming and attractive man in private life, he is a terror when
> he is at the conductor's desk. He is meticulously conscientious
> and has a passion for accuracy – which he enforces with
> an unparalleled authority and energy. Utterly ruthless and
> looking neither right nor left, he insists on everybody doing
> the utmost of which they are capable. In this respect he
> resembles Gustav Mahler.[79]

Devoted to Toscanini, Alda wrote in her memoirs:

> [There] was a perpetual quarrel between Gatti and Toscanini.
> Gatti contended that an opera house, like a soup factory,

existed to make money for its shareholders. Toscanini held
that it existed as a place in which the best opera could be given.
And that unless the best was given – with the best musicians
and singers available – then the opera house, whatever the box-
office receipts amounted to, was a flat failure and a disgrace.[80]

On 17 February 1916, Alda starred as Molly Pepper in a specially
created operetta, *Melinda and her Sisters*, which was performed at the
Waldorf-Astoria Hotel in New York. It was developed as a fund-raiser for
the women's suffrage movement, the libretto by activist Alva Vanderbilt
Belmont, the music by writer and socialite Elsa Maxwell, who was to
become a long-time close friend of Frances. The single performance of
that operetta raised $8000. While a few individual states had enabled
women to vote, national suffrage for women in the USA did not come
about until the Nineteenth Amendment to the Constitution was passed
in August 1920.

The United States finally joined the war in April 1917 and from that
time on Frances increasingly supported the Allies in patriotic ways.
She regularly sang 'The Star-Spangled Banner', 'Rule Britannia' and 'La
Marseillaise' at performances and recorded the last two, plus 'God Save
the King' between May and July 1917. Of these it was the French anthem
which was the best-seller. Frances explained her patriotic performances
in public:

> Would Madame Alda appear on a program with Madame
> Sarah Bernhardt and Ignace Paderewski at a benefit for the
> War? Would Madame Alda dress like Columbia and stand
> on the steps of the Public Library? ... Would Madame Alda
> appear on the Hippodrome stage with ex-President Theodore
> Roosevelt and sing 'The Star-Spangled Banner'?[81]

Right: Frances Alda in 1918

Yes, she would and did. In June 1918 Alda organised a fund-raising gala at the Metropolitan Opera House as part of the US Navy's Music Festival, which featured a wide range of her celebrity friends, including Caruso, John McCormack, Martinelli, Mischa Elman, Claudia Muzio, Scotti, de Luca, De Segurola and many others. The event raised over $50 000 and the Assistant Secretary to the Navy at the time, Franklin D Roosevelt, wrote her a personal letter of thanks.[82] The Great War was effectively over in Europe by mid-September 1918 and in October Germany asked the Allies for an armistice. On 9 November Kaiser Wilhelm II abdicated and two days later the war officially ended.

Following the cessation of hostilities, Alda continued her work at the Met – on 22 November 1918 as Saamcheddine in Henri Rabaud's comic opera *Mârouf* (in which she had first appeared on 19 December 1917 with de Luca and De Segurola). This was followed five days later by another Mimì.

Normal service had been resumed. Alda was at the peak of her powers and her reputation. After the war, what might the future hold for her?

Notes

1   *New York Times*, 2 November 1893, 11

2   *New York Times*, 21 March 1909, 39; Cottenet was also a part-time composer, among his output a 'Meditation' written for (and recorded by) the great violinist Fritz Kreisler

3   Harvey Sachs, *Toscanini* (2017), 200; Alda, 7; Dippel held the role at the Met 1908–10, an arrangement thoroughly disliked by both Gatti and Alda; he went on the become General Director of the Philadelphia-Chicago Opera Company in 1910

4   *New York Times*, 24 January 1908, 1

5   *Cincinnati Enquirer*, 12 February 1908, 2

6   *Salt Lake Telegram*, 7 March 1908, 2

7   *Democrat and Chronicle* (Rochester, NY), 16 August 1908, 14

8   Emmy Destinn was a particular favourite of Alda's among her soprano competitors: 'She was magnificent. Nobody ever sang Butterfly as Destinn did. Of course, she was stout … but her manner of singing was so perfect, her voice so divine – like drops of water – and the pathos she put into the role … All these made her unforgettable'; Alda, 129
9   *New York Tribune*, 17 November 1908, 7
10 Harvey Sachs, *Toscanini: Musician of Conscience*, 219; Toscanini will have rehearsed Wagner with the Met orchestra at his first encounter with them in order to make a point – he was not just an Italian
11 Alda, 97–98
12 Alda, 99
13 *La Prensa* (Buenos Aires), 1 July 1908
14 Susana Salgado, *The Teatro Solís*, 130–32
15 Alda, 101
16 Alda, 114
17 *New York Times*, 15 September 1908, 1
18 Edith Wharton, *The Age of Innocence*, 7
19 Alda, 109
20 Alda, 5; in fact, Alda was not 23 but 29 years old
21 *New York Times*, 8 December 1908; *Evening World* (New York), 8 December 1908, 13; *Sun*, 8 December 1908, 7
22 Alda, 6–7
23 *New York Times*, 18 December 1908, 2; *Indianapolis Star*, 27 December 1908, 17
24 Alda, 13–14
25 Alda, 118–19
26 *New York Tribune*, 18 December 1908
27 *Baltimore Sun*, 11 February 1909, 9
28 *New York Times*, 27 February 1909, 9
29 *New York Tribune*, 20 March 1909
30 *Inter-Ocean* (Chicago), 25 April 1909, 9
31 *Harrisburg Telegraph* (Pennsylvania), 18 October 1909, 2; *Australasian* (Melbourne), 23 October 1909, 39
32 *New York Press*, 18 November 1909
33 Alda, 144
34 *New York Times*, 3 December 1909, 11
35 Alda, 140
36 Alda, 139
37 *Musical Courier* (New York), nd, quoted in *Sunday Times* (Sydney), 13 March 1910, 18
38 Alda, 180–82; *Star-Gazette* (Elmira, New York), 8 February 1910, 7; the 'several sopranos' included Johanna Gadski
39 JB Steane, *The Grand Tradition*, 127
40 *Indianapolis Star*, 2 March 1910, 4; New Zealand Herald, 4 March 1910, 5
41 Alda, 145
42 *New York Times*, 4 April 1910, 9
43 *Inter-Ocean* (Chicago), 8 April 1910, 6
44 In reality, she was only ten years younger than Gatti
45 Alda, 146 and 159
46 Alda, 100–01
47 *Baltimore Sun*, 27 April 1910, 2
48 Alda, 151
49 Alda, 173
50 *Nebraska State Journal*, 8 May 1910, 23
51 *Washington Post*, 5 June 1910, 9; Alda, 151–53
52 Waxed cloths for wrapping a corpse

53   Alda, 153–57
54   *Chicago Tribune*, 16 June 1910, 8; *Portsmouth Herald* (New Hampshire), 26 October 1910, 7; *Philadelphia Enquirer*, 7 February 1911, 2; at the Boston Opera in the 1909–10 season Alda sang Gilda, Marguérite (*Faust*), Mimì and Margherita (*Mefistofele*); the following season in Boston she was Margherita and Desdemona (with Slezak), Marguérite and Massenet's Manon; she returned to Boston in 1912–13 as Desdemona
55   *St Louis Star and Times*, 29 January 1911, 11
56   *Evening World* (New York), 4 March 1911, 11
57   In Bruce Beresford's film drama of Alma Mahler's life, *Bride of the Wind* (2001), Renée Fleming sang 'Laue Sommernacht' as Frances Alda
58   *New York Times*, 19 February 1911, 63; Zoltan Roman, *Gustav Mahler's American Years, 1907–1911: A Documentary History*, 462
59   Alma Mahler, *Gustav Mahler: Memories and Letters*, 188
60   *Evening World* (New York), 22 February 1912, 7
61   Henry Russell, *The Passing Show*, 166
62   Alda, 22; however, Eames's main target throughout her career was Nellie Melba
63   André Benoist (ed John Anthony Maltese), *The Accompanist: An Autobiography of André Benoist*, 172–79
64   *New York Times*, 28 February 1913
65   Alda, 186–87
66   Alda, 191–92
67   *Philadelphia Inquirer*, 24 December 1913, 8
68   'Vecchia zimmara' sung by Caruso on Victor matrix B-17198-1 (recorded 23 February 1916 but not issued); RCA-Victor later released this in 1949 on 87499 exclusively for Wally Butterworth's radio programme 'Voices That Live' with Butterworth and Alda speaking on the reverse side in New York in 1949 about the incident in Philadelphia
69   *Evening World*, 11 April 1914, 7
70   Letter from John Gray to Adrienne Simpson, 29 March 1988
71   Alda, 223–25
72   *Des Moines Tribune*, 4 November 1915, 5
73   *Washington Herald*, 27 July 1913, 18
74   *Atlanta Constitution*, 28 February 1916, 13
75   *New York Sun*, 23 December 1916.
76   *Brooklyn Daily Eagle*, 29 December 1916, 6
77   Alda, 217–18
78   Harvey Sachs, *Toscanini*, 2017, 293–99; Sachs seems to think, without any evidence, that Alda and Toscanini had an affair, purely on the basis that he often did that
79   Leo Slezak, *Song of Motley*, 43–44
80   Alda, 206–07
81   Alda, 230
82   *Brooklyn Daily Eagle*, 11 June 1918, 6; Alda, 229

Chapter 10
Frances Alda: Radio Star

1

By the time the Great War ended, both Alda and Gatti were well established at the Metropolitan Opera, their careers flourishing. But their marriage was in many ways already over. From the start of their relationship, they seemed an unlikely couple: Gatti introverted, shrewd, gloomy; Alda, in her own words 'impulsive, fiery-tempered, ardent'. While Gatti declared his love for Alda in a stream of letters and telegrams to South America when she was performing there in 1908, Alda never mentions that she had reciprocal feelings. While he endlessly pressed her to marry him, she constantly prevaricated. Moreover, once Alda had discovered that she could work more and earn more by constantly touring in concert, their lives were geographically separated for much of the time. It gradually became clear to all that this was a marriage in name only. Nevertheless, when rumours swirled around America in June 1926 that Alda was to 'seek her freedom', they denied it.[1] In previous years, Alda had from time to time given in-depth interviews to journalists on how to have a successful marriage and related topics. How their inner circle of friends must have smiled.

In her memoirs published in 1937, Alda comes clean about the fact that she had affairs. On a date she did not disclose, she wrote: 'I remember one evening whilst I was singing at the Metropolitan, I knew that four of my beaus were in the audience … As the opera went on, I proceeded to sing to each one in turn.'[2] The beau she wrote about in some detail was a young British aristocrat, 'Lord Robin Innes-Ker'. She says that this affair took place during the winter of 1917–18 in New York:

> My marriage to Gatti was frankly, on my part at least, a
> marriage after the European pattern; a sensible arrangement
> between a man and a woman who liked each other and who
> would be mutually benefited by sharing the same name and
> the same home.

For sure, Alda had benefited from (and been hindered by) her relationship with Gatti from the start. It is less easy to identify how Gatti had benefited from his relationship with Alda. Innes-Ker was apparently at that time just one of six Lords Innes-Ker. In fact, this one seems to have been not 'Robin' but Robert Innes-Ker, youngest son of the 7th Duke of Roxburghe, and married to the musical comedy star Jose Collins. He was in the Irish Guards in the First World War, was wounded in 1914, and by 1917–18 was doing a recruitment job in the USA for the Royal Flying Corps. According to Alda:

> He was young, six feet tall, and magnificent in his Guards'
> uniform of grey and scarlet, when I first caught sight of him

across the dining-room of the Ritz. He was with Ella Widener.
But he was looking at me … I could guess, too, that his good
looks and debonair charm were raising no small havoc among
New York's society women.[3]

Herself included. Within a week they were seeing each other every day
and he was constantly sending Frances flowers and notes … 'Of course,
people knew about it.'

In September 1928, Innes-Ker long gone, Alda sued Gatti for divorce
on the grounds of incompatibility. It was finalised in November.[4] They
had been together for twenty years, married for eighteen, and remained,
said Frances, good friends.[5]

2

Quite soon after the end of the war, Alda formed a new touring company
– the Metropolitan Opera Quartet – one that would last for a decade and
more.[6] The original members were Alda (soprano), Carolina Lazzari
(mezzo), Giovanni Martinelli (tenor) and Giuseppe de Luca (baritone).

Of Italian/French parentage, Lazzari was born in 1891 at Milford,
Massachusetts, and was first spotted by Cleofonte Campanini, who
hired her to sing La Cieca in Ponchielli's *La Gioconda*, followed by
Giglietta in the American première of Mascagni's *Isabeau* at the
Chicago Opera in 1917. She sang only once at the Met – as Amneris in
Aida on Christmas Day 1920.

Both men were established stars of the opera stage. Italian tenor
Martinelli was born in 1885, starting his operatic career in 1910 at the
Teatro dal Verme in Milan, singing the title role in Verdi's *Ernani*. In
1912 he was chosen by Toscanini to sing Dick Johnson in the Italian
première of Puccini's *La fanciulla del West* at La Scala, and from
that moment on his career blossomed with successful runs at Covent

Garden, the Met and elsewhere. After the death of Caruso in 1921, he was regarded by many as the natural successor. He sang in 663 performances at the Met over thirty-two seasons, frequently appearing with Alda.

De Luca was the oldest member of the quartet, born in 1876 in Rome. His first role was in 1897 as Valentin in *Faust* at Piacenza, and in his first season with La Scala he created the role of Sharpless in *Madama Butterfly*. He gradually became famous in Europe, North and South America, and was a principal baritone at the Met for over thirty years. He sang in 725 performances there, including dozens of performances with Alda between 1915 and 1929.[7]

Having established a clear brand for her ensemble, so long as Alda appeared, there could be personnel changes from time to time. The first such (in 1919) was American tenor Charles Hackett, who was brought in to replace the highly in-demand Martinelli. He was born at Worcester, Massachusetts in 1899, so he was just nineteen when he joined the MOQ.[8] His operatic debut seems to have been as a fifteen-year-old in 1914 – as Wilhelm Meister in *Faust* at Genoa. For his Met opening in January 1919, he was Almaviva in *Il barbiere di Siviglia*. In addition to all the quartet concerts he appeared in, he occasionally sang with Alda in opera. In one of these in Boston in 1921, Olin Downes praised his 'finished vocalism … finely sustained phrases … polished tone production … light but beautiful voice'.[9] He sang Roméo to Melba's Juliette at her Covent Garden Farewell on 8 June 1926.

The next change to the original MOQ line-up was Chilean baritone Renato Zanelli for de Luca in 1922.[10] Zanelli was born at Valparaiso in 1892, starting his operatic life (as had de Luca before him) as Valentin in *Faust* at Santiago in 1916, and going on to build a successful international career. He started at the Met as Amonasro in *Aida* in November 1919. In turn, by October 1924 Zanelli had been replaced by a baritone who was to become a legend of American opera, Lawrence Tibbett.[11] The *Evening News* in Harrisburg, Pennsylvania, commented:

The booking of a quartet of such a musical calibre as the Alda
Metropolitan Quartet may be considered a feat in itself, for it
is but rarely that four topnotchers can be signed up to sing solo
and concerted numbers in the same program.[12]

Tibbett was born at Bakersfield, California, in 1896, making his
operatic debut as Amonasro at Los Angeles in 1923. He was introduced
to Alda as a young man by his teacher (and regular Alda accompanist)
Frank La Forge. She thought Tibbett promising and asked him to
come back again in six months. This he did and, impressed, Frances
introduced him to Gatti. Alda took Tibbett on several of her tours. He
opened at the Met as Lovitsky in *Boris Godunov* on 24 November1923, in
time graduating to larger roles, including Ford (his breakthrough role),
Germont, Rigoletto, Amonasro and Scarpia. He was to sing twenty-
seven seasons with the company, in the process becoming an American
icon and, in the early 1930s, a star in many Hollywood movies. Alda
was not best pleased when Tibbett broke his contract with her and her
quartet, his career in rapid ascent.[13]

A typical appearance for the MOQ was at Lincoln, Nebraska, in
October 1919. Entertainment for the quartet was laid on in a local hotel
after the concert by the organisers:

Mme Alda and her associates were exceedingly jolly and
gracious during the evening ... Mme Alda remembered her
former appearances in the city with much pleasure ... She
talked entertainingly of the different cities she had visited
and she compared the beauty of the ports putting Sydney,
Australia, at the top of the list. She admitted to a prejudice in
favor of things Australian, as she had been educated there.[14]

This latter observation becomes ironic, given the animosity towards
Australia and Australians that came out of her mouth after touring
there in 1927. While the MOQ concert tours were the backbone of

Alda's performing life through the early 1920s, she still undertook solo appearances, including her annual concerts at Carnegie Hall in New York, and from time to time sharing the stage with fellow-Australian pianist-composer Percy Grainger.[15] Alda's constant concertising provided American composers with the opportunity to write new songs for her to sing, including several by long-time accompanist Frank La Forge.

3

While concerts had taken over the bulk of Alda's appearances by the early 1920s, she still sang regularly with the Metropolitan Opera.[16] She continued as Mimì in *Bohème*, Marguérite in *Faust*, the title role in *Manon Lescaut* and Nannetta in *Falstaff*, but she also added five important new roles there – Margherita in Boito's *Mefistofele* (a role she had sung previously at La Scala), Rozenn in Lalo's *Le Roi d'Ys*, and the title roles in Catalani's *Loreley*, Flotow's *Martha* and Giordano's *La cena della beffe*, plus the last of her new American operas, as Cleopatra in Henry Kimball Hadley's *Cleopatra's Night*.

First to be performed of the new roles was the Hadley opera on 31 January 1920. *Cleopatra's Night* was his fourth opera and from the start was regarded very highly by the New York critics, several of whom thought it the best of all the American operas so far produced at the Met. It 'bids fair to have come to stay', asserted the *Evening World*, adding that 'Frances Alda as Cleopatra and Orville Harrold as Meiamoun were recalled many times.'[17] Unusually for a new American work, the opera had no fewer than nine performances over two seasons at the Met.

The following month, the Chicago Opera came to give a season at the Lexington Theatre in New York, including in their programme Bellini's *Norma*, which had not been performed in the city since 1891 (with Lilli Lehmann in the title role). Norma in 1920 was the Russian-

Polish soprano Rosa Raisa, and the Chicago company was under the directorship of Scottish-American diva Mary Garden. A long-time friend of Alda, Garden asked her to join her in the director's box, 'and let us show the world there are two women opera singers who can be friends'. According to Alda, Garden entered the box:

> ... in all her war paint! Diamond and emerald bracelets
> from her wrists to her elbows. Diamonds and a bird of
> paradise in her hair. She turned toward me ... 'Sit forward,
> Alda, sit forward. Let the people see you.' *Norma* began.
> When the curtain fell after the First Act, Mary leaned far
> out over the parapet and clapped and clapped and clapped.
> 'Bravo! Bravo! Bravo!' she shouted, while again the house
> turned and craned and stared at her. Then to me ... 'Bloody
> opera, Alda, isn't it'.[18]

Next at the Met came Boito's *Mefistofele* (a work that Alda had previously sung with Chaliapin at La Scala in 1908). The revival opened on 26 November 1920, and in the role of Faust was the young Italian tenor Beniamino Gigli, who was making his debut at the house.[19] Gigli was already such a major prospect for the future that all critical eyes were focused on him, not always in a friendly way. Richard Aldrich in the *New York Times* did not appreciate his 'persistent disposition to sing to the audience, to the neglect of Margherita ... also to cultivate the high note and make whatever there is to be made of it in the way of applause.' Aldrich thought Alda's Margherita was 'somewhat mature in aspect, less beautiful to listen to'.[20]

Alda opened as Rozenn in Édouard Lalo's *Le Roi d'Ys* on 5 January 1922. In recent years Frenchman Lalo has been most known for his 'Symphonie espagnole' for violin and orchestra, but in the nineteenth century he was highly regarded as a progressive composer. At the Met in 1922, it had a first-rate cast with the brilliant young soprano Rosa Ponselle as Margared, Gigli as Mylio, Léon Rothier as the King and

Giuseppe Danise as Karnac. This was Alda's first performance of the season, having taken the period up to the New Year to finish her concert tour. For Oscar Thompson in *Musical America*:

> … the Rozenn of Mme Alda was of a winsome simplicity
> and lovely to look at … [but] the best singing of the evening
> undoubtedly was that of Mr Gigli.[21]

However, William B Murray in the *Brooklyn Daily Eagle* thought the only singers worth praise were Rothier and Alda, who 'sang with beauty of voice and in a language that would have been comprehensible on the Rue de la Paix'. As for the rest, 'they produced much beautiful tone, but …' that seemed to be all.[22]

Alfredo Catalani's *Loreley* re-opened at the Met on 6 December 1922 with Alda in the title role. Catalani was one of Toscanini's closest friends, and his opera, *La Wally*, which had had its American première at the Met in 1909, had established the composer as a leader in the verismo movement. *Loreley* had first been performed at the Teatro Regio in Turin in February 1890, but its Met première had to wait until January 1922 with Claudia Muzio in the title role and Gigli as Walter. Alda replaced Muzio in its second season at the Met, Gigli returning to sing Walter. Taking over from Muzio would not be the easiest thing in the world for Frances – Muzio was ten years younger and was to become one of the best loved sopranos in opera around the world through the 1920s and early 1930s, especially revered in the verismo repertoire. Nevertheless, critical and audience response to Alda as the Loreley was intensely positive. RM Knerr in *Musical America* wrote:

> *Loreley* emerged … with a new and resplendent protagonist of
> the titular role in the person of Frances Alda. The part seems
> ideally fitted to this artist, and she sang it very well indeed,
> with lyric phrases of unusual beauty in the higher register.[23]

Alda had recorded the aria 'Ah, dunque ei m'amera' from *Loreley* for Victor a whole decade earlier, in 1912, and that is now widely regarded as one of her finest and most moving performances on record. After *Loreley*, the next role new to Alda was Martha in Flotow's opera on 14 December 1923. A great favourite at the house, this was another role that suited Alda's particular qualities very well, her assumption of the part strongly appealing again to RM Knerr in *Musical America*:

> Mme Alda disclosed her clear and sympathetic voice to especial advantage in the passages of the score in which tender sentiment abounds. She brought a pictorial quality to the role that was most effective. Her singing in the 'Spinning Wheel' quartet of Act 2 was brilliant.[24]

As with *Loreley*, Victor had made recordings from *Martha* in 1912 – with Alda, Josephine Jacoby, Caruso and Marcel Journet. Four of those recordings include Alda, all ensemble pieces, and they are great treasures, especially for the interactions of Alda and Caruso. Frances was the fourth Simonsen woman to sing the title role in *Martha*, following her grandmother Fanny and her aunts Martina Simonsen and Frances Saville.

Alda's final new role at the Met was Ginevra in Giordano's *La cena della beffe* (*The Jester's Supper*) on 2 January 1926. Toscanini had conducted the very successful première at La Scala twelve months earlier, so this was its first performance in America. In fact, Alda had been able to try out the role in August the previous year in a return trip to perform at Buenos Aires, this time at the Teatro Colón. She was there while the thirty-one-year-old playboy Prince of Wales was visiting, and she sang a duet with him, Irving Berlin's 'All Alone', at a party at the British Embassy.[25]

The Met cast for *La cena della beffe* was again stellar, with Gigli as Giannetto and Titta Ruffo as Neri, Tullio Serafin the conductor. One of the most brutal of verismo operas, it has never won sufficient favour to demand a regular place in the repertoire, yet much of the music has Giordano at his best. WJ Henderson in the *Sun* was full of praise for the cast, especially for Alda:

> Mme Alda found one of her most well-chosen parts in
> Ginevra, the Florentine siren, to whom love was a succession of
> voluptuous adventures. She looked, sang and acted well.[26]

Victor recorded two of Ginevra's arias with Alda in 1925 and 1926. Both show her at her most persuasive.

4

Of the four who had worked at the Metropolitan Opera so successfully together – Alda, Gatti-Casazza, Caruso and Toscanini – by 1921 there were three, Toscanini having left in 1915. Then came one of the major sadnesses of Frances Alda's life, the death of her close friend, the great tenor Caruso, in Naples on 2 August 1921.

Alda and Caruso's last performance together at the Met (or anywhere) had been on 15 January 1920 in *Manon Lescaut* with their friends and colleagues Scotti and De Segurola. Caruso's health started a rapid decline in the winter of 1920–21, and his own last performance at the Met was as Éléazar in Halévy's *La Juive* on Christmas Eve of 1920. Devoted to Caruso, in her memoirs Frances wrote:

> The great tenor was the finest artist, the truest friend, the
> kindest person I ever knew in the theatre … 'Why not try it
> this way?' he would often suggest, and then show his ideas how
> a phrase should be sung, or a bit of business played. And his
> ideas were always good.[27]

Enrico Caruso

Alda had first sung with Caruso in *Rigoletto* at Covent Garden on 13 June 1906, and she wrote later: 'What thrilled me most about that performance of *Rigoletto* was finding that Caruso's voice and mine blended so perfectly.'[28] The truth of this observation is very evident from the recordings they left to us. An indication of the closeness of their relationship is contained in this story from one of their performances at the Met together of *La bohème*. It was the heyday of the practical joke:

As Mimì, I wore a crinoline, with ruffled white pantalettes showing beneath the hem. The pantalettes were fastened about my waist with a button and buttonhole. At the point where I bent over to pick up the key, I felt (and with what consternation!) the button give way. Beneath my crinoline I could feel the muslin pantalettes slipping down ... I got behind the sofa, I let the pantalettes slip to the floor, I then stepped out of them, and then came forward again, congratulating myself on my cleverness and presence of mind. Then, to my horror, I saw the dangerous gleam in Caruso's eye ... Still singing, he stooped, picked up the pantalettes, lifted them so that no one in the audience could fail to recognise them for what they were, and bowing to me, laid them on the sofa, while the audience roared with laughter.[29]

In 1914 Caruso had written in Alda's autograph book (in Italian): 'I wish I were able to sing with my pen the praises I would address to you, my dear and good lady and friend, but it is poor, and nothing remains for me but to tell you you have in me a heart, a soul, and an affectionate and devoted friend.'[30]

On 27 November 1921, twenty-five days after Caruso's death, the Met mounted a special Memorial Concert, the proceeds to go to the Verdi Home for Aged Musicians in Milan. Alda sang Cézar Franck's 'Panis Angelicus'.

5

Alda was sought out in 1925 by an experienced Australian music critic and teacher, AL Kelly, who interviewed her in her New York home. He was clearly impressed by her, both as a musician and as a woman:

> Frances Alda is not an emotional singer or a stirring actress,
> but she knows the stage thoroughly, and uses her beautiful
> voice with fine taste and absolutely sound musicianship ... But
> her many years at the Metropolitan have not Americanised her
> speech or dulled her Australian frankness ... It was a pleasure
> to meet an artist with views so positive and with such a hearty
> informality of expression: a singer of high distinction, and a
> shrewd, frank, and kindly woman.[31]

While Alda still had three flourishing income streams – at the Metropolitan Opera, with nationwide concert tours, and through studio recordings – a fourth major opportunity opened up for her in 1925: performing on radio.

That year saw a step-change in the effectiveness of radio as a communicator of music with the introduction of highly effective microphones. American radio stations were rapidly equipping themselves with this new technology, while looking around for the musical talent that might exploit it, and Frances Alda was one of the first to be tapped. The pioneering New York radio station WEAF, owned by telecommunications giant and microphone manufacturer Western Electric, started the first series of dedicated opera and song programmes, together with Alda's recording company, Victor. WEAF's first programme featured soprano Lucrezia Bori and Irish tenor John McCormack, but the second, on 15 January 1925, starred Frances Alda. It broadcast an array of Alda's recordings, the companies realising that, with improved sound quality, radio broadcasts would drive both live radio audiences and record sales.[32] For the broadcast, WEAF was hooked up with seven other radio stations in eastern cities. Much was made in the press of this star of the Metropolitan Opera making her radio debut.[33] Millions were said to have listened to the broadcast, an unimaginable figure compared with the few who could attend either opera house or concert hall performances.[34] Alda was very clear about the potential:

In the years whilst I had been singing to four thousand
people crowded into an opera house, science had invented a
means by which a singer could sing to four million persons
at a time ... I felt that I knew America, and I wanted to sing
to the whole country.[35]

In March Alda starred again, this time with Spanish tenor Miguel
Fleta, and there was much discussion in the press of the relative
merits of theatre and radio.[36] In January 1926, Alda featured in a WJZ
programme (a six station hook-up) with celebrated Italian baritone
Titta Ruffo,[37] and by April that year the radio manufacturer Atwater
Kent became a major player on the scene, starting the first American
radio symphony orchestra and establishing the Atwater Kent Hour
(broadcast on WEAF), in which Alda was a regular featured artist.[38]
By the end of 1926 WEAF was boasting a fourteen-station network
for its broadcasts featuring Alda, and in 1927 General Motors, seeking
to build positive attitudes towards its cars, started a rival series of
programmes with a twenty-eight-station network featuring other opera
stars. Competition was hotting up.[39] The following year the Atwater
Kent series was going out to twenty-six stations, 'coast to coast' as their
advertisements asserted, and Frances Alda was the featured artist in
a programme on 7 October which was devoted entirely to the operas
of Puccini.[40]

The network must have thought they were really on to something
with the Puccini broadcast, because in November 1929 a new series was
announced which would bring six different whole Puccini operas to the
nation in English – each one a two-hour programme – starting with
Madame Butterfly on 16 November.[41] *Butterfly* was followed by *Tosca*,
The Girl of the Golden West, *Manon Lescaut*, *Turandot* and finally *La
bohème* (on 19 April 1930).[42] Alda used a luncheon at the Park Lane
Hotel on 48th Street to signal both the coming close of her long career
at the Met and the planned season of broadcast operas. At the lunch,
she said:

Giacomo Puccini

Alda's Puccini operas on radio

> I am about to say farewell to the opera house. I have finished
> twenty-two years with the Metropolitan Opera Company.
> During all that time I am proud to say that I have never missed
> a scheduled performance ... I have striven always to give the
> best that was in me ... Everyone loves good music, though not
> everyone can attend the operas ...[43]

And with that she talked of the forthcoming pioneering series of
Puccini operas on the radio. It would be a real breakthrough for
broadcast opera.[44] Her principal co-stars in the series were American
tenor Mario Chamlee and Italian baritone Pasquale Amato. While
Chamlee had sung with Alda at the Met on only thirteen occasions,
Amato had performed with her from the start of her tenancy there in
1908 – singing Rigoletto to her Gilda at her debut. It was ironic that in

a long operatic career featuring much Puccini, Alda had only sung on stage in two of the six operas to be broadcast – *La bohème* and *Manon Lescaut*. In 1929–30 they were all broadcast live, but sadly without the technological means at that time to record them.[45]

During the weeks that the Puccini operas were being broadcast, Alda gave her final performance at the Met – on 28 December 1929 in the title role of *Manon Lescaut*. If it was assumed that she was intending to retire from all performing, nothing could be further from the truth. In fact, she simply gave up the opera house in order to focus on radio, with its enormous reach and its 'vastly increased remuneration'. In January 1930 it was announced that Alda had signed an exclusive one-year contract worth $250 000 with the Judson division of Columbia Concerts (roughly equivalent to $US3.8 million in today's money), which would commit her to two fifteen-minute programmes each week – 104 programmes in all.[46] At the time, this was the highest amount paid to any radio star.[47]

That commitment having been delivered, Alda went on in January 1932 to sign a further exclusive contract, this time with WEAF's owner, the NBC network. It was NBC which had commissioned the Puccini operas.[48] However, it was around this time that the American networks started to pay more attention to changing musical tastes around the country, changes which later prompted Alda to condemn 'all crooner and boop-a doop songs as passé'. Perhaps this was an early skirmish in the constant battle against the perceived plague of 'dumbing down'.[49] It was a battle that Alda was bound to lose, and her radio career wound down gradually over the next three years, effectively at an end by 1936. Nevertheless, looking back, Alda thoroughly enjoyed her career as a radio star:

> Of all the audiences I ever faced, the microphone gave me the greatest thrill. It wasn't a curious round black hole on the end of a pipe that I was singing to. It was uncounted thousands of human beings. Who were they? Where were they?[50]

6

Since the end of the Great War in 1918, Alda's previously established career as a bestselling recording artist had carried on unabated. In February 1919 she made the first-ever recording of an aria that was generally unknown at the time, but has since become a great favourite around the world – 'O mio babbino caro' from Puccini's *Gianni Schicchi* – and the trio (with Martinelli and Journet) from the Prison Scene in Gounod's *Faust*, which was not published. She returned to the Victor studios in mid-year, to make one new recording – of the spiritual 'Deep River' – and was back again in December, when she recorded two more songs. Between 1920 and 1924, she visited the Camden studios eleven times, the sessions mostly setting down more songs, chosen primarily because they would broadcast well, plus two arias, both unpublished, from Mascagni's *L'amico Fritz*,[51] and (in the last of those sessions) an elegant rendition of Irving Berlin's 'What'll I do?'. That recording was first broadcast by WEAF on 15 January 1925 and as a consequence it became one of the earliest songs whose record sales outsold the sheet music.

All of Alda's studio recordings up to this time had been made acoustically, but in 1925, the microphone having arrived, the process was transformed, making a step-change in sound fidelity. Alda made her first electrical recordings for Victor in May that year, returning again to the studios each year until 1928. Although she was coming towards the end of her career in the opera house, these late discs show Alda still at the height of her powers. Of particular note are two arias from Giordano's *La cena della beffe* – great favourites among collectors – and, in her final sessions, two arias from Puccini's *Manon Lescaut* and two touching Maori songs which she learned during her 1927 tour of New Zealand – 'Waiata Maori', collected and arranged by Alfred Hill, and 'A Maori slumber song (Hine e hine)' by Princess Te Rangi Pai.[52]

Alda's recording career stretched from 1909 to 1928 and gives us a very clear picture of her vocal abilities. Unlike several of her contemporaries (including Melba), she seems to have been quite at home in the recording studio, uninhibited and singing with freedom. Noticeable throughout is her excellent breath control, enabling her to sing whatever she addressed with consummate musicianship. She sang always with clean attack and controlled legato, usually with good intonation. She was equally happy in both head and chest voice, and in managing between the two – something she would have learned from Marchesi. Her recordings are full of presence and feeling. She knew what suited her particular voice and personality, steering clear of both bel canto and the arrival of Wagner and his followers. Only her somewhat clouded diction has been a cause for occasional adverse comment.

As early as 1921 Alda was thinking about returning to perform in the countries where she was born and grew up, New Zealand and Australia. She had begun discussions with the top agent-impresarios in the territories, J & N Tait, but the proposed performances fell through when the diva became indisposed through illness.[53] Frances rekindled these intentions six years later, but was by now working with a recent agent start-up – Mr P Haskevitch of Concert Tours Ltd in Sydney.[54] Maybe they were offering better terms than the Taits.

7

For Australian musicians and singers returning home to perform, having established themselves in Europe or North America, there seem to have been four cardinal rules: first, maintain all your personal connections with family and friends, so that they can support you and act as cheerleaders; second, over the years, ensure that your personal profile remains salient in Australia, with media coverage of all your international successes; third, on arrival, leverage your 'backstory' with all its local assets – education, interesting childhood anecdotes, early successes and so on; fourth, appoint an experienced and first-rate local agent who can squeeze every drop out of your engagements. While for her return visits Nellie Melba ticked every box, Alda had none of these on her return to Australia. The consequence was that she was treated as just another visiting artist. And she had not set foot in the country for twenty-six years.

For Alda, things went wrong in Australia from the start. In January Haskevitch proudly announced his forthcoming star tourists – violinist Efrem Zimbalist (and his wife soprano Alma Gluck) and Frances Alda – in that order, with not a word about Alda's Australian roots. Had she known, Frances would have been appalled to be treated as the also-ran in that particular list.[55] On top of that, Australia in the years 1926 and 1927 was overrun with high profile visiting artists, among them two Russians, the celebrated bass Feodor Chaliapin and the star ballet dancer Anna Pavlova, plus a Cossack choir; two international pianists – expatriate Australian Percy Grainger and the great Pole, Paderewski; and two outstanding fiddlers, the young Russian Jascha Heifetz and the aforementioned Efrem Zimbalist.

But more significantly than any of them for Alda, there was a yearlong series of farewell concerts from Australia's most famous daughter, Dame Nellie Melba. These farewells followed her major Farewell to her artistic home, Covent Garden, in June 1926. And, to top it all, on 9 May in the presence of the Duke of York (later King George VI), together with all the great and good of Australia, Melba sang 'God Save the King' at the opening of the new Australian Parliament building in Canberra. Altogether, it was a highly competitive scene, but one in which a well-presented prima donna with Australian roots still might do quite well.

In the circumstances, inappropriately billed as 'The Voice of the Century', Alda opened at the Town Hall in Sydney on 11 August 1927. By this time, the major news stories about her in the local press were a series of scurrilous articles, filled with half-truths and blatant untruths. In response, the *Sunday Times* in Sydney took the moral high ground under the banner headline: 'OPERATIC SENSATION – Wicked Lies about Madame Frances Alda.'

The gist of the article was a repetition of 'insidious and abominable … perversions and distortions of fact … diabolic lies' previously printed in *Smith's Weekly,* together with the *Sunday Times*'s refutations of same. The potentially damaging part of the story was that Frances had been supported financially before leaving Australia in 1900 by the pastoralist Sir Rupert Clarke, with the clear implication that she had had an intimate relationship with him. If she knew about the story at all, it appears that she ignored it.[56]

Since 1899, there had been in the Australian press occasional veiled intimations of a close relationship between Sir Rupert and young Francie Adler. Clarke had at that time been lessee of the Theatre Royal in Melbourne and the Criterion in Sydney – it was at the latter house that Francie had been performing with Harry Rickards's company that year.[57] The whole saga was reminiscent of the problems that Melba had had during her first return to Australia in 1902, when *Truth* journalist John Norton had falsely accused the diva of being a drunkard who cancelled concerts.

In 1989, thirty-seven years after Alda's death, a man called Norbert Saville died at St Marys in the outer western suburbs of Sydney. Saville was supposedly Alda's illegitimate son. He had been born on 29 November 1898, two years before Alda and her brother left for Europe.[58] In February 1898, when a child might have been conceived, Francie Adler was 'resting' following her performance as Ethel in *The Gay Parisienne* at the Princess Theatre in Melbourne. In late November 1898, when the child was born, she was preparing to open in *Ali Baba and the Forty Thieves* at Her Majesty's Theatre in Sydney.

Norbert Saville had a very large collection of original 78 rpm records (mostly pre–First World War) and from time to time wrote articles about opera in the 1920s and about early singers. The house in which he lived his last day as an alcoholic was derelict with no toilet. No solid evidence has surfaced that this man was in fact Alda's son, but allegedly she spent time with him on her return to Australia in 1927, and many who knew him did believe that she was his mother.[59] If Norbert Saville was indeed Frances Alda's son, it seems possible, even likely, that the father was Sir Rupert Clarke.

Reviews of her first concert in Sydney were mildly enthusiastic: 'Artistic Singing' was the headline in the *Sydney Morning Herald*, which went on to praise the 'wealth of her vocal resources ... her voice clear and sympathetic'.[60] A good report, but not one to set box office tills alight. More positive in tone was a review in the *Sunday Times* a few days later, which talked of:

> ... large audiences at the Town Hall [who] were roused to
> an immense pitch of enthusiasm by the singing of Madame
> Frances Alda, who comes to us in the full plenitude of
> her powers.[61]

It seems that audiences were satisfactory, both in numbers and enthusiasm, as her short season in Sydney progressed, and by the last week of August Alda had moved on to her childhood hometown, Melbourne. While *Table Talk* covered her associations with the city and her Simonsen relations, the rest of the media either did not know about them, or chose to ignore them.[62] In Melbourne, Alda might have been expected to perform, as in Sydney, at the Town Hall, but in fact she was booked into the less prestigious Auditorium in Collins Street. None of the advertising for her Melbourne concerts mentioned anything about her local associations. Just as in Sydney, the Melbourne press was mildly enthused: 'An attractive singer' was the tepid headline to a report in *The Age* following her opening concert on 27 August, and *The Argus* review chose to focus on the flowers, frocks and hair.[63]

By the fifth concert at the Auditorium, *The Age* was complaining that 'Madame Alda, from her extensive knowledge of vocal works, might have found more vital and valuable selections for her recital,' citing several works that she had sung in earlier recitals,[64] and, of the following night's concert, *Table Talk* was not impressed that she had publicly admonished her accompanist, Max Rabinowitsch for dragging the tempo in a song.[65] Never one to miss the opportunity to disparage a famous artist, Australian writer Thorold Waters described the scene in more elaborate detail:

> I saw [Chaliapin] try to cover a mistake of his own by
> pounding the piano and storming at his accompanist, a fellow
> Russian. The scene was repeated by the soprano Frances
> Alda with the same victim while she was in Australia, but I
> was overjoyed when in bringing down her hand angrily on
> the Steinway grand she broke a bracelet, its glittering jewels
> scattering to all points.[66]

While Alda was in the city, she caught up with her brother Alby and his family. Together she and Alby drove to visit the house in Carlisle Street, St Kilda, where they had had their childhoods:

> Grandmother's house there had been sold long before, but
> the present owners welcomed us and let us walk through
> those well-remembered rooms, and see again the familiar
> patterns the sunlight made on the walls and floors, and catch
> a whiff of lavender that still haunted the room that was my
> grandmother's.[67]

Alda's farewell concert in Melbourne on 9 September was followed by three concerts at the Town Hall in Adelaide, before she moved on to the country of her birth, New Zealand.

8

Would Alda's reception in New Zealand be warmer than that she had received in Australia? It might well be. For one thing, she had been born there; and, while Australia had Nellie Melba as a national icon, Frances Alda was up to that time internationally by far the most successful singer born in New Zealand – retaining that crown until the arrival of Kiri Te Kanawa (who was born sixty-five years after Alda).[68]

By this stage, Alda had jettisoned her tour manager in Australia, Mr Haskevitch, and had in his place the very experienced manager of opera companies, DD O'Connor. At short notice, she had also taken on board a new accompanist, Cyril Towsey, dispensing with the services of the unfortunate Rabinowitsch. Dunedin-born Towsey had been a pupil of Busoni in Berlin. In 1906 he had accompanied Princess Te Rangi Pai on tour in New Zealand, and by 1908 he was in Britain accompanying Blanche Marchesi, Count John McCormack and violinist Joseph Szigeti.[69] Publicity ahead of the tour focused on Alda's special ties to New Zealand and on her glittering career in the major opera houses of Europe and at the Met. She was positioned constantly as 'one of the world's great sopranos'.[70] The opening concert was at the Town Hall in Auckland, where 'the audience was delighted with the finished singing, and the varied programme, which was out of the usual run.' The *Auckland Star* continued:

> The soprano possesses a voice of extensive compass, suited admirably for operatic and concert purposes. Her high notes are full and telling, and shine out brilliantly in the climaxes, the middle and low intervals are of rich timbre … Madame phrases with rare art, and delightfully expresses the mood of her solos.[71]

All was very well in the Land of the Long White Cloud. However, back in Melbourne a sinister press row was erupting. The director of the Albert Street Conservatorium in Melbourne (the institution prominently supported by Melba), Fritz Hart, criticised some remarks made by Alda in Adelaide to the effect that the musical tastes of Melbourne audiences never 'soared above "I passed by your window" and the like'.[72] In his response, Hart blamed visiting international stars (like Madame Alda), who included rubbish in their own programmes. In a letter to the *Melbourne Herald*, Alda accused Hart, saying that what he had said was both untrue and impertinent. Hart then countered that what Alda had written was full of 'irrelevancies'.[73] Altogether it made a good press story, but it clearly stung Alda, and placed her, not the English-born Hart, as the outsider.

Alda gave three concerts each in Auckland and Wellington. In all of them she sang her usual mix of arias and songs organised into four groups: the first group was of seventeenth- and eighteenth-century bel canto songs that she might have learned with Marchesi in Paris; the second, of late nineteenth- and early twentieth-century songs, usually French; the third, of arias from her major roles, often by Puccini; and the fourth, of recent and current popular songs. Alda's sets were interspersed by piano solos played by her accompanist.

Her Wellington concerts opened at the Town Hall on 1 October and the *Evening Post* remarked that the visit of the diva was 'an event of some musical importance' but was dismayed that the hall was not full. However, the audience that was there was thrilled, among other items, by her performance of 'Un bel dì vedremo' from *Madama Butterfly* and 'clamoured for more'.[74] Anticipation of her arrival in her birthplace, Christchurch, was rising, driven by complimentary media attention, the *Press* going overboard in anticipating her:

> By universal consent the greatest operatic soprano of the day
> is Madame Frances Alda, the reigning prima donna of the
> Metropolitan Opera House, New York … She was born in
> Christchurch, New Zealand …[75]

She opened there on 8 October, the *Press* declaring 'her first triumph', before adding that:

> ... a very large audience [was] waiting with ill-suppressed excitement for the first tell-tale notes to fall from the famous singer ... [and] a world of beauty and romance may be crystallised in a single note

... and so on.[76] She gave a second concert in Christchurch on the 13th, equally gratefully received. In the days between her final concert in New Zealand and leaving the country, Alda visited Rotorua in the heart of North Island. Then as now, a centre for Maori culture, she heard perhaps for the first time Maori songs, which had a profound effect on her. In her memoirs she wrote:

> All my life has been lived among peoples whose civilisation is accounted very old and conventionalised. I have never felt any appeal in crudities and unsophistication. But in those beautiful Maoris, the handsomest people on earth, flowed something so natural, so smooth, so gentle that it was perfect art ... One of the Maori songs haunted me for days.[77]

That song was 'Hine e hine' by Princess Te Rangi Pai, which Alda was later to use to introduce her weekly radio programme in America, using her commercial recording of it, one of her most touching. A few days later Alda sailed on the *Aorangi* from Auckland via Fiji to Hawaii and on to Vancouver. Never one to miss an opportunity, when the ship stopped for half a day on 4 November at Honolulu, Alda gave a noonday concert at the Princess Theater,[78] just as her grandparents had on a similar voyage forty-five years before.

In her researches into Alda's origins with members of her father's family, Adrienne Simpson was able to establish that, during her time in New Zealand in 1927, Frances had met joyfully with Davis relations,

Princess Te Rangi Pai

including some who remembered her as a small child in Christchurch. She particularly enjoyed meeting with a cousin in Auckland whose wife, Marion Davis, was a principal singer in light opera, and also with Ernest Davis, who would later become mayor of Auckland. She took a trip from Wellington to Palmerston North, where she visited an uncle. 'She was impressed by the prosperity and stature of her father's family and delighted by New Zealand,' wrote Simpson.[79]

Arriving at Vancouver, Alda gave an extraordinary interview while waiting for her baggage to clear. Clearly, the difference in her treatment between Australia and New Zealand had left a deep wound:

> Miss Alda said: 'Never again! I have done with Australia.
> What a place it is! The people are simply loathsome, and the

hotels are abominable. The theatres are unendurable, and
the railways insufferable … I would rather have sung in this
customs shed. 'New Zealand is different,' said Miss Alda. 'It is
a lovely place, with a lovely people and a lovely climate'[80]

How was it that such an outpouring of bile came from someone
usually so skilled in handling press reporters? Of course, after such a
long journey, she may have been extremely tired, but equally she was
clearly saying out loud what was on her mind. By this stage of her
career, Alda had all sorts of diva-ish characteristics. She expected to be
heard and obeyed. She thought that her opinions were more important
than other people's. What she had perhaps forgotten is that Australians
have little tolerance for such attitudes and behaviour, and like nothing
better than to cut down to size people who get above themselves – the
'tall poppy syndrome'.

One outcome of all this kerfuffle was that, while Alda had always
previously described herself as either Australian or English, for the
future she was to be a proud New Zealander.[81] However, clearly, by the
time she came to write her memoirs in 1937, her love for Australia had
fully revived.

Returned to New York from her tour of Australia and New Zealand in
November 1927, Frances Alda quickly picked up her career with the Met
again, singing a series of Mimìs, Manon Lescauts and Marthas, all with
Beniamino Gigli; and several Marguérites to Chaliapin's Méphistophélès
in *Faust*. Of her Mimì with Gigli on 29 November at Philadelphia, the
first after her return, the *Philadelphia Inquirer* reported:

> As for Madame Alda, she has returned from her protracted
> tour of her native New Zealand and Australia with her tones
> fresher and firmer than they have been for seasons.[82]

As mentioned previously, Alda's final performance at the Met, on
28 December 1929, was in *Manon Lescaut* with Gigli.

9

Frances Alda's performing career – opera, concerts, studio recordings and radio – was effectively over by 1936. What was she to do with the rest of her life? She was a wealthy woman. Although she lived life to the full – an expensive undertaking – for many years she also benefited from the financial guidance of her friend, the entrepreneur-investor Harrison Williams. Nevertheless, when the Crash came in October 1929, Alda was 'gasping for breath' when 'everybody's securities began tobogganing out of sight.' After a few days, she called Williams, who gave her advice and practical support, and she emerged from the experience virtually intact.[83]

By 1936, Alda at fifty-seven had been singing professionally for forty years. How did she account for such a long career? In an article based on an interview with James Francis Cooke, first published in 1921, Alda gave the credit to her teacher, Mathilde Marchesi:

> Marchesi, with her famous wisdom on vocal matters, advised twenty minutes a day and then not more than ten minutes at a time ... Most girls over-exercise their voices during the years when they are too delicate ... The girl who hopes to become a prima donna will dream of her work morning, noon and night ... Even now I study pretty regularly two hours a day, but I rarely sing more than a few minutes.[84]

Alda had been talking for several years of writing her memoirs, and now in the early 1930s would be an ideal time to finish and publish them. They might have multiple objectives: they might tell the story of her origins and life; they might relate all the exciting and funny things that had happened to her; they might settle some scores. She hired a ghost-writer, and between them they conjured up something unique in the long history of such tomes: Alda's memoirs are elegantly written, revealing and full of wit. *Men, Women and Tenors*, which came out in 1937, is a genuine page-turner. Of course, it is also filled with little inaccuracies, exclusions and occasional untruths. But which book of that sort is not? Unlike most, in its candour it caused quite a stir in the press, with journalists lifting and retelling favourite anecdotes from the pages. Reviewing the book, *TIME* magazine reflected:

> As memoirs of operatic divas go, one in which the author
> admits she is plump, is not too boastful about herself or too
> jealous of her peers, is on its face worthy …[85]

In November Alda put on a lavish launch party for the press, where she admitted to one of them: 'The two biggest mistakes I ever made were first to marry Gatti-Casazza and second to divorce him.'[86] And in January 1939 she charmed a journalist of the *Palm Beach Post* in Florida in a lengthy interview, in which she divulged that the experience of singing with Caruso was still one she treasured. 'As many times as I sang with him, he always made me cry.' She also disclosed that she was planning a second volume of memoirs, although this never came about.[87]

By this stage, her candour about colleagues knew no bounds. When the great Italian tenor Beniamino Gigli, with whom she had shared the stage at the Met so often after the death of Caruso, criticized American singers, Alda told a reporter that Gigli was 'a nasty little pig'.[88] Although she had sung with him so often, she never recorded or broadcast with Gigli, and he scarcely features in Alda's memoirs.

Having noted that Alda had a certain fluidity concerning her nationality, it is also worth noting that, in her memoirs, at no point does she mention her Jewish heritage. Indeed, she may well have sought to conceal it, including changing her birth surname in her memoirs, consistently presented there as Davies rather than Davis.[89]

10

During her years in retirement, Alda occupied herself with teaching young singers. None of them seem to have amounted to much, apart from Gertrude Ribla, who sang at the Met in 1949–50 as Aida, Leonora in *Il trovatore* and Gerhilde in *Die Walküre*. However, the pupil she describes at some length in her memoirs was the six-times-married Polish soprano, Ganna Walska. Walska was said to have had a terrible voice (and with it a minimal career). She was pelted with rotten vegetables by the audience during Giordano's *Fedora* in Havana – it was this event that Orson Welles remembered in his film, *Citizen Kane*. Initially, Alda refused to teach her: 'If you want my honest advice', I told her, 'learn to cook. You'll never be a singer.'[90]

Aside from the teaching, Alda entertained regularly at Great Neck, many of her guests being rich and/or famous:

> There have been half a dozen kings and several queens;
> great ladies and ballet girls; bank presidents and tenors;
> movie stars, ambassadors, crooners, debutantes, admirals,
> advertising men, politicians … Charlie Chaplin came to lunch
> and suddenly stood up and acted a scene from his picture,
> *The Gold Rush* …[91]

Throughout this time Alda had altercations with servants and tradespersons, the problems all stemming from her high-handed attitude towards them. As early as 1927, she had refused to pay $1100 to the man who had decorated her home at Great Neck, threatening to shoot him, because he was 'incompetent'.[92] In 1941 she was sued for $25 000 damages by her cook, Louise Blazej, who asserted that Alda had struck her, causing her to burn her arm on the oven, because the dinner was late. The case was dismissed.[93] Another Alda cook, Mrs Barbara Neill, accused the diva of stealing stamps worth 300 points

Alda at home

from her ration book in 1945. Frances seemed to think that the points were really hers, and, in a confused situation, Alda was sent for trial on charges of petty larceny, and in due course was cleared.[94]

Alda could mix kindness and imperiousness in equal measure, as shown by this incident recalled by her younger colleague, soprano Rosa Ponselle:

The limousine pulled up in front of her home. It was beautiful. Once we got inside, Alda reached for a bellcord and summoned her five servants. They stood in front of her like an army at attention. In an unbroken string of words, she said to them, 'This is Rosa Ponselle, the greatest soprano who ever lived, so have a look and get back to work!' Like obedient soldiers, they gawked, smiled, did an about-face and then left.[95]

Two years after their divorce in 1928, the sixty-one-year-old Gatti-Casazza married a thirty-three-year-old première danseuse at the Met, Rosina Galli. They had known each other for decades. After twenty-seven years in the job, Gatti finally retired from directing the Metropolitan Opera in 1935, and on 19 March the Met put on a Gala Performance in his honour with the cream of that generation of singers, including Rosa Ponselle, Lucrezia Bori, Kirsten Flagstad, Elisabeth Rethburg, Giovanni Martinelli, Lauritz Melchior, Richard Crooks, Friedrich Schorr and Ezio Pinza. Alda, Caruso and Toscanini, who had been with Gatti at the Met from 1908, had all moved on. Gatti died aged seventy-one in his hometown, Ferrara, in 1940.[96]

In April 1941 Alda also remarried – to advertising executive Ray Vir Den.[97] They were happy together, living mainly at her house at Great Neck, and she continued to teach a small group of pupils. In March of 1952 dinner guests at Casa Mia included the Duke and Duchess of Windsor, and later that summer they were vacationing, as they did most years, with friends on the Lido at Venice. Frances Alda died there of a cerebral haemorrhage on 18 September 1952. She was said to be sixty-nine years old, but having moved her birth year forward by four years, she was in reality seventy-three. Ironically, that evening she had planned to be at the opera house, La Scala in Milan, at an orchestral concert given by her old friend Arturo Toscanini, who thought she was in the audience, only to be told later of her demise. Toscanini had sent flowers and a note to Frances and Ray's hotel room that morning.[98] Alda's ashes were taken by Ray back to America and were buried in the cemetery at Great Neck.[99] The *New York Herald*'s take on her life was:

> Mme Alda, one of the most striking figures of an era that ran to colourful prima donnas, said of herself that she 'had red hair and the temperament to go with it.' She was given to plain speaking and acquired both a reputation for wit and a number of enemies.[100]

Aside from news reports of her death in Australia and New Zealand, there was a solitary family notice in *The Age* in Melbourne, placed by her pharmacist brother Alby and his children:

> Alda, Frances – On September 18 in Venice, loving sister of Albert Adler, and aunt of Leonora and John.[101]

At her death she was said to have been one of the wealthiest of retired opera singers, having earned great sums throughout her career and having invested wisely.[102] Her husband Ray Vir Den died three years later in November 1955, and on 19 March 1956 many of Alda's possessions, including autographed photographs and a record collection, were sold by the New York dealer, Plaza Art Galleries.[103] For the biographer, it is near catastrophic that Alda's letters, both to and from, seem not to have survived. In her memoirs she writes frequently and with pride of her correspondence with Gatti, Caruso, Toscanini and so many others. Was it dumped in the trash by Vir Den or his family, not understanding its importance? Or does it rest undisturbed in some academic library? Thank goodness for Alda's charming and eloquent book.

Thus came to a close the story of an extraordinary family of singers, one which stretched over a hundred years and more. Summing up her own life, Alda wrote in her memoirs:

I have been enjoying tremendously the adventure of being alive. I have had success and failure; and perhaps more than my fair share of fame in an art that I love passionately … I have known love and ecstasy; deep hurt and bitterness and loss; and some strong, sustaining friendships. And whether I owe this to an irrepressible sense of humor or to an almost equally irrepressible pride, I can't say; there has grown up in me a tolerance for the extraordinary, sometimes ridiculous, often exasperating creatures that are men and women.[104]

In many ways, she captured the essence of her personality in her remembrance of herself as a child:

Certainly a great deal of the secret of Frances Alda was to be found in the impulsive, fiery-tempered, ardent little girl playing prima donna in the lath and burlap theatre in the garden at St Kilda.[105]

Notes

1   *Star-Gazette* (Elmira, New York), 29 June 1926, 20; *Tribune* (Seymour, Indiana), 20 September 1926, 8; *Lansing State Journal* (Michigan), 13 November 1926, 17
2   Alda, 101
3   Alda, 230–32
4   *St Louis Post-Dispatch*, 8 September 1928, 3; *Pittsburgh Post-Gazette*, 17 November 1928, 1
5   It is noticeable, however, that Alda is scarcely mentioned in Gatti's memoirs of 1941
6   *Argus-Leader* (Sioux Falls, South Dakota), 24 August 1918, 7
7   Alda and de Luca performed together at the Met in *La bohème, Manon Lescaut, Manon, Mârouf, Faust* and *Martha*
8   *Cincinnati Enquirer*, 31 August 1919, 44

9   *Boston Post*, 17 January 1921, 15
10 *Pittsburgh Press*, 29 January 1922, 39
11 *Chicago Tribune*, 19 October 1924, 68
12 *Evening News* (Harrisburg, Pennsylvania), 21 November 1924, 1
13 Alda, 255–58
14 *Nebraska State Journal*, 26 October 1919, 31
15 *Democrat and Chronicle* (Rochester, New York), 3 August 1919, 31; *New York Times*,
    13 October 1920, 18; *New York Herald*, 1 February 1922, 10 & 3 December 1922, 80
16 Alda's appearances continued at the Met through the 1920s: 1920 (19), 1921 (16), 1922
    (23), 1923 (17), 1924 (24), 1925 (25), 1926 (17), 1927 (16), 1928 (12), 1929 (3, her last
    performance at the house being on 28 December 1929 in the title role of *Manon Lescaut*)
17 *Evening World* (New York), 6 February 1920, 23
18 Alda, 242–43, *New York Herald*, 4 February 1920, 13
19 The 1920 Mefistofele was Adamo Didur, the role being taken from 1922 by Chaliapin
20 *New York Times*, 27 November 1920
21 *Musical America*, nd (1922)
22 *Brooklyn Daily Eagle*, 6 January 1922, 6
23 *Musical America*, nd (1922)
24 *Musical America*, nd (1923)
25 *Evening News* (Harrisburg, Pennsylvania), 12 May 1925, 6; *Quad-City Times* (Davenport,
    Iowa), 28 August 1925, 10; at the Colón, Alda sang in *Martha*, *La bohème*, *Mefistofele*,
    Manon Lescaut and *La cena della beffe*
26 *New York Sun*, 3 January 1926
27 Alda, 10
28 Alda, 64
29 Alda, 141
30 Alda, 240
31 *The Triad* (Sydney), 1 June 1926, 11–12
32 *Courier-News* (Bridgewater, New Jersey), 7 January 1925, 8; *Pittsburgh Press*, 11 January
    1925, 24; *Alexandria Times-Tribune* (Indiana), 12 January 1925, 3
33 *Pittsburgh Daily Post*, 16 January 1925, 1
34 *Indianapolis News*, 16 January 1925, 20
35 Alda, 281
36 *Telegraph* (Brisbane), 30 March 1925, 16
37 *Cincinnati Enquirer*, 12 January 1926, 9
38 *Pittsburgh Post-Gazette*, 18 April 1926, 58
39 *Honolulu Advertiser*, 29 October 1927, 5
40 *Brooklyn Daily Eagle*, 30 September 1928, 88; *Los Angeles Times*, 2 October 1928, 29
41 *Pittsburgh Press*, 10 November 1929, 77; *Brooklyn Daily Eagle*, 16 November 1929, 10
42 The first radio broadcast from the Metropolitan Opera (*Hänsel und Gretel*) was not until
    Christmas Day 1931
43 Cutting from unidentified US newspaper in Simpson files at New Zealand National
    Library, 12 November 1929
44 The first networked broadcast of a complete opera from the Met was Humperdinck's
    Hansel and Gretel on Christmas Eve 1931
45 Broadcast on Saturday evenings, the series opened with *Madama Butterfly* on 16
    November 1929 (Alda as Butterfly, Chamlee as Pinkerton, Amato as Sharpless); then
    Tosca on 21 December (Alda in the title role, Chamlee as Cavarodossi, Amato as Scarpia);
    The Girl of the Golden West on 18 January 1930 (Alda as Minnie, Chamlee as Dick
    Johnson, Amato as Jack Rance, a role he had created); *Manon Lescaut* on 15 February
    (Alda as Manon, Chamlee as Des Grieux, Amato as Lescaut); *Turandot* on 15 March (Alda
    as Liu, Chamlee as Calaf, no Amato, Della Baker in the title role); *La bohème* on 19 April
    (Alda as Mimì, Chamlee as Rodolfo, Amato as Marcello, with 19-year-old Thelma Kessler

as Musetta; the broadcasts were conducted by Gennaro Papi. Studio recordings made by Alda of arias/duets from Puccini operas include two from *Manon Lescaut* (both recorded twice), four from *Madama Butterfly*, one from *Tosca*, three from *La bohème*, one from *Gianni Schicchi* – see Appendix 3

46   *Oakland Tribune*, 24 November 1929, 66; *Oshkosh Northwestern* (Wisconsin), 29 January 1931, 16; Arthur Judson was a leading artists' and orchestra manager who founded CBS

47   *Detroit Free Press*, 1 February 1931, 9

48   *Quad-City Times* (Davenport, Iowa), 18 January 1932, 5; *Miami News*, 24 January 1932, 19

49   *Los Angeles Times*, 14 February 1932, 15

50   Alda, 281

51   *L'amico Fritz* was concurrently being performed at the Met with Lucrezia Bori as Suzel

52   Alda's most recent discographer, Larry Lustig, has identified in total 172 recordings for Victor – see Appendix 3

53   *Sydney Morning Herald*, 5 March 1921, 8

54   *Sydney Morning Herald*, 8 January 1927, 16

55   *Sydney Mail*, 12 January 1927, 37

56   *Sydney Morning Herald*, 27 July 1927, 2; *Smith's Weekly*, 6 August 1927, 1; *Sunday Times* (Sydney), 7 August 1927, 1; Sir Rupert Clarke had died in Monte Carlo in 1926

57   Relationships between members of the British (and Australian) aristocracy and showgirls were comparatively commonplace in the fin-de-siècle, some of them becoming Countesses, Marchionesses and even Duchesses – see Madeleine Bingham, *Earls and Girls: Dramas in High Society*, 1980

58   On his birth certificate, Henry Norbert Saville's mother is given as Annie M Saville; no father is listed; place of birth – Sydney; Annie Saville was born at Goulburn in 1871 and died at Hurstville in 1928

59   Letters to Adrienne Simpson from: Jeff Brownrigg, 26 September 1989; Michael Quinn, 24 July 1990 and 10 November 1992; Peter Burgis, 5 February 1990 and 29 April 1990

60   *Sydney Morning Herald*, 12 August 1927, 12

61   *Sunday Times* (Sydney), 14 August 1927, 9

62   *Table Talk* (Melbourne), 25 August 1927, 66

63   *Age* (Melbourne), 29 August 1927, 11; *Argus*, 29 August 1927, 18

64   *Age*, 7 September 1927, 12

65   *Table Talk*, 8 September 1927, 58

66   Thorold Waters, *Much Besides Music*, 230

67   Alda, 272

68   Alda's nearest 'competitor' among New Zealand-born singers of her own generation was Rosina Buckman (1881–1948), who had a reasonably successful career at Covent Garden and elsewhere, and was a celebrated Butterfly

69   *Bedford Record*, 27 October 1908, 7; Cyril Towsey mysteriously disappeared in 1932, never to be found

70   *New Zealand Herald* (Auckland), 10 September 1927, 14; *New Zealand Herald*, 27 September 1927, 10

71   *Auckland Star*, 28 September 1927, 20

72   'I passed by your window' by May Brahe was popularised by Eileen Boyd and others in 1927

73   *Telegraph* (Brisbane), quoting the *Melbourne Herald*, 29 September 1927, 6

74   *Evening Post* (Wellington), 3 October 1927, 6

75   *Press* (Christchurch), 6 October 1927, 7

76   *Press*, 10 October 1927, 2

77   Alda, 274–75

78   *Honolulu Advertiser*, 5 November 1927, 2

79   Adrienne Simpson and Peter Downes, *Southern Voices*, 20–21

80 *New Zealand Herald*, 14 November 1927, 9
81 Was Alda in reality by this stage an American?
82 *Philadelphia Inquirer*, 30 November 1927, 3
83 Alda, 196–97
84 Frances Alda, 'What the American girl should know about an operatic career', 10
85 *TIME*, 8 November 1937
86 *Morning Call* (Allentown, Pennsylvania), 26 November 1937, 30
87 *Palm Beach Post* (Florida), 1 January 1939, 9
88 *Tampa Times* (Florida) 27 February 1939, 5
89 Davis is a frequently used anglicisation of David, whereas Davies is often Welsh in origin
90 Alda, 290
91 *Hearst's International* combined with *Cosmopolitan*, December 1936, 32
92 *Scranton Republican* (Pennsylvania), 6 April 1927, 1
93 *St Louis Star and Times*, 24 October 1941, 16
94 *New York Times*, 2 March 1945, 21; 3 March 1945, 13; 8 March 1945, 25; 24 March 1945, 19; 10 May 1945, 25; 11 May 1945, 21
95 Rosa Ponselle and James A Drake, *Ponselle: A Singer's Life*, 181–82
96 *Evening News* (Harrisburg, Pennsylvania), 3 September 1940, 2
97 *Chicago Tribune*, 27 April 1927, 66
98 *Times* (Shreveport, Louisiana), 20 September 1952, 1; *Miami News*, 21 September 1927, 38
99 *Morning News* (Wilmington, Delaware), 24 September 1952, 8
100 *New York Herald*, 19 September 1952
101 *Age* (Melbourne), 20 September 1952, 22
102 *Marshall News Messenger* (Texas), 9 November 1952, 23
103 *New York Times*, 11 March 1956, 118; Alda's prized collection of letters to and from Caruso, Toscanini and many others does not appear in that auction catalogue
104 Alda, 4
105 Alda, 74

Appendices

Appendix 1 The Simonsen family

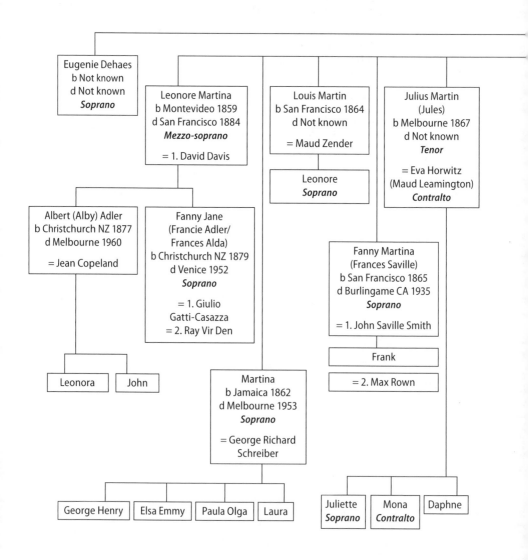

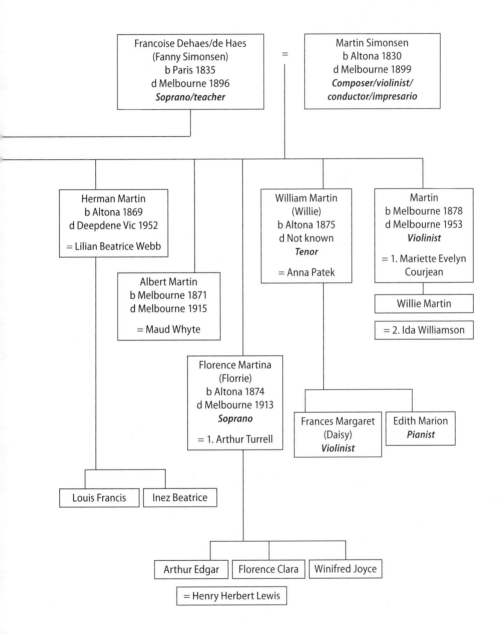

Appendix 2
Opera/role debuts by Simonsen singers

This is a list of opera and operetta debuts in roles performed by the various members of the Simonsen family. It is a work-in-progress and does not include pantomimes, vaudevilles, burlesques and music hall performances. Conspicuous by their absence are 'baroque' composers (aside from a single performance of Handel's *Acis and Galatea*), deemed at the time to be old-fashioned and unperformable. Also, perhaps more surprisingly, there is no Gluck.

It was claimed that Fanny Simonsen sang ninety different roles through her career. Here forty-eight of them have been identified, most of the others probably being roles from which she sang excerpts in concert.

*World première
**National première

1. Daniel Auber, *Les diamants de la couronne* (also later performed as *The Crown Diamonds*)
   FRANÇOISE DE HAES (ROLE UNKNOWN): Opéra-Comique, Paris, 1854/57
   FANNY SIMONSEN (CATARINA): WS Lyster's Royal Italian and English Opera Company, Princess Theatre, Melbourne, 17 June 1867
2. Giacomo Meyerbeer, *L'étoile du nord*
   FRANÇOISE DE HAES (ROLE UNKNOWN): Opéra-Comique, Paris, 1854/57
3. Victor Massé, *Galathée*
   FRANÇOISE DE HAES (ROLE UNKNOWN): Opéra-Comique, Paris, 1854/57
4. Adolphe Adam, *Le toréador*
   FRANÇOISE DE HAES (ROLE UNKNOWN): Opéra-Comique, Paris, 1854/57
5. Aimé Maillart, *Les dragons de Villars* (*The Hermit's Bell*)
   FRANÇOISE DE HAES (ROLE UNKNOWN): Théâtre-Lyrique, Paris, 1856/57
   **FANNY SIMONSEN (ROSE MOINEAU): Simonsen's Royal English, Italian and

Opera Bouffe Company, Queen's Theatre, Dunedin, 7 April 1876
MARTINA SIMONSEN (GEORGETTE): with FANNY SIMONSEN (ROSE); Simonsen's
Royal English and Italian Opera Company, Sloan's Theatre, Invercargill,
12 December 1880

6. Gaetano Donizetti, *Lucia di Lammermoor*
FANNY SIMONSEN (TITLE ROLE): WS Lyster's Royal Italian and English Opera
Company, Theatre Royal, Melbourne, 25 June 1866
FRANCES SIMONSEN (ALISA): Simonsen's Royal English and Italian Opera
Company, Princess Theatre, Dunedin, 11 January 1881
MARTINA SIMONSEN (TITLE ROLE): Simonsen's Royal English and Italian Opera
Company, Princess Theatre, Wanganui, 20 May 1881
JULES SIMONSEN (ARTURO): Tancioni Cuttica's Opera Company, Princess
Theatre, Melbourne, 14 May 1892
FRANCES SAVILLE (TITLE ROLE): Aquarium Theatre, St Petersburg, 6 June 1893

7. Vincenzo Bellini, *La sonnambula*
FANNY SIMONSEN (AMINA): WS Lyster's Royal Italian and English Opera
Company, Theatre Royal, Melbourne, 28 June 1866
MARTINA SIMONSEN (AMINA): Simonsen's Royal English and Italian Opera
Company, Royal Princess Theatre, Bendigo, 26 October 1880
FRANCES SIMONSEN (TERESA): with MARTINA SIMONSEN (AMINA); Simonsen's
Royal English and Italian Opera Company, Sloan's Theatre, Invercargill,
1 December 1880

8. Daniel Auber, *La muette de Portici* (*Masaniello*)
FANNY SIMONSEN (ELVIRA): WS Lyster's Royal Italian and English Opera
Company, Theatre Royal, Melbourne, 29 June 1866

9. Giacomo Meyerbeer, *L'Africaine*
FANNY SIMONSEN (SÉLIKA): WS Lyster's Royal Italian and English Opera
Company, Theatre Royal, Melbourne, 1 July 1866
FANNY SIMONSEN (INEZ): WS Lyster's Royal Italian and English Opera
Company, Theatre Royal, Melbourne, 13 November 1866

10. Friedrich von Flotow, *Martha*
FANNY SIMONSEN (TITLE ROLE): WS Lyster's Royal Italian and English Opera
Company, Theatre Royal, Melbourne, 6 July 1866
FRANCES SAVILLE (NANCY): Montague-Turner Opera Company, Theatre Royal,
Rockhampton, 21 June 1883
MARTINA SIMONSEN (TITLE ROLE): Emilie Melville Opera Company, Bijou
Theatre, Melbourne, 12 April 1884
JULES SIMONSEN (LIONEL): Simonsen's Opera Company, Theatre Royal, Broken
Hill, 10 April 1890
FRANCES SAVILLE (TITLE ROLE): Court Opera, Vienna, 4 May 1901
FRANCES ALDA (TITLE ROLE): Metropolitan Opera, New York, 14, December 1923

11. Giuseppe Verdi, *La traviata*
    FANNY SIMONSEN (VIOLETTA): WS Lyster's Royal Italian and English Opera
    Company, Theatre Royal, Melbourne, 25 July 1866
    MARTINA SIMONSEN (VIOLETTA), FRANCES SIMONSEN (ANNINA): Simonsen's
    Royal English and Italian Opera Company, Sloan's Theatre, Invercargill,
    10 December 1880
    JULES SIMONSEN (GASTONE): Tancioni Cuttica's Opera Company, Princess
    Theatre, Melbourne, 21 May 1892
    FRANCES SAVILLE (VIOLETTA): Kroll Theatre, Berlin, 17 September 1893
    WILLIE SAVILLE (ALFREDO): with FRANCES SAVILLE (VIOLETTA); Prague,
    9 May 1903
    FRANCES ALDA (VIOLETTA): Théâtre de la Monnaie, Brussels, 21 April 1907
12. Giacomo Meyerbeer, *Les Huguenots*
    FANNY SIMONSEN (MARGUÉRITE DE VALOIS): WS Lyster's Royal Italian and
    English Opera Company, Theatre Royal, Melbourne, 28 July 1866
    LEONORE SIMONSEN (URBAIN): Madame Fabbri's Opera Company, Mission
    Street Opera House, San Francisco, 1884
    FANNY SIMONSEN (VALENTINE): Simonsen's Royal Italian Opera Company,
    Theatre Royal, Melbourne, 30 September 1887
    FRANCES SAVILLE (MARGUÉRITE DE VALOIS): Royal Opera House, Covent
    Garden, London, 3 June 1897 (In the event, Saville withdrew from this
    performance and it is unclear whether she took the role in any of the subsequent
    performances; probably her debut in the role was at the Court Opera in Vienna,
    29 October 1902)
    FRANCES ALDA (MARGUÉRITE DE VALOIS): Théâtre de la Monnaie, Brussels,
13. Giacomo Meyerbeer, *Le prophète*
    FANNY SIMONSEN (BERTHA): WS Lyster's Royal Italian and English Opera
    Company, Theatre Royal, Melbourne, 30 July 1866
14. Vincenzo Bellini, *I puritani*
    FANNY SIMONSEN (ELVIRA): WS Lyster's Royal Italian and English Opera
    Company, Victoria Theatre, Adelaide, 25 August 1866
15. Wolfgang Amadeus Mozart, *Le nozze di Figaro* (*The Marriage of Figaro*)
    FANNY SIMONSEN (COUNTESS): WS Lyster's Royal Italian and English Opera
    Company, Victoria Theatre, Adelaide, 14 September 1866
    FANNY SIMONSEN (SUSANNA): Simonsen's Royal English, Italian and Opera
    Bouffe Company, Theatre Royal, Auckland, 13 September 1876
    FRANCES ALDA (COUNTESS): Théâtre de la Monnaie, Brussels, 27 January 1906
16. Giacomo Meyerbeer, *Robert le diable* (*Roberto il diavolo*)
    FANNY SIMONSEN (ISABELLA): WS Lyster's Royal Italian and English Opera
    Company, Theatre Royal, Melbourne, 29 October 1866
    FRANCES SAVILLE (ISABELLE): Court Opera, Vienna, 12 November 1899

17. Carl Maria von Weber, *Der Freischütz*
    FANNY SIMONSEN (AGATHE): WS Lyster's Royal Italian and English Opera
    Company, Theatre Royal, Melbourne, 12 November 1866
    MARTINA SIMONSEN (AENNCHEN), FRANCES SIMONSEN (FIRST BRIDESMAID):
    with FANNY SIMONSEN (AGATHE); Simonsen's Royal English and Italian Opera
    Company, Theatre Royal, Christchurch, 14 February 1881
    MARTINA SIMONSEN (AGATHE), LEONORE SIMONSEN (AENNCHEN): Simonsen's
    Royal English and Italian Opera Company, Queen's Theatre, Dunedin,
    14 June 1881

18. Vincenzo Bellini, *Norma*
    FANNY SIMONSEN (TITLE ROLE): Lyster and Smith's Royal Italian and English
    Opera Company, Theatre Royal, Melbourne, 10 March 1870
    MARTINA SIMONSEN (ADALGISA): Simonsen's Royal English and Italian Opera
    Company, Royal Princess Theatre, Bendigo, 29 October 1880
    FRANCES SIMONSEN (CLOTILDE): with FANNY (NORMA) AND MARTINA
    (ADALGISA); Simonsen's Royal English and Italian Opera Company, Sloan's
    Theatre, Invercargill, 3 December 1880
    FRANCES SAVILLE (ADALGISA): Montague-Turner Opera Company, Theatre
    Royal, Grafton, 16 May 1883
    LEONORE SIMONSEN (ADALGISA): Madame Fabbri's Opera Company, Mission
    Street Opera Company, San Francisco, 11 September 1884

19. Michael William Balfe, *The Bohemian Girl*
    FANNY SIMONSEN (ARLINE): Lyster and Smith's Royal Italian and English Opera
    Company, Theatre Royal, Melbourne, 12 March 1870
    MARTINA SIMONSEN (ARLINE): Simonsen's Royal English and Italian Opera
    Company, Royal Princess Theatre, Bendigo, 28 October 1880
    LEONORE SIMONSEN (QUEEN OF THE GYPSIES), FRANCES SIMONSEN (BUDA):
    Simonsen's Royal English and Italian Opera Company, Sloan's Theatre,
    Invercargill, 4 December 1880
    FRANCES SAVILLE (QUEEN OF THE GYPSIES): Montague-Turner Opera Company,
    Theatre Royal, Grafton NSW, 5 May 1883
    FRANCES SAVILLE (ARLINE): Montague-Turner Opera Company; Academy of
    Music, Adelaide, 20 October 1883
    Jules Simonsen (Thaddeus): Imperial Opera House, Sydney, 20 January 1894

20. Vincent Wallace, *Maritana*
    FANNY SIMONSEN (TITLE ROLE): Lyster and Smith's Royal Italian and English
    Opera Company, Theatre Royal, Melbourne, 26 March 1870
    LEONORE SIMONSEN (LAZARILLO), FRANCES SIMONSEN (MARCHIONESS): with
    FANNY SIMONSEN (MARITANA); Simonsen's Royal English and Italian Opera
    Company, Theatre Royal, Hobart, 24 November 1880
    MARTINA SIMONSEN (TITLE ROLE), FRANCES SAVILLE (LAZARILLO): Simonsen

Royal English and Italian Opera Company, Gaiety Theatre, Sydney, 21 July 1882

JULES SIMONSEN (DON CAESAR DE BAZAN): Simonsen's Opera Company, Exhibition Theatre, Geelong, 27 December 1889

21. Gioacchino Rossini, *Il barbiere di Siviglia* (*The Barber of Seville*)

    FANNY SIMONSEN (ROSINA): Lyster and Smith's Royal Italian and English Opera Company, Theatre Royal, Melbourne, 7 April (?) 1870

22. Giuseppe Verdi, *Il trovatore*

    FANNY SIMONSEN (LEONORA): Lyster and Smith's Royal Italian and English Opera Company, Theatre Royal, Melbourne, 5 May 1870

    LEONORE SIMONSEN (AZUCENA), FRANCES SIMONSEN (INEZ): with FANNY SIMONSEN (LEONORA); Simonsen's Royal English and Italian Opera Company, Sloan's Theatre, Invercargill, 2 December 1880

    FRANCES SAVILLE (AZUCENA): Montague-Turner Opera Company, Victoria Theatre, Newcastle NSW, 1 May 1883

    JULES SIMONSEN (MANRICO): Simonsen's Opera Company, Theatre Royal, Broken Hill, April/May 1890

    FRANCES SAVILLE (LEONORA): Carl Rosa Company, Theatre Royal, Glasgow, 25 November 1893

23. Giuseppe Verdi, *Un ballo in maschera*

    FANNY SIMONSEN (OSCAR): Lyster and Smith's Royal Italian and English Opera Company, Theatre Royal, Melbourne, 8 September 1870

    FANNY SIMONSEN (AMELIA), MARTINA SIMONSEN (OSCAR), LEONORE SIMONSEN (ULRICA): Simonsen's Royal English and Italian Opera Company, Princess Theatre, Dunedin, 6 January 1881

24. Gioacchino Rossini, *Guillaume Tell* (*William Tell*)

    FANNY SIMONSEN (MATHILDE): Lyster and Smith's Royal Italian and English Opera Company, Prince of Wales Theatre, Sydney, 21 November 1870

    FRANCES SAVILLE (MATHILDE): Court Opera, Vienna, 2 May 1899

25. Jacques Offenbach, *La Grande-Duchesse de Gérolstein* (*The Grand Duchess of Gerolstein*)

    **FANNY SIMONSEN (TITLE ROLE): Lyster and Smith's Royal Italian and English Opera Company, Princess Theatre, Melbourne, 27 February 1871

    LEONORE SIMONSEN (WANDA), FRANCES SIMONSEN (CHARLOTTE): with FANNY SIMONSEN (TITLE ROLE); Simonsen's Royal English and Italian Opera Company, Theatre Royal, Auckland, 7 May 1881

    FRANCES SAVILLE (WANDA): WITH FANNY SIMONSEN (TITLE ROLE); Simonsen's Royal English and Italian Opera Company, Gaiety Theatre, Sydney, 2 June 1882

26. Michael William Balfe, *Satanella*

    FANNY SIMONSEN (TITLE ROLE): Lyster and Smith's Royal Italian and English Opera Company, Princess Theatre, Melbourne, 28 March 1871

    MARTINA SIMONSEN (TITLE ROLE), LEONORE SIMONSEN (LILIA), FRANCES

SIMONSEN (BERTHA): Simonsen's Royal English and Italian Opera Company, Theatre Royal, Auckland, 2 May 1881
FRANCES SAVILLE (LILIA): Simonsen's Royal Italian and English Opera Company, Gaiety Theatre, Sydney, 20 May 1882
JULES SIMONSEN (COUNT RUPERT): Simonsen's Opera Company, Royal Princess Theatre, Bendigo, 13 January 1890

27. Vincent Wallace, *Lurline*
FANNY SIMONSEN, (TITLE ROLE): Lyster and Smith's Royal Italian and English Opera Company, Princess Theatre, Melbourne, 10 April 1871

28. Jacques Offenbach, *Le violoneux* (*Breaking the Spell*)
**FANNY SIMONSEN (LEAD ROLE): Simonsen's English Opera Company, White's Assembly Rooms, Adelaide, 20 June 1871

29. Jacques Offenbach, *La rose de Saint-Flour* (*The Rose of Auvergne*)
**FANNY SIMONSEN (TITLE ROLE): Simonsen's English Opera Company, White's Assembly Rooms, Adelaide, 17 July 1871

30. Comyn Vaughan, *£. S. D* (a musical charade)
**FANNY SIMONSEN (ROLE UNKNOWN): Simonsen's English Opera Company, Freemasons Hall, Wagga Wagga NSW, 14 October 1871

31. Michael William Balfe, *The Rose of Castile*
FANNY SIMONSEN (ELVIRA): Simonsen's Royal English Opera Company, Victoria Theatre, Sydney, 17 February 1872

32. Charles Gounod, *Faust*
FANNY SIMONSEN (MARGUÉRITE): Simonsen's Opera di Camera, Prince of Wales Theatre, Auckland, 26 April 1872
LEONORE SIMONSEN (SIEBEL), FRANCES SIMONSEN (MARTHE): with FANNY SIMONSEN (MARGUÉRITE); Simonsen's Royal English and Italian Opera Company, Theatre Royal, Wellington, 18 February 1881
LEONORE SIMONSEN (MARGUÉRITE), FRANCES SAVILLE (SIEBEL): Simonsen's Royal English and Italian Opera Company, Gaiety Theatre, Sydney, 9 June 1882
FRANCES SAVILLE (MARGUÉRITE): Théâtre de la Monnaie, Brussels, 19 October 1892
JULES SIMONSEN (TITLE ROLE); Farley's Opera Company, Opera House, Sydney, 10 July 1897
FRANCES ALDA (MARGUÉRITE): Théâtre de la Monnaie, Brussels, 2 November 1904

33. Gaetano Donizetti, *Lucrezia Borgia*
FANNY SIMONSEN (TITLE ROLE): Simonsen's Royal English, Italian and Opera Bouffe Company, Queen's Theatre, Dunedin, 22 March 1876
LEONORE SIMONSEN (MAFFIO ORSINI): Simonsen's Royal English and Italian Opera Company, Theatre Royal, Hobart, 16 November 1880
EUGÉNIE DEHAES (SMALL ROLE): with FANNY AND LEONORE SIMONSEN AS

ABOVE; Simonsen's Royal English and Italian Opera Company, Sloan's Theatre, Invercargill, 30 November 1880

FRANCES SAVILLE (MAFFIO ORSINI): Montague-Turner Opera Company, Academy of Music, Adelaide, 22 November 1883

34. Charles Lecocq, *La fille de Madame Angot*
**FANNY SIMONSEN (CLAIRETTE): Simonsen's Royal English, Italian and Opera Bouffe Company, Queen's Theatre, Dunedin, 27 March 1876
LEONORE SIMONSEN (CLAIRETTE), FRANCES SAVILLE (AMARANTE), FANNY SIMONSEN (MLLE LANGE): Simonsen's Royal English and Italian Opera Company, Gaiety Theatre, Sydney, 1 July 1882
FRANCES SAVILLE (MLLE LANGE): Majeroni and Wilson Comic Opera Company, New Opera House, Sydney, 12 January 1885
JULES SIMONSEN (ANGE PITOU): Simonsen's Opera Company, Theatre Royal, Broken Hill, 16 April 1890
JULES SIMONSEN (POMPONNET); Nellie Stewart Opera Company, Opera House, Melbourne, 6 December 1890
FRANCES ALDA (CLAIRETTE): Metropolitan Opera, New Theatre, New York, 14 December 1909

35. Jacques Offenbach, *La Périchole*
**FANNY SIMONSEN (TITLE ROLE): Simonsen's Royal English, Italian and Opera Bouffe Company, Theatre Royal, Christchurch, 15 May 1876

36. Daniel Auber, *La part du diable (Carlo Broschi)*
**FANNY SIMONSEN (TITLE ROLE): Simonsen's Royal English, Italian and Opera Bouffe Company, Theatre Royal, Wellington, 28 June 1876

37. Charles Lecocq, *Giroflé-Girofla*
FANNY SIMONSEN (TITLE ROLES): Simonsen's Royal English, Italian and Opera Bouffe Company, Theatre Royal, Hobart, 3 April 1877
MARTINA SIMONSEN (TITLE ROLES), FRANCES SAVILLE (PEDRO): Simonsen's Royal English and Comic Opera Company, Sloan's Theatre, Invercargill, 4 November 1882
JULES SIMONSEN (MARASQUIN): Simonsen's Opera Company, Theatre Royal, Broken Hill, 5 April 1890

38. Otto Nicolai, *Die lustigen Weiber von Windsor (The Merry Wives of Windsor)*
**FANNY SIMONSEN (MRS FORD): Simonsen's Royal English, Italian and Opera Bouffe Company, Royal Princess Theatre, Bendigo, 18 July 1877

39. Johann Strauss II, *Die Fledermaus (The Bat)*
**FANNY SIMONSEN (ROSALINDA): Simonsen's Royal English, Italian and Opera Bouffe Company, White's Rooms, Adelaide, 30 August 1877
FRANCES SAVILLE (FAUSTINE): Court Opera, Vienna, 30 October 1898

40. Arthur Sullivan, *HMS Pinafore*
MARTINA SIMONSEN (JOSEPHINE), LEONORE SIMONSEN (LITTLE BUTTERCUP),

FRANCES SIMONSEN (HEBE): Simonsen's Royal English and Italian Opera Company, Theatre Royal, Hobart, 20 November 1880

FRANCES SAVILLE (LITTLE BUTTERCUP): Majeroni and Wilson Comic Opera Company, New Opera House, Sydney, 27 February 1885

FRANCES SAVILLE (JOSEPHINE): Majeroni and Wilson Comic Opera Company, Theatre Royal, Adelaide, 18 April 1885

JULES SIMONSEN (RALPH RACKSTRAW): Mechanics' Institute, Albury NSW, 18 September 1889

41. Adrien Boïeldieu, *La dame blanche* (*The White Lady of Avenel*)

     **FANNY SIMONSEN (ANNA), MARTINA SIMONSEN (JENNY), FRANCES SIMONSEN (MARGUERITE): Simonsen's Royal English and Italian Opera Company, Sloan's Theatre, Invercargill, 6 December 1880

42. Franz von Suppé, *Boccaccio*

     FANNY SIMONSEN (TITLE ROLE), LEONORE SIMONSEN (FIAMETTA), FRANCES SAVILLE (ISABELLA): Simonsen's Royal English and Italian Opera Company, Theatre Royal, Adelaide, 22 September 1882

     **MARTINA SIMONSEN (LEONETTO): with FANNY, LEONORE AND FRANCES AS ABOVE; Simonsen's Royal English and Comic Opera Company, Sloan's Theatre, Invercargill, 1 November 1882

     JULES SIMONSEN (TITLE ROLE): Simonsen's Opera Company, Wagga Wagga, 14 July 1894

43. Jacques Offenbach, *Les brigands* (*The Bandits*)

     **MARTINA SIMONSEN (FIORELLA), FRANCES SAVILLE, (FRAGOLETTO): Simonsen's Royal English and Comic Opera Company, Theatre Royal, Christchurch, 5 January 1883

44. Georges Bizet, *Carmen*

     MARTINA SIMONSEN (TITLE ROLE): Verdi's Opera Company, Opera House, Melbourne, 4 August 1883

     FRANCES SAVILLE (MICAËLA): Academy Theatre, Moscow, 29 March 1895

     FRANCES ALDA (MICAËLA): Metropolitan Opera, New York, 19 November 1914

45. Wolfgang Amadeus Mozart, *Don Giovanni*

     FANNY SIMONSEN (DONNA ANNA), MARTINA SIMONSEN (ZERLINA): Verdi's Opera Company, Opera House, Melbourne, 7 September 1883

     FRANCES SAVILLE (ZERLINA): Metropolitan Opera, New York, 16 April 1896

46. Gioacchino Rossini, *Mosè in Egitto* (*Moses in Egypt*)

     MARTINA SIMONSEN (SINAIDE): Verdi's Opera Company, Opera House, Melbourne, 25 August 1883

47. Friedrich von Flotow, *L'ombra*

     **MARTINA SIMONSEN (VESPINA): Graziosi's Opera Company, Victoria Hall, Melbourne, 13 October 1883

48. Ambroise Thomas, *Mignon*
    Frances Saville (Philine): Montague-Turner Opera Company, Theatre Royal, Rockhampton, 30 June 1883
    Frances Alda (Philine): Teatro de la Opera, Buenos Aires, 30 June 1908
49. Robert Planquette, *Rip Van Winkle*
    Frances Saville (Gretchen): Theatre Royal, Hobart, 29 May 1884
50. Fromental Halévy, *La Juive*
    Leonore Simonson (role unknown): Madame Fabbri's Opera Company, Mission Street Opera House, San Francisco, 1884
51. Richard Wagner, *Lohengrin*
    Leonore Simonsen (Ortrud): Madame Fabbri's Opera Company, Mission Street Opera House, San Francisco, 2 September 1884
    Frances Saville (Elsa): Aquarium Theatre, St Petersburg, 16 July 1893
52. Ludwig van Beethoven, *Fidelio*
    Fanny Simonsen (Marcelline): Melbourne Liedertafel, Town Hall, Melbourne, 15 September 1884
53. Luscombe Searelle, *Bobadil*
    *Frances Saville (Lulu): Majeroni and Wilson Comic Opera Company, New Opera House, Sydney, 22 November 1884
    Frances Saville (Princess Zorayda): Majeroni and Wilson Comic Opera Company, New Opera House, Sydney, 9 January 1885
54. Jacques Offenbach, *La belle Hélène*
    Frances Saville (Orestes): Majeroni and Wilson Comic Opera Company, New Opera House, Sydney, 7 February 1885
    Frances Saville (title role): Majeroni and Wilson Comic Opera Company, Bijou Theatre, Melbourne, 29 June 1885, 2
55. Luscombe Searelle, *Isidora*
    Frances Saville (Sabina): Majeroni and Wilson Comic Opera Company, New Opera House, Sydney, 22 August 1885
56. George Frideric Handel, *Acis and Galatea*
    Frances Saville (Galatea): Sydney Philharmonic Society, Exhibition Building, Sydney, 27 January 1886
57. Henri Kowalski, *Verçingétorix*
    Frances Saville (Luctera): Sydney Philharmonic Society, Great Hall, Sydney University, 1 July 1886
58. Amilcare Ponchielli, *La Gioconda*
    **Fanny Simonsen (La Cieca): Simonsen's Royal Italian Opera Company, Theatre Royal, Melbourne, 5 November 1887
59. Robert Planquette, *Les cloches de Corneville* (*The Chimes of Normandy*)
    Jules Simonsen (Grenicheux): Simonsen's Opera Company, School of Arts, Bathurst, 2 August 1890

60. Walter Slaughter, *Marjorie*
   **FRANCES SAVILLE (TITLE ROLE): Williamson Garner and Co, Princess Theatre, Melbourne, 20 December 1890

61. Arthur Sullivan, *The Pirates of Penzance*
   FRANCES SAVILLE (MABEL): Williamson Garner and Co, Princess Theatre, Melbourne, 17 January 1891

62. John F Sheridan, *Bridget O'Brien Esq*
   JULES SIMONSEN (ROLE UNKNOWN): Sheridan's company, Theatre Royal, Adelaide, 20 July 1891

63. John F Sheridan, *Uncle Tom's Cabin*
   JULES SIMONSEN (PHINEAS FLETCHER): Sheridan's company, Theatre Royal, Hobart, 17 September 1891

64. Charles Gounod, *Roméo et Juliette*
   FRANCES SAVILLE (JULIETTE): Théâtre de la Monnaie, Brussels, 7 September 1892
   FRANCES ALDA (JULIETTE): Théâtre de la Monnaie, Brussels, 17 March 1906

65. Giuseppe Verdi, *Rigoletto*
   FRANCES SAVILLE (GILDA): Aquarium Theatre, St Petersburg, 18 June 1893
   FRANCES ALDA (GILDA): Théâtre de la Monnaie, Brussels, 30 October 1905

66. Pietro Mascagni, *Cavalleria rusticana*
   FRANCES SAVILLE (SANTUZZA): Aquarium Theatre, St Petersburg, 15 August 1893

67. Giuseppe Verdi, *Otello*
   FRANCES SAVILLE (DESDEMONA): Monte Carlo Opera, 20 January 1894
   FRANCES ALDA (DESDEMONA): Metropolitan Opera, New York, 17November 1909

68. Richard Wagner, *Tannhäuser*
   FRANCES SAVILLE (ELISABETH): Carl Rosa Company, Theatre Royal, Manchester, 11 April 1894

69. Victor Massé, *Paul et Virginie*
   FRANCES SAVILLE (VIRGINIE): Opéra-Comique, Paris, 18 December 1894

70. Giuseppe Verdi, *Falstaff*
   FRANCES SAVILLE (ALICE FORD): Metropolitan Opera, New York, 22 January 1896
   FRANCES ALDA (NANNETTA): Metropolitan Opera, Academy of Music, Philadelphia, 16 March 1909

71. August Juncker, *The Romance of Corsica*
   *JULES SIMONSEN (ROLE UNKNOWN): Opera House, Sydney, 27 February 1897

72. Hector Berlioz, *The Damnation of Faust*
   **JULES SIMONSEN (FAUST): Sydney Town Hall, 13 May 1897
   FRANCES ALDA (MARGUÉRITE): Théâtre de la Monnaie, Brussels, 23 February 1906

73. Jules Massenet, *Manon*
    FRANCES SAVILLE (TITLE ROLE): Royal Opera House, Covent Garden, London, 21 May 1897
    FRANCES ALDA (TITLE ROLE): Opéra-Comique, Paris, 15 April 1904

74. Richard Wagner, *Siegfried*
    FRANCES SAVILLE (WOODBIRD): Royal Opera House, Covent Garden, London, 23 June 1897

75. Ferd Regnal (Frédéric d'Erlanger), *Inez Mendo*
    *FRANCES SAVILLE (TITLE ROLE): Royal Opera House, Covent Garden, London, 10 July 1897

76. Ivan Caryll, *The Gay Parisienne*
    FRANCIE ADLER (ETHEL): Williamson and Musgrove, Her Majesty's Theatre, Sydney, 31 July 1897

77. Giacomo Puccini, *La bohème*
    **FRANCES SAVILLE (MIMÌ): Theater an der Wien, Vienna, 5 October 1897
    FRANCES ALDA (MIMÌ): Metropolitan Opera, New York, 2 December 1909

78. Ruggiero Leoncavallo, *Pagliacci* (*Der Bajazzo*)
    **FRANCES SAVILLE (NEDDA): Court Opera, Vienna, 29 December 1897

79. Ambroise Thomas, *Hamlet*
    FRANCES SAVILLE (OPHÉLIE): Teatr Wielki, Warsaw, 3 January 1897
    FRANCES ALDA, (OPHÉLIE): Théâtre de la Monnaie, Brussels, 22 March 1905

80. Lacôme and Caryll, *Ma mie Rosette*
    FRANCIE ADLER (CLOCHETTE): Williamson and Musgrove, Theatre Royal, Perth, 14 May 1898

81. Arthur Sullivan, *The Yeomen of the Guard*
    FRANCIE ADLER (KATE): Williamson and Musgrove, Theatre Royal, Perth, 25 May 1898

82. Alfred Cellier, *Dorothy*
    FRANCIE ADLER (PHYLLIS TUPPETT): Williamson and Musgrove, Theatre Royal, Perth, 2 June 1898

83. Arthur Sullivan, *The Gondoliers*
    FRANCIE ADLER (FIAMETTA): Williamson and Musgrove, Theatre Royal, Adelaide, 16 July 1898

84. Robert Planquette, *The Old Guard* (*Les voltigeurs du 32ieme*)
    FRANCIE ADLER (FOLLOW THE DRUM): Williamson and Musgrove, Theatre Royal, Adelaide, 30 July 1898

85. Arthur Sullivan, *The Mikado*
    FRANCIE ADLER (PEEP-BO): Williamson and Musgrove, Her Majesty's Theatre, Sydney, 25 August 1898
    JULES SIMONSEN (NANKI-POO): Carl Marten Opera Company, Macdonough Theater, Oakland CA, 8 September 1898

86. Edmond Audran, *La poupée* (*The Doll*)
    **FRANCIE ADLER (MARIE): Williamson and Musgrove, Her Majesty's Theatre, Sydney, 10 September 1898

87. Richard Wagner, *Götterdämmerung*
    FRANCES SAVILLE (GUTRUNE): Royal Opera House, Covent Garden, London, 11 June 1898

88. Oscar Weil, *Suzette*
    JULES SIMONSEN (ROLE UNKNOWN): Tivoli Theatre, San Francisco, February 1899

89. Wolfgang Amadeus Mozart, *Così fan tutte*
    FRANCES SAVILLE (FIORDILIGI): Court Opera, Vienna, 4 October 1900

90. Wolfgang Amadeus Mozart, *Die Zauberflöte* (*The Magic Flute*)
    FRANCES SAVILLE (QUEEN OF THE NIGHT): Court Opera, Vienna, 25 November 1900

91. Jacques Offenbach, *Les contes d'Hoffmann*
    FRANCES SAVILLE (OLYMPIA, ANTONIA AND GIULIETTA): Court Opera, Vienna, 12 November 1901
    FRANCES ALDA (GIULIETTA): Metropolitan Opera, New York, 6 December 1913

92. Jules Massenet, *Hérodiade*
    FRANCES ALDA (SALOMÉ): Théâtre de la Monnaie, Brussels, 6 February 1905

93. Paul Gilson, *Princesse Rayon de Soleil*
    FRANCES ALDA (TITLE ROLE): Théâtre de la Monnaie, Brussels, 9 September 1905

94. Jules Massenet, *Chérubin*
    **FRANCES ALDA (ENSOLEILLAD): Théâtre de la Monnaie, Brussels, 16 December 1905

95. André Messager, *Madame Chrysanthème*
    **FRANCES ALDA (TITLE ROLE): Théâtre de la Monnaie, Brussels, 9 November 1906

96. Gustave Charpentier, *Louise*
    FRANCES ALDA (TITLE ROLE): Teatro alla Scala, Milan, 6 February 1908

97. Arrigo Boito, *Mefistofele*
    FRANCES ALDA (MARGUERITA): Teatro alla Scala, Milan, 11 April 1908

98. Giacomo Puccini, *Le villi*
    **FRANCES ALDA (ANNA): Metropolitan Opera, New York, 17 December 1908

99. Walter Damrosch, *Cyrano*
    *FRANCES ALDA (ROXANA): Metropolitan Opera, New York, 27 February 1913

100. Victor Herbert, *Madeleine*
    *FRANCES ALDA (TITLE ROLE): Metropolitan Opera, New York, 24 January 1914

101. Wolf-Ferrari, *Il segreto di Susanna*
    FRANCES ALDA (TITLE ROLE): Metropolitan Opera, New York, 30 March 1914

102. Alexander Borodin, *Prince Igor*
    **FRANCES ALDA (YAROSLAVNA): Metropolitan Opera, New York, 30 December 1915

103. Giacomo Puccini, *Manon Lescaut*
    FRANCES ALDA (TITLE ROLE): Metropolitan Opera, New York, 6 January 1916
104. Giuseppe Verdi, *Aida*
    FRANCES ALDA (TITLE ROLE): Metropolitan Opera, Auditorium, Atlanta,
    27 April 1916
105. Riccardo Zandonai, *Francesca da Rimini*
    **FRANCES ALDA (TITLE ROLE): Metropolitan Opera, New York,
    22 December 1916
106. Adriano Ariani, *St Francis of Assisi*
    *FRANCES ALDA (CLARA AND VOX TENTATIONIS): Metropolitan Opera, New
    York, 15 April 1917
107. Henri Rabaud, *Mârouf*
    *FRANCES ALDA (SAAMCHEDDINE): Metropolitan Opera, New York, 19
    December 1917
108. Henry Kimball Hadley, *Cleopatra's Night*
    *FRANCES ALDA (TITLE ROLE): Metropolitan Opera, New York, 31 January 1920
109. Édouard Lalo, *Le roi d'Ys*
    FRANCES ALDA (ROZENN): Metropolitan Opera, New York, 5 January 1922
110. Alfredo Catalani, *Loreley*
    FRANCES ALDA (TITLE ROLE): Metropolitan Opera, New York, 6 December 1922
111. Umberto Giordano, *La cena della beffe* (*The Jester's Supper*)
    **FRANCES ALDA (GINEVRA): Teatro Colón, Buenos Aires, August 1925
112. Giacomo Puccini, *Madama Butterfly*
    FRANCES ALDA (TITLE ROLE): NBC/WEAF, New York, 16 November 1929
113. Giacomo Puccini, *Tosca*
    FRANCES ALDA (TITLE ROLE): NBC/WEAF, New York, 21 December 1929
114. Giacomo Puccini, *The Girl of the Golden West*
    FRANCES ALDA (MINNIE): NBC/WEAF, New York, 18 January 1930
115. Giacomo Puccini, *Turandot*
    FRANCES ALDA (LIÙ): NBC/WEAF, New York, 15 March 1930

Appendix 3
Discographies of Frances Saville and Frances Alda

Frances Saville
by Nathan B Davis
(First published in *The Record Collector*, Vol 32, Nos 6&7, June 1987)

Bettini cylinders, New York, 1895/96
1. *Rigoletto* (Verdi), 'Caro nome'
2. *Carmen* (Bizet), Aria, Act 3

Bettini cylinders, New York, 1898/99
3. *Rigoletto*, 'Caro nome'
4. 'Wiegenlied' (Brahms)

Black Label G &T, Vienna, 1902, 7 inch
5. 'Wiegenlied', matrix 2375B, catalogue 43184
6. 'Ich hälte nicht daran gedacht' (Meyer-Helmund), mat 2376B-F, cat 43185
7. 'Heidenröslein' (Schubert), mat 2439B, cat 43300

Black Label G&T, Vienna, 1902, 10 inch
8. *Manon* (Massenet), Aria from Act 1, mat 873x, cat 43280
9. Gavotte? (unpublished), mat 874x
10. *Manon*, Gavotte, mat 874½x, cat 43224
11. *Hoffmanns Erzählungen* (Offenbach), 'Horst du', mat875x, cat 43225
12. 'Morgen send' ich dir die Veilchen' (Meyer-Helmund), mat 876x, cat 43285
13. *Hoffmanns Erzählungen* (Offenbach), Puppenarie, mat 951x, cat 43240
14. *Lohengrin* (Wagner), Elsas Gesang an die Lüfte, mat 952x, cat 43241
15. (Unpublished), mat 953x
16. 'Ninon' (Tosti), mat 954x, cat 43287
17. 'Maman, dites-moi' (traditional), mat 955x, cat 33333
18. *Martha* (Flotow), 'Letzte Rose', mat 956x, cat 43277

Frances Alda
by Larry Lustig

Alda was exclusively contracted to Victor for her entire recording career.
B-/BVE- 10 in. (25 cm); C-/CVE- = 12 in. (30 cm)
Parentheses around a catalogue number indicate assigned but not issued.

Mat. No cat. no.	Vic. s/s cat. no.	Vic. d/s s/s cat. no.	Gram. Co. d/s cat. no.	Gram. Co.	other

ACOUSTIC RECORDINGS

Camden, NJ

27 December 1909, with orchestra
1. *Il Trovatore*: Quel suon, quelle preci ... Ah, che la morte ognora (Miserere);
    (Verdi) with Enrico Caruso
    C-8506-1   unpublished
    (Vinyl pressings exist. This was first issued on LP RCA Victor ARM1-3373)

New York

**6 January 1910, with Metropolitan Opera Chorus and Orchestra,
cond. Walter Rogers**
2. *Il Trovatore*: Quel suon, quelle preci ... Ah, che la morte ognora (Miserere);
    (Verdi) with Enrico Caruso

C-8506-2	hold				
C-8506-3			2-054007	DK 119	78518 (Ger.)
C-8506-3 S/8	89030	8042			AGSB 62
	766-6018 (Arg.)				

(S/8 indicates a dubbing)

Camden, NJ

25 January 1910, with Victor orchestra
3. *Otello*: Salce, salce (Verdi)
    C-8577-1   88214   15-1000
    C-8577-2   destroy
4. *Otello*: Ave Maria, piena di grazia (Verdi)
    C-8578-1   destroy
    C-8578-2   88213   15-1000

New York

25 April 1910, with Victor orchestra, except where noted
5. *Falstaff*: Sul fil d'un soffio etesio (Verdi)
    C-8883-1   88247   IRCC 111   AGSB 16

6. *La Bohème*: Addio, senza rancor (Puccini)
   C-8884-1   destroy
7. *La Bohème*: Sì, mi chiamano Mimì (Puccini)
   C-8885-1   destroy
   C-8885-2   master/destroy
8. La Serenata (Cesareo/Tosti) with piano
   C-8886-1   88248
9. Oh! Si les fleurs avaient des yeux (Buchillot/Massenet) with piano
   B-8887-1   87066

Camden, NJ

14 April 1911, with orchestra

10. Oh! Si les fleurs avaient des yeux (Buchillot/Massenet)
    B-8887-2   87066
11. From the land of the sky-blue water (Eberhart/Cadman)
    B-10187-1   destroy/hold
12. *Manon Lescaut*: L'ora, o tirsi (Puccini)
    B-10188-1   87079   HRS 1014
13. Cradle song (Wiegenlied) (Ebeling/Humperdinck)
    B-10189-1   destroy
14. *More Daisies*: The Cuckoo (Rands/Lehmann)
    B-10190-1   destroy

30 October 1911, with orchestra

15. Cradle song (Wiegenlied) (Ebeling/Humperdinck)
    B-10189-2   87090
16. *More Daisies*: The Cuckoo (Rands/Lehmann)
    B-10190-2   87086
    B-10190-3   destroy
17. *Loreley*: Ah, dunque ei m'amera! ... Amor, celeste ebbrezza (Catalani)
    C-11150-1   destroy
18. L'âme évaporée et souffrante (Romance) (Bourget/Debussy)
    B-11151-1   destroy
19. *Manon Lescaut*: In quelle trine morbide (Puccini)
    B-11152-1   destroy

New York

7 January 1912, with orchestra, cond. Walter Rogers

20. *Martha*: Siam giunti, o giovinette (Flotow); with Josephine Jacoby,
    Enrico Caruso & Marcel Journet
    C-11437-1   destroy
    C-11437-2   95207   10002   2-054030   DM 100   78528 (Ger.)

21. *Martha*: Questa camera è per voi … Che vuol dir ciò? (Flotow); with Jacoby, Caruso & Journet

C-11438-1	95208	10002	2-054031	DM 100	78529 (Ger.)

22. *Martha*: Presto, presto andiam (Flotow); with Jacoby, Caruso & Journet

C-11439-1	95209	10003	2-054032		78529 (Ger.)
				DM 101	78530 (Ger.)
C-11439-2	destroy				

23. *Martha*: T'ho raggiunta, scagurata … Dormi pur (Flotow); with Jacoby, Caruso & Journet

C-11440-1	95210	10003	2-054037	DM 101	78531 (Ger)
		16-5002			78528 Ger)

24. *I Lombardi*: Qual voluttà trascorre (Verdi); with Caruso & Journet

C-11441-1	95211	10010	2-054029	DM 126	78542
		16-5002			

Camden, NJ

4 April 1912, with Victor orchestra

25. *Loreley*: Ah, dunque ei m'amera! … amor, celeste ebbrezza (Catalani)

C-11150-2	88325	IRCC 111

26. L'âme évaporée et souffrante (Romance) (Bourget/Debussy)

B-11151-2	87096
B-11151-3	hold/destroy

27. Manon Lescaut: In quelle trine morbide (Puccini)

B-11152-2	87106	HRS 1014

4 November 1912, with orchestra

28. *Les Contes d'Hoffmann*: Elle a fui, la tourterelle (Offenbach)

C-12559-1	88399	2-033064	DB 635

29. The birth of morn (Dunbar/Leoni)

B-12560-1	87116

30. Ich liebe dich (Herrosee/Beethoven)

B-12561-1	87117

31. The dawn (Teschemacher/d'Hardelot)

B-12562-1	87115

32. *Manon*: Obéissons, quand leur voix appelle (Gavotte) (Massenet)

B-12563-1	87111	7-33022	DA 159

33. Murmuring zephyrs, Op. 21, no 4 (English words by Wilcox/Jensen) with André Benoist (piano)

B-12564-1	87118	2-3359	DA 503

34. Old black Joe (words & music Foster) with André Benoist (piano)?

B-12565-1	destroy

New York

7 April 1913, with Frank La Forge (piano) and Gutia Casini (cello)
35. But lately in the dance I embraced her (Fet; Baum/Arensky)
    B-13082-1   destroy
    B-13082-2   64338
36. Old black Joe (words & music Foster)
    C-13083-1   destroy
    C-13083-2   destroy
37. *Les Contes d'Hoffmann*: Belle nuit, ô nuit d'amour (Barcarolle) (Offenbach)
    B-13084-1   master/hold
38. *4 Lieder* Op. 27, no 4: Morgen (R. Strauss)
    B-13085-1   destroy
    B-13085-2   64339   538   2-43425

10 April 1913, with Victor orchestra
39. *Madama Butterfly*: Ancora un passo or via (Puccini)
    B-13108-1   destroy
    B-13108-2   64334   528   7-53046   DA 136
40. *Madama Butterfly*: Un bel dì, vedremo (Puccini)
    C-13109-1   74335   6037   2-053200   DB 596
                8044

Camden, NJ

20 February 1914, with orchestra
41. *Il Segreto di Susanna*: O gioia, la nube leggera (Wolf-Ferrari)
    C-14495-1   74388   AGSB 16
42. *Carmen*: Je dis que rien ne m'épouvante (Bizet)
    C-14496-1   destroy
43. *La Bohème*: Donde lieta uscì (Puccini)
    B-14497-1   (64417)   AGSA 14
44. *Madeleine*: A perfect day (Herbert) with the Victor Herbert Orchestra
    C-14498-1   74385   6370   03742   cond. Victor Herbert

New York

9 April 1914, with Frank La Forge (piano) and Imperial Russian Balalaika Court Orchestra
45. Night (Russian folk song)
    B-14687-1   destroy
46. *Jocelyn*: Cachés dans cet asile (Berceuse) (Godard)
    C-14688-1   hold

47. *Melodies, piano,* Op. 3, no. 1: Solitude (Melody in F) (d'Offoel/Rubinstein)
    B-14689-1   64450   533   7-33009

with La Forge (piano) & Casini (cello)

48. *Mass* Op. 12: Panis angelicus (Franck)
    C-14690-1   74399   6353
49. *Tosca*: Vissi d'arte (Puccini)
    C-14696-1   destroy
50. An open secret (anon./Woodman)
    B-14697-1   destroy

22 April 1914, with Frank La Forge (piano)

51. *Tosca*: Vissi d'arte (Puccini) with Gutia Casini (cello)
    C-14696-2   destroy
    C-14696-3   74400   6037
52. *Sari*: Love's own sweet song (Cushing; Heath/Kálmán)
    B-14740-1   destroy
    C-14740-1   74401   6307   03405
53. Ouvre tes yeux bleus (Robique/Massenet)
    B-14741-1   destroy
    B-14741-2   64451

10 December 1914, with orchestra, cond. Walter Rogers

54. *Carmen*: Je dis que rien ne m'épouvante (Bizet)
    C-14496-2   74353   6038   2-033048   DB 155
    C-14496-3   destroy
55. *Carmen*: Parle-moi de ma mère (Bizet) with Enrico Caruso
    C-15483-1   destroy
    C-15483-2   destroy
    C-15483-3   assigned 89083 but not published, one test exists

15 March 1915, with Frank La Forge (piano) and Mischa Elman (violin)

56. Chanson d'amour (Grandmougin/Hollman)
    C-15792-1   88521   2-033083   DB 516
                89128
57. Tes yeux (?/Rabey)
    B-15793-1   87216   3030   7-33014   DA 503
                87556
    C-15793-1   hold
58. Ave Maria (Bach BWV 846/Gounod)
    C-15794-1   88522   8001
                89129

59. Angel's serenade (Marcello/Braga)
    C-15795-1   88523   8001
                            89130
    C-15795-2   destroy

Camden, NJ

10 June 1915, with orchestra, cond. Walter Rogers
60. Mighty lak' a rose (Stanton/Nevin)
    B-16087-1   destroy
    B-16087-2   destroy
61. Dreams (Porteous/Strelezki)
    C-16088-1   destroy

15 July 1915, with orchestra, cond. Walter Rogers
62. *La Bohème*: Sì, mi chiamano Mimì (Puccini)
    C-8885-3   74448   6038   2-053182   DB 155
63. Mighty lak' a rose (Stanton/Nevin)
    B-16087-3   64308   535   2-3167   DA 138
64. Chanson provençale (dell'Acqua)
    C-16209-1   destroy
    C-16209-2   74449   2-033080   DB 516
65. Ma curly-headed babby (trad./Clutsam) with P. Bianculli (mandolin)
    C-16210-1   destroy
    C-16210-2   destroy

24 January 1917, with orchestra, cond. Josef Pasternack
66. The Star (Lummis/Rogers) with Francis Lapitano (harp)
    B-19119-1   destroy
    B-19119-2   64658
67. Somewhere a voice is calling (Newton/Tate) with Lapitano (harp)
    B-19120-1   destroy
68. Deep River (trad, arr Fisher) with the Orpheus Quartet: William Hooley,
    Reinald Werrenrath, Lambert Murphy & John Barnes Wells
    C-19121-1   destroy
    C-19121-2   master (74507)/destroy

16 February 1917, with orchestra, cond. Josef Pasternack
69. Somewhere a voice is calling (Newton/Tate) with Francis Lapitano (harp)
    B-19120-2   64654   535   2-3276   DA 138
70. I love you truly (words & music Jacobs-Bond)
    B-19186-1   destroy
    B-19186-2   64662   531   2-3358   DA 135

71. *The Big Show*: Poor Butterfly (Golden/Hubbell)
    B-19187-1   64653   530   2-3530
    B-19187-2   hold/ destroy
72. Just-a-wearyin' for you (Stanton/Jacobs-Bond) with Lapitano (harp)
    B-19188-1   64674   531
73. Simple aveu (Love token) (Bordèse/Thomé)
    B-19189-1   64675   538   2-3498
    B-19189-2   destroy

24 May 1917, with orchestra, cond. Josef Pasternack
74. *Lakmé*: Dans la forêt près de nous (Delibes)
    B-19891-1   hold/destroy
    B-19891-2   64715   533   7-33039   DA 159
75. *Alfred*: Rule Britannia (Thomson/Arne)
    B-19892-1   hold/destroy
    B-19892-2   64692   2-3500
76. For your country and my country (words & music Berlin)
    B-19893-1   destroy
    B-19893-2   64689   2-3500
    B-19893-3   destroy
77. Sing me love's lullaby (Terriss/Morse)
    B-19894-1   hold/destroy
    B-19894-2   64716   536   2-3492

New York

1 June 1917, with orchestra, cond. Josef Pasternack
78. La Marseillaise (de l'Isle) with Metropolitan Opera Chorus
    B-19972-1   destroy
    B-19972-2   64693   534   7-33034
    B-19972-3   destroy

Camden, NJ

20 July 1917, with orchestra, cond. Josef Pasternack
79. Deep River (trad, arr Fisher) with the Orpheus Quartet: William Hooley,
    Reinald Werrenrath, Lambert Murphy & Harry Macdonough
    B-19121-1   hold/destroy
    B-19121-2   64687   527
80. God save the King (Carey) with Orpheus Quartet: William Hooley, Reinald
    Werrenrath, Lambert Murphy & Harry Macdonough
    B-20434-1   destroy
    B-20434-2   64717   534

81. You're way out there (Maxwell)
    B-20435-1 destroy (take one pressing extant)
    B-20435-2 destroy

New York

16 April 1918, with Victor Orchestra, cond. Josef Pasternack
82. Laddie o' mine (Johnstone/Krams)
    B-21769-1 destroy
    B-21769-2 64779
83. Sorter miss you (words & music Smith) with Lapatino (harp)
    B-21770-1 64780
    B-21770-2 hold
84. The magic of your eyes (words & music Penn)
    B-21771-1 hold
    B-21771-2 64782   529   2-3531
85. The Girl Who Waits at home (Laddie in Khaki) (words & music Novello)
    B-21772-1 destroy
    B-21772-2 64781

Camden, NJ

20 September 1918, with orchestra, cond. Josef Pasternack
86. *Madama Butterfly*: Tutti i fior (Puccini) with Sophie Braslau
    C-22244-1 88597   8044   2-054090   DB 596
               89131
    C-22244-2 destroy
87. *La Bohème*: O soave fanciulla (Puccini) with Giovanni Martinelli
    C-22245-1 destroy
    C-22245-2 88598   8002   2-054091   DK 100
               89132
88. Madama Butterfly: Dicon ch'oltra mare ... O quanti occhi fisi (Puccini)
    with Martinelli
    C-22246-1 89163   8002   2-054123   DK 100
    C-22246-2 hold

11 February 1919, with orchestra, cond. Josef Pasternack
89. *Gianni Schicchi*: O mio babbino caro (Puccini)
    B-22578-1 destroy
    B-22578-2 64802   528   7-53033   DA 136
                                               AGSA 14
    B-22578-3 hold

90. *Faust*: Alerte! Alerte! Où vous êtes perdus (Gounod) with Martinelli
    & Marcel Journet with Bourdon (piano)
    B-22579-1   destroy
    B-22579-2   destroy
    B-22579-3   destroy

1 December 1919, with orchestra, cond. Josef Pasternack
91. The Bells of St Mary's (Furber/Adams) with Bourdon (celeste)
    B-23505-1   destroy
    B-23505-2   destroy
    B-23505-3   64844   525   2-3471
92. If you could care (As you were) (Wimperis/Darewski) with Bourdon (piano)
    & William Reitz (bells)
    B-23506-1   destroy
    B-23506-2   64859   530   2-3491
93. Thoughts of you (Grey/Novello) with Bourdon (piano)
    B-23507-1   destroy
    B-23507-2   destroy
    B-23507-3   destroy

17 May 1920, with orchestra, cond. Josef Pasternack
94. Thoughts of you (Grey/Novello) with Bourdon (piano)
    B-23507-4   destroy
    B-23507-5   destroy
95. I'd build a world in "The heart of a rose" (David/Nicholls)
    B-24118-1   destroy   with Rattay (violin)
    B-24118-2   64893   529   2-3501
    B-24118-3   destroy
96. By the Waters of Minnetonka (Cavanass/Lieurance) with Rattay (violin)
    & Lapitino (harp)
    B-24119-1   64908   527   2-3520
    B-24119-2   destroy
97. *La Wally*: Ebben? ne andrò lontana (Catalani)
    B-24120-1   destroy
    B-24120-2   destroy

4 October 1920, with orchestra, cond. Josef Pasternack
98. Thoughts of you (Grey/Novello) with Bourdon (piano)
    B-23507-6   destroy
    B-23507-7   64927   526   2-3550
99. *La Wally*: Ebben? ne andrò lontana (Catalani)
    B-24120-3   hold
    B-24120-4   64981   537   7-53048   DA 123

100. *Mefistofele*: L'altra notte (Boito)
    C-24609-1 74651   6353   2-053185   DB 635
    C-24609-2 hold

5 January 1921, with orchestra, cond. Josef Pasternack

101. I passed by your window (Taylor/Brahe)
    B-24780-1 destroy
    B-24780-2 master/destroy

102. An open secret (anon./Woodman)
    B-24781-1 destroy
    B-24781-2 destroy
    B-24781-3 destroy

25 February 1921, with orchestra, cond. Josef Pasternack

103. I passed by your window (Taylor/Brahe)
    B-24780-3 destroy
             B-24780-4 64948   532   2-3567   DA 137

104. An open secret (anon./Woodman)
    B-24781-4 64960   524   2-3582
    B-24781-5 destroy
    B-24781-6 destroy

105. The Singer (Maxwell)
    B-24961-1 destroy
    B-24961-2 destroy
    B-24961-3 destroy

106. Mother of my heart (Montanye/Grey)
    B-24962-1 destroy
    B-24962-2 destroy
    B-24962-3 64988   536   2-3608

13 June 1921, with orchestra, cond. Josef Pasternack

107. The Singer (Maxwell)
    B-24961-4 hold
    B-24961-5 hold
    B-24961-6 hold

23 September 1921, with orchestra, cond. Josef Pasternack and Meyer Gorodetzer (violin)

108. Every bit of loving in the world (Furber/Novello)
    B-25570-1 destroy
    B-25570-2 destroy
    B-25570-3 destroy

109. Carissima (words & music Penn)
    B-25571-1   destroy
    B-25571-2   destroy

13 December 1921, with orchestra, cond. Josef Pasternack

110. Every bit of loving in the world (Furber/Novello)
    B-25570-4   destroy
    B-25570-5   destroy
    B-25570-6 66056   526   2-3670

111. Carissima (words & music Penn)
    B-25571-3   destroy
    B-25571-4   destroy
    B-25571-5 66036   897   2-3655

112. Bless you (Furber/Novello) with Bourdon (celeste)
    B-25901-1   destroy
    B-25901-2 66027   524   2-3640   DA 135
    B-25901-3   hold

7 June 1922, with orchestra, cond. Rosario Bourdon

113. The Singer (Maxwell)
    B-24961-7   destroy
    B-24961-8   destroy
    B-24961-9   destroy
    B-24961-10 66093   532   2-3708   DA 137

114. Rimpianto (Serenade) (Silvestri/Toselli) with Rattay (violin)
    B-26517-1   destroy
    B-26517-2   destroy

2 January 1923, with orchestra, cond. Josef Pasternack, with Bourdon (piano)

115. *Guillaume Tell*: Selva opaca (Rossini)
    B-27368-1   destroy
    B-27368-2   destroy
    B-27368-3   destroy
    B-27368-4   master/hold/destroy

116. Daddy (Lemon/Behrend) with Lapitino (harp)
    B-27369-1   destroy
    B-27369-2   master/hold/destroy
    B-27369-3   destroy

18 January 1923, with orchestra, cond. Josef Pasternack, with Bourdon (piano)

117. *Guillaume Tell*: Selva opaca (Rossini)

    B-27368-5   destroy

    B-27368-6   hold

    B-27368-7   66134   537   7-53057   DA 123

    B-27368-8   destroy

with orchestra, cond. Rosario Bourdon, with Lapitino (harp)

118. Daddy (Lemon/Behrend)

    B-27369-4   destroy

    B-27369-5   hold

    B-27369-6   destroy

    B-27369-7   66152   897

8 March 1923, with orchestra, cond. Rosario Bourdon

119. Vale (D'Arcy/Russell)

    B-27595-1   hold

    B-27595-2   (66244)   1005   2-3863   DA 639

    B-27595-3   destroy

120. If winter comes (Summer will come again) (Arkell/Tennent) with Alexander Schmidt (violin)

    B-27596-1   destroy

    B-27596-2   hold

    B-27596-3   66140   525   2-3764

19 March 1923, with orchestra, cond. Rosario Bourdon

121. *Faust*: Alerte! Alerte! Ou vous êtes perdues (Gounod) with Martinelli, Mardones & Charles Linton (piano)

    C-27701-1   destroy

    C-27701-2   destroy

    C-27701-3   (95214)

122. *Faust*: Je ris de me voir si belle (Gounod)

    B-27702-1   hold

    B-27702-2   destroy

    B-27702-3   hold

7 June 1923, with orchestra, cond. Rosario Bourdon

123. *L'Amico Fritz*: Non mi resta che il pianto (Mascagni) with Ted Levy (piano)

    B-28101-1   destroy

    B-28101-2   hold

    B-28101-3   master/hold

124. *L'Amico Fritz*: Son pocchi fiori (Mascagni) with Levy (piano) & Lapitino (harp)
    B-28102-1   destroy
    B-28102-2   destroy
    B-28102-3   master/hold (test pressing exists)
125. Coming home (Eardley-Wilmot/Willeby)
    B-28103-1   destroy
    B-28103-2   destroy
    B-28103-3   (66175)   946   03819   DA 575
                                          (2-3804)

8 June 1923, with orchestra, cond. Rosario Bourdon
126. *Faust*: Je ris de me voir si belle (Gounod)
    B-27702-4   destroy
    B-27702-5   master/destroy
    B-27702-6   destroy
127. Memory's garden (G. Denni/L. Denni)
    B-28104-1   destroy
    B-28104-2   (66174)   946   03818   DA 575
                                          (2-3803)
    B-28104-3   hold

20 February 1924, with orchestra, cond. Rosario Bourdon
128. Robin Adair (Keppel/trad.) with Reibold (celeste)
    B-29489-1   destroy
    B-29489-2   hold
    B-29489-3   destroy
129. If God left only you (Mitchell/Densmore) with Alexander Schmidt (violin)
    B-29490-1   destroy
    B-29490-2   (1148)
    B-29490-3   destroy
    (1148 was assigned but not published. The number was used for the electrical
    recording of 19 May 1925)
130. Last rose of summer (Moore) with Lapitino (harp)
    B-29491-1   destroy
    B-29491-2   hold
    B-29491-3   destroy
131. I heard you go by (Stuart/Wood) with Schmidt (violin)
    B-29492-1   (66245)   1005   (2-3864)   DA 639
    B-29492-2   destroy
    B-29492-3   destroy
132. *Sari*: Love's own sweet song (Kálmán) with Alfred Lennartz (cello)
    C-29493-1   destroy
    C-29493-2   destroy

4 April 1924, with orchestra, cond. Rosario Bourdon

133. *Faust*: Je ris de me voir si belle (Gounod)

    B-27702-7   destroy

    B-27702-8   destroy

    B-27702-9   destroy

134. Robin Adair (Keppel/trad.) with Reibold (celeste)

    B-29489-4   destroy

    B-29489-5   master/destroy

135. Last rose of summer (Moore) with Lapitino (harp)

    B-29491-4   hold

    B-29491-5   destroy

    B-29491-6   destroy

    B-29491-7   destroy

136. *Sari*: Love's own sweet song (Kálmán) with Alfred Lennartz (cello)

    C-29493-3   destroy

    C-29493-4   6370

137. *Faust*: Il était un roi de Thulé (Gounod)

    B-29859-1   destroy

    B-29859-2   destroy

12 June 1924, with orchestra, cond. Rosario Bourdon

138. *Music Box Revue*: What'll I do (Berlin) with Reibold (celeste)

    B-30270-1   1032   DA 641

    B-30270-2   destroy

    B-30270-3   destroy

139. Love has a way (words & music Schertzinger) with Schmidt (violin)

    B-30271-1   destroy

    B-30271-2   1032   DA 641

    B-30271-3   destroy

29 January 1925, with orchestra, cond. Rosario Bourdon

140. Please keep out of my dreams (Bayes/Maxwell) with Schmidt (violin)
    & Reibold (celeste)

    B-31815-1   destroy

    B-31815-2   destroy

141. Indian dawn (Roos/Zamecnik) with Alfred Lennartz (cello) & Clement
    Barone (flute)

    B-31819-1   destroy

    B-31819-2   destroy

142. *Rose Marie*: Indian love call (Friml)

    B-31820-1   destroy

    B-31820-2   destroy

ELECTRIC RECORDINGS

Camden, NJ

19 May 1925, with orchestra, cond. Rosario Bourdon
143. Robin Adair (Keppel/trad.)

BVE-29489-6	destroy		
BVE-29489-7	destroy		
BVE-29489-8		1188	

144. If God left only you (Mitchell/Densmore)

BVE-29490-4		1148	

145. Indian dawn (Roos/Zamecnik)

BVE-31819-3		1094	DA 718
BVE-31819-4	destroy		

146. *La Cena delle Beffe*: Sempre così (Giordano)

BVE-32816-1	destroy		
BVE-32816-2	destroy		
BVE-32816-3	destroy		

20 May 1925, with orchestra, cond. Rosario Bourdon
147. *Faust*: Je ris de me voir si belle (Gounod)

BVE-27702-10	destroy		
BVE-27702-11	destroy		

148. Please, keep out of my dreams (Bayes/Maxwell)

BVE-31815-3	destroy		
BVE-31815-4		1094	DA 718
BVE-31815-5		1094	
BVE-31815-6	destroy		

149. *La Cena delle Beffe*: Ed io non ne godevo… Sempre così (Giordano)

BVE-32816-4	destroy		
BVE-32816-5	destroy		
BVE-32816-6		1359	AGSA 9

12 February 1926, with orchestra, cond. Rosario Bourdon
150. *La Cena delle Beffe*: Sempre così (Giordano)

BVE-32816-7	destroy		
BVE-32816-8	destroy		
BVE-32816-9	destroy		

151. *La Cena delle Beffe*: Mi chiamo Lisabetta (Giordano)

BVE-34561-1	hold		
BVE-34561-2		1359	AGSA 9

152. Howdy do Mis' Springtime (Gordon/Guion)
     BVE-34562-1   destroy
     BVE-34562-2   hold
     BVE-34562-3   hold
153. Nobody else (words & music Penn)
     BVE-34563-1   destroy
     BVE-34563-2   hold
     BVE-34563-3   1148

5 April 1926, with orchestra, cond. Rosario Bourdon
154. Mighty lak' a rose (Stanton/Nevin)
     BVE-16087-4   1189
     BVE-16087-5   destroy
     BVE-16087-6   destroy
155. Somewhere a voice is calling (Newton/Tate)
     BVE-19120-3   destroy
     BVE-19120-4   destroy
156. *La Cena delle Beffe*: Sempre così (Giordano)
     BVE-32816-10   destroy
     BVE-32816-11   destroy

6 April 1926, with orchestra, cond. Rosario Bourdon
157. Last rose of summer (Moore)
     BVE-29491-8   destroy
     BVE-29491-9   destroy
     BVE-29491-10   destroy

Camden, NJ, Church Building

8 June 1926, with orchestra, cond. Rosario Bourdon
158. Somewhere a voice is calling (Newton/Tate)
     BVE-19120-5   1189
     BVE-19120-6   destroy
159. Ever of Thee I'm fondly dreaming (Linley/Hall)
     BVE-35483-1   destroy
     BVE-35483-2   hold
     BVE-35483-3   1176   DA 822
160. Carmena (Walton/Lane Wilson)
     BVE-35484-1   destroy
     BVE-35484-2   destroy
     BVE-35484-3   destroy
     BVE-35484-4   destroy

9 June 1926, with orchestra, cond. Rosario Bourdon

161. Somewhere a voice is calling (Newton/Tate)
     BVE-19120-7   destroy

162. The Bells of St Mary's (Furber/Adams)
     BVE-23505-4   destroy
     BVE-23505-5   destroy
     BVE-23505-6   1176   DA 822

163. Last rose of summer (Moore)
     BVE-29491-11   1188
     BVE-29491-12   destroy

8 April 1927, with orchestra, cond. Rosario Bourdon

164. Deep River (trad, arr La Forge) with Shannon Quartet: Wilfred Glenn, Elliot
     Shaw, Lewis James & Franklyn Baur
     BVE-19121-3   1268   DA 991
     BVE-19121-4   destroy
     BVE-19121-5   destroy

165. By the Waters of Minnetonka (Cavanass/Lieurance) with Shannon Qt: Glenn,
     Shaw, James & Baur
     BVE-24119-3   1268   DA 991
     BVE-24119-4   destroy
     BVE-24119-5   hold

Liederkrantz Hall, New York

6 March 1928, with orchestra, cond. Rosario Bourdon

166. *Manon Lescaut*: L'ora o tirsi (Puccini)
     BVE-10188-2   1474   DA 1156
                                                      AGSA 8
     BVE-10188-3   hold

167. A Maori slumber song (Hine e hine) (Te Rangi Pai)
     BVE-43126-1   master/hold
     BVE-43126-2   hold

168. Waiata Maori (arr Hill)
     BVE-43127-1   destroy
     BVE-43127-2   master/hold

28 March 1928, with La Forge (piano)

169. A Maori slumber song (Hine e hine) (Te Rangi Pai)
     BVE-43185-1   1330   DA 986
     BVE-43185-2   hold

170. Waiata Maori (arr Hill)
    BVE-43186-1   hold
    BVE-43186-2   1330   DA 986

26 June 1928
171. *Manon Lescaut*: In quelle trine morbide (Puccini)
    BVE-45658-1   destroy
    BVE-45658-2   hold
    BVE-45658-3   1474   DA 1156
                                    AGSA 8

Broadcast? 1949 (issued by RCA)
172. Why Caruso recorded the Coat song (Alda talking with Wally Butterworth)
    D9-CB-2234-1B   87499   DL 100
    (reverse: Enrico Caruso La Bohème: Vecchia zimarra (matrix B-17198-1)

Frances Alda as pianist

Mrs Jesse Donahue made eight records for Victor in New York which are described as "Special records for personal use" (private records). In her autobiography *Men, Women and Tenors* Frances Alda mentions Donahue as being a personal friend. Alda appears to have acted as director for the five sessions involved and provided the piano accompaniment for several of the titles.

Say not life is a dream (???)
BS102013-1-1A   5 June 1936   with piano
BS102042-1-1A   12 June 1936   with orchestra

Madama Butterfly: **Un bel dì (Puccini)**
CS102014-1-1A   5 June 1936   with piano
CS102044-1-1A   12 June 1936   with orchestra

La Bohème: **Si, mi chiamano Mimì (Puccini)**
BS102015-1-1A   5 June 1936   with piano
BS102043-1-1A   12 June 1936   with orchestra

Ave Maria (Bach-Gounod)
BS03465-1-1A   11 December 1936   piano and violin
BS03465-2-2A-3   13 December 1936   piano and violin

Ecstasy (words & music Beach)
BS03805-1-1A   18 December 1936   piano

Frances Alda on Vitaphone Films

February 1927: The Star Spangled Banner (Key/Smith)
With Vitaphone Symphony Orchestra cond. Herman Heller
Apr 1929: The Last Rose of Summer (Moore/trad) and Birth of Morn (Dunbar/Leoni)
  With Frank La Forge (piano)
November 1929: *Otello*: Ave Maria (Verdi) With Frank La Forge (piano) and
  Clarence Dickerson (organ)

Frances Alda reissues on LP and CD

(These lists are not intended to be exhaustive but to represent the most easily
obtainable reissues of Alda's records on LP and CD.)

LP

Club 99: CL99-45: Frances Alda: 1, 5, 8, 12, 19, 25, 41, 43, 44, 64, 89, 99, 100, 117, 149,
  151
Club 99: CL99-91: Frances Alda, Vol. 2: 3, 15, 16, 28, 30, 32, 38, 39, 40, 51,
  53, 54, 57, 62, 66, 73, 74, 87
Pearl: Opal 807: Frances Alda: 5, 9, 25, 26, 28, 29, 32, 38, 39, 41, 51, 53, 64, 89
Court Opera Classics CO 383: Frances Alda: 2, 3, 4, 5, 12, 25, 27, 28, 38, 39, 40, 62, 87,
  88, 89, 100
Olympus: ORL 306: Enrico Caruso, Vol. 6: 1, 2
Olympus: ORL 310: Enrico Caruso, Vol. 10: 20-24
Olympus: ORL 313: Enrico Caruso, Vol. 13: 55 (take 3)
RCA Camden: CDN 1030: Giovanni Martinelli: 88
EJS: GM 100: Giovanni Martinelli: 87
EMI: RLS 743: The Record of Singing, Vol. 2: 25
EJS 142: Potpourri (2): 55 (take 3)
OASI 514: S. Braslau: 86

CD

Romophone 81034: Frances Alda: The Complete Victor Recordings 1909-15: all
  published records 2-64 plus unpublished 1 and 55 (take 3)
VAI 1126: Frances Alda: 1, 10, 16, 25, 32, 40, 41, 43, 44, 48, 52, 86, 89, 100, 123 (take
  ?), 148 (take 5), 149, 151, 158, 162, 166 (take 2), 169, 170, 171
ATOLL A9701: Alda in Opera and Song: 2, 3, 24, 40, 54, 57, 62, 87, 88, 89, 92, 99, 100,
  103, 111, 112, 115, 138, 169, 172
Great Voices of the Opera III LC05057: Primadonnas: 2, 3, 4, 5, 25, 27, 28, 43, 87, 89
Biddulph LAB 039: Mischa Elman: 56, 57, 58, 59
Pearl EVC II: The Caruso Edition, Vol. 2: 1, 2, 20-23
Pearl EVC III: The Caruso Edition, Vol. 3: 24, 55 (take 3)
Naxos 8.110719: Caruso Complete Recordings, Vol. 4: 1, 2

Naxos 8.110721: Caruso Complete Recordings, Vol. 6: 20-23
Naxos 8.110724: Caruso Complete Recordings, Vol. 7: 24
Naxos 8.110750: Caruso Complete Recordings, Vol. 9: 55 (take 3) (two versions?)
Romophone 82012: Giovanni Martinelli: 87, 88
Marston 53017: Richard Strauss Lieder: 38
Kiwi Pacific: Southern Voices: 89

Acknowledgments
My grateful thanks to John T. Hughes, John Holohan, John Bolig, Roger Neill and Peter Chaplin for useful additions to, or for checking, the discography.

Bibliography

Books and major catalogues

Alda, Frances, *Men, Women and Tenors*, AMS Press, New York, 1971 (reprinted from Boston edition of 1937)

Anderson, Gae, *Tivoli King: Life of Harry Rickards*, Vaudeville Showman, Allambie, Sydney, 2009

Barker, Lady, *Station Life in New Zealand*, Macmillan, London, 1883

Bassett, Judith, Sinclair, Keith and Stenson, Marcia, *The Story of New Zealand*, Reed, Auckland, 1985

Bauer-Lechner, Natalie, *Recollections of Gustav Mahler*, Cambridge University Press, Cambridge, 1980

Bebbington, Warren, ed., *A Dictionary of Australian Music*, Oxford University Press, Melbourne, 1998

Becker, Heinz and Gudrun, *Giacomo Meyerbeer: A Life in Letters*, Christopher Helm, London, 1983

Benoist, André, *The Accompanist: An Autobiography of André Benoist* (edited by John Anthony Maltese), Paganiniana Publications, Neptune, New Jersey, 1978

Blainey, Ann, *I Am Melba: A Biography*, Black Inc, Melbourne, 2008

Blainey, Geoffrey, *The Tyranny of Distance*, Macmillan, Melbourne, 1966

——, *A History of Victoria*, Cambridge University Press, Melbourne, 1984/2006

Bonyhady, Tim, *Good Living Street: Portrait of a Patron Family, Vienna 1900*, Pantheon, New York, 2011

Brisbane, Katharine, ed., *Entertaining Australia: The Performing Arts as Cultural History*, Currency Press, Sydney, 1991

Brockway, Wallace and Weinstock, Herbert, *The World of Opera*, Methuen, London, 1941/1962

Brownrigg, Jeff, *A New Melba? The Tragedy of Amy Castles*, Crossing Press, Sydney, 2006

Cairns, David, *Mozart and his Operas*, Penguin, London, 2007

Caruso, Dorothy, *Enrico Caruso: His Life and Death*, T Werner Laurie, London, 1946

Caruso Jr, Enrico and Farkas, Andrew, *Enrico Caruso: My Father and My Family*, Amadeus Press, Portland, Oregon, 1997

Chatfield-Taylor, Joan, *San Francisco Opera: The First Seventy-Five Years*, Chronicle, San Francisco, 1997

Christiansen, Rupert, *Prima Donna: A History*, Penguin, Harmondsworth, Middlesex, 1984

Clément, Catherine, *Opera, Or the Undoing of Women* (translated by Betsy Wing), University of Minnesota Press, Minneapolis, 1988

Cone, John Frederick, *Adelina Patti: Queen of Hearts*, Scolar Press, Aldershot, Hampshire, 1994

Cowgill, Rachel and Poriss, Hilary, eds, *The Arts of the Prima Donna in the Long Nineteenth Century*, Oxford University Press, Oxford, 2012

Crankshaw, Edward, *The Fall of the House of Habsburg*, Sphere-Longmans, London, 1963

Davis, Peter G, *The American Opera Singer: The Lives and Adventures of America's Great Singers in Opera and Concert from 1825 to the Present*, Doubleday, New York, 1997

Davis, Richard, *Anna Bishop: The Adventures of an Intrepid Prima Donna*, Currency Press, Sydney, 1997

de La Grange, Henry-Louis, *Mahler: Volume One*, Victor Gollancz, London, 1976

——— *Gustav Mahler: Vienna: The Years of Challenge (1897–1904)*, Oxford University Press, Oxford, 1995

———, *Gustav Mahler: Vienna: Triumph and Disillusion (1904–1907)*, Oxford University Press, Oxford, 1999

Denholm, David, *The Colonial Australians*, Penguin, Harmondsworth Middlesex, 1979

Dent, Edward J, *Mozart's Operas: A Critical Study*, Oxford University Press, London, 1913

Dicker, Ian G, *JCW: A Short Biography of James Cassius Williamson*, Elizabeth Tudor Press, Sydney, 1974

Dizikes, John, *Opera in America: A Cultural History*, Yale University Press, New Haven, Connecticut, 1993

Downes, Peter, *The Pollards: A Family and its Child and Adult Opera Companies in New Zealand and Australia 1880–1910*, Steele Roberts, Wellington, 2002

Drake, James A, *Rosa Ponselle: A Centenary Biography*, Amadeus Press, Portland Oregon, 1997

Eaton, Quaintance, *Opera Caravan: Adventures of the Metropolitan on tour 1883–1956*, John Calder, London, 1957

———, *The Boston Opera Company: The Story of a Unique Musical Institution*, Appleton-Century, New York, 1965

———, *The Miracle of the Met: An Informal History of the Metropolitan Opera 1883–1967*, Meredith, New York, 1968

Finck, Henry T, *My Adventures in the Golden Age of Music*, Funk & Wagnalls, New York, 1926

Freund, Peter with Smith, Val, *Her Maj: A History of Her Majesty's Theatre, Ballarat*, published by the theatre, 2007

Gale, Maggie B and Gardner, Viv, eds, *Women, Theatre and Performance: New Histories, New Historiographies*, Manchester University Press, Manchester, 2000

Gammond, Peter, *Offenbach*, Omnibus, London, 1980

Gänzl, Kurt and Lamb, Andrew, *Gänzl's Book of the Musical Theatre*, Bodley Head, London, 1988

Garden, Mary and Biancolli, Louis, *Mary Garden's Story*, Michael Joseph, London, 1952

Gattey, Charles Neilson, *Queens of Song*, Barrie and Jenkins, London, 1979

Gatti-Casazza, Giulio, *Memories of the Opera*, Scribner, New York, 1941

Gers, Arthur de, *Théâtre Royal de la Monnaie, 1856–1926: Troupes, créations, artistes en representation*, Des Presses P Dykmans, Brussels, 1926

Gigli, Beniamino, *The Memoirs of Beniamino Gigli* (translated by Darina Silone), Cassell, London, 1957

Gorky, Maxim, *Chaliapin: An Autobiography as Told to Maxim Gorky* (translated by Nina Froud and James Hanley), Columbus Books, London, 1967

Gosling, Nigel, *Paris 1900–1914: The Miraculous Years*, Weidenfeld and Nicolson, London, 1978

Greenfeld, Howard S, *Caruso: An Illustrated Life*, Collins and Brown, London, 1991

Greenwood, Gordon, *Australia: A Social and Political History*, Angus and Robertson, Sydney, 1955

Gyger, Alison, *Opera for the Antipodes: Opera in Australia 1881–1939*, Currency Press, Sydney, 1990

——, *Civilising the Colonies: Pioneering Opera in Australia*, Pellinor, Sydney, 1999

Hamilton, David, ed., *The Metropolitan Opera Encyclopedia: A Comprehensive Guide to the World of Opera*, Simon and Schuster, New York, 1987

Hanslick, Eduard, *Vienna's Golden Years of Music 1850–1900* (translated and edited by Henry Pleasants III), Victor Gollancz, London, 1951

Harding, James, *Gounod*, George Allen and Unwin, London, 1973

——, *Folies de Paris: The Rise and Fall of French Operetta*, Chappell/Elm Tree Books, London, 1979

Harewood, The Earl of, ed and revised, *Kobbé's Complete Opera Book*, Putnam, London, 1954

Heinz, William F, *New Zealand's Last Gold Rush*, Reed, Wellington, 1977

Hetherington, John, *Melba: A Biography*, Faber and Faber, London, 1967 (republished by Melbourne University Press, Melbourne, 1995)

Hill, Alfred, *The Leipzig Diary* (edited by Donald Maurice), Wirripang, Wollongong NSW, 2008

Hughes, Robert, *The Fatal Shore: The Epic of Australia's Founding*, Vintage, New York, 1986/88

Hurst, PG, *The Age of Jean de Reszke: 40 Years of Opera 1874–1914*, Johnson, London, 1958

———, *The Golden Age Recorded*, Oakwood Press, Surrey, 1963

Irvin, Eric, *Dictionary of the Australian Theatre 1788–1914*, Hale and Iremonger, Sydney, 1985

Irvine, Demar, *Massenet: A Chronicle of His Life and Times*, Amadeus Press, Portland, Oregon, 1994

James, Alan, *Gilbert & Sullivan*, Omnibus, London, 1989

Klein, Herman, *Musical Notes*, Novello Ewer, London, 1890

———, *Great Women Singers of My Time*, George Routledge, London, 1931

———, *The Golden Age of Opera*, George Routledge, London, 1933

Kobbé, Gustav, *The Complete Opera Book*, GP Putnam, London, 1922

Kolodin, Irving, *The Story of the Metropolitan Opera*, Knopf, New York, 1953

Kutsch, KJ and Riemens, Leo, *A Concise Dictionary of Singers: From the beginning of recorded sound to the present*, Chilton Book Company, Philadelphia, 1962/1969

Love, Harold, *The Golden Age of Australian Opera: WS Lyster and His Companies 1861–1880*, Currency Press, Sydney, 1981

Mackenzie, Barbara and Mackenzie, Findlay, *Singers of Australia: From Melba to Sutherland*, Lansdowne, Melbourne, 1967

McColl, Sandra, *Music Criticism in Vienna 1896–1897: Critically Moving Forms*, Oxford University Press, Oxford, 1996

Mahler, Alma, *Gustav Mahler: Memories and Letters* (edited by Donald Mitchell and Knud Martner), Cardinal, London, 1946/1990

Mahler-Werfel, Alma, *Diaries 1898–1902* (selected and translated by Antony Beaumont), Cornell University Press, Ithaca, New York, 1997

Mahler, Gustav, *Letters to his Wife*, Faber and Faber, London, 1995/2004

Marchesi, Blanche, *Singer's Pilgrimage*, Grant Richards, London, 1923

Marchesi, Mathilde, *Marchesi and Music: Passages from the Life of a Famous Singing-Teacher*, Harper, London, 1897

Marsh, Robert C, *150 Years of Opera in Chicago* (completed by Norman Pellegrini), Northern Illinois University Press, DeKalb, Illinois, 2006

Martin, George, *Verdi at the Golden Gate: Opera and San Francisco in the Gold Rush Years*, University of California Press, Berkeley, California, 1993

Martner, Knud, ed., *Selected Letters of Gustav Mahler*, Faber and Faber, London, 1979

Matenson, Winsome E, *A Melbourne Family 1848–1948*, Self-published, Melbourne, 1989

Mayer, Martin, *The Met: 100 Years of Grand Opera*, Thames and Hudson, London, 1983

Melba, Nellie, *Melodies and Memories*, Thornton Butterworth, London, 1925

Missen, Margery, *Tarraville's Queen of Song*, Yarram Victoria, nd, (c. 2000)

Moran, William R, ed., *Nellie Melba: A Contemporary Review*, Greenwood, Connecticut, 1985

Murphy, Agnes G, *Melba: A Biography*, Doubleday Page, New York, 1909

Neill, Roger, *Legends: The Art of Walter Barnett*, National Portrait Gallery, Canberra, 2000

———, *Divas: Mathilde Marchesi and Her Pupils*, NewSouth (University of New South Wales Press), Sydney, 2016

Newcomb, Ethel, *Leschetizky As I Knew Him*, Appleton, Boston, 1921; republished by Da Capo, New York, 1967

Nicolson, Juliet, *The Perfect Summer: Dancing into Shadow in 1911*, John Murray, London, 2006

Osborne, Richard, *Rossini*, JM Dent, London, 1986

Phillips-Matz, Mary Jane, *Verdi: A Biography*, Oxford University Press, Oxford, 1993

Pleasants, Henry, *The Great Singers: From the Dawn of Opera to Our Own Time*, Victor Gollancz, London, 1967

Ponselle, Rosa and Drake, James A, *Ponselle: A Singer's Life*, Doubleday, New York, 1982

Proust, Marcel, *À la recherche du temps perdu*, Grasset and other publishers, Paris, 1913–27

Radic, Thérèse, *Melba: The Voice of Australia*, Macmillan, Melbourne, 1986

Reid, JC, ed., *A Book of New Zealand*, Collins, Glasgow, 1964

Rodmell, Paul, *Opera in the British Isles, 1875–1918*, Ashgate, Farnham, Surrey, 2013

Roman, Zoltan, *Gustav Mahler's American Years, 1907–1911: A Documentary History*, University of California Press, Berkeley, California, 1991

Rosenthal, Harold, *Two Centuries of Opera at Covent Garden*, Putnam, London, 1958

Rosenthal, Harold and Warrack, John, *Concise Oxford Dictionary of Opera*, Oxford University Press, London, 1964/1966

Rosselli, John, *Singers of Italian Opera: The History of a Profession*, Cambridge University Press, Cambridge, 1992

Russell, Henry, *The Passing Show*, Thornton Butterworth, London, 1926

Rutherford, Susan, *The Prima Donna and Opera 1815–1930*, Cambridge University Press, Cambridge, 2006

Sachs, Harvey, *Toscanini*, Harper and Row, New York, 1978

———, ed., *The Letters of Arturo Toscanini*, Knopf, New York, 2002

Salgado, Susana, *The Teatro Solís: 150 Years of Opera, Concert and Ballet in Montevideo*, Wesleyan University Press, Middletown, Connecticut, 2003

Schorske, Carl E, *Fin-de-Siècle Vienna: Politics and Culture*, Vintage, New York, 1981

Scott, Michael, *The Record of Singing* (two volumes), Duckworth, London, 1977

———, *The Great Caruso*, Hamish Hamilton, London, 1988

Seltsam, William H, *Metropolitan Opera Annals*, HW Wilson, New York, 1947

Shaw, Bernard, *London Music in 1888–89 As Heard by Corno Di Bassetto*, Constable, London, 1937

————, *Music in London 1890–94* (three volumes), Constable, London, 1932

Shrimpton, AW and Mulgan, Alan E, *Maori and Pakeha: A History of New Zealand*, Whitcombe and Tombs, Auckland, 1930

Simpson, Adrienne, ed., *Opera in New Zealand: Aspects of History and Performance*, Witham Press, Wellington, 1990

————, *Opera's Farthest Frontier: A History of Professional Opera in New Zealand*, Reed, Auckland, 1996

Simpson, Adrienne and Downes, Peter, *Southern Voices: International Opera Singers of New Zealand*, Reed, Auckland, 1992

Slezak, Leo, *Song of Motley: Being the Reminiscences of a Hungry Tenor*, William Hodge, London, 1938

Soubies, Albert and Malherbe, Charles, *Histoire de l'Opéra-Comique: La seconde Salle Favart – 1840-1860*, Librairie Marpon et Flammarion, Paris, 1892

Steane, JB, *The Grand Tradition: Seventy Years of Singing on Record 1900–1970*, Scribner's, New York, 1974

Steen, Michael, *Enchantress of Nations: Pauline Viardot: Soprano, Muse and Lover*, Icon, Cambridge, 2007

Stockdale, Freddie, *Emperors of Song: Three Great Impresarios*, John Murray, London, 1998

Tait, Viola, *A Family of Brothers: The Taits and JC Williamson, A Theatrical History*, Heinemann, Melbourne, 1971

Taubman, Howard, *Toscanini*, Odhams, London, 1951

Thomson, John Mansfield, *A Distant Music: The Life and Times of Alfred Hill 1870–1960*, Oxford University Press, Auckland, 1980

————, *The Oxford History of New Zealand Music*, Oxford University Press, Auckland, 1991

Tremain, Rose, *Music and Silence*, Vintage, London, 2000

————, *The Colour*, Chatto and Windus, London, 2003

Trollope, Anthony, *Australia* (two volumes), Chapman and Hall, London, 1873 (republished Alan Sutton, Gloucester, 1987)

————, *New Zealand*, Chapman and Hall, London, 1874

Turnbull, Michael TRB, *Mary Garden*, Scolar Press, Aldershot Hampshire, 1997

Van Straten, Frank, *Tivoli*, Thomas C Lothian, Melbourne, 2003

Vergo, Peter, *Art in Vienna 1898–1918: Klimt, Kokoschka, Schiele and Their Contemporaries*, Phaidon, London, 1975

Vestey, Pamela, *Melba: A Family Memoir*, Phoebe, Melbourne, 1996

Wagner, Alan, *Prima Donnas and Other Wild Beasts*, Crowell-Collier, New York, 1961

Walsh, TJ, *Monte Carlo Opera 1879–1909*, Gill and Macmillan, Dublin, 1975

Waters, Thorold, *Much Besides Music: Memoirs*, Georgian House, Melbourne, 1951

Weber, William, *Music and the Middle Class: The Social Structure of Concert Life in London, Paris and Vienna Between 1830 and 1848*, Croom Helm, London, 1975
——, *The Musician as Entrepreneur: Managers, Charlatans and Idealists*, Indiana University Press, Bloomington, Indiana, 2004
Weinstock, Herbert, *Donizetti: And the World of Opera in Italy, Paris and Vienna in the First Half of the Nineteenth Century*, Methuen, London, 1964
——, *Vincenzo Bellini: His Life and His Operas*, Weidenfeld and Nicolson, London, 1971
Wharton, Edith, *The Age of Innocence*, D Appleton and Company, New York, 1920 (republished by Constable/Penguin, London, 1966/1974)
Wiesmann, Sigrid, ed., *Gustav Mahler in Vienna*, Rizzoli, New York, 1976
Wild, Nicole and Charlton, David, *Théâtre de l'Opéra-Comique Paris: Répertoire 1792–1972*, Mardaga, Sprimont, Belgium, 2005
Woollacott, Angela, *To Try Her Fortune in London: Australian Women, Colonialism and Modernity*, Oxford University Press, New York, 2001
Wyndham, H Saxe and L'Epine, Geoffrey, *Who's Who in Music: A Biographical Record of Contemporary Musicians*, Sir Isaac Pitman, London, 1913
Zweig, Stefan, *The World of Yesterday: An Autobiography*, Viking, New York, 1943

Letters, diaries, dissertations, essays, articles, sleeve notes, small catalogues etc

Arts Centre Melbourne archives: Simonsen family letters, notebooks, programmes, cuttings etc
State Library of Victoria archives: similar
Performing Arts Library, Museum of Performance and Design, San Francisco: similar

Alda, Frances, 'Men, Women and Opera Singers', *Hearst's International combined with Cosmopolitan*, New York, December 1936
——, 'What the American girl should know about an operatic career', biographical sketch by James Francis Cooke, first published in *Great Singers on the Art of Singing: Educational Conferences with Foremost Artists,* Theo Presser, Philadelphia, 1921, republished in *Great Singers on the Art of Singing*, Dover, Mineola, NY, 1996
Anae, Nicole, 'Operatic performances two hundred miles in the Australian bush: Staging rural reality, the case of Madame Fannie Simonsen in Wagga Wagga, 1866', *Rural Society*, Charles Sturt University, October 2010
Bebb, Richard, 'Frances Alda', Pearl/Opal LP sleeve notes, 1982

Bergsagel, John, 'The Impact of Italy on Danish Music', <https://arkivet. thorvaldsensmuseum.dk>, 1997

Bethea, Stephanie, 'The Flute Music of Carl Reinecke', doctoral dissertation, University of Washington Graduate School, 2008

Biddlecombe, George, 'The Bohemian Girl: Balfe and English opera', in 'Balfe: The Bohemian Girl', Argo/Decca, London, 1991

Bredin, Henrietta, 'Flushed with Success: Henrietta Bredin on singing and the menopause', OPERA, March 2018, 260–65

Davis, Dudley David, 'The Other Side of the Record: A History of the Davis Family', excerpts from unpublished manuscript, 1980

Davis, Nathan B, 'Frances Saville', The Record Collector, Vol 32, Nos 6 &7, June 1987

Doggett, Anne, 'And for harmony most ardently we long: Musical life in Ballarat 1851–1871', doctoral thesis, School of Behavioural and Social Sciences and Humanities, University of Ballarat, March 2006

——, 'Beyond Gentility: Women and music in early Ballarat, History Australia, Vol 6, No 2, 37.1–37.17, 2009

Favia-Artsay, Aida, 'Frances Alda', The Record Collector, Vol 6, No 10, October 1951

——, 'Frances Alda: A personal remembrance', in 'Frances Alda: Acoustic and electric recordings 1910–1928', VAI Audio, 1995

Gyger, Alison, 'Italian Opera in Nineteenth Century Australia', in 'The Italian Connection: Italian artists in 19th century Australia', seminar papers, SH Ervin Gallery, Sydney, October 1993

Hall, Stephen, 'Opera before the Opera House', Sydney Opera House first season program, 1973

Harewood, Lord, 'Review of Opera for the Antipodes by Alison Gyger', OPERA, January 1992, 33

Heckscher, Frank, 'Origins of the Heckscher Family', privately published, Yateley, England, October 2009 (revised February 2013)

Hefling, Stephen E, 'Mahler's Decade in Vienna: Singers of the Court Opera 1897–1907', Marston Records, 2003

Hellwig, Klaus, 'Carl Heinrich Reinecke: Piano Concertos 1–4', CPO/Westdeutscher Rundfunk Köln, Georgsmarienhütte, 1994

Henig, Stanley, 'Vienna: The Mahler Years 1897–1907', Symposium Records, London, 2004

Henstock, Michael E, 'The Harold Wayne Collection: Vol 7', Symposium Records, London, 1990

Irvin, Eric, 'Sydney's Early Opera Performances', OPERA, September 1969, 764–82

Jacobson, Robert, 'RCA/MET 100 Singers/100 Years', LP box notes, RCA Victor, Sydney, 1984

Murphy, Kerry, 'Melba's Paris Debut: Another white voice?', Musicology Australia, Vol 33, No 1, 3–13, June 2011

————, 'The French Connection: 19th century Australia had a link, through music, to continental Europe', *Australian Financial Review*, 28 December 2011, Review 5

————, 'Henri Kowalski (1841–1916): A French musician in colonial Australia', *Australian Historical Studies*, Vol 48, Issue 3, 2017, 346–62

Neill, Dora, 'How far was education for women before 1900 aimed at improving their domestic accomplishments?', A-level history course work, 2019

Neill, Roger, 'Bewitching: Frances Alda, the once forgotten rival of Nellie Melba', *Portrait* magazine, National Portrait Gallery, Canberra, Winter 2006

————, 'Melba: Melba's first recordings', Historic Masters, London, 2008

————, 'The Year in Music', in *Glorious Days: Australia 1913*, National Museum Australia, Canberra, 2013

————, 'Melba's Farewell: Dame Nellie Melba's famous farewell from Covent Garden and other recordings', Decca Eloquence, Sydney, 2017

Neill, Roger and Locantro, Tony, 'From Melba to Sutherland: Australian singers on record', Decca Eloquence, Sydney, 2016

Neubacher, Jürgen, 'Georg Philipp Telemann: Festive compositions for Altona', CPO, Georgsmarienhütte, 2017

O'Brien, Betty T, 'Australian Contralto Ada Crossley (1871–1929): A critical biography', PhD thesis, University of Melbourne, 2010

Osborne, Charles, 'Review of *Opera's Farthest Frontier* by Adrienne Simpson', *OPERA*, July 1997, 73

Pesman, Ros, 'Australian Women Encounter the East: The boat stops at Colombo', *Journal of the Royal Australian Historical Society*, June 1998

Rocha, Esmeralda Monique Antonia, 'Imperial Opera: The nexus between opera and imperialism in Victorian Calcutta and Melbourne, 1833–1901', PhD thesis, University of Western Australia, 2012

Schnitzler, Arthur, *The Spring Sonata* (translated by JH Wisdom and Marr Murray, 1914), contained within *Vienna 1900*, Penguin, Harmondsworth, Middlesex, nd

Shengold, David, 'An Uncivil Tongue', *Opera News*, New York, October 2009

Simpson, Adrienne, 'The Greatest Ornaments of their Profession: The New Zealand tours by the Simonsen Opera Companies 1876–1889', *The Canterbury Series of Bibliographies*, Catalogues and Source Documents in Music 7, Christchurch, 1993

————, 'Footlights and Fenians: The adventures of a touring concert party in gold rush New Zealand', *Australasian Drama Studies*, No 24, University of Queensland, 1994

————, 'Alda in Opera and Song: Historic recordings 1910–1928', ATOLL Records, 1997

————, 'Frances Saville: Australia's forgotten prima-donna', *Australian Music Research* 4, University of Melbourne, 1999

Steane, John, 'Frances Alda: The complete Victor recordings (1909–15)', Romophone, 1999

Van Gessel, 'Between Tourism and Fandom: The operatic exploits of Ferdinand de Beaufort (1797–1868)', Tijdschrift Van De Koninklijke vereniging voor Nederlandse Muziekgeschiedenis, DEEL LXIX, 2019

Williams, Beth Mary, 'Lineages of Garcia-Marchesi and other Traditional Italian Vocal Pedagogy in Australia' (two volumes), PhD dissertation, University of Melbourne, September 2002

Not known, 'Le Theatre Royal de la Monnaie', Vol 1, Rubini Collection, LP box notes, 1980

Online archives

Australian Dictionary of Biography, <www. adb.anu.edu.au>

BBC Proms archive, <www.bbc.co.uk/programmes/articles/>

British Newspaper Archive,

CHARM (Centre for the History and Analysis of Recorded Music), <www.charm. rhul.ac.uk/index.html>

Dictionary of New Zealand Biography, <www.mch.govt.nz/what-we-do/websites-we-run/dictionary-new-zealand-biography>

Gallica (France),

La Voce Antica (Italy),

Metropolitan Opera Archive (New York), <www.archives.metoperafamily.org/archives/frame.htm>

Newspapers.com (USA),

Papers Past (New Zealand), <www.paperspast.natlib.govt.nz/cgi-bin/paperspast>

Royal Opera House Collections, <www.rohcollections.org.uk/performances.aspx>

The Stage Archive (London), <www.archive.thestage.co.uk/Default/Skins/TheStage/>

Trove (Australia),

Wiener Staatsoper Archive (Vienna),

Index